PYTHON

SECOND EDITION

PROGRAMMING IN CONTEXT

BRADLEY N. MILLER
DAVID L. RANUM

Luther College

JONES & BARTLETT
LEARNING

World Headquarters
Jones & Bartlett Learning
5 Wall Street
Burlington, MA 01803
978-443-5000
info@jblearning.com
www.jblearning.com

Jones & Bartlett Learning books and products are available through most bookstores and online booksellers. To contact Jones & Bartlett Learning directly, call 800-832-0034, fax 978-443-8000, or visit our website, www.jblearning.com.

Production Credits

Executive Publisher: Kevin Sullivan
Senior Developmental Editor: Amy Bloom
Director of Production: Amy Rose
Marketing Manager: Lindsay White
V.P., Manufacturing and Inventory Control: Therese Connell

Composition: Northeast Compositors, Inc.
Cover and Title Page Design: Kristin E. Parker
Cover and Title Page Image: © 1shostak/Shutter-Stock, Inc.
Printing and Binding: Edwards Brothers Malloy
Cover Printing: John Pow Company

To order this product, use ISBN: 978-1-4496-9939-0

Library of Congress Cataloging-in-Publication Data
Miller, Bradley N.
  Python programming in context / Bradley N. Miller, David L. Ranum. — Second edition.
      pages cm
  Includes bibliographical references and index.
  ISBN 978-1-4496-9197-4 (pbk.) — ISBN 1-4496-9197-8 (pbk.) 1. Python (Computer program language)
I. Ranum, David L. II. Title.
  QA76.73.P98M544 2014
  005.13'3—dc23
                          2012029912

6048
Printed in the United States of America
17 16 15 14 13   10 9 8 7 6 5 4 3 2 1

PREFACE

Introduction

We (the authors, David and Brad) like to ski and we are pretty good at it, too. But that level of competence only comes with practice, lots and lots of practice. The designers of ski runs help with that practice by coding runs based on ability level. Green is for beginner, blue is for intermediate, and black runs are for advanced skiers. However, this does not suggest that green runs are void of the important skills that skiers need to become better. Beginning runs still require turns, speed control, and the ability to start and stop.

One of the most unsettling things that we observe on the mountain occurs when a beginning skier ventures out on the blue or black runs before they are ready. It can be an extremely frustrating experience watching them as they slowly attempt to pick their way down the hill, often falling, sometimes crying. The bottom line is that if you start out on the black runs, you are likely to get frustrated and give up. You will often fail before you have the chance to succeed.

Computer science deals with people who have problems to solve, and with algorithms, they can find the solutions to these problems. Computer science was never intended to be the study of programming. To be a computer scientist means first and foremost that you are a problem solver, capable of constructing algorithms either from scratch or by applying patterns from past experience.

Learning computer science is not unlike learning to ski in that the only way to be successful is through deliberate and incremental exposure to the fundamental ideas of the discipline. A beginning computer scientist needs practice in order to establish a thorough understanding

v

of a concept before continuing on to the more complex parts of the curriculum. In addition, a beginner needs the opportunity to be successful and gain confidence.

As students progress through the introductory computer science sequence, we want them to focus on aspects of problem solving, algorithm development, and algorithm understanding. Unfortunately, many modern programming languages require that students jump into more advanced programming concepts too early in their development. This practice sets them up for possible failure, not because of the computer science, but because of the language vehicle being used.

This book is designed to be a first course in computer science that focuses on problem solving, rather than language features. Therefore, we have structured the book around problems of general interest, rather than a traditional language-element structure. You will not see chapter titles in this book like "loops" and "conditionals." You will see chapter titles such as "Astronomy" and "Bears, Fish, and Plants, Oh My!" The content is still there, but structured a little differently.

We use Python as the programming language because it has a clean, simple syntax and an intuitive user environment. The basic collections are very powerful and yet easy to use. The interactive nature of the language creates an obvious place to test ideas without the need for a lot of coding. Finally, Python provides a textbook-like notation for representing algorithms, alleviating the need for an additional layer of pseudocode. This allows the illustration of many relevant, modern, and interesting problems that make use of algorithms.

Key Features

Throughout the book, concepts are introduced using a spiral model. Because the syntax of Python is so easy to learn, we can introduce all of the standard programming constructs very quickly. As students progress through the book, more of the details and background for these constructs are introduced. Thus, students are exposed to important computer science concepts when the concepts are needed to solve a problem.

An illustration of how this spiral approach touches on a specific topic in different ways can be seen in our presentation of functions. Students begin to write functions with parameters in Chapter 1. Chapter 2 introduces functions with return values. In Chapter 6, students learn about passing functions as parameters to other functions and the details of Python's scoping rules. In Chapter 8, students learn about Python's keyword and optional parameters. Chapter 9 covers recursive functions. In Chapter 10, students learn about writing functions that are methods of a class.

Throughout this second edition, we have made a number of small corrections and revisions that aim to provide clearer presentation of material. We have updated all references to the cTurtle module to reflect the standard Python 3 turtle module and have also updated all references to the urllib module. Additionally, we have enhanced the ancillary materials that accompany the text. New Test Bank questions and PowerPoint Lecture Outlines are available for free instructor download, and all source code and Answers to the Chapter Exercises have been updated. Every new copy of the second edition also includes access to Turing's Craft Codelab (a detailed description of CodeLab can be found after this preface).

How to Use This Book

Chapter Organization

This book is organized into three parts. Chapters 1–5 introduce all of the key control structures and Python data types, emphasizing straightforward imperative programming ideas such as variables, loops, and conditionals. By the end of the first five chapters, all of the major Python data types are covered. This includes integers, floats, strings, lists, dictionaries, and files.

In the very first chapter, we introduce the idea of an object as something you can use. In a sense, programming in Python is an objects-always approach. Students begin by using common programming concepts, while employing the modules that Python provides. These modules allow us to address more interesting problems without introducing unnecessary complexity. For example, we cover simple graphics in Chapter 1 by using a turtle graphics module. We cover image processing through the use of a simple image object that automatically loads an image from a file but allows the students to get and set the values of pixels.

The next chapters provide more details about the concepts introduced in Chapters 1–5. Chapters 6–9 provide students with an opportunity to get more comfortable with basic programming concepts while introducing additional problem-solving patterns. Additionally, students learn more about the internal mechanisms of Python.

The last chapters emphasize object-oriented programming and introduce the concepts needed to design and build classes. When these topics are introduced, students are comfortable with the idea of using an object; therefore, building their own objects is a natural next step. Our first examples emphasize the importance of the interaction between multiple real-world objects. After implementing simple classes, we introduce inheritance in a natural way by implementing a graphics library and by implementing video games as an extension of the turtle module.

Using the Book

There are several possible ways to use this book. Figure P.1 gives you an overview of some possibilities. One path is to move through the book sequentially. Instructors could either cover the entire book in a single semester, or, because there is enough exploratory material to last an entire year, instructors could cover the material in two semesters. A second path would be to cover Chapters 1–5 and then move to Chapters 10–13. This approach provides a balance between imperative and object-oriented programming that fits easily into a single semester. If instructors have additional time, they can cover Chapters 1–5 and then pick and choose from Chapters 6–9 before continuing to Chapters 10–13. Another suggestion would be to teach Chapters 1–9 in an introductory course that covers only imperative programming and the use of objects.

Using the Exercises

There are three kinds of exercises in this book. First, there are exercises in which students run the code that has been presented as a part of the section. These exercises have students use the code to learn or explore on their own. Second, there are exercises that have students modify or extend the code provided in the section. Many times a simple version of the code is provided and students are asked to modify the code to improve it or add additional features. Third, at the end of each chapter there are programming exercises that provide complete projects. These projects are related to the materials covered in the chapter, but do not extend or modify the code already provided.

Throughout the book we have included exercises as a part of each section. These exercises are structured so that they can be used in several ways:

- If you are reading this book as a self-study, the exercises provide breaking points where you have the opportunity to stop reading and try them.
- Instructors may find that many of the exercises contain material to cover in a lecture that complements the material the students have read.

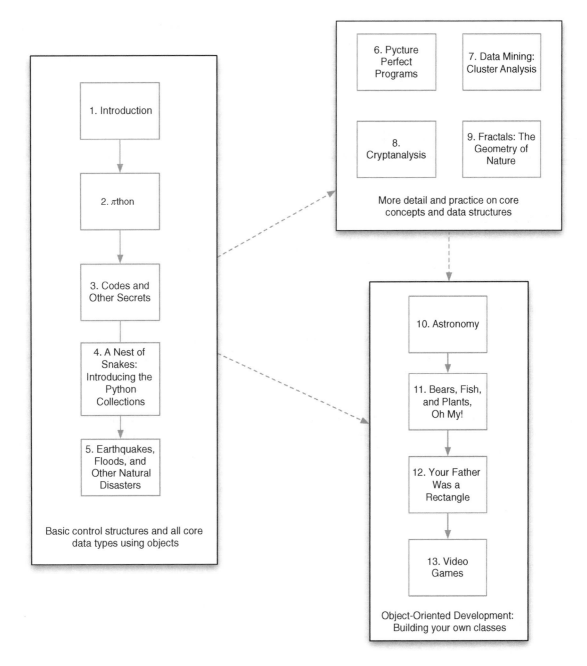

Figure P.1   Road Map

- In a traditional lecture course, the exercises can also be used as homework problems. We have had good luck in the introductory CS course using many small programming assignments. Often the students are able to do more than 30 small programming assignments during a single semester.
- We have also used this book as part of a "hands on" introduction to computer science. A small amount of lecture can be used to reinforce the main points of a chapter, but the majority of the class time is used to work on the exercises that complement the reading. This approach follows a growing trend in computer science education and was very well received by our students.

Key Topics by Chapter

Table P.1 maps the problems that are introduced in each chapter with the key computer science concepts that are established in the chapter.

Supplements

Instructor's supplements, including Answers to Chapter Exercises, a Test Bank, and Power-Point Lecture Outlines are available for instructor download. Complete source code is also provided for students and instructors. For more information and to request access, contact your account representative or visit go.jblearning.com/Python2e.

In addition, instructors now have the opportunity to assign additional online programming activities to their students with Turing's Craft CodeLab. A CodeLab student access code is provided with every new copy of the text. More information about this online service and how to get started can be found after this preface.

Chapter	Problem	Key Computer Science Concepts
Introduction	Drawing polygons and approximating a circle	Numeric data types, assignment statements, using `turtle` objects, loops, functions
πthon	Various methods for approximating Pi	Accumulator pattern, simple selection statements, Boolean expressions, functions that return values, `math` module, `random` module
Codes and Other Secrets	Cipher algorithms—transposition, mono and poly alphabetic substitution algorithms	String data type, modulo arithmetic, selection statements, iteration over strings
A Nest of Snakes: Introducing the Python Collections	Computing simple statistics	Python list, tuple, and dictionary data types
Earthquakes, Floods, and Other Natural Disasters	Computing statistics with large data sets	Reading from files, `while` loops, `urllib` module for reading web pages
Pycture Perfect Programs	Digital image processing, pixel manipulations, enlarge and reduce images, edge detection algorithms	Nested loops, passing functions as parameters, scoping rules
Data Mining: Cluster Analysis	Cluster analysis and visualization of large data sets	Python list and dictionary data types, reading from files, `while` loops
Cryptanalysis	Methods for cracking transposition and substitution ciphers; frequency analysis	Storing nontrivial data in lists and dictionaries, string processing, regular expression module
Fractals: The Geometry of Nature	What are fractals, how can we use them to simulate trees, shrubs, snowflakes, and other natural objects	Recursion, grammars, and production rules
Astronomy	Calculating and plotting the interaction of large celestial bodies	Introduce object-oriented design and construction of classes, instance variables, methods
Bears, Fish, and Plants, Oh My!	Simulating predator–prey relationships	Using objects as part of a simulation. Many objects with simple behaviors can lead to interesting complex results.
Your Father Was a Rectangle	Designing an object-oriented graphics library, circle, square, polygon, etc.	Inheritance, polymorphism, using the `turtle` module to implement a higher-level graphics library
Video Games	Designing and implementing a video game similar to those from the 1980s	Event-driven programming, inheritance, static variables, static methods

Table P.1   Problems and Key Concepts

Acknowledgments

We would like to thank the following reviewers of the first edition for their constructive comments and suggestions, as well as the many other instructors who provided feedback after the first edition published:

Susan Eileen Fox, Macalester College
David R. Musicant, Carleton College
Christine Shannon, Centre College

We would also like to thank our Luther Computer Science colleagues Kent Lee, Steve Hubbard, and Walt Will. We are grateful to our students in CS150 who used early drafts of this book.

Thank you to the staff at Jones & Bartlett Learning for their help and guidance through the publishing process: Tim Anderson, Senior Acquisitions Editor; Amy Bloom, Senior Developmental Editor; and Amy Rose, Director of Production.

We hope that you enjoy reading and using this book as much as we have enjoyed researching and writing it. Please do not hesitate to contact us with problems or suggestions about how to improve this text.

Brad Miller
David Ranum

Turing's Craft CodeLab Student Registration Instructions

turingscraft

CodeLab is the web-based interactive programming exercise service that accompanies this text. It is designed to reduce attrition and raise the overall level of the class. Since 2002, CodeLab has analyzed over forty-two million exercise submissions from more than 110,000 students.

CodeLab has over 400 short exercises, each focused on a particular programming idea or language construct. The student types in code and the system immediately judges its correctness, offering hints when the submission is incorrect. Through this process, the student gains mastery over the semantics, syntax, and common usage of the language elements.

For the Students

CodeLab offers a tree-based, table-of-content navigation system augmented by prev/next buttons that permit sequential traversal. Exercises are organized within a hierarchy of topics that match the textbook's organization and can be reconfigured as needed by the instructor. The student interface offers three tabs for each exercise: a work-area tab containing the instructions of the exercise and a text area for typing in a submission; a results tab that indicates the correctness of the student's submission and provides an analysis of the submission code in the event of an error; and a solutions tab which, by default, is invisible but may be made available at the discretion of the instructor. The solutions tab contains one or more solutions to the exercise; the results tabs contains one or more of the following: correctness indicator, ad hoc hints, marked-up submission indicating possible errors, compiler messages, table of passed and failed test cases. In addition, the usual online amenities of preferences, account management, documentation, and customer support options are provided.

A unique student access code can be found at the beginning of this text. Length of student access is 52 weeks for this edition of the text.

Students can also purchase the access code online at

jblearning.turingscraft.com.

For the Instructors

CodeLab provides the preceding student interface and, in addition, provides

- a **Course Manager** that permits the instructor to rearrange, rename, and/or omit topics and exercises. It also allows instructors to assign deadlines, specify dates when solutions can be seen by students, dates past which student work will not be "counted," and dates prior to which the exercises will be invisible to students.
- a **Grading Roster** that presents a graphical spreadsheet view of student work, where each row corresponds to a student and each column to an exercise. It is also possible to email and/or download rosters in CSV format.
- an **Exercise Creation Tool** that permits instructors to create their own exercises.

Custom CodeLab

CodeLab is customized to this text as follows:

1. The organization of the CodeLab matches the organization of the text.

2. For each chapter that covers an appropriate standard introductory programming topic, the CodeLab offers CodeLab exercises, taken from either the standard set of existing CodeLab exercises or added to fill in any gaps in coverage.

Demonstration Site for CodeLab

A Jones & Bartlett Learning demonstration site is available online at

jblearning.turingscraft.com

Visitors to this site will be directed to a landing page that provides an overview of the product. By clicking on the selected Jones & Bartlett Learning textbook cover, you will be led to more detailed product description pages. In the detailed product description pages there are further descriptions, examples of or links to examples of specific examples of custom CodeLab tie-ins with this text, and a link to a fully functional demo version of the Custom CodeLab. The latter offers full functionality and contains all of the exercise content of the particular Custom CodeLab. To make use of this link, instructors will need a unique Section Creation access code provided by their Jones & Bartlett Learning Computer Science Account Specialist at 1-800-832-0034, or online at www.jblearning.com.

Using this CodeLab Section Creation Code permits instructors to use the online tool to create their own unique CodeLab sections based on the Custom CodeLab. This permits instructors to have instructor accounts that enable access to the Course Manager, roster, and exercise creation tools described on the previous page.

Additonally, Turing's Craft provides online documentation and support for both prospective adopters and actual faculty users of this text. In creating sections for classroom adopting, instructors will receive CodeLab Section Access Codes that should be provided to their students—enabling their students to associate their accounts (i.e., join their instructor's CodeLab section).

System Requirements: CodeLab runs on recent versions of most browsers (e.g., Internet Explorer, Firefox, Safari) on Windows and MacOS and on many versions of Linux. CodeLab does require the installation of the latest Flash Reader, available from www.adobe.com. (Most systems come with Flash pre-installed.) More details about CodeLab browser compatibility can be found at:

www.turingscraft.com/browsers.html

CONTENTS

9   Fractals: The Geometry of Nature   305

CHAPTER 1

Introduction

1.1 Objectives

- To provide examples of computer science in the real world
- To provide an overview of common problem-solving strategies
- To introduce Python's numeric data types
- To show examples of simple programs
- To introduce loops and simple functions
- To introduce turtle graphics

1.2 What Is Computer Science?

Computers are a vital part of our lives. They help to control the planes we fly in and the cars we drive in. They keep track of the buying and selling of stocks in financial markets around the world. They control complex surgical machinery and the pacemakers that are embedded in our bodies. Computers help us to communicate quickly and efficiently with others throughout the world. If you are reading this book, it is likely that you have used a personal computer for writing a paper, surfing the Web, or sending an email. You may have more experience. Perhaps you have hooked up a home network, or even built your own web page. However, even though computers have become appliances that are part of the backdrop of our lives, the chances are that you have not explored the world of programming.

The important question that we must answer in this chapter is "what is computer science?" The problem with answering this question is that the term is misleading right from the start. A look in a dictionary will tell you that science is the theoretical and experimental study of the natural world. It seeks to understand how things work by forming hypotheses, conducting experiments, and analyzing results. Given that definition, you might think that computer science is the exploration and discovery of how a computer works. As a novice, that might be interesting to you, but as a discipline it makes little sense given that computers are manufactured by humans. Computer science is not like biology or physics, disciplines where we are trying to understand the working of the human body, or how the universe works. In the words of Edsgar Dijkstra: "Computer science is no more about computers than astronomy is about telescopes."

So, what is computer science? **Computer science** is the study of **algorithms**.

To put it another way, computer science is primarily about problem solving and computational process. For beginning computer scientists, finding the solution to a problem is often the easiest part. Turning the solution into a set of step-by-step instructions that can be performed by a computer (creating a computational process) is often difficult. Computer scientists often call this set of instructions a **program**. You may think of it as something like a recipe for a beginning cook. First, bring the water to a boil, then add the macaroni, and so on.

Since you are familiar with using advanced programs that are designed to make the computer look intelligent, it is important to dispel that idea right away. Here are six important things to remember about computers as you are learning to program:

1. Computers are dumb.

2. Computers only do what you tell them to do.

3. Computers do what you tell them to do really fast, so they appear smart (but they are not).

4. Computers don't remember anything unless you tell them how to remember.

5. Computers take your instructions literally. If you tell them to do something dumb, they do it.

6. A computer only does what it is told and in exactly the order you tell it.

1.3   Why Study Computer Science?

Now that you have a better idea of what computer science is, you may be wondering why you should learn any more about it. Our belief is that computer science is for everyone. Some of the biggest computer success stories come from people who were not even computer scientists by training but came to computer science later in their careers because they had an interesting problem to solve. For example, a physicist by the name of Tim Berners-Lee at the European Laboratory for Particle Physics (CERN) needed a better way for physicists around the world to share information. The solution to this information-sharing problem became what is today called the World Wide Web. Berners-Lee wrote the computer programs for the first web server and browser. Today he is Director of the World Wide Web Consortium and a professor at the MIT Computer Science and Artificial Intelligence Laboratory.

1.3.1 Everyday Applications of Computer Science

Even if you know you want to be a computer scientist, the fact is that few computer scientists work only on problems limited to computers such as building a better operating system or improving a local area network. Most computer scientists work with people, writing programs in areas such as biology, chemistry, business, economics, publishing, automotive design, or entertainment. Look around you and think about the computer applications you use many times each day: from your browser to an instant messaging program and emails, from word processing to iTunes, cell phones, and iPods.

In addition to our desktop computers, there are the computers we use daily that we do not even think about. For example, the computer in your car that checks your gas mileage several times every second; that examines the wear on your brake pads; that monitors your speed and emissions; that updates your GPS display to keep track of your exact position and plots it on a map on the dashboard display. More and more appliances have computer capabilities as part of their function.

If you go to the doctor and need medical imaging such as a CAT scan or MRI, you are relying on sophisticated computer programs to make and interpret the images of your body. If you look in the cockpit of a newer airplane, you will see that the entire cockpit is nothing more than a bunch of displays with virtual switches on them. In addition, the pilot of the airplane has spent many hours training in a simulated environment controlled by a computer.

There are the computer programs that run behind the scenes that make the world a more orderly place to live. As a student, you probably know that a computer keeps track of your lunch money or credit at the cafeteria, your grade point average, and how much money you owe the college this month. The computers in the library keep track of which books the library owns, who has books checked out, and when they are due back in the library.

If you have ever flown in an airplane, you may not have realized how much the routing and positioning of airplanes rely on computers. Each airplane is tracked by two different radar systems, plus a transponder in the airplane itself that transmits information to a computer to identify itself, along with its current position and altitude. On the ground a multitude of computers share this information to help route the airplane on a safe and efficient path from takeoff to touchdown. Even after the plane is on the ground, computers continue to track it as it moves from the runway to its gate.

When you arrange for a package to be delivered by UPS, that package is routed and tracked by a very sophisticated computer program. At the UPS worldport in Louisville, Kentucky, every package is automatically photographed, measured, and weighed, and it has the information on its super-barcode analyzed by computers to determine its trajectory along some of the 17,000 conveyor belts. This requires awesome computing power: more data are processed here every 30 minutes than in an entire day of trading on the New York Stock Exchange. Eventually every package slides down a chute and is placed into a bag or an air-freight container. And before dawn it is off again to complete its journey in another aircraft or in one of a fleet of waiting trucks [Eco06].

In large cities all the stoplights are controlled by computers. Sensors in the road monitor traffic conditions. Large simulations are used to determine how to keep traffic flowing as quickly as possible. When high traffic is detected in an area, the computer adjusts the timing of the stoplights to increase the flow of traffic [How97].

Computers are providing key help on the forefront of biological research with proteins. Before proteins can carry out their important functions as biology's workhorses, they assemble themselves and undergo the process of protein "folding." While critical and fundamental to virtually all of biology, in many ways the process remains a mystery. Moreover, when proteins do not fold correctly, there can be serious consequences—from Alzheimer's disease to mad cow, Huntington's and Parkinson's disease, as well as many cancers and cancer-related syndromes. The folding@home project is using computers throughout the world to try to understand how protein folding works. For example, the best-known gene that helps to fight cancer is called p53. Roughly half of all known cancers result from mutations in this gene. One of the first published results from the folding@home project involves an investigation into p53 folding. Researchers at Stanford say "We predict how p53 folds and in doing so, we can predict which amino acid mutations would be relevant. When compared with experiments, our predictions have appeared to agree with the experiment and give a new interpretation to existing data." [fold]

In the war on terror, computers are not only busy inside government agencies analyzing millions of emails from suspected terrorists but also working on ways to respond to every possible kind of attack. For example, suppose that the smallpox virus were released into the population of a city like Portland, Oregon. What would be the best response to prevent an epidemic? Should the government institute a policy of mass vaccination? Should only exposed individuals and their circle of contacts be quarantined and/or vaccinated? Should major centers where people congregate, like schools and malls, be closed? These questions can best be answered by using massive computer simulation programs that can anticipate the movements of individuals in a large city, along with various strategies for reducing the spread of a disease [BES05].

Countless motion pictures today are produced with various kinds of computer-generated special effects. Obviously there are the computer-animated movies such as *Toy Story*, *Cars*, and *Shrek*, but the line is continually blurring between live action and computer-generated films. For example, the vast battles between the Orcs and the humans in the *Lord of the Rings* movies were completely computer-generated, including the actions of each individual battle participant. In the traditionally animated movie *The Lion King*, the wildebeest stampede was computer-generated. For his role in *The Polar Express*, Tom Hanks wore a special suit with sensors on it so that his body motions were continuously monitored. After the live action part of the film was completed, a new skin was computer-generated and put on the body that followed the live movements of the actor.

1.3.2   Why Computer Science Is Important

In one sense, studying computer science is important because it gives you a better understanding of how the technological world around you works. After reading this book, you may have a new appreciation for the applications you use every day. Hopefully, you will even aspire to write your own improved version of some application.

In another sense, computer science helps to prepare you for your future. Many of the interesting jobs are going to be at the intersection of computer science and some other domain. Speaking at the Microsoft Research Faculty summit, Bill Gates made this observation: "The nature of these jobs is not just closing the door and coding. The greatest missing skill is somebody who's good at understanding engineering and bridges that to working with customers and marketing." Recently a manager at a successful software company said, "I sometimes turn away applicants who have perfect scores on the standardized tests." The reason he said this was that these applicants may be technically perfect, but they lack the ability to communicate with people and solve real-world problems.

Most importantly, a first course in computer science will help you in the following ways:

- You will be able to apply new problem-solving skills.
- You will learn to apply logic.
- You will learn about process (a series of actions or steps taken in order to achieve a specific outcome).

- You will understand and apply abstraction.
- You will learn to think and communicate more clearly.

1.4   Problem-Solving Strategies

Problem solving happens on three different levels:

- **Strategy:** A high-level idea for finding a solution.
- **Tactics:** Methods or patterns that work in many different settings.
- **Tools:** Specific tricks and techniques that are used in specific situations.

Paul Zeitz [Zei99] provides us with a helpful analogy for illustrating the three different levels of problem solving:

> You are standing at the base of a mountain, hoping to climb to the summit. Your first strategy may be to take several small trips to various easier peaks nearby, so as to observe the target mountain from different angles. After this, you may consider a somewhat more focused strategy, perhaps to try climbing the mountain via a particular ridge. Now the tactical considerations begin: how to actually achieve the chosen strategy. For example, suppose that our strategy suggests climbing the south ridge of the peak, but there are snowfields and rivers in our path. Different tactics are needed to negotiate each of these obstacles. For the snowfield, our tactic may be to travel early in the morning while the snow is hard. For the river, our tactic may be scouting the banks for the safest crossing. Finally, move into the most tightly focused level, that of tools: specific techniques to accomplish specialized tasks. For example, to cross the snowfield we may set up a particular system of ropes for safety and walk with ice axes. The river crossing may require the party to strip from the waist down and hold hands for balance. These are all tools. They are very specific. You would never summarize, "To climb the mountain we had to take our pants off and hold hands," because it was a minor—though essential—component of the entire climb. On the other hand, strategic and sometimes tactical ideas are often described in your summary: "We decided to reach the summit via the south ridge and had to cross a difficult snowfield and a dangerous river to get to the ridge."

As you progress through this book, you will encounter several different problem-solving strategies. In addition, you will see that computer science uses many different problem-solving tactics. In particular you will learn to recognize patterns in the problems you solve that lead to patterns in the programs you write. Finally, as you use the Python programming language you will learn about the tools that Python provides to write your solution as a program.

A simple example will illustrate some of what we are talking about. The question is as follows: "A class has 12 students. At the beginning of class each student shakes hands with each of the other students. How many handshakes take place?"

Your first instinct might be to simply say that since each person must shake hands with 11 other people the answer is $12 \cdot 11 = 132$ handshakes, but you would be wrong. To help you make progress toward the correct answer, you can employ a strategy called **simplification**. Simplification is a strategy that reduces a problem to a trivial size.

Let's assume that instead of 12 people there is only one person in the classroom. When there is only a single person, no handshakes will take place. But what happens when a second person enters the classroom? Upon entering the room, the second person must shake hands with the first (and only other) person in the room for one handshake. Now suppose a third person enters the classroom. The third person must shake hands with the first two, making a total of $2 + 1 + 0 = 3$ handshakes. The fourth person who enters the room must shake hands with the three people already in the room, so our total handshake count is now $3 + 2 + 1 + 0 = 6$. By this time you should see a pattern of **generalization**—a technique that enables you to go from some specific examples to a solution that can be implemented as a program.

In our handshaking problem the pattern is telling us that the Nth person to enter the classroom shakes hands with $N - 1$ other people, and the total number of handshakes is the sum $1 + 2 + 3 + \ldots N - 1$. At this point we might simply write a computer program that adds up the numbers from 1 to $N - 1$ for us. Adding numbers is something that computers are particularly good at. However, we will also point out that there is a general solution for this problem for adding a sequence of numbers:

$$sum = \frac{n \cdot (n + 1)}{2}$$

For our handshake problem, we need to add up the numbers from 1 to 1 less than the number of students. Given that there are 12 students, $n = 11$. Plugging 11 into the formula gives us:

$$\frac{11 \cdot 12}{2} = 66$$

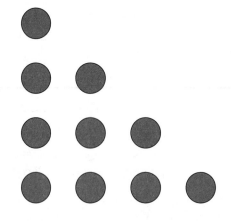

Figure 1.1   Representing the sum of the numbers from 1 to N graphically

You can verify this result yourself by simply adding the numbers from 1 to 11.

In fact we can *prove* that the formula gives us the correct answer by using **representation**, another important strategy that will solve our problem. Proving that $\sum_{i=1}^{n} i = \dfrac{n \cdot (n+1)}{2}$ is true for all values of n using mathematical induction would be a daunting task for most people. However, let's visualize the problem of adding up the numbers from 1 to N as shown in Figure 1.1.

In this representation of the problem, we show each of the numbers we want to add as a row of circles, thus representing the addition of $1 + 2 + 3 + 4$. Now we could just count the circles to get our answer, but that is not very interesting and does not prove anything. The interesting part comes in Figure 1.2, where we have taken all four rows of dots, duplicated them, and flipped them diagonally. The dots now form a rectangle that is 4 rows high and 5 columns wide. It is now easy to see that the total number of dots is just $4 \cdot 5 = 20$. But we have twice as many dots as we started with, so the number of dots we started with is $20 \div 2 = 10$.

If you generalize our example a little bit, it is easy to see that this graphical trick works no matter how many rows of dots we use. Therefore, we have shown a proof for an interesting mathematical sequence, but because we chose a good representation for the problem we have not had to do anything more complicated than simple multiplication and division.

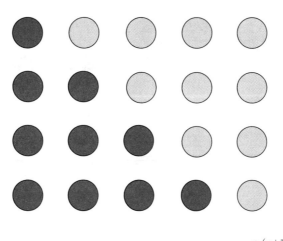

Figure 1.2   The sum of the numbers 1 to N is $\frac{n\cdot(n+1)}{2}$

1.5   Python Overview

In this book the language you will use to write your computer programs is called **Python**. Why did we choose Python instead of a language like C++ or Java? The answer is simple: We want you to focus on learning the problem-solving strategies and techniques that a computer scientist uses. **Programming languages** are tools and Python is a good beginning tool. Languages like Java and C++ are fine tools as well, but they require you to keep track of many more details and they are harder to learn than Python.

The best way to learn Python is to try it out—so let's get started. The first thing we are going to do is start the Python interpreter. Depending on your operating system, there are any number of ways to do this. For example, you might start a program called IDLE—named after Eric Idle of Monty Python fame. Or you might just type `Python` at the command prompt. No matter how you start it, you will know you are successful when you see a window such as the one shown in Figure 1.3. In this case, we have started the Python interpreter from a terminal window on a MacBook Pro. For detailed instructions on installing and starting Python on your system, refer to Appendix A.

As you progress through this chapter, you will see that example programs are in boxes called **listings**, and commands that you can type interactively at the Python shell are in boxes called **sessions**. Whenever you see a session box, we strongly encourage you to try the session for yourself. Also, once you have typed in the example we have shown, feel free to try some variations in order to find out for yourself what works and what does not.

```
● ○ ○                    ⌂ davidranum — Python — 102×27
david-ranums-powerbook-g4-90:~ ranumdav$ python3
Python 3.2.3 (v3.2.3:3d0686d90f55, Apr 10 2012, 11:25:50)
[GCC 4.2.1 (Apple Inc. build 5666) (dot 3)] on darwin
Type "help", "copyright", "credits" or "license" for more information.
>>> ▌
```

Figure 1.3   The Python shell

As we begin to explore Python, we will answer three important questions you should ask about any programming language:

- What are the primitive elements?
- How can we combine the primitive elements?
- How can we create our own abstractions?

1.5.1   Primitive Elements

At the deepest level, the one primitive element in Python is the **object**. In fact, everything in Python is an object, and you will read this refrain often in this book. By now you are probably wondering what we mean by *object*. After all, if you look around you will see many objects: this book, pencils, pens, your chair, a computer. What do these items have to do with Python? Like you, Python thinks of the things in its world as objects. Python even considers numbers to be objects—an idea that may be a bit confusing to you as you probably don't think of numbers as objects. But Python does, and we'll see why this is important shortly.

Python classifies the different kinds of objects in its world into **types**. Some of the easiest types to work with are numbers. Python knows about several different types of numbers:

- Integer numbers
- Floating point numbers
- Complex numbers

Integer Numbers

Integers are the whole numbers that you learned about in math class. We will introduce more of Python's primitive types as we progress through this chapter. But before we move on let's look at Python's integers in more detail. We can already do a lot with Python just using integers. For starters, we can use the Python shell we started a few moments ago as a calculator. Let's try a few mathematical expressions. Type in the following examples using the Python interpreter. After you have typed in an expression, press the return key to see the result.

```
>>> 2+2
4
>>> 100-75
25
>>> 7*9
63
>>> 14//2
7
>>> 15//2
7
>>> 15 % 2
1
```

Session 1.1   Simple integer math

The examples in Session 1.1 illustrate some very important Python concepts that you should become familiar with as soon as possible. The first concept is Python's **evaluation loop**.

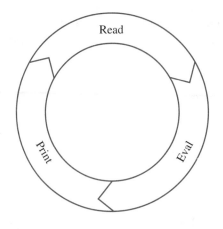

Figure 1.4   The Read–Eval–Print loop in Python

At a high level, the Python interpreter is really very simple. It does three things over and over again: (1) read, (2) evaluate, and (3) print. These are illustrated in Figure 1.4.

First, Python *reads* one line of input. In the first example, Python reads 2 + 2, then it *evaluates* the expression 2 + 2 and determines that the answer is 4. Finally, Python *prints* the resulting value of 4. After displaying the result, Python prints the characters >>> to show you that it is waiting to read another expression. The three characters >>> are called the Python **prompt**.

In general, a Python **expression** is a combination of operators and operands. When we evaluate an expression, we get a result. In the examples in our Python session, the operators are familiar mathematical operators '+', '−', '*', and '//'. You may be more used to × and ÷ for multiplication and division, but you will not find those symbols on a standard keyboard, so Python, and almost all other programming languages use "*" and "/".

One thing that may surprise you in the example is the result of the expression 15//2. Of course, we all know that 15 divided by 2 is really 7.5. However, because both operands are integer objects and // is the integer division operator, Python produces an integer object as a result. Integer division works like the division you learned when you were young. 15 divided by 2 equals 7, remainder 1. You can find out the remainder part of the result using the modulo operator (%). For example, 15 % 7 evaluates to the remainder value of 1.

Integer division is really useful in some cases, but it can also trip you up. What if you want to divide 15 by 2 and get 7.5 as the answer? In order to get the result as a **floating point** number you must use the floating point division operator '/'.

Exercises

1.1 Find the sum of the numbers 8, 9, and 10.

1.2 Find the product of the numbers 8, 9, and 10.

1.3 Compute the number of seconds in a year.

1.4 Compute the number of inches in 1 mile.

1.5 Compute the number of 2 ft square tiles to cover the floor of a 10 by 12 ft room.

1.6 Compute the number of handshakes required for each person in your class to shake hands with every other person exactly one time.

1.7 Find the average age of five people around you using integer division. Doublecheck your answer.

Floating-Point Numbers

Floating-point numbers are Python's approximation of what you called real numbers in math class. We say that floating-point numbers are an approximation because unlike real numbers, floating-point numbers cannot have an infinite number of digits following the decimal point. In Python you can tell the difference between a floating-point number and an integer because a floating-point number has a decimal point. Session 1.2 presents some examples of math using floating-point numbers.

```
>>> 2.0 + 2.0
4.0
>>> 2 + 2.0
4.0
>>> 15 / 2
7.5
>>> 2.0 ** 50
1125899906842624.0
>>> 2.5 ** 25
8881784197.0012531
>>> 2.0 ** 500
3.2733906078961419e+150
>>> 1.33e+5 + 1.0
133001.0
```

Session 1.2   Floating-point math

Notice that we have added something new in this example: the ** symbol, which is called the exponentiation operator. So 2.0 ** 50 is really two to the fiftieth power. You should also notice that when the result of a floating-point operation gets really big, Python uses scientific notation to express the results. The Python number 3.273e+150 really means 3.273 times 10 to the 150th power, or 3273 followed by 147 zeros! A very big number indeed. Notice also that you can use floating-point numbers in scientific notation as part of a Python expression.

Exercises

1.8 Find the average age of five people around you using floating-point division. Double-check your answer.

1.9 Find the volume of a sphere with a radius of 1 using the formula $4/3\pi r^3$.

1.10 Compute 1/3 of 15. Did you get the right answer?

1.11 The Andromeda galaxy is 2.9 million light years away. There are 5.878×10^{12} miles per light year. How many miles away is the Andromeda galaxy?

1.12 How many years would it take to travel to the Andromeda galaxy at 65 miles per hour?

Although 3.273e + 150 is a good approximation, we know that there are not really 147 zeros in the result. One of the disadvantages of using scientific notation is that you lose some *precision* in your result. If you want to get very exact results, integers allow us to do calculations to unlimited precision. Session 1.3 shows the real value of 2 ** 500 using integers.

```
>>> 2 ** 500
32733906078961418700131896968275991522166420460430647894832913680961337964046745548832700923259041571508866841275600710092172565458853930533285275893
76
>>>
```

Session 1.3   The use of integers to obtain very precise answers for large numbers

---

Exercises

1.13 Compute the factorial of 13.

1.14 Compute 2 to the 120th power.

1.15 If the universe is 15 billion years old, how many seconds old is it?

1.16 How many handshakes would it take for each person in Chicago to shake hands with every other person?

Complex Numbers

The final primitive numeric type in Python is the **complex number**. As you may remember, complex numbers have two parts to them, a real part and an imaginary part. In Python a complex number is displayed as *real* + *imaginary*j. For example, 5.0 + 3j has a real part of 5.0 and an imaginary part of 3. Although we mention complex numbers here to give you a complete list of the numeric primitives, we will not go into any additional details at this point.

Summary of Numeric Types

What happens when we mix integers and floating-point numbers? Let's look at the examples shown in Session 1.4 to find out.

```
>>> 100 * 3.4
340.0
>>> 100000000000000000000000000 * 3.4
3.4000000000000003e+26
>>> 10000000 * 1000000
10000000000000
>>> 1000000000 / 1000000000
1
>>> 1000 // 10.0
100.0
>>> 1000 / 10.2
98.039215686274517
>>> 1000 // 10.2
98.0
>>> 5 + 4+3j
(9+3j)
```

Session 1.4   Mixing integers, long integers, floats, and complex numbers

When mixing different types of numbers, you can figure out what the result will be converted to by applying the following rules:

1. If either argument is a complex number, the other is converted to complex.

2. If either argument is a floating-point number, the other is converted to floating point.

3. For all other arguments, both must be plain integers and no conversion is needed.

Notice that when using floating-point numbers with the integer division operator the result is a floating-point number with the fractional part truncated. You can also tell Python to explicitly convert a number to either an integer or floating-point number by using the `int` or `float` functions. For example, `float(5)` will convert the integer 5 to the floating-point number 5.0. When converting floating-point numbers to integers, Python always truncates the fractional part of the number. For example, `int(3.99999)` will convert the floating-point number 3.99999 to the integer 3.

In summary, we have seen that Python supports several different types of primitive objects in the number family: integers for ordinary simple math; or, when precision is required or when dealing with very large numbers; floating-point numbers, for working with scientific applications or accounting applications where we need to keep track of dollars and cents. We have seen that Python can be used to make simple numerical calculations. However, at this point, Python is nothing more than a calculator. In the next section we will add some additional Python primitives that will give us a lot more power.

1.5.2 Naming Objects

Very often we have an object that we would like to remember. Python allows us to **name** objects so that we can refer to them later. For example, we might want to use the name *pi* rather than the value 3.14159 in a mathematical expression. We might also want to give a name to a value that we are going to use over and over again rather than recalculating it each time.

In Python we can name objects using an **assignment statement**. A statement is like an expression except that it does not produce a value for the read–eval–print loop to print. An assignment statement has three parts: (1) the left-hand side, (2) the right-hand side, and (3) the assignment operator (=). The left side contains the name we are assigning to and the right side can be any Python expression.

```
name = python expression
```

When the Python interpreter evaluates an assignment statement, it first evaluates the expression that it finds on the right-hand side of the equals sign. Once the right-hand side expression has been evaluated, the resulting object is referred to using the name found on the left side of the equals sign. In computer science, we call these names **variables**. More formally, we define a variable to be a named reference to a data object. In other words, a variable is simply a name that allows us to locate a Python object.

Suppose we want to calculate the volume of a cylinder where the radius of the base is 8 cm and the height is 16 cm. We will use the formula *volume = area of base * height*. Rather than calculate everything in one big expression, we will divide the work into several assignment statements. First, we will name the numeric objects "pi," "radius," and "height." Next, we will use the named objects to calculate the area of the base and finally the volume of the cylinder. Session 1.5 shows how we use this sequence of assignment statements and Python arithmetic to solve our problem.

```
>>> pi = 3.14159
>>> radius = 8.0
>>> height = 16
>>> baseArea = pi * radius ** 2
>>> cylinderVolume = baseArea * height
>>> baseArea
201.06175999999999
>>> cylinderVolume
3216.9881599999999
>>>
```

Session 1.5   Calculating the volume of a cylinder with assignment statements

After studying Session 1.5, you may have some questions:

- How is the use of the equals sign in Python different from what you learned in math class?
- If you change the value for `baseArea` will `cylinderVolume` automatically change?
- Why doesn't Python print out the value of `pi` after the first assignment statement?
- What names are legal in Python?

Let's look at these questions one at a time. The equals sign in Python is very different from what you learned in math class. In fact, you should think of it not in terms of equality but rather as the assignment operator, which has the job of associating a name with an object. Figure 1.5 illustrates how names are associated with objects in Python. All the names and objects in this figure come from Session 1.5. The relationships between names and the objects they reference are indicated by the arrows between them.

Another way of thinking about assignment is to imagine that an assignment statement is like taking a sticky label with a name written on it and attaching it to an object. You know that you can put more than one sticky label on an object in the real world, and the

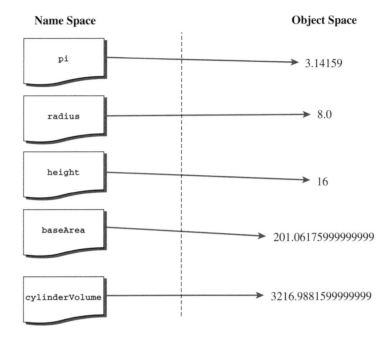

Figure 1.5 A reference diagram illustrating simple assignment in Python

analogy holds true in the Python world as well. A Python object can have more than one name. For example, suppose you made the following additional assignment $x = 8.0$. After executing that statement, you could add another label called **x** with another arrow pointing at the object 8.0, as shown in Figure 1.6.

Variables can take the place of the actual object in a Python expression. When Python evaluates the expression **pi * radius ** 2**, it first looks up **pi** and **radius** to see what objects they refer to and then substitutes the values into the expression. The expression thus becomes **3.14159 * 8.0 ** 2**. Next, Python evaluates **8.0 ** 2** to get an intermediate result of **64.0**. Python then evaluates **3.14159 * 64.0** to get the value **201.06176**. After the right-hand side of the expression is evaluated, Python assigns the name **baseArea** to **201.06176**.

Let's look at one more example using assignment. Consider the Python statements in Session 1.6.

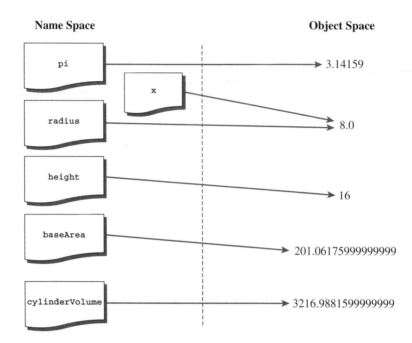

Figure 1.6   Reference diagram after x = 8.0

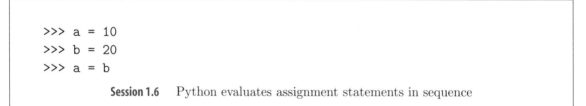

```
>>> a = 10
>>> b = 20
>>> a = b
```

Session 1.6   Python evaluates assignment statements in sequence

After these three assignment statements, what object does **a** refer to? As you think about this question it is very important to remember that Python evaluates the statements from top to bottom, one after another. Let's rephrase what is going on in the order that Python performs its work.

1. Assign the name **a** to the integer object 10.

2. Assign the name **b** to the integer object 20.

3. Find the object named **b**, then assign the name **a** to that object.

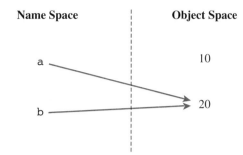

Figure 1.7 Result of assignment a = b

The answer to our question is that **a** now refers to the object 20. This is shown in Figure 1.7. In addition, since we have not changed what **b** refers to since the original assignment, **b** continues to refer to the object 20. If you are confused by this example, try to draw the reference diagram yourself one step at a time.

Now that you understand more about the assignment operator you will understand that attaching the name `baseArea` to a different object will have no impact on the name `cylinderVolume`. To make the new value for `baseArea` change the value of `cylinderVolume`, you will need to ask Python to execute the statement `cylinderVolume = baseArea * height`.

Since assignment is a statement rather than an expression, it does not return a value. This means that there is nothing for the read–eval–print loop to print out. That is why you do not see any output following the assignment statements in Sessions 1.5 and 1.6.

A name on a line all by itself is a very simple Python expression. Notice that just typing a name causes Python to find the value for the object and return it as the result of the expression. You can see examples of this in Session 1.5.

There are several important rules to remember about naming things in Python. Names can include any letter, number, or an _ (underscore). Names must start with either a letter or an _. Python is case sensitive, which means that the names `baseArea`, `basearea`, and `BaseArea` are all different. Some names are reserved by Python for its own use. These are called **keywords** and correspond to important Python capabilities that you will learn about. Table 1.1 shows you all of Python's reserved keywords.

and	continue	else	for	import	not	raise
assert	def	except	from	in	or	return
break	del	exec	global	is	pass	try
class	elif	finally	if	lambda	print	while

Table 1.1   Python's reserved words

Exercises

1.17 Given the following Python statements:

```
a = 79
b = a
a = 89
```

(a) Draw a reference diagram to show the labels and objects after the first two statements.

(b) Draw a reference diagram to show the labels and objects after the last statement.

1.18 Which of the following are legal variable names:

(a) _abc123

(b) 123abc

(c) abc123_

(d) _123

1.19 Consider the following statements:

```
a = 10
b = 20
c = a * b
d = a + b
```

Draw a reference diagram to show all the objects and names after evaluating these statements

1.20 What are the values of a and b after Python evaluates each of the following four statements?

```
a = 10
b = 20
a = b
b = 15
```

1.21 Consider the following statements:

```
idx = 0
idx = idx + 1
idx = idx + 2
```

What is the value of `idx` after Python evaluates each of the three statements?

1.5.3 Abstraction

Abstraction is defined as a concept or idea not associated with any specific instance. For example, you can think of mathematical functions on your calculator such as square root, sine, and cosine as abstractions. These functions can calculate a value for *any* number, but the method of calculating a square root is independent of the particular number. In that way we can think of a function that calculates a square root as being the general idea. The square root function works equally well for all numbers because it is a general function. We do not have a special square root function for each possible number, just one function that works for all numbers.

One way of thinking about functions is as a "black box." You send information into the black box on one side and new information comes out on the other side. You don't know exactly what goes on inside the box but you do know the behavior that the box should exhibit. Figure 1.8 illustrates this concept for the square root function.

The Python language contains many such abstractions. Many of the new things we will see in Python from here on are in fact abstractions built using the Python primitives we have already talked about or will talk about in the first few chapters of this book. In other words, much of Python is written in Python.

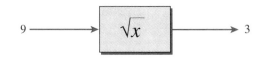

Figure 1.8   A black box view of the square root function

The turtle Module

Many of the additional parts of Python functionality are found in **modules**—an optional part of Python that implements an abstraction that is designed to make programming easier. In order to get the power of a module, you have to tell Python to load the module you want. The statement you need to use to load a module is **import** *modulename.*

When you **import** a module, an object is created inside Python. That object has the type *module* and has a name attached to it that matches the name you used on the import line. Every object in Python has three important characteristics: (1) an identity, (2) a type, and (3) a value. In addition, some Python objects have special values called attributes, and some Python objects also have **methods** that allow us to ask the object to do something interesting. Let's look at a simple example before we go any further.

The example we will use is the **turtle** module. The **turtle** module provides us with a simple graphics programming tool known as a turtle. Very simply, a turtle is an object that we can control. A turtle can move forward or backward, and it can turn in any direction. When a turtle moves, it draws a line if its tail is down. A turtle is a Python object that has both attributes and methods. Some of the attributes of a turtle are shown in Table 1.2.

position	The coordinates of the turtle on the screen
heading	The direction the turtle is facing
color	The color of the turtle
tail position	The turtle's tail can be up or down

Table 1.2   Turtle attributes

Name	Parameter(s)	Description
Turtle	None	Creates and returns a new turtle object
forward	Distance	Moves the turtle forward
backward	Distance	Moves the turle backward
right	Angle	Turns the turtle clockwise
left	Angle	Turns the turtle counterclockwise
up	None	Picks up the turtle's tail
down	None	Puts down the turtle's tail
color	Color name	Changes the color of the turtle's tail
fillcolor	Color name	Changes the color that the turtle will use to fill a polygon
heading	None	Returns the current heading
position	None	Returns the current position
goto	x, y	Moves the turtle to position x, y
begin_fill	None	Remembers the starting point for a filled polygon
end_fill	None	Closes the polygon and fills it with the current fill color
dot	None	Leaves a dot at the current position

Table 1.3 Summary of simple turtle methods

The methods of the turtle are summarized in Table 1.3. To start, we will just concern ourselves with a few of them. For example, we can tell the turtle to go forward, backward, turn left, turn right, or ask for its position. The turtle has a tail that can be up or down. When the tail is down and the turtle moves, it draws a line. If the tail is up and the turtle moves, nothing is drawn. Session 1.7 shows a Python session where we create a turtle object and try out some of the turtle's capabilities.

Let's look at this example line by line. In line 1 we use an import statement to load the turtle module. In line 2 we ask Python to evaluate the name turtle. Python rewards us by telling us the identity of the object that turtle is assigned to. If you look at the identity, you will see it is telling the location of the source code for the module. This location will vary according to the kind of computer you are using. If we were really adventurous, we could go there and look at the Python methods that are stored in the turtle.py file.

```
>>> import turtle
>>> turtle
<module 'turtle' from
'/Library/Frameworks/Python.framework/Versions/3.2/lib
/python3.2/turtle.py'>
>>> gertrude = turtle.Turtle()
>>> gertrude
<turtle.Turtle object at 0x101393950>
>>> gertrude.forward(100)
>>> gertrude.right(90)
>>> gertrude.forward(50)
>>> gertrude.position()
(100.00,-50.00)
>>> gertrude.heading()
270.0
>>>
```

Session 1.7   Using the `turtle` module

Once we have the `turtle` module loaded, we will start to use the methods in the module to do something interesting. In line 6 we have an assignment statement, in which we are making a new `Turtle` object and giving it the name `gertrude`.

Before we go any further with this example, we need to explain line 6 in more detail. In particular the expression `turtle.Turtle()` contains a new operator—the dot (.). The **dot operator** tells Python to look up the name right in front of the dot and return the object it names. This process is referred to as **dereferencing**. In this case the dereferencing operation allows Python to find the `turtle` module. Once we have the module, Python continues looking for the name to the right of the dot. In this case Python looks for the name `Turtle`. A good way to think of this is that Turtle is "inside" the `turtle` module. So the first . gets us to the `turtle` module and then inside the `turtle` module we find the object named `Turtle`.

We can then see that `turtle.Turtle()` is a method that creates a new object. The type of the new object is `Turtle`. A method that creates a new object is called a **constructor**. New turtles that we construct are called **instances** of the type `Turtle`.

If you are typing this session interactively as you are reading, you will see that when a turtle is created a new window appears on the screen. The triangle in the middle of the screen is the turtle. When a new instance of `Turtle` is first created, it is at position (0, 0) in the middle of the window. The turtle's initial heading is 0 degrees, or straight to the right. The color attribute for the new turtle is black. As you move the turtle around, it remembers its latest position, what direction it is facing, and whether its tail is up or down.

The next two lines simply demonstrate that when you evaluate a name that corresponds to a more complicated object you get back Python's representation of that object. Unlike a number where the representation is self-evident, a turtle's representation gives you a unique identification for the object. In this case we see that `gertrude` is `<turtle.Turtle object at 0x101393950>`. To be even more specific, the result is telling us that the type of `gertrude` is `turtle.Turtle`. Furthermore, the turtle can be found at location `0x101393950` in the computer's memory.

Now that we have our new turtle object, named `gertrude`, the next three lines instruct `gertrude` to do some drawing. As you might guess, the line `gertrude.forward(100)` causes the turtle to move forward 100 units. Once again, the dot notation is very important to understanding how Python interprets the statement. First, the dot tells Python to dereference the name `gertrude`. When Python finds the object, it evaluates the method `forward` that is "inside" the turtle. The forward method knows that it needs to move forward 100 units because we pass it a parameter of 100. Just as mathematical functions like $\cos(20)$ or $\sqrt{20}$ take parameters, Python functions and methods may also accept parameters.

Functions are abstractions of generalized behaviors. **Parameters** are the way we tell the function *specifically* what it should do. In this case we want `gertrude` to move forward 100 units, then turn right 90 degrees, then move forward again, but this time by only 50 units. If you try to run this example on your own, your window should look just like Figure 1.9.

The last four lines of Session 1.7 show that we can also use methods to ask the turtle for information about itself. First, we ask `gertrude` to tell us where it is with the method call `gertrude.position()`. `gertrude` replies that it is at (100.0, −50.0). What is in fact happening is that the `position()` method returns the value (100.0, −50.0) and the print part of the read–eval–print loop prints out that value. All functions can return values, and so they can be included in Python expressions. The fact that the `position` method returns a value is no different than the cosine function returning a value. Similarly the heading method tells us that `gertrude` is currently facing 270 degrees.

Notice that in the world of our turtle, the coordinates (0, 0) are in the center of the window. The x coordinate grows in a positive direction as the turtle moves toward the right. If the turtle moves toward the left side of the window, the x coordinates get smaller and are

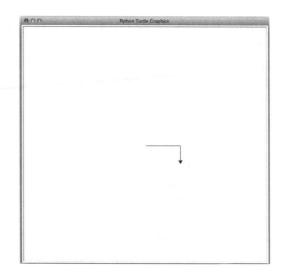

Figure 1.9   Using methods to control a turtle

negative to the left of the middle of the window. Similarly, the y coordinate grows as the turtle moves toward the top of the window and gets smaller as the turtle moves toward the bottom. One pixel on your computer screen corresponds to 1 unit of turtle movement. If the turtle's heading is 0 degrees, it is facing to the right; 90 degrees is up, 180 degrees is to the left, and 270 degrees is down.

The turtle objects found in the **turtle** module have many other methods. Table 1.3 shows just a few of them. We'll introduce additional methods as we have need for them in future examples.

Exercises

1.22 Create a turtle called **sven**. Now tell **sven** to go forward 10. What is **sven**'s position now?

1.23 Create a turtle called **ole** and tell **ole** to turn right 45 degrees and go forward 50. Notice that you now have two turtles in the same window.

1.24 On a sheet of graph paper sketch out a simple line drawing of something. Using the turtle methods in Table 1.3, recreate your line drawing.

Writing Your Own Functions

We are not limited to the functions that the authors of Python have given us. We, too, can write our own functions to add our own abstractions to the Python language. In fact, functions are just another kind of Python object with a couple of special capabilities. We define a function in Python using the *def* statement. Listing 1.1 shows a general template for using the *def* statement to define a function.

```
1    def functionName (param1, param2, ...):
2        statement1
3        statement2
4        ...
```

Listing 1.1   A template for function definition

The *def* statement begins by giving the function a name. Next we specify any parameters we want our function to accept. In Python we can have zero or more parameters for any function we write. All the parameters must be listed inside the parentheses that follow the function name. Next we have a colon character, which tells the Python interpreter that the sequence of indented statements that follow are all part of the function. Python knows to stop reading lines for the *def* statement when it encounters a line that is not indented. We call a group of Python statements that are indented at the same level a block.

Now let's try to write a real function. Suppose that we are working on a graphics program that requires us to draw a lot of squares. Telling the turtle how to draw a square each time we need one is tiresome and repetitious. In fact, a square is an example of an abstraction. We know that a square is a geometric shape that has four sides of equal length, and four 90-degree corners. What we don't know is how long the sides are for any particular square.

Our goal is to write a function that can use any turtle to draw a square of any size. That statement suggests that we need two pieces of information to solve our problem—namely, the turtle that will draw the square and the size of the square. These pieces of information will become the parameters to our function.

The next step is to use the parameters along with the built-in methods of a turtle. We can draw a square by moving the turtle forward and turning right by 90 degrees four times in a row. Listing 1.2 shows a complete Python function for drawing a square with a turtle.

Notice that the statements in the function are the same turtle commands that we typed in interactively when we first started using the turtle. When the commands are inside the function, they are just grouped together so that we can have all the commands run as if we had typed them one after another. This is one of the great powers of writing a function.

```
1    def drawSquare(myTurtle,sideLength):
2        myTurtle.forward(sideLength)
3        myTurtle.right(90)     # side 1
4        myTurtle.forward(sideLength)
5        myTurtle.right(90)     # side 2
6        myTurtle.forward(sideLength)
7        myTurtle.right(90)     # side 3
8        myTurtle.forward(sideLength)
9        myTurtle.right(90)     # side 4
```

Listing 1.2   A function to draw a square using a turtle

It is also important to remember that Python will do the commands in exactly the order they are typed in the function.

One final thing to note about the code in Listing 1.2 is the # character as seen on Lines 3, 5, 7, and 9. This is known as the **comment marker**. Any text following the comment marker is ignored by the Python interpreter. Comments allow the programmer to place descriptive documentation into Python code that will not impact the execution of the program.

Type the **drawSquare** function into a text file exactly as shown here. After you type in the function, save it to a file called **ds.py**. You have just created your first module! In the same way that **turtle** is a module created by other Python programmers, you have created a module called **ds**. We can now use the **drawSquare** function, as shown in Session 1.8. After running the commands in this session, you should have an image that looks like Figure 1.10.

```
>>> from ds import *
>>> import turtle
>>> t = turtle.Turtle()
>>> drawSquare(t,150)
>>>
```

Session 1.8   A Python session to demonstrate calling a function

There is a lot going on in this simple example, but there are only a couple of new things that you have not seen before. First, we import the **turtle** and **ds** modules. We then make a new **turtle** object named t, and next we call **drawSquare**. Python knows that it should treat the object **drawSquare** like a function call because of the parentheses after the name. The parentheses are operators that tell Python to treat the object as a function. You can even show yourself that **drawSquare** is a plain old object by simply typing **drawSquare**

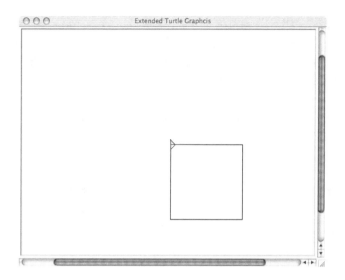

Figure 1.10   The result of the statements in Session 1.8

without the parentheses after the name. If you do so, Python will tell you something like `<function drawSquare at 0x11a1270>`.

When we call the function `drawSquare`, we pass it two objects, `t` and `150`. When a function is called, the objects are matched up with the parameter names they were given when we defined the function. The first parameter in the list names the first object, the second parameter in the list names the second object, and so on. This means that inside the `drawSquare` function `t` goes by the name `myTurtle`. The turtle object now has two names. Similarly, inside the `drawSquare` function, `150` now has the name `sideLength`.

Figure 1.11 shows a reference diagram to help you understand how all the names and objects are matched up. This diagram is simplified somewhat, but we will add more details to such diagrams in later chapters. The important thing to notice is the relationship between the names of the parameters of a function and the objects that are passed to the function when it is called.

In particular, notice the difference in location between the `Turtle` constructor and the `drawSquare` function. When we execute the statement `import turtle`, we are creating a module, and any functions inside the module are "hidden" from us unless we use the `turtle` prefix. However, if we use the statement `from ds import *`, all the functions defined in the file `ds.py` are visible to us without the `ds` prefix.

In Figure 1.11 there are three names: (1) `turtle`, which references the turtle module we imported previously; (2) `t`, which references the turtle object we created with the call to the turtle constructor (`turtle.Turtle()`). You can see the turtle constructor inside the `turtle` module. (3) `drawSquare` references the function object we defined for drawing squares. In the function object named `drawSquare`, you can see that there are two additional names: (1) `myTurtle`, which references the turtle object named `t`, and (2) `sideLength`, which references the integer object 150 and has no other name.

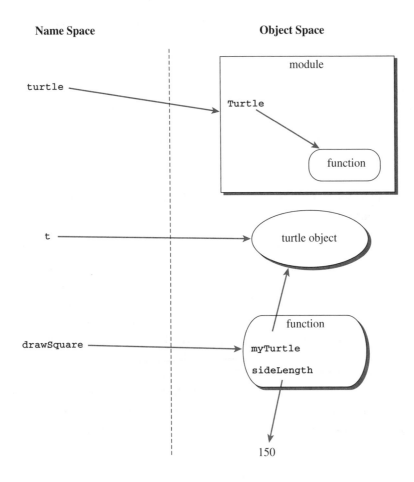

Figure 1.11   A reference diagram for the function `drawSquare`

Exercises

1.25 Modify the `drawSquare` function to draw a rectangle whose width is twice the `sideLength`.

1.26 Create a new function called `drawRectangle` that takes three parameters: `myTurtle`, `width`, and `height`.

1.27 Suppose that in Session 1.8 we had used the expression `import ds` instead of `from ds import *`. Continue the rest of the session. Draw a reference diagram that illustrates this session.

1.28 Call your function as follows: `drawRectangle(t,50,300)`.

1.29 Draw a reference diagram for the previous problem.

1.5.4   Repetition

Although the `drawSquare` function we discussed earlier worked just fine, there is one thing that is unsatisfying about our solution. We had to duplicate the move forward and turn to the right statements four times. In order to eliminate this duplication, Python provides us with a statement that allows us to repeat a block of code multiple times. This statement is called a *for* loop. The *for* loop is an example of using *repetition* in our program.

Before we rewrite our `drawSquare` function, let's look at the structure of a *for* loop to get a better idea of how this statement works:

```
for i in range(n):
    statement1
    statement2
    . . .
```

Notice that the *for* loop template has some similarity to the *def* template. There is a beginning line ending with a colon, followed by an indented block of code. All you need to know about a *for* loop at this point is that each statement in the indented block will be evaluated **n** times, where **n** is the parameter to the `range` function. We will talk more about the `range` function as well as the **i** and *in* part of the statement shortly. If the first line was `for i in range(10):`, then each statement would be evaluated ten times.

Now let's see how we can use this idea of simple repetition to make our `drawSquare` function more elegant. In fact, all we are going to do is wrap the two lines that tell the turtle to move forward and turn right inside a loop that will be evaluated four times. You can see the new and improved **drawSquare** function in Listing 1.3.

```
1    def drawSquare(myTurtle,sideLength):
2        for i in range(4):
3            myTurtle.forward(sideLength)
4            myTurtle.right(90)
```

Listing 1.3   A better version of the **drawSquare** function

Drawing a Spiral

Our goal for this section is to understand how we can use the *for* loop to have the turtle create a more complicated square spiral pattern. To create a spiral pattern, we need to have the sides of our square grow each time the turtle moves forward. We can make that happen easily when we understand the two components from the *for* statement we ignored a moment ago. First, let's look at the **range** function. If you ask Python to evaluate the expression **range(5)**, you will get back an object representing the sequence of numbers [0, 1, 2, 3, 4].

The **range** function is very versatile in that it can create all kinds of sequences depending on the parameters that we supply. There are three ways we can call **range**:

- **range(stop):** Creates a sequence of numbers starting at 0 going up to **stop-1**.
- **range(start, stop):** Creates a sequence of numbers beginning at **start** going up to **stop-1**.
- **range(start, stop, step):** Creates a sequence of numbers beginning at **start** going up to **stop-1** counting by **step**.

Exercises

1.30 Use the **range** function to create a sequence of the multiples of 5 up to 50.

1.31 Use the **range** function to create a sequence of numbers from −10 to 10.

1.32 Use the **range** function to create a sequence of numbers from 10 to −10.

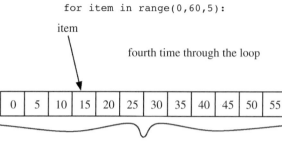

Figure 1.12   A loop variable naming each item in a sequence

Now that you have a better understanding of the **range** function, let's look at the **loop variable**—the variable that always follows the keyword *for*. In Listing 1.3 the loop variable is named **i**. The way the *for* loop works in Python is that the loop variable starts out as the name for the first item in the sequence produced by the **range** function the first time through the loop. The second time through, the loop variable is the name for the second item in the sequence and so on until there are no more items in the sequence. We can use any valid Python name for the loop variable.

Figure 1.12 shows the sequence produced by the call to **range** and the item in the list named by **item** during the fourth repetition of the loop. Note that 55 is the last item in the sequence because the upper bound, 60, is never included in the result of the **range** function.

Loop variables can be used in expressions and function calls like any other Python names. To solve the spiral problem, we will use a loop variable in a function that draws a spiral. The parameters to this function will be the turtle and a bound for the longest side on the spiral. We will start with the first side having length 1, then each time through the loop we will increase the length of the side of the spiral by 5. Listing 1.4 shows the function drawSpiral.

```
1    def drawSpiral(myTurtle,maxSide):
2        for sideLength in range(1,maxSide+1,5):
3            myTurtle.forward(sideLength)
4            myTurtle.right(90)
```

Listing 1.4   A Python function to draw a spiral

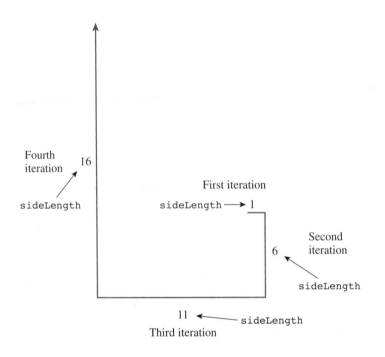

Figure 1.13   The first four iterations of the loop in `drawSpiral(t,150)`

Figure 1.13 illustrates the first four iterations of the *for* loop in Listing 1.4. In the first iteration, the turtle draws a line that is 1 unit long because `sideLength` refers to the first item in the sequence produced by `range(1,maxSide+1,5)`, which is 1. In the second iteration, `sideLength` refers to the number 6, so the turtle draws a line that is 6 units long. In the third iteration, `sideLength` refers to 11; in the fourth iteration, `sideLength` refers to the fourth number in the sequence, which is 16.

Exercises

1.33 Modify the spiral function to turn more than 90 degrees for each iteration.

1.34 Modify the spiral function to turn less than 90 degrees for each iteration.

1.35 Modify the spiral function to use the loop variable as the number of degrees to turn.

1.36 Modify the spiral function to use a second turtle and create two spirals in opposite directions.

1.37 Write a function `drawTriangle` that takes two side lengths and the angle between them and draws the triangle. (Hint: You need to remember the starting point.)

1.38 Write a function that draws a series of 10 squares, with each square being 5 pixels smaller on each side. The squares should all start at the same location.

1.39 Redo the last question so that the squares are all centered.

1.40 Use the turtle to plot the function $y = x^2$.

1.41 Use the turtle to plot the function $y = \frac{x}{2} + 3$.

Drawing a Circle

Our final problem for this chapter is to write a function that uses a turtle to draw a circle of a given radius. Although this may seem like a daunting task, we will help ourselves by solving a simpler problem first and then using what we learn to solve the more general problem. The first thing we must recognize is that the turtle's functionality allows us to draw only straight lines. We will approximate a curved line by drawing many short straight lines.

Suppose that our problem was to draw a triangle rather than a circle. Starting from the `drawSquare` function, it is not too hard to imagine how we would modify `drawSquare` to write `drawTriangle`. We would change the call to `range(4)` to be `range(3)` since we only need three sides. The other change we need to make is the number of degrees we pass as the parameter for our right turn function.

How many degrees do we need to turn each time to draw an equilateral triangle? When we are all done, we want our turtle to be pointed in the same direction it was when we started. That means that as we draw the three sides of our triangle the turtle is going to turn through 360 degrees. That matches our `drawSquare` function where we made four 90 degree turns ($4 \cdot 90 = 360$). So to draw a triangle we will use $360 \div 3 = 120$ for our turning angle. Listing 1.5 shows the small changes made to the `drawSquare` function.

```
def drawTriangle(myTurtle,sideLength):
    for i in range(3):
        myTurtle.forward(sideLength)
        myTurtle.right(120)
```

Listing 1.5 A Python function to draw a triangle

Name	Sides	range()	Angle
Triangle	3	3	$360/3 = 120$
Square	4	4	$360/4 = 90$
Pentagon	5	5	$360/5 = 72$
Octagon	8	8	$360/8 = 45$

Table 1.4   Number of sides versus turning angle for several polygons

We now have two simple examples of polygons, the equilateral triangle and the square. It is relatively easy to imagine how to write a function to draw a pentagon or an octagon by following the pattern we have established with the triangle and square. In fact, Table 1.4 illustrates the values we would supply to the **range** and **right** functions for several different polygons.

What Table 1.4 suggests is that we can write a function that is more abstract than **drawSquare**, **drawTriangle**, or even **drawOctagon**. The abstraction is a regular polygon. Creating one function that can replace many simpler functions at a higher level of abstraction is a common and important problem-solving technique in computer science.

Given what we have learned, we can write a function that draws any regular polygon if we pass the function a third parameter. The third parameter tells the function how many sides we want. Once we know how many sides are required, we can easily have Python calculate the turning angle for us using the formula **turnAngle = 360 / numSides**. You can see the new **drawPolygon** function in Listing 1.6.

```
1    def drawPolygon(myTurtle, sideLength, numSides):
2        turnAngle = 360 / numSides
3        for i in range(numSides):
4            myTurtle.forward(sideLength)
5            myTurtle.right(turnAngle)
```

Listing 1.6   A Python function to draw any size regular polygon

Session 1.9 along with Figure 1.14 illustrate several calls to the **drawPolygon** function. Note that the call **drawPolygon(t,20,20)** makes a pretty good approximation of a circle. Note also that we are assuming that the **drawPolygon** function has been saved in a file called **dp.py**.

```
>>> from dp import *
>>> import turtle
>>> t = turtle.Turtle()
>>> t.up()
>>> t.backward(200)
>>> t.left(90)
>>> t.down()
>>> drawPolygon(t,100,4)
>>> drawPolygon(t,100,8)
>>> drawPolygon(t,50,20)
>>> drawPolygon(t,20,20)
```

Session 1.9   Testing the `drawPolygon` function

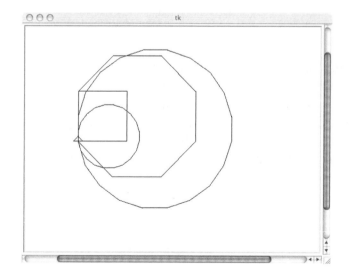

Figure 1.14   Several polygons drawn by the `drawPolygon` function

We have worked our way through the problem of drawing a circle by using a large degree polygon as an approximation. Now let's return to the original problem statement, which asks us to draw a circle of a given radius. So, the last trick is to figure out how to use the radius to compute the number of sides and the side length.

Suppose that to get the smoothest circle possible, even a very large circle, we choose to always have 360 sides to our polygon. This means that the turtle will always turn 1 degree and should give us a smooth circle even for a large radius.

Only one question remains: How do we decide what side length to use for a given radius? One good approximation is to use the relationship of the radius of a circle to the circumference. If we are doing a good job of approximating a circle, then the circumference of a circle should be very close to the sum of the individual sides of the polygon. Recall that the circumference of a circle can be calculated from the radius using the formula $circumference = 2 \cdot \pi \cdot radius$. Once we have the circumference, we can calculate an individual side length by dividing by the number of sides, which we have decided will be 360. Listing 1.7 shows the **drawCircle** function, which makes use of our **drawPolygon** function to draw a circle with a given radius.

```
1    def drawCircle(myTurtle,radius):
2        circumference = 2 * 3.1415 * radius
3        sideLength = circumference / 360
4        drawPolygon(myTurtle,sideLength,360)
```

Listing 1.7   A Python function to draw a circle

The **drawCircle** function is extremely simple because we have reduced the problem of drawing a circle to drawing a polygon with a particular number of sides and side lengths. We first calculate the circumference and then calculate the side length given the circumference and number of sides. Since we already know how to draw a polygon, we do not have to redo that work. We can build on what we have already done and use the **drawPolygon** function. Session 1.10 and Figure 1.15 illustrate the use of the **drawCircle** function to draw both a large and a small circle.

```
>>> from dp import *
>>> import turtle
>>> t = turtle.Turtle()
>>> t.up()
>>> t.backward(200)
>>> t.left(90)
>>> t.down()
>>> drawCircle(t,20)
>>> drawCircle(t,200)
>>>
```

Session 1.10 Drawing a circle

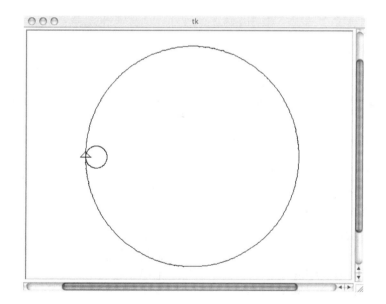

Figure 1.15 Drawing a circle for a given radius

Exercises

1.42 Modify the `drawCircle` function so that the circle is drawn with the center at the turtle's present position.

1.43 The `drawCircle` function is somewhat inefficient: for small circles, 360 sides is really overkill and for very large circles 360 sides might be too few. See if you can devise a way to make the number of sides and turning angle dependent on the radius so that smaller circles use fewer sides and larger circles use more.

1.6   Summary

This chapter introduced the following fundamental building blocks of programming and Python:

- Primitive types
- Expressions
- Naming objects
- Using modules and functions provided by Python
- Writing your own functions to extend the functionality provided by Python

In addition, the approach we followed to use the turtle to draw a circle illustrates an important problem-solving pattern that you will use many times as you progress through this book. That pattern can be summarized as follows:

- Simplify in order to understand the problem better.
- Generalize to solve many problems with one function.
- Build on what you have learned to solve more complex problems.

In subsequent chapters we will continue to use these basic building blocks. There will be more tools to add to your toolbox. We have glossed over a few details on some of the ideas introduced in this chapter but will return to them later. Keep in mind the idea behind this book: to focus on problem solving while continually adding to your knowledge of programming and computer science.

Key Terms

abstraction	dot operator	loop variable	Python
algorithm	expression	module	repetition
assignment statement	floating-point number	name	representation
block	generalization	object	sequence object
complex number	instance	parameter	simplification
computer science	integer	program	type
constructor	keywords	programming language	variable
dereferencing	list	prompt	

Python Keywords

```
def    from     in
for    import   range
```

Bibliography

[BES05]   Chris L. Barrett, Stephen G. Eubank, and James P. Smith. If smallpox strikes portland. *Scientific American*, March 2005.

[Eco06]   Economist. The physical internet. *The Economist*, June 2006.

[fold]   Stanford folding@home project. http://folding.stanford.edu

[How97]   Kenneth R. Howard. Unjamming traffic with computers. *Scientific American*, 1997.

[Zei99]   Paul Zeitz. *The Art and Craft of Problem Solving*. Wiley, 1999.

Programming Exercises

1.1 Using the **drawSquare** function, you can have the turtle draw an interesting flowerlike shape by drawing many squares. Each square is drawn after turning the turtle by some number of degrees between each square. Write a function **drawflower** that takes the number of squares to draw as a parameter (**numSquares**) and draws a flower by repeating the square **numSquares** times. You will need to figure out how far to turn the turtle based on **numSquares**.

1.2 Write a function to make the turtle draw a five-pointed star.

1.3 Write a function to make the turtle draw an n-pointed star when n is restricted to be odd.

1.4 Write a function to have the turtle draw a simple line drawing of anything you want.

1.5 There are two more functions that the turtle understands: **begin_fill()** and **end_fill()**. When **begin_fill** is called, the turtle keeps track of its starting point, and all the lines it has drawn until **end_fill** is called. When **end_fill** is called, the turtle fills in the space enclosed by the lines that the turtle has drawn. Use these new functions to draw a more interesting picture.

CHAPTER 2

πthon

2.1 Objectives

- To understand how computers can help solve real problems
- To further explore numeric expressions, variables, and assignment
- To understand the accumulator pattern
- To utilize the math library
- To further explore simple iteration patterns
- To understand simple selection statements
- To use random numbers to approximate an area

2.2 What Is Pi?

In this chapter we will continue to explore computer science, problem solving, and the Python programming language by considering one of the most famous numbers of all: the number pi, often represented by the Greek letter π. Almost everyone has at one time or another used the value pi. In fact, we used π in Chapter 1 in our circle calculations.

Pi is defined to be the ratio of a circle's circumference to its diameter (see Figure 2.1). This relationship, $\pi = C/d$, gives rise to the familiar equation $C = \pi d$ used to compute the circumference of a circle given the diameter. Since the diameter of a circle is twice the radius, this can also be written $C = 2\pi r$ where r is the radius.

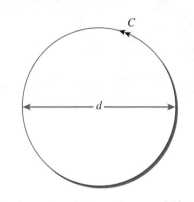

Figure 2.1   Pi—the ratio of circumference (C) to diameter (d)

Other common formulas that utilize pi include the area of a circle with radius r, $A = \pi r^2$, the volume of a sphere with radius r, $V = \frac{4}{3}\pi r^3$, and the surface area of a sphere with radius r, $S = 4\pi r^2$. In this chapter, we are more interested in the value of pi itself, not in the way that pi is used.

The value of pi has been a matter of interest for thousands of years. Writings from ancient Egypt and Babylon as well as the Bible contain references to this mystical number. In your math class, it is likely that you were told to use 3.14 or 3.14159 as the value of pi. In fact, these values worked fairly well for many of the problems that you were asked to solve. However, it turns out that the exact value of pi is not as simple as this would make it seem.

Pi is known in mathematics as an irrational number. This means that pi is a floating-point number with an infinite, nonrepeating pattern of decimal digits. The actual value of pi is

$$3.14159265358979323846264338327950288419716939937510...$$

where the ... indicates the infinite digits.

Because pi cannot be stated exactly, the best that we can do is provide an approximation, for example 3.14. Other usual approximations are $\frac{22}{7}$, $\frac{355}{113}$, and the more complex $\frac{9801}{2206\sqrt{2}}$.

Session 2.1 shows the interactive Python environment as we evaluate each of these approximations.

```
>>> 22/7
3.1428571428571428
>>> 355/113
3.1415929203539825
>>> import math
>>> 9801/(2206*math.sqrt(2))
3.1415927300133055
>>>
```

Session 2.1   Simple approximations for pi

There is one Python element that is new in Session 2.1: the statement `import math`. Recall that the `import` statement allows us to gain access to a Python module that contains additional functionality that we might find useful. In this case, we need to compute the square root of 2. After loading the math module, we can use the `sqrt()` function to do this for us.

2.3   More About the math Module

As we mentioned earlier, there are many mathematical helper functions available in the math module. Unfortunately, it is sometimes difficult to know what they are and what they are called. To remedy this, Python has a built-in help subsystem that allows you to see the documentation for a particular module. To use help, simply give the command `help("modulename")` where the module name is the particular module you are interested in. For example, Session 2.2 shows the result of asking for help on the math module. You might find it interesting that in addition to typical math functions such as `sin`, `log`, and `pow`, the math module contains two constants, `e` and `pi`.

```
>>> help("math")
Help on module math:
NAME
    math
FILE
    .../lib-dynload/math.so
MODULE DOCS
    http://www.python.org/doc/current/lib/module-math.html
DESCRIPTION
    This module is always available.  It provides access to the
    mathematical functions defined by the C standard.
FUNCTIONS
    acos(...)
        acos(x)
        Return the arc cosine (measured in radians) of x.
    asin(...)
        asin(x)
        Return the arc sine (measured in radians) of x.

    .
    .many more functions here...
    .

    sqrt(...)
        sqrt(x)
        Return the square root of x.
    tan(...)
        tan(x)
        Return the tangent of x (measured in radians).

    tanh(...)
        tanh(x)
        Return the hyperbolic tangent of x.
DATA
    e = 2.7182818284590451
    pi = 3.1415926535897931
>>>
```

Session 2.2   Asking for help on a Python module

In the sections that follow, we will explore a number of interesting techniques for approximating pi. Remember that none of them can give us an exact answer.

Exercises

2.1 Run the help command as follows: `help('turtle')`. Note the quotes around `turtle`.

2.2 Run the help command as follows: `help(turtle)`. What is the difference?
[handwritten: error not def]

2.3 `import turtle` and repeat the last exercise.

2.4 Run the help command on the `math.sin` function.

2.5 Explore the `random` module using the help facility. What does the `randrange` function do? What does the `randint` function do?
[handwritten: 'random. randrange']

2.4 The Archimedes Approach

The first technique we will consider, attributed to the mathematician Archimedes, makes use of a many-sided polygon to approximate the circumference of a circle. Recall that pi is related to the circumference of a circle by the equation $C = 2\pi r$ where r is the radius of the circle. Given a circle of radius 1, sometimes called a unit circle, this equation can be rearranged to give $\pi = \frac{C}{2r}$ or simply $\pi = \frac{C}{2}$.

The **Archimedes approach**, shown in Figure 2.2, will use the distance around a polygon that is inscribed within a unit circle. By using a polygon with increasing numbers of sides (therefore decreasing side length), the total distance around the polygon will come closer and closer to the actual circumference of the circle. Does this sound familiar? Of course, no matter how large the number of sides, we will never truly reach the actual circle.

Figure 2.2 shows more of the details that will be needed to understand how this **approximation** will work. If we assume that the polygon has n sides of length s, we can then focus our attention on a small slice of the polygon. In the triangle shown, the side labeled h will have a length of 1 since we are assuming a unit circle. The angle labeled B can be easily computed by remembering that there are 360 degrees in a circle. This means that angle B is $360 \div n$. Therefore, angle A is $\frac{1}{2}B$. In addition, we also know that the highlighted triangle is a right triangle so that the side opposite angle A has a length of $\frac{1}{2}s$

Now we have to use a bit of trigonometry. In a right triangle (see Figure 2.3), the ratio of the opposite side to the long side (or hypotenuse) is equal to the sine of angle A. Because our triangle has a hypotenuse of length 1, we know that $\frac{1}{2}s$ will simply be equal to the

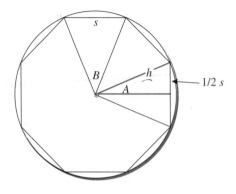

Figure 2.2   Developing the Archimedes Approach using an 8-sided polygon

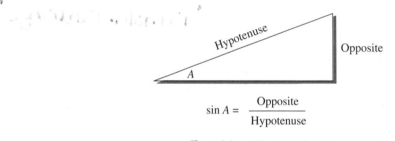

$$\sin A = \frac{\text{Opposite}}{\text{Hypotenuse}}$$

Figure 2.3   The `sin` function

sine of angle A. How do we compute the sine of angle A? The answer is to use the math library. As with `sqrt` earlier, the `sin` function (as well as all of the other trigonometric relationships) is available once we import the math module.

2.4.1   The Python Implementation

Session 2.3 shows that it is possible to implement Archimedes' algorithm by using the interactive Python environment. We can simply type in and evaluate statements that follow the steps outlined here. Note that the last step evaluates the value of `pi` as computed in the previous statement.

```
>>> import math
>>> numsides = 8
>>> innerangleB = 360.0/numsides
>>> halfangleA = innerangleB/2
>>> onehalfsideS = math.sin(math.radians(halfangleA))
>>> sideS = onehalfsideS * 2
>>> polygonCircumference = numsides * sideS
>>> pi = polygonCircumference / 2
>>> pi
3.0614674589207183
>>>
```

converts degrees to radians

Session 2.3   The Archimedes approach: Interactive implementation

2.4.2   Developing a Function to Compute Pi

What if we now want to change the number of sides and try the calculation again? Unfortunately, we would need to retype all of the statements since the calculations need to be redone. A better way to do this is to use abstraction.

Recall that abstraction allows us to think about a collection of steps as a logical group. In Python, we can define a function that not only serves as a name for a sequence of actions but also returns a value when it is called. We have already seen this type of behavior with the sqrt function. When we call sqrt(16), it *returns* 4.

Listing 2.1 shows the function definition template as shown earlier with one additional statement. The **return** statement causes two related actions. First, the expression contained in the statement will be evaluated, producing a result object. Second, the function will terminate immediately and the reference to the result object will be returned to the calling statement. It is important to realize that no matter where the return statement occurs, it will be the final statement performed as **return** causes the function to terminate. For this reason, **return** is typically the last statement in the function.

In the case of the Archimedes pi approximation, we need to develop a function that has the behavior shown in Figure 2.4. This function will need one parameter—namely, the number of sides we wish to use in the polygon. The function will return the value of pi using the steps as we developed them earlier.

Listing 2.2 shows the **archimedes** function. As you look at each statement, you should note that we have used variable names that match those we used as we worked through the

```
1    def functionName(param1,param2,...):
2        statement1
3        statement2
4        ...
5        return expression
```

Listing 2.1   Template for a function definition with *return*

Figure 2.4   Abstraction with the Archimedes approximation

previous problem-solving process. This makes it easier to see how the steps we discovered in the solution can be mapped into Python statements. In fact, one of the characteristics of a well-written function is the ability to read the code and see the underlying algorithm.

```
1    import math
2
3    def archimedes(numsides):
4
5        innerangleB = 360.0/numsides
6        halfangleA = innerangleB/2
7
8        onehalfsideS = math.sin(math.radians(halfangleA))
9
10       sideS = onehalfsideS * 2
11
12       polygonCircumference = numsides * sideS
13       pi = polygonCircumference/2
14
15       return pi
```

Listing 2.2   Implementing the Archimedes approximation as a function

Before moving on we should note one additional use of the math library. Recall that the `sin` function takes an angle and returns the ratio of opposite side to hypotenuse. However, it assumes that the angle will be in radians instead of degrees. When we compute angle B by dividing 360 by the number of sides, we get a value in degrees. Fortunately, the math library contains a function (called **radians**) that will convert a value in degrees to the equivalent value in radians.

Session 2.4 shows how we can use the **archimedes** function. The first evaluation shows that the name **archimedes** evaluates to a reference to a function object. The subsequent lines invoke the function passing different numbers of sides. Note that the accuracy of the pi approximation gets better and better as we increase the number of sides in the polygon.

```
>>> archimedes
<function archimedes at 0x103e0b0>
>>> archimedes(8)
3.0614674589207183
>>> archimedes(16)
3.1214451522580524
>>> archimedes(100)
3.1410759078128301

>>> for sides in range(8,100,8):
        print(sides,archimedes(sides))

8 3.06146745892
16 3.12144515226
24 3.13262861328
32 3.13654849055
40 3.13836382911
48 3.13935020305
56 3.13994504528
64 3.14033115695
72 3.1405958903
80 3.14078526073
88 3.14092537783
96 3.14103195089
>>>
```

Session 2.4   Using the **archimedes** function

In the final code fragment of the session, we use a *for* statement to call the **archimedes** function, repeatedly using a *range* construct to automatically provide different numbers of sides. Recall that **range(8,100,8)** will produce values for the variable sides starting at 8 and stopping at or before 99, increasing by 8 every time.

You will also notice another new Python function, *print*. The *print* function shows both the number of sides used and the result returned from the function. In a sense, this is nothing more than explicitly calling the print action as was described as part of the read–eval–print loop. It is possible to print more than one value by including multiple parameters.

Exercises

2.6 Repeat the loop in Session 2.4. In addition to the value of pi, print out the difference between the value calculated by the `archimedes` function and `math.pi`. How many sides does it take to make the two close?

2.7 Modify the `archimedes` function to take the radius as a parameter. Can you get a better answer more quickly using a larger circle?

2.5   Accumulator Approximations

The pi approximation techniques that follow will use mathematics based on what are called infinite series and infinite product expansions. The basic idea is that by adding or multi-plying an infinite number of arithmetic terms, we can get closer and closer to the actual value we are trying to compute. Although the mathematics of these approaches is beyond the scope of this book, the patterns provide excellent examples of arithmetic processing.

2.5.1   The Accumulator Pattern

In order to use these techniques, we will need to introduce another important problem-solving pattern known as the **accumulator pattern**. This common pattern comes up very often. Your ability to recognize the pattern and then implement it will be especially useful as you encounter new problems that need to be solved.

As an example, consider the simple problem of computing the sum of the first five integer numbers. Of course, this is really quite easy since we can just evaluate the expression $1 + 2 + 3 + 4 + 5$. But what if we wanted to sum the first ten integers? Or perhaps the first hundred? In this case we would find that the size of the expression would become quite long. To remedy this, we can develop a more general solution that uses iteration.

Examine the Python code shown in Session 2.5. As you can see, the variable `acc` starts off with a value of 0, sometimes called the **initialization**. Recall that the statement `for x in range(1,6):` will cause the loop variable `x` to iterate over the values from 1 to 5. Figure 2.5 shows how this can then be used to create the **running sum**. Every time we pass through the body of the `for` loop, the assignment statement `acc = acc + x` is performed. Since the right-hand side of the statement is evaluated first, it is the current value of `acc` that is used in the addition. To complete the assignment statement, the name `acc` will now be updated to refer to this new sum. The final value of `acc` is then 15.

```
>>> acc=0
>>> for x in range(1,6):
        acc = acc + x

>>> acc
15
>>>
```

Session 2.5 Computing a running sum with iteration and an accumulator variable

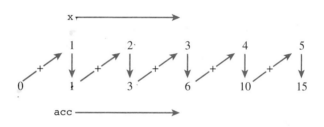

Figure 2.5 Using the accumulator pattern

This may seem strange to see the same name appearing on both the left-hand and right-hand sides of the assignment statement. However, if you remember the sequence of events for an assignment statement you will not be confused.

1. Evaluate the right-hand side

2. Let the variable left-hand side refer to the resulting object

The variable `acc` is often referred to as the **accumulator variable** since it is continuously updated with the current value of the running sum. Now, whether we want the sum of the first five integers or the first 5000, the task is the same. Simply change the upper bound on the iteration and allow the accumulator pattern to do its work. It is very important to note that the entire process depends on correctly initializing the accumulator variable. If `acc` does not start at 0 in this case, the ending sum will not be correct.

Exercises

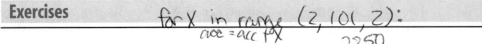

for X in range (2, 101, 2):
acc = acc + X
2250

2.8 Compute the sum of the first 100 even numbers. 2250

2.9 Compute the sum of the first 50 odd numbers. 625

2.10 Compute the average of the first 100 odd numbers.

2.11 Write a function that returns the average of the first N numbers where N is a parameter.

2.12 Write a function called factorial that computes the product of the first N numbers where N is a parameter.

2.13 Each number in the Fibonacci sequence is the sum of the previous two numbers. The first two numbers in the sequence are 1 and 1. Compute the tenth Fibonacci number.

2.14 Write a function to compute the Nth Fibonacci number where N is a parameter. You may assume that N will be greater than or equal to 3.

2.5.2   Summation of Terms: The Leibniz Formula

We can now turn our attention back to computing approximations of pi. As we suggested earlier, there are a number of formulas that use the idea of infinite expansion. One of these is the **Leibniz formula**: $\frac{\pi}{4} = \frac{1}{1} - \frac{1}{3} + \frac{1}{5} - \frac{1}{7} + \frac{1}{9}$.... A bit of algebra—namely multiplying every fraction by 4—will give us a much easier form: $\pi = \frac{4}{1} - \frac{4}{3} + \frac{4}{5} - \frac{4}{7} + \frac{4}{9}$....

In order to successfully turn this formula into Python, we must look for the following patterns:

- All the numerators are 4.
- The denominators are all odd numbers.
- The sequence alternates between addition and subtraction.

We will deal with each of these patterns shortly.

The accuracy of the approximation will depend on how many terms we decide to use. More terms will lead to a better approximation. Given that, we can think about the abstraction pattern and construct a function that will need the number of terms as a parameter and will return the value of pi that those terms produce (see Figure 2.6).

Because the right-hand side of this formula is a sum of terms, we are inclined to think about the accumulator pattern. To set up this pattern, we will need an accumulator variable and

Figure 2.6 Abstraction for the Leibniz formula

an iteration. In this case, since the number of terms will be a parameter to the function, we can start with the following structure:

```
def leibniz(terms):
    acc = 0

    for aterm in range(terms):
        #body goes here

    return acc
```

Since each term is a fraction, we have to build both the numerator and denominator. Each fraction will have a common numerator of 4. The denominator in each case will change, starting at 1 and increasing by 2 each time. We can achieve this effect using the accumulator pattern. In this case we will start the accumulator variable **den** at 1 and the statement **den = den + 2** will cause an accumulation each time through the iteration.

```
def leibniz(terms):
    acc = 0
    num = 4
    den = 1

    for aterm in range(terms):

        den = den + 2

    return acc
```

We now need to determine how to compute each fraction term. To start, we can divide the numerator by the denominator. However, we still need to make some of the terms positive

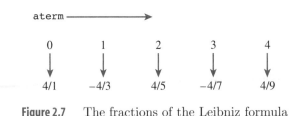

Figure 2.7   The fractions of the Leibniz formula

and some negative. An interesting way to do this is to take advantage of the loop variable `aterm`.

Figure 2.7 shows the first five fractions of the sequence and how each term is related to the value of the loop variable `aterm`. Notice that when `aterm` is 0 or an even number, the term is positive; when `aterm` is 1 or an odd number, the term is negative.

One way to produce this pattern is to raise -1 to the power of `aterm`. This will cause a sequence of alternating 1 and -1 that can be multiplied by the fraction. The result can then be added to the accumulator variable, as shown in Listing 2.3. Each time through the iteration, `nextterm` is computed by dividing the numerator by the denominator and multiplying the result by a power of -1. Session 2.6 shows the function in action. Note again that increasing the number of terms gives a better approximation.

```
1  def leibniz(terms):
2      acc = 0
3      num = 4
4      den = 1
5
6      for aterm in range(terms):
7          nextterm = num/den * (-1)**aterm
8
9          acc = acc + nextterm
10
11         den = den + 2
12
13     return acc
```

Listing 2.3   A function to compute pi using the Leibniz formula

```
>>> leibniz(100)
3.1315929035585537
>>> leibniz(1000)
3.1405926538397941
```

Session 2.6   Using the `leibniz` function

Exercises

2.15 Run the `leibniz` function using 10,000 and 100,000 terms.

2.16 Compare the results of the `leibniz` function with `archimedes`. How does the number of terms compare with the number of sides?

2.17 Modify the `leibniz` function so that you can alternate signs without using `(-1)**term`.

2.5.3   Product of Terms: The Wallis Formula

Our second example of the accumulator pattern will use an infinite product instead of an infinite sum. The **Wallis formula**, 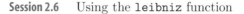 $\frac{\pi}{2} = \frac{2}{1} \times \frac{2}{3} \times \frac{4}{3} \times \frac{4}{5} \times \frac{6}{5} \times \frac{6}{7} \times \frac{8}{7}...$, will again require that we decide how many terms we want to use. In this case, you can see that the right-hand side makes use of the multiplication operator.

One thing to immediately note is the impact this multiplication will have on the initialization of the accumulator variable. If we use 0 as before, we will always get a result of 0. In order to start out the process, we will want to use 1.

The next pattern we should consider is the fractions themselves. At first glance it might seem that they are unrelated. However, if you look at them in pairs (see Figure 2.8), you can see that they are related. Each pair of fractions shares a common numerator, starting with 2 in the first pair and increasing by 2 for each subsequent pair.

Using abstraction once again, we can now begin to construct a function that will accept the number of pairs as the input parameter and will return the value of pi produced by the infinite product. We can initialize our accumulator variable to 1 and our numerator to 2.

Pair 1   Pair 2   Pair 3

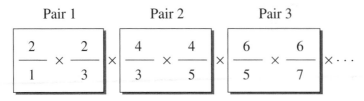

Figure 2.8   Fraction pairs in the Wallis formula

```
def wallis(pairs):
    acc = 1
    num = 2

    for apair in range(pairs):
        #compute a fraction pair

        num = num + 2
```

Our next step is to calculate the actual fractions. Since we have already noted that they come in pairs, we need to look for the relationship between the numerator and denominator within each pair. Given a specific numerator, the denominators can be seen to be one less and one more. In other words, if the numerator is n, the left fraction of the pair has a denominator of $n-1$ and the right fraction of the pair has a denominator of $n+1$. We can now calculate the two fractions and perform the accumulating multiplication.

```
def wallis(pairs):
    acc = 1
    num = 2

    for apair in range(pairs):
        leftterm = num/(num-1)
        rightterm = num/(num+1)

        acc = acc * leftterm * rightterm
```

A final observation to note: In the original Wallis formula the value of the infinite product is equal to $\frac{\pi}{2}$. This means that we must multiply the resulting product by 2 to get the approximation of pi that will be returned by the function. Listing 2.4 shows the complete function. Note also that the multiplication statement before the return is at the same level as the `return`, not inside the `for` loop. We only want that multiplication to be done once. Session 2.7 shows the result of invoking the function on a number of different pairs.

```
1  def wallis(pairs):
2      acc = 1
3      num = 2
4      for apair in range(pairs):
5          leftterm = num/(num-1)
6          rightterm = num/(num+1)
7
8          acc = acc * leftterm * rightterm
9
10         num = num + 2
11
12     pi = acc * 2
13     return pi
```

Listing 2.4   A function to compute pi using the Wallis formula

```
>>> wallis(100)
3.1337874906281575
>>> wallis(1000)
3.1408077460303785
>>> wallis(10000)
3.1415141186818549
```

Session 2.7   Using the `wallis` function

Exercises

2.18 Run the `wallis` function using 10,000 and 100,000 terms.

2.19 Compare the results of the `wallis` function with `archimedes` and `leibniz`. How does the number of pairs compare with terms and sides?

2.20 It is also possible to write the `wallis` function by pairing the fractions by their denominators. Rewrite the `wallis` function using this pairing. *Hint:* The first term will not be part of a pair.

2.6   A Monte Carlo Simulation

Our final technique for approximating pi will make use of probability and random behavior. These types of solutions are often referred to as **Monte Carlo simulations** because they use features that are similar to "games of chance." In other words, instead of knowing specifically what will happen during the simulation, a random element will be introduced into the simulation so that it will behave differently each time.

To set up our simulation, consider Figure 2.9. Pretend that we are looking at a dartboard in the shape of a square that is 2 units wide and 2 units high. A circle has been inscribed within the square so that the radius of the circle is 1 unit.

Now assume that we cut out the upper right-hand quadrant of the square (see Figure 2.10). The result will be a square that is 1 unit high and 1 unit wide with a quarter-circle tran-scribed inside. This piece is what we will use to "play" our simulation. The area of the original square was 4 units. The area of the original circle was $\pi r^2 = \pi$ units since the circle had a radius of 1 unit. After we cut the upper-right quarter, the area of the quarter-circle is $\frac{\pi}{4}$ and the area of the entire quarter square is 1.

The simulation will work by randomly "throwing darts" at the dartboard in Figure 2.10. We will assume that every dart will hit the board but that the location of that strike will be random. It is easy to see that each dart will hit the square but some will also land inside the quarter-circle. The number of darts that hit inside or outside the quarter-circle will be proportional to the areas of each. More specifically, the fraction of darts that land inside the quarter-circle will be equal to $\frac{\pi}{4}$.

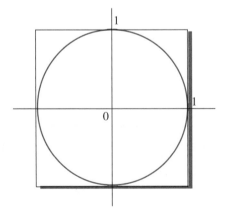

Figure 2.9   Setting up the Monte Carlo simulation

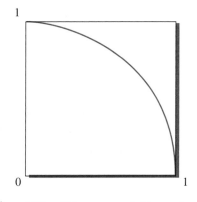

Figure 2.10   The upper-right quadrant

In order to implement this simulation, we will use the **random** module. You may find it useful to invoke the **help** command on the module to explore the functionality. For our purposes here, we will use only the **random** function—a random number generator that returns a floating-point number between 0 and 1 each time it is called. Session 2.8 shows the **random** function in action.

```
>>> import random
>>> random.random()
0.57346717619779752
>>> random.random()
0.54832767404135008
>>> for i in range(5):
        print (random.random())
0.355533646663
0.607688967224
0.464142190998
0.814134550939
0.712540183514
>>>
```

Session 2.8   Exercising the **random** function

We will use these random numbers to simulate the random dart throw we described earlier. For each round of the simulation, we will randomly generate two numbers between 0 and 1.

These will represent the position that each dart lands on our square. We can think of the board as having a horizontal and a vertical axis, both labeled between 0 and 1. If we let the first number represent the horizontal distance and the second represent the vertical distance, then the two numbers give us an exact location for the point.

Now recall that the location of the random point is important in that we need to know whether it occurs inside or outside the quarter-circle. Our plan is to keep track of the number of points that land inside that circle and then use that number to compute our estimate for π. In order to do this, we need to be able to decide whether the point is in the circle. This will require a few new ideas.

2.6.1   Boolean Expressions

To solve the problem of deciding whether a point is inside or outside of the circle, we need to be able to ask a question. In computer science, questions are often referred to as **Boolean expressions** because the result of asking them is one of the Boolean data values `True` or `False`. These Boolean values are another primitive type in Python.

```
>>> 6
6
>>> 4.5
4.5
>>> True
True
>>> False
False
>>>
```

The easiest type of Boolean expression to write compares the results of two expressions. To make this comparison, the common **relational operators** from mathematics such as equal to, less than, and greater than are used. Table 2.1 shows the operators and their meaning in Python.

Comparisons between two data values using a relational operator are called **relational expressions**. Like other expressions in Python, a result is produced when relational expressions are evaluated. In this case, the result will be a Boolean value. Session 2.9 shows a few simple examples of relational expressions. Note that the variable `apple` is assigned the value 25 and is then used in an equality comparison. It is important to distinguish between

Relational Operator	Meaning
<	Less than
<=	Less than or equal to
>	Greater than
>=	Greater than or equal to
==	Equal
!=	Not equal

Table 2.1   Relational operators and their meaning

the use of the assignment operator, =, and the equality operator, ==. Note also that in the last example the value of the variable is compared against the result of an arithmetic expression—namely, $5 * 5$.

```
>>> 6<10
True
>>> 4!=4
False
>>> apple = 25
>>> apple == 25
True
>>> apple == 5 * 5
True
>>>
```

Session 2.9   Evaluating simple relational expressions

2.6.2   Compound Boolean Expressions and Logical Operators

In Python **compound Boolean expressions** are composed of simple Boolean expressions that are connected by the **logical operators** **and**, **or**, and **not**. Table 2.2 defines the behavior of the Python logical operators. Note that *any* Python expression can be used as part of a Boolean expression. Most often the expressions will be relational expressions.

It is important to understand that Python evaluates a Boolean expression exactly as indicated in Table 2.2. Python uses **short-circuit evaluation** of a Boolean expression. This

x and y	If x is False, return x; otherwise return y.
x or y	If x is False, return y; otherwise return x.
not x	If x is False, return True; otherwise return False.

Table 2.2   Logical operator behavior

means that Python evaluates only as much of the expression, from left to right, as it needs to in order to determine if the expression is True or False.

For example, in the Boolean expression 3 < 7 or 10 < 20: Python needs to evaluate only the expression 3 < 7 since it would not matter whether 10 < 20 is True or False. Similarly, Python would need to evaluate only the 10 > 20 part of the Boolean expression 10 > 20 and 3 < 7 since the full expression will be False regardless of whether 3 < 7. Session 2.10 shows the logical operators in action.

```
>>> 6<10 and 3 < 7
True
>>> 4!=4  or 5 < 8
True
>>> 6 < 10 and 10 < 6
False
>>> not 6 < 10
False
>>>
```

Session 2.10   Evaluating compound Boolean expressions

Exercises

2.21 What is the result of evaluating the Boolean expression False or True?

2.22 What is the result of evaluating the Boolean expression True and False?

2.23 What is the result of evaluating the Boolean expression not 7 > 3? Fals e

2.24 What is the result of evaluating the Boolean expression not (True or False)?

2.25 What is the result of evaluating the Boolean expression (not True) and (not False)?

2.26 Write an equivalent Boolean expression for `(not (True and False))`.

2.27 Write a compound Boolean expression that returns `True` if the value of the variable `count` is between 1 and 10 inclusive.

2.6.3 Selection Statements

Once we are able to ask a question by writing a Boolean expression, we can turn our attention to using that question for making a decision. In computer science, decisions are often called **selection** because we wish to select between possible outcomes based on the result of the question we have asked. For example, when we go outside in the morning we might ask the question "Is it raining?" If it is raining, we will grab an umbrella. Otherwise, we will pack our sunglasses. We are selecting which item to take with us based on the condition of the weather.

Up until now, the statements in our Python programs have been executed in sequence—one at a time, in the order that they were written. We now introduce a new statement called a **selection statement**, also known as an if statement. The selection statement will contain a question and other groups of statements that may or may not be executed, depending on the result of the question. Most programming languages provide two versions of this useful statement: the `ifelse` and the `if`.

The `ifelse` statement looks like this:

```
if <condition>:
    <statements>
else:
    <statements>
```

The keyword `if` is followed by a Boolean expression that is used as a condition for the selection. When the Boolean expression is evaluated, the result will either be `True` or `False`. If it is `True`, the first group of statements is executed in sequence and the second group is skipped. Notice that each group of statements is indented just like a *for* loop or function definition.

On the other hand, if the condition is `False`, the first group is skipped and the second group is executed in sequence (see Figure 2.11). In this way, it is possible to perform different actions based on the result of the question that was asked.

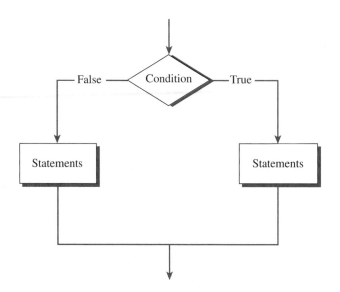

Figure 2.11   The logical flow of an `ifelse` statement

For example, in Session 2.11 the variables a and b are assigned initial values. The `ifelse` statement that follows asks the question whether a is greater than b. Since a is greater than b, the first group of statements (in this case only one) is performed and the value of the variable c is set to 10. We can check that this did occur by evaluating the variable c after the statement is done.

```
>>> a=5
>>> b=3
>>> if a>b:
        c=10
    else:
        c=20

>>> c
10
>>>
```

Session 2.11   Executing a simple `ifelse` selection statement

The other variation of the if statement does not provide an else clause. It looks like the following:

```
if <condition>:
    <statements>
```

As before, the condition is evaluated and the result will be either **True** or **False**. If the result is **True**, the first group of statements is executed in sequence. However, if the condition is **False**, nothing is performed, the statement completes, and the program goes on to the next statement in sequence (see Figure 2.12).

For example, in Session 2.12 the variables a and b are again assigned initial values. The if statement that follows asks the question whether a is greater than b. Since it is, the group of statements (again, in this case only one) is performed and the value of the variable c is set to 10. However, if the condition evaluates to **False** (as in the second selection), then the value of the variable c would not have been modified. In this case, the value for c remains the same as it was before the selection.

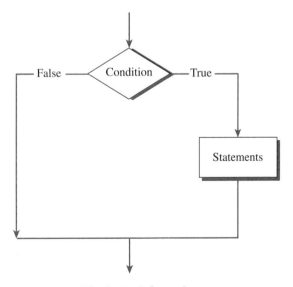

Figure 2.12   The logical flow of an if statement

```
>>> a=5
>>> b=3
>>> c = 44
>>> if a>b:
        c=10

>>> c
10
>>> if b>a:
        c=25

>>> c
10
```

Session 2.12   Executing a simple `if` selection statement

Since the statements contained within a selection statement can be any legal Python statement, it is certainly possible to place one `if` statement inside of another. This is sometimes referred to as **nested selection**. The following `ifelse` statement has two nested `ifelse` statements:

```
if <condition>:
    if <condition>:
        <statements>
    else:
        <statements>
else:
    if <condition>:
        <statements>
    else:
        <statements>
```

The result of this structure is to decide between four groups of statements. If the outer condition is `True`, then the first nested `ifelse` is performed. If the nested condition is also `True`, then the first group of statements is performed. However, if the nested condition is `False`, the second group of statements is executed. Likewise, if the outer condition is

False, the second nested `ifelse` will be performed. In this way we are able to decide between four groups of statements by using the results of two conditions.

A common pattern for nested selection is called tail nesting. With tail nesting, all of the nested selection occurs in the `else` of the previous `ifelse` statement. The structure looks like this:

```
if <condition>:
    <statements>
else:
    if <condition>:
        <statements>
    else:
        if <condition>:
            <statements>
        ...
```

This tail nesting pattern is so common that Python provides a shorter version known as the `elif` statement. Here the `else` and the next `if` are combined to allow us to simply list the conditions and associated statements one at a time without additional indentation. Note that the last case still uses a simple `else`.

```
if <condition>:
    <statements>
elif <condition>:
    <statements>
elif <condition>:
    <statements>
elif <condition>:
    <statements>
...
else:
    <statements>
```

Exercises

2.28 How does Python know to which **if** an **else** belongs?

2.29 Write a selection statement that sets the value of a variable named **answer** to 1 if a variable named **result** is equal to 100. Set **answer** to 2 otherwise.

2.30 Write a nested selection using **ifelse** that sets the value of a variable **gradepoint** to 4 if a variable named **score** is greater than 90, 3 if **score** is between 80 and 89, 2 if **score** is between 70 and 79, 1 if **score** is between 60 and 69, and 0 otherwise.

2.31 Rewrite the selection in Exercise 2.30 using an **elif** statement.

2.32 A year is a leap year if it is divisible by 4 unless it is a century that is not divisible by 400. Write a function that takes a year as a parameter and returns **True** if the year is a leap year and **False** otherwise.

2.33 A fruit company sells oranges for 32 cents a pound plus $7.50 per order for shipping. If an order is over 100 pounds, shipping cost is reduced by $1.50. Write a function that will take the number of pounds of oranges as a parameter and return the cost of the order.

2.34 Write a function that takes three integers as parameters and returns the largest.

2.35 Write a function that takes two parameters—a pay rate and the number of hours worked—and returns the pay. Any hours over 40 are paid at time and a half.

2.6.4   Completing the Implementation

We are now ready to complete our Monte Carlo approximation of π. Again we will use the abstraction idea to build a function that will return the approximate value of π. For this function, we will use the number of darts as the input parameter. The more darts we throw, the better our approximation should be.

Recall the basic steps of the simulation. First, pick a random point on the square board. Next, decide whether that point is also in the transcribed circle, keeping a count of those that fall in the circle. After all the random points have been tested, the approximate value of π will be four times the fraction of darts that land inside the circle.

To keep a count of the number of points that fall in the circle, we will once again use the accumulator pattern with a variable initialized to 0. Every point that lands in the circle will cause our accumulator variable to be incremented by 1. Remember that the initialization needs to occur outside the iteration.

To process each point, we must first generate the two values that will make up the random location. For this we will use the `random` function from the `random` module. Since we will think of the first value as the horizontal measure and the second as the vertical, we will use `x` and `y` as the names.

```
def montePi(numDarts):

    inCircle = 0

    for i in range(numDarts):
        x = random.random()
        y = random.random()


    return pi
```

We now need to decide whether the random point is inside the circle. For this we can use the formula for finding the distance between a point and the origin $(0,0)$: $d = \sqrt{x^2 + y^2}$. The `math` module will provide us with the `sqrt` function.

Once we have the distance, we can use our selection statement to decide whether we want to count the point. Again, remember that if the point is within 1 unit of the center, it is in the circle and we should perform our increment step. A simple `if` statement will work nicely.

```
def montePi(numDarts):
    ...
    d = math.sqrt(x**2 + y**2)

    if d <= 1:
        inCircle = inCircle + 1
    ...
```

Finally, as shown in Listing 2.5, the calculation of `pi` is the ratio of the number of points that occur in the circle to the number of total points. That ratio must then be multiplied by 4 to get the approximation. Session 2.13 shows the function at work. Note that as we increase the number of points (darts) used in the simulation, the accuracy improves.

```
1   import random
2   import math
3
4   def montePi(numDarts):
5
6       inCircle = 0
7
8       for i in range(numDarts):
9           x = random.random()
10          y = random.random()
11
12          d = math.sqrt(x**2 + y**2)
13
14          if d <= 1:
15              inCircle = inCircle + 1
16
17      pi = inCircle/numDarts * 4
18
19      return pi
```

Listing 2.5   A function to compute pi using the Monte Carlo simulation

```
>>> montePi(100)
3.0
>>> montePi(1000)
3.1080000000000001
>>> montePi(10000)
3.1543999999999999
>>>
```

Session 2.13   Using the `montePi` function

Exercises

2.36 Run the `montePi` function using 10,000, 100,000, and more terms.

2.37 Compare the results of the `montePi` function with the functions we have written in previous sections.

2.38 Write a function `isInCircle` that takes a point and a radius as a parameter. The function should return `True` if the point is inside the circle and `False` otherwise.

2.39 Modify `montePi` to use the `isInCircle` function you wrote in the previous exercise.

2.6.5   Adding Graphics

As a final variation on this simulation, we will use our `Turtle` to provide a graphical animation of the algorithm. Recall that a turtle object can provide a basic graphics capability. We can use this to show the random points as they are being generated. In addition, depending on the location of the point, we can use color to show the location as either inside or outside the circle.

To begin using the turtle we must import the `turtle` module. In all of our previous turtle examples, the turtle window was created automatically when we created a new turtle object. The `turtle` module makes it possible to create the drawing window, or screen, separately, and then add the turtle later. By doing this, we can call methods to manipulate the drawing window.

The way we create a drawing window is to use the `Screen` constructor contained in the `turtle` module. The statement `wn = turtle.Screen()` will create a new drawing window and name it `wn`. If we want to change the background color of the drawing window, we can use the `bgcolor` method. For example, `wn.bgcolor("light green")` will change the color of the window from the default white to a light shade of green.

Now, it is possible to create the drawing window and then the drawing turtle.

```
import turtle
wn = turtle.Screen()
drawingT = turtle.Turtle()
```

Our next step will be to set up the "dartboard" that was described earlier. Remember that the simulation works by generating numbers between 0 and 1 as locations for the random

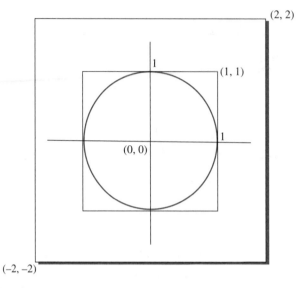

Figure 2.13   Setting the world coordinates for the graphical simulation

points. In order to show this, we can adjust the coordinate system used by the drawing turtle so that the drawing window more closely contains the points. Figure 2.13 shows the original diagram for the simulation with a window set up to contain it.

To modify the coordinate system of the drawing window, we will use a `Screen` method called `setworldcoordinates`. This method will take four pieces of information: (1) the x-coordinate of the lower-left corner, (2) the y-coordinate of the lower-left corner, (3) the x-coordinate of the upper-right corner, and (4) the y-coordinate of the upper-right corner. These two points will denote the coordinates of the lower-left and upper-right corners of the window used by the drawing turtle.

```
wn.setworldcoordinates(-2,-2,2,2)
```

It is important to note that we could have made this window any size we wish. However, the larger the window, the smaller the actual area of the simulation.

Now that the window is set up we will draw the initial horizontal and vertical axes so that when we begin to plot points, it is clear where they are being placed. Remember that the drawing turtle will draw a line whenever its tail is in the down position. So all we need to do is raise the tail, go to the starting position for the first axis, lower the tail, and then go to the ending position for the axis. The Python code to accomplish this is shown on the next page.

```
drawingT.up()
drawingT.goto(-1,0)
drawingT.down()
drawingT.goto(1,0)
```

Likewise, we can do the same thing for the vertical axis:

```
drawingT.up()
drawingT.goto(0,1)
drawingT.down()
drawingT.goto(0,-1)
```

The remaining portion of the program will simply ask the drawing turtle to place dots at the random points as they are generated. To do this, we can go to the location and then use the dot method to ask the turtle to make a dot at the current location. The only additional feature that we will add is color. If the location is inside the circle, we can change the color of the drawing turtle to a new color—say, "blue." Otherwise, if it is outside the circle, we can use a different color, such as "red."

Since there are now two choices depending on the location of the point, it makes sense to use the *ifelse* version of the selection statement described earlier. If the location is inside the circle, change the tail color to blue and count the point. Otherwise, if the point is outside the circle, change the tail color to red. In Python, this translates to the following:

```
drawingT.goto(x,y)

if d <= 1:
    circle = circle + 1
    drawingT.color("blue")
else:
    drawingT.color("red")

drawingT.dot()
```

Listing 2.6 shows the complete function including the commands to use the turtle to show the simulation in progress. It is important to note that the dot gets drawn after the *if*

```
1  import random
2  import math
3  import turtle
4
5  def showMontePi(numDarts):
6      wn = turtle.Screen()
7      drawingT = turtle.Turtle()
8
9      wn.setworldcoordinates(-2,-2,2,2)
10
11     drawingT.up()
12     drawingT.goto(-1,0)
13     drawingT.down()
14     drawingT.goto(1,0)
15
16     drawingT.up()
17     drawingT.goto(0,1)
18     drawingT.down()
19     drawingT.goto(0,-1)
20
21     circle = 0
22     drawingT.up()
23
24     for i in range(numDarts):
25         x = random.random()
26         y = random.random()
27
28         d = math.sqrt(x**2 + y**2)
29
30         drawingT.goto(x,y)
31
32         if d <= 1:
33             circle = circle + 1
34             drawingT.color("blue")
35         else:
36             drawingT.color("red")
37
38         drawingT.dot()
39
40     pi = circle/numDarts * 4
41
42     wn.exitonclick()
43
44     return pi
```

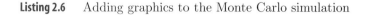

Listing 2.6   Adding graphics to the Monte Carlo simulation

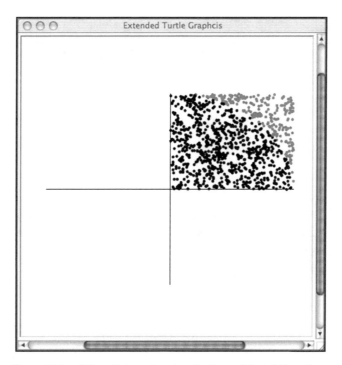

Figure 2.14   Visualizing the simulation with 1,000 points

statement. This needs to be done only once for each iteration. Figure 2.14 shows what the simulation might look like. You can see how the quarter-circle is beginning to emerge. As more and more points are used, this would become even more clear.

We have used one additional `Screen` method at the end of the `showMontePi` function. It is called `exitonclick`. This method tells the drawing window to "freeze" until the user clicks somewhere inside the window. If you don't use this method, the turtle drawing window will be automatically closed when the program terminates. In our case, we have placed a call to `exitonclick` immediately before returning from the function.

Exercises

2.40 Adjust the world coordinates so that the window contains only the upper-right quadrant of the circle.

2.41 Modify the simulation to plot points in the entire circle. You will have to adjust the calculated value of π accordingly.

2.7   Summary

This chapter has introduced the following additional building blocks of programming and Python:

- Math modules
- Boolean expressions
- Selection statements

One very important pattern, the accumulator pattern, was also introduced. This pattern uses an accumulator variable that is continuously updated as part of an iteration. It is important to initialize the accumulator variable to an appropriate starting value. Finally, we used the Monte Carlo simulation technique, which is based on random numbers, to approximate the value of `pi`.

Key Terms

accumulator pattern	initialization	relational expression
accumulator variable	Leibniz formula	relational operator
approximation	logical operator	running sum
Archimedes approach	Monte Carlo simulation	selection statement
Boolean expression	nested selection	short-circuit evaluation
compound Boolean expression	pi	tail nesting
degrees	radians	Wallis formula

Python Keywords

and	help	math	random
elif	if else	not	return
False	if	or	sin
for	import	print	True

Bibliography

[AAR04] Runde Angel, Christine Abbot, and Dennis Runde. *A Survey of Mathematics with Applications*. Prentice Hall, 2004.

[BB87] J. M. Borwein and P. B. Borwein. Ramanujan and pi. *Scientific American*, 1987.

[Wei02] Eric W. Weisstein. *CRC Concise Encyclopedia of Mathematics*. Chapman & Hall/ CRC, 2002.

Programming Exercises

2.1 Write a function to compute the circumference of a circle with a radius of r. Use r as the parameter to the function. Use π from the math module.

2.2 Write a function to compute the area of a circle with a radius of r. Use r as the parameter to the function. Use π from the math module.

2.3 Write a function to compute the volume of a sphere with a radius of r. Use r as the parameter to the function. Use π from the math module.

2.4 Write a function that will return an approximate value for π by evaluating the equation $\pi = 16(arctan\frac{1}{5}) - 4(arctan\frac{1}{239})$, where $arctan$ is the arc tangent function from the math library.

2.5 Write a function that will return an approximate value for π by evaluating the equation $\pi = \frac{ln(640320^3 + 744)}{\sqrt{163}}$, where ln is the **log** function from the math library.

2.6 Write a function **isEven** that takes a number as a parameter and returns **True** if the number is even and **False** otherwise.

2.7 Write a function that will return an approximate value for π by evaluating the equation $\pi = \sqrt{12}(1 - \frac{1}{3\times3} + \frac{1}{5\times3^2} - \frac{1}{7\times3^3} + ...$ Use a parameter called n to denote the number of terms to include in the summation.

2.8 We have used the square root function from the math library a number of times in this chapter. Write your own square root approximation function using the equation $X_{k+1} = \frac{1}{2} \times (X_k + \frac{n}{X_k})$ where $X_0 = 1$. This equation says that the $\sqrt{n}$ can be found by repeatedly computing the next X_i term. The larger the number of terms used, the better the answer. Allow your function to have two input parameters, the number that you want the square root of and the number of terms to compute.

2.9 Buffon's needle is a very old (eighteenth-century) simulation for approximating pi. Research this simulation and implement it using Python and turtle graphics. How good is the approximation?

CHAPTER 3

Codes and Other Secrets

3.1 Objectives

- To introduce the string data type
- To demonstrate the use of string methods and operators
- To introduce simple cryptographic algorithms

3.2 Introduction

For almost as long as people have been writing, people have also been trying to hide what they were writing from others. Herodotus describes the use of "secret writing" that saved Greece from being conquered by Xerxes and the Persians. The Kama Sutra, based on writings dating back to the fourth century BCE, instructs women in the art of secret writing in order to hide the details of their liaisons. In this chapter we explore some simple forms of secret writing using Python.

Today this art of secret writing is called **cryptography**. You use cryptography nearly every day without even thinking about it. Not because you are sending secret messages to your friends, (although there are several cryptographic add-ons for email these days) but whenever you use your browser. When you make a purchase on the Web or check your grades or bank online, you are using cryptography.

Before we dive into cryptography we must learn about another important Python data type called the **string**—a data structure that allows us to represent the written word in our programs. After the numeric data types introduced in "Introduction" (Chapter 1), the next most common type of data used in programming is the string.

You are already more familiar with strings than you think. Strings are simply **sequences of characters**, such as the letters of the alphabet and all the other symbols commonly used in writing. Most often, these sequences of characters are put together to form familiar words, but as we will see in this chapter, character sequences can be used for many other interesting purposes.

In Python you will know that an object is a string because it is surrounded by either single quotes (') or double quotes ("). Like numbers, strings are objects that can be named by variables. Python Session 3.1 illustrates a number of simple strings.

Like the numeric data types, Python provides us with operators we can use on strings to transform them. In the next four sections we will examine some commonly used string operators.

Strings can contain any characters: letters, numbers, punctuation marks, and even quotation marks. When you want to have a string that contains a single quote, you use double quotes around the outside of the string. When you want to have double quotes inside your string, you use single quotes around the outside. If your string does not contain either single or double quotes, it does not matter whether you use single or double quotes around the outside.

```
>>> "hello"
'hello'
>>> 'world'
'world'
>>> a = "hello"
>>> a
'hello'
>>> b = 'world'
>>> "let's go"
"let's go"
>>> 'she said "how are you?" then left'
'she said "how are you?" then left'
>>>
```

Session 3.1   A variety of simple strings

3.2.1 Concatenation

As a first example of an operator applied to a string, we will look at the addition operator (+). When + is applied to two strings, we call it the **concatenation** operator. When you concatenate two strings, you simply put the two strings one after the other, as shown in Session 3.2. Notice that the concatenation operator does not automatically add a space between two strings. To add a space, you must concatenate a string that contains only a space.

```
>>> "hello " + "world!"
'hello world!'
>>> fname = 'John'
>>> lname = 'Smith'
>>> fname + lname
'JohnSmith'
>>> fullName = fname + ' ' + lname
>>> fullName
'John Smith'
>>>
```

Session 3.2 String concatenation

3.2.2 Repetition

The next operator we can apply to a string is the **repetition** operator (*). As you might guess, this operator takes a string and repeats it as many times as you would like. For example, suppose you want to create the string `'gogogo'`. Rather than typing 'go' multiple times, you can simply apply the repetition operator as follows: `'go'*3`

As with their numeric counterparts, the repetition operator has a higher precedence than concatenation. We can thus construct strings using both operators together, as shown in Session 3.3.

```
>>> 'go'*3
'gogogo'
>>> 'go '*3 + 'twins '*2
'go go go twins twins '
>>> ('hello ' + 'world ')*3
'hello world hello world hello world '
>>>
```

Session 3.3   String repetition

3.2.3   Indexing

We next examine the **index** operator [], an operator that has no mathematical counterpart. This operator is useful when we want to get at particular characters in a string. For example, if we want to get at the first character of a string, we can use the index operator as follows: 'John'[0]. The first character in a string is at index 0, the second character is at index 1, and so on. In addition, Python allows us to index the string in reverse. The last character in a string has index value −1, the second to last character has index value −2, and so on. Figure 3.1 shows the relationship between index values and the characters in a string.

When indexing a string, it is often important to know the overall **length** of that string. The len function tells us how many characters are in a string. It is important to understand the relationship between the length of a string and the index of the last character in the string. For example, although the len('abc') returns 3, we would use 'abc'[2] to access the character 'c'.

We can go one step further and combine the **range** function with the **len** function to allow us to access each character in a string. Session 3.4 illustrates some uses of the index operator.

Positive indexes	0	1	2	3	4	5	6	7	8	9	10	11
String	P	Y	T	H	O	N		R	O	C	K	S
Negative indexes	−12	−11	−10	−9	−8	−7	−6	−5	−4	−3	−2	−1

Figure 3.1   Index values for each character in a string

```
>>> name = "Roy G Biv"
>>> first = name[0]
>>> first
'R'
>>> middleChar = name[4]
>>> middleChar
'G'
>>> for i in range(len(name)):
...     print(name[i])
...
R
o
y

G

B
i
v
>>> name[-1]
'v'
>>> name[len(name)-1]
'v'
```

Session 3.4   String indexing

3.2.4   Slicing

The **slice** operator `[:]` is similar to the index operator except that it can get multicharacter parts of the string. We often call these parts of a string **substrings**. For example, we can get the first three characters of a string as follows: `"john[0:3]"`. The first number after the left square bracket gives the starting index of the first character in the substring. The number after the `':'` is the index that is one after the last character selected for the substring. This is similar to the bounds of the **range** function where the upper bound is not included.

The proper prefixes of a string are all the substrings that start with the first character of the string and are shorter than the original string. We can easily generate the prefixes of a string using the slice operator. Notice that the last example in Session 3.5 does not include the `'v'` since the upper bound on the range function stops one character before the required index. Also, notice that the first substring created is the empty string.

```
                  0123
>>> name = 'Roy G Biv'
>>> name[0:3]
'Roy'
>>> name[6:9]        ← minus 1
'Biv'
>>> for i in range(len(name)):
...     print(name[0:i])
...
...

R
Ro
Roy
Roy
Roy G
Roy G
Roy G B
Roy G Bi
```

Session 3.5   String slicing

Two additional operators, **in** and **not in**, determine whether one string is contained in another. Table 3.1 provides a short summary of the string operators we have introduced so far.

Operator	Example	Result	Description
+	"hello " + "world"	"hello world"	**Concatenation**, joins two strings together
*	"abc"*3	"abcabcabc"	**Repetition**, repeats the string
[i]	"abc"[1]	'b'	**Index**, returns the character at position i
[i:j]	"abcdef"[0:2]	"ab"	**Slice** returns the substring from i to j-1
len()	len('abc')	3	Determines the **length** of a string.
in	'bc' in 'abc'	True	Determines whether one string contains another
not in	'bc' not in 'abc'	False	Determines whether one string does not contain another

Table 3.1   Summary of the string operators

Exercises

3.1 Create a string variable that is initialized to your entire name—first, middle, and last.

3.2 Using the slice operator, print your first name.

3.3 Using the slice operator, print your last name.

3.4 Using the slice and concatenation operators, print your name in the form "Lastname, Firstname."

3.5 Print the length of your first name.

3.6 Assume you have two variables: `s='s'`, and `p='p'`. Using concatenation and repetition, write an expression that produces the string `mississippi`.

3.7 Modify the prefix example in Session 3.5 to print all prefixes of "Roy G Biv," including the entire string.

3.2.5 String Methods

In addition to the string operators, strings are objects that have methods just like turtles. Some of these methods are summarized in Table 3.2. Several help you to format your strings to fit in a certain amount of space, such as `ljust`, `rjust`, and `center`. Others convert the string to be all uppercase or lowercase.

The most useful methods for us in this chapter are those that allow us to search for one string within another. The `count` method finds the number of occurrences of one string within another. The `index` and `find` methods are similar in that they return the index of the first occurrence of one string within another. However, they differ in their behavior when the string we are looking for is not found. The `find` method returns −1 if the string you are looking for is not found. The `index` method generates an error and halts your program if the string is not found. Session 3.6 illustrates the use of these string methods.

Method	Use	Explanation
center	astring.center(w)	returns the string astring surrounded by spaces to make astring w characters long.
count	astring.count(item)	Returns the number of occurrences of item in astring.
ljust	astring.ljust(w)	Returns astring left justified in a field of width w.
rjust	astring.rjust(w)	Returns astring right justified in a field of width w.
upper	astring.upper()	Returns astring in all uppercase.
lower	astring.lower()	Returns astring in all lowercase.
index	astring.index(item)	Returns the index of the first occurrence of item in astring, or an error if not found.
find	astring.find(item)	Returns the index of the first occurrence of item in astring, or −1 if not found.
replace	astring.replace(old,new)	Replaces all occurrences of old substring with new substring in astring

Table 3.2   Summary of string methods

```
>>> "hello".ljust(10)
'hello     '
>>> "hello".rjust(10)
'     hello'
>>> "hello".center(10)
'  hello   '
>>> astring = "golden gopher football"
>>> astring.count('o')              occurrence
4
>>> astring.count('oo')
1
>>> astring.find('b')        index
18
```

Session 3.6   Demonstrating string methods (continues on next page)

```
>>> astring.index('b')
18
>>> astring.find('oo')
15
>>> astring.find('badger')
-1
>>> astring.index('cyclone')
Traceback (most recent call last):
  File "<stdin>", line 1, in <module>
ValueError: substring not found
>>> 'ab cd ef'.replace('cd','xy')
'ab xy ef'
>>>
```

Session 3.6   Demonstrating string methods (continued)

Exercises

3.8 Using the count method, find the number of occurrences of the character 's' in the string 'mississippi'.

3.9 Replace all occurrences of the substring 'iss' with 'ox'.

3.10 Find the index of the first occurrence of 'p' in 'mississippi'.

3.11 Make the word 'python' centered and all capital letters in a string of length 20.

p = 'python'. upper()

p. center(lo)

3.2.6 Character Functions

As you will see shortly, one of the things our string-based algorithms will do is convert a character into a number and back again. Python contains some built-in functions for converting a character to a number and vice versa. The functions ord and chr do the job for us. In addition, the str function converts a number into its string form. Session 3.7 presents an example.

```
>>> ord('a')
97
>>> ord('c')
99
>>> ord('z')
122
>>> chr(104)
'h'
>>> chr(97+13)
'n'
>>> str(10980)
'10980'
>>>
```

Session 3.7   Using ord, chr, and str

It may seem a bit odd to you that the letter 'a' is represented by the number 97. Why not 1 or 0? Each character that we see is actually stored in the memory of a computer as a series of 1's and 0's. The sequence of 1's and 0's that correspond to the letter 'a' is represented as decimal number 97. The mapping from letters to numbers is defined by the **American Standard Code for Information Interchange (ASCII)** and has been in use since the 1970s.

For our purposes, we would much prefer the letter 'a' to map to the number 0 and the letter 'z' to map to the number 25. To illustrate the use of the **find** method and string indexing, we define our own helper functions for mapping from characters to numbers and back in Listing 3.1.

In **indexToLetter**, we use the **elif** form of an *if* statement. This form allows us to check for a sequence of conditions on a variable. For example, if the index of a character is greater than 26, we print an error message. Or if the index is less than 0 we print an error message. Otherwise, we just return the letter from the alphabet at the index provided.

```
1     def letterToIndex(ch):
2         alphabet = "abcdefghijklmnopqrstuvwxyz "
3         idx = alphabet.find(ch)
4         if idx < 0:
5             print ("error: letter not in the alphabet", ch)
6         return idx
7
8     def indexToLetter(idx):
9         alphabet = "abcdefghijklmnopqrstuvwxyz "
10        if idx > 25:
11            print ('error: ', idx, ' is too large')
12            letter = ''
13        elif idx < 0:
14            print ('error: ', idx, ' is less  than 0')
15            letter = ''
16        else:
17            letter = alphabet[idx]
18        return letter
```

Listing 3.1   Two helper functions for string lookups

Exercises

3.12 What is the difference between ord('A') and ord('a')?
65   97

3.13 Write a function that takes a single character digit and returns its integer value.

3.14 Write the `letterToIndex` function using `ord` and `chr`.

3.15 Write the `indexToLetter` function using `ord` and `chr`

3.16 Write a function that takes an exam score from 0–100 and returns the corresponding letter grade. Use the same grading scale your professor does for this class.

3.3   Encoding and Decoding Messages

Cryptography is the science of making messages secure, of transforming readable messages into unreadable messages and back again. In this chapter we refer to messages that are readable as **plaintext**. Messages that are unreadable are called **ciphertext**. The process of turning plaintext into ciphertext is called **encryption**. The reverse process of turning

Figure 3.2   Encrypting and decrypting a message

ciphertext into plaintext is called **decryption**. Figure 3.2 shows an overview of the encryption and decryption processes. Algorithms for both encryption and decryption are the subject of this section.

One of the easiest ways to encrypt a message is to simply scramble the letters. For example, the word "apple" could be randomly transformed to "lapep." In fact, there are 120 different possible arrangements of the word "apple." However, if the encryption algorithm randomly scrambles the letters, the task of the decryption algorithm is pretty hard. Encryption and decryption algorithms must work together in some agreed upon way, with the encryption algorithm scrambling letters and the decryption algorithm unscrambling them.

3.4   Transposition Cipher

3.4.1   Encrypting Using Transposition

One way to scramble the letters of a message is to separate the message into two groups of characters: the first group composed of the even-numbered characters and the second group composed of the odd-numbered characters. If we create one string out of the even-numbered characters and another out of the odd, we can concatenate the two new strings together to form the ciphertext string. Because this results in a string with the characters shuffled to new positions, we call this a **transposition cipher**. In some books you will find this cipher called the **rail fence cipher**. Figure 3.3 illustrates the idea behind this encryption algorithm.

Now that we have a scheme for scrambling the plaintext message, let's write a Python function that takes the plaintext message as a parameter and returns the ciphertext message. The key to this algorithm lies in our ability to put the even characters from the plaintext in one string and the odd characters in another. One way to do this is to use a counter and a string iterator. A string iterator is a *for* loop where the loop variable takes on the value of each character in the string. As we iterate over each character of the string, we increment the counter. If the counter is an even number, we concatenate the current character to our even character string. If the counter is odd, we concatenate the character to our odd

Original   It was a dark and stormy night

Even   I _ a _ _ a k a d s o m _ i h

Odd   t w s a d r _ n _ t r y n g t

Break up the plaintext into even and odd characters

twsadr_n_tryngt + I_a__akadsom_ih

Combine the even and odd parts to make the ciphertext

Figure 3.3   Encrypting a string using an even–odd shuffle

character string. This transposition cipher is sometimes called the rail fence cipher where each rail contains part of the original string. In this case, since we are dividing the string into two parts, we call it a two-rail cipher.

How can we tell if a number is even or odd? Recall that for any even number N, when you divide N by 2, there is no remainder. For any odd number N, N divided by two has a remainder of one. In Python, we can obtain the remainder by using the modulo operator. For any even number N, N % 2 is 0. For any odd number N, N % 2 is 1. We can use the expression `counter % 2 == 0` as the condition in an *if* statement as a test for whether the counter is even or odd. Listing 3.2 shows the encryption algorithm using the strategy described here.

```
1  def scramble2Encrypt(plainText):
2      evenChars = ""
3      oddChars = ""
4      charCount = 0
5      for ch in plainText:
6          if charCount % 2 == 0:
7              evenChars = evenChars + ch
8          else:
9              oddChars = oddChars + ch
10         charCount = charCount + 1
11     cipherText = oddChars + evenChars
12     return cipherText
```

Listing 3.2   Scrambling a plaintext message

The scramble2Encrypt function makes use of the **accumulator pattern** in several different places. First, evenChars and oddChars accumulate characters. The accumulator pattern works just as well when concatenating strings as it does for adding numbers. When we apply the accumulator pattern to strings, we build up a string that starts from nothing (the empty string ''), growing the string one character at a time. The next use of the accumulator pattern is a familiar numeric accumulator using the charCount variable.

On line 5 of Listing 3.2 we begin a loop that will iterate over each character in the plainText string. When we iterate over a string, the loop variable references each character in the string one after another. On line 6 we make use of the test we devised to decide if charCount is even or odd. If charCount is even, we concatenate the old value of evenChars with the current character referenced by the loop variable ch. Because concatenation creates a new string, evenChars references this newly constructed string when we perform the assignment. If charCount is odd, we concatenate oddChars and ch to create a new string referenced by oddChars.

Finally, after all characters in the plaintext string have been processed, we create the cipherText string by concatenating oddChars and evenChars. The order of variables in the concatenation is not accidental. We put oddChars first for a reason: If there is an odd number of characters in our string, oddChars will be one character shorter than even characters. Can you explain why? We will see in a moment that this is important when we want to split the ciphertext back into two pieces.

Session 3.8 shows the output of the scramble2Encrypt function for five different test inputs. Notice that some of the test cases are just nonsense strings, but they are chosen carefully to make it easy to see if the function is working the way we think it should. Also notice that we test some boundary cases like a string of length 1 and even an empty string.

```
>>> scramble2Encrypt('abababab')
'bbbbaaaa'
>>> scramble2Encrypt('ababababc')
'bbbbaaaac'
>>> scramble2Encrypt('I do not like green eggs and ham')
' ontlk re gsadhmId o iegeneg n a'
>>> scramble2Encrypt('a')
'a'
>>> scramble2Encrypt('')
''

>>>
```

Session 3.8   Testing scramble2Encrypt

3.4.2   Decrypting a Transposed Message

Our next task is to write a function to decrypt a message that was encrypted by our `scramble2Encrypt` function. The input to our decrypt function will be the ciphertext produced by our encrypt function. The decrypt function will return the restored plaintext copy of the string.

To restore the plaintext string, we start out by splitting the ciphertext in half. The first half of the string contains the odd characters from our original message, and the second half of the string contains the even characters. To restore the plaintext version of the string, we start with an empty plaintext string and concatenate the characters from the even and odd strings onto the end of the plaintext string. We alternate taking a character from the even string first, then the odd string, and so on. Figure 3.4 gives an example of putting the plaintext back together again.

One detail to consider when reconstructing the plaintext message is that we may have one more character in the even character string than we do in the odd character string. We can easily check for this by comparing the lengths of the two strings. If the odd-numbered character string is shorter than the even, we simply concatenate the last character from the even string onto the plaintext. Listing 3.3 shows the Python code for implementing the decryption function.

To split the ciphertext string into two halves, we use the slicing operator as shown on lines 3 and 4 of Listing 3.3. To find the middle of the string we use integer division to divide the length of the string by 2. We use a simple slicing operator shortcut on these lines. When the number is omitted before the `:`, the slice operator starts at the beginning of the string. When the number after the `:` is omitted, the slice operation continues until the end of the string. A useful side effect of this shortcut is that we can make a copy of a string using the following slice operator: `duplicateStr = oldStr[:]`.

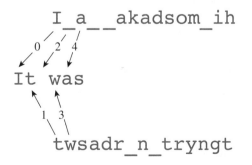

Figure 3.4   Decrypting a message by alternating characters from the ciphertext

```
1    def scramble2Decrypt(cipherText):
2        halfLength = len(cipherText) // 2
3        oddChars = cipherText[:halfLength]
4        evenChars = cipherText[halfLength:]
5        plainText = ""
6
7        for i in range(halfLength):
8            plainText = plainText + evenChars[i]
9            plainText = plainText + oddChars[i]
10
11        if len(oddChars) < len(evenChars):
12            plainText = plainText + evenChars[-1]
13
14        return plainText
```

Listing 3.3   Decrypting a transposed message

In the loop that starts on line 7, we use the string indexing operator to get the next character from each of the two halves. Once again, we are using an accumulator pattern to build the plaintext string. Finally, we check for the case when the number of characters in the ciphertext is odd, and add the final character from `evenChars` to the end of the plaintext string.

Session 3.9 shows how you can test the decrypt function. Notice that since `scramble2Encrypt` returns a string, we can use the function call directly as a parameter to the `scramble2Decrypt` function. It is easy to test whether the decrypt function works because it should print out the exact same string that we provided as a parameter to the encrypt function. Once again, we have tried an easy case, plus a couple of boundary cases.

```
>>> scramble2Decrypt(scramble2Encrypt('abababc'))
'abababc'
>>> scramble2Decrypt(scramble2Encrypt('a'))
'a'
>>> scramble2Decrypt(scramble2Encrypt(''))
''
>>> scramble2Decrypt(scramble2Encrypt('I do not like green eggs and ham'))
'I do not like green eggs and ham'
>>>
```

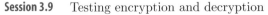

Session 3.9   Testing encryption and decryption

Exercises

3.17 With paper and pencil, use the transposition algorithm to encrypt the sentence "the quick brown fox jumps over the lazy dog." Check your answer by calling the scramble2Decrypt function.

3.18 Write a python function stripSpaces(myString) that takes a string representing a phrase as a parameter and returns the paragraph with the order of the letters intact but the spaces between each word removed.

3.19 The transposition cipher can be generalized to any number of rails. Write a function to implement a three-rail fence cipher that takes every third character and puts it on one of the three rails.

3.4.3 Asking for Input

Now that we have functions for encrypting and decrypting a message, it would be nice if there was an easier way to get a message to pass to the encrypt function. Most programs today use a dialog box as a way of asking the user for some input. While Python provides a way to create dialog boxes, there is a much simpler method to use. Python provides us with a function that allows us to ask a user to enter some data and returns a reference to the data in the form of a string. The function is called **input**.

Python's **input** function takes a single parameter that is a string. This string is often called the **prompt** because it contains some helpful text prompting the user to enter something. For example, you might call input as follows: msg = input('Enter a message to encrypt: '). Now whatever the user types after the prompt will be stored in the msg variable.

Using the input function, we can easily write another function that will prompt the user to enter a message and then print out the encrypted message when it is done. Listing 3.4 illustrates how to incorporate input into your program.

```
def encryptMessage():
    msg = input('Enter a message to encrypt: ')
    cipherText = scramble2Encrypt(msg)
    print('The encrypted message is: ', cipherText)
```

Listing 3.4 Using input

3.5   Substitution Cipher

The transposition cipher is only interesting because it provides us with a simple example. It is not a very secure form of encryption. An attacker who is trying to read your secret messages and knows you are using a transposition cipher will find it very easy to use the same algorithm to decrypt your message.

There is another kind of cipher, called the **substitution cipher**, which substitutes one letter for another throughout a message. For example, you may say that 'a' = 't'. In this case, the letter 't' would be inserted into the ciphertext in each place where there was an 'a' in the plaintext. Substitution ciphers have been used since the time of Caesar. They continue to be popular today, where they most often appear as the "Cryptoquip" in the daily newspaper.

The substitution cipher has one big advantage over the transposition cipher: It uses a **key**. If attackers are trying to read your secret messages, knowing that you are using a substitution cipher only helps them a little. They would also need to know how the letters were rearranged. We call this rearranged version of the plaintext alphabet the ciphertext alphabet or key. Figure 3.5 illustrates the encryption process using a key. If we just consider the 26 letters of the alphabet, there are 26 factorial, or 403,291,461,126,605,635,584,000,000 different possible rearrangements of the alphabet. So we have a lot of keys to choose from!

Let's look at a simple example of a substitution cipher in action. We will encrypt the word 'flow' using the key 'bpzhgocvjdqswkimlutneryaxf'. Letters are matched up according to their position in the alphabet. For example, the sixth letter in the plaintext alphabet is 'f', which corresponds to the sixth letter in the key, which is 'o'. Figure 3.6 illustrates the process. Each letter in the word 'flow' is mapped from the regular alphabet into the corresponding letter in the key. In this case, 'f' maps to 'o', 'l' maps to 's', 'o' maps to 'i', and 'w' maps to 'y'.

Our next step is to turn this mapping process into a Python function. The important step in the encryption process is to take a letter from the plaintext alphabet and map it into a

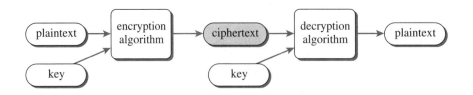

Figure 3.5   Using a key to make encryption more secure

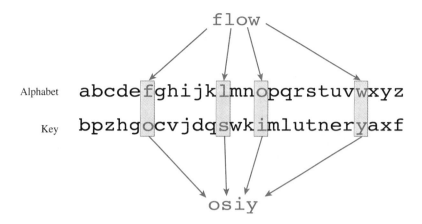

Figure 3.6 A substitution cipher

letter in the ciphertext alphabet. We can do this using the string **index** method. Recall that `astring.index(ch)` returns the first occurrence of `ch` in the string `astring`. Using this technique, we can create an alphabet string `"abcdefghijklmnopqrstuvwxyz"` and use the **index** method to return the position of any letter in the alphabet. Once we know the position of a letter in the plaintext alphabet, we can use the index operator to look up a different letter in the key. For example, let's find a mapping from the plaintext alphabet to the ciphertext alphabet for the letter `'h'`.

```
>>> alphabetString = "abcdefghijklmnopqrstuvwxyz"
>>> key = "zyxwvutsrqponmlkjihgfedcba"
>>> i = alphabetString.index('h')
>>> print(i)
7
>>> print(key[i])
s
```

Now that we know how to map characters from the plaintext to the ciphertext alphabet, what remains is to apply this mapping process to each character of the plaintext message, and to construct the final message. For these last two steps, we use iteration and the accumulator pattern. Listing 3.5 shows a function to encrypt a string using a given key.

```
1   def substitutionEncrypt(plainText,key):
2       alphabet = "abcdefghijklmnopqrstuvwxyz "
3       plainText = plainText.lower()
4       cipherText = ""
5       for ch in plainText:
6           idx = alphabet.find(ch)
7           cipherText = cipherText + key[idx]
8       return cipherText
```

Listing 3.5   Encrypting a message using a substitution cipher

If you look at the code carefully, you will notice that the alphabet contains the 26 lowercase letters of the alphabet along with a space. We add the space at the end of the alphabet and the key so we can preserve the spaces between the individual words in our secret message. This is a bad idea from a cryptographer's point of view, but it makes it easier for us to demonstrate these algorithms. A better approach would be to strip out all of the spaces from plaintext before applying any substitutions. This would effectively reduce the string "the quick brown fox" to the string "thequickbrownfox." Removing the spaces makes cracking the code much harder, but it also makes the decrypted message more difficult to read. We will keep the spaces intact to make it easier to read.

Session 3.10 shows the substitutionEncryption algorithm in action. Notice that even though we encrypt the same plaintext message, we get different ciphertext messages when we use different keys. This is what makes the substitution cipher superior to the transposition cipher. Even though an attacker may know that we are using a substitution cipher, that does not do her any good if she does not have the key. The substitutionDecrypt function is nearly the same as the substitutionEncrypt function.

```
>>> testKey1 = "zyxwvutsrqponmlkjihgfedcba "
>>> testKey2 = "ouwckbjmpzyexavrltsfgdqihn "
>>> cipherText = substitutionEncrypt("the quick brown fox",testKey1)
>>> print(cipherText)
gsv jfrxp yildm ulc
>>> cipherText = substitutionEncrypt("the quick brown fox",testKey2)
>>> print(cipherText)
fmk lgpwy utvqa bvi
>>>
```

Session 3.10   Using the substitutionEncrypt function

Exercises

3.20 Make up your own key and encrypt a message. Exchange your key and the ciphertext with a partner to see if you can decrypt each other's message.

3.21 Write the `substitutionDecrypt` method.

3.22 Rewrite the `substitutionEncrypt` function, but remove all spaces from the plaintext message.

3.6 Creating a Key

The strength of the substitution cipher lies in the ability of two people to share a key. That key must represent a scrambled version of the 26 letters of the alphabet. As a first approach, let's write a Python function that returns a randomly scrambled version of the alphabet.

The main idea in this algorithm is that we want to randomly select one letter from the alphabet to include in our key, and then to randomly select another letter and another until we have selected all 26 letters in a random order. This seems pretty simple at first, but we must be careful to keep track of the letters we have already selected so that our key does not contain duplicate letters.

Let's think of the problem in a slightly different way. Suppose that we start with a string that contains all 26 letters in the alphabet. Next we pick a random number from 0 to 25. This random number gives us the index of the first letter we will use in the key. We concatenate the letter retrieved from the alphabet to our key string. To make sure that we do not pick the same letter again, we will also remove it from our alphabet string. Since the alphabet string is now one character shorter we must pick a random number from 0 to 24. We can repeat this process of picking random numbers and removing characters until we have used up all the letters in our original alphabet string.

To implement this solution, let's break it up into two subproblems. First, we write a function that takes a string and an index value and returns a new string with the character at the given index position removed. Next, we write a function that starts with a full alphabet and returns the scrambled alphabet as our key.

Listing 3.6 provides us with a short Python function for removing a character from a string. This version of the function uses the slice operator to first get the substring from the beginning up to but not including the character we want to delete, and then to get the substring from the character after the one we want to delete up to the end. We can use string concatenation to combine these two pieces into our final string.

```
1   def removeChar(string,idx):
2       return string[:idx] + string[idx+1:]
```

Listing 3.6   Removing one character from a string

Let's test the removeChar function using a simple string and several different index values. Notice that we get an unexpected result when we use the index value −1. Before reading on, see if you can explain why we get the unexpected result for index −1.

```
>>> removeChar('abcdefg',0)
'bcdefg'
>>> removeChar('abcdefg',6)
'abcdef'
>>> removeChar('abcdefg',3)
'abcefg'
>>> removeChar('abcdefg',-1)
'abcdefabcdefg'
>>> removeChar('abcdefg',-2)
'abcdeg'
```

This example illustrates the importance of testing even the simplest of functions. The reason we get the result we do when using character index −1 is as follows. The first slice operation (string[:-1]) works just fine. It returns the entire string except for the last character. However, the second slice operation (string[-1+1:]) returns the entire string. We can move forward with this broken version of the removeChar function since our key-generating function will never try to remove a negative index.

Now that we have the removeChar function, let's turn our attention to the main key-generating function, keyGen(). Listing 3.7 shows the Python code for the strategy we outlined above. The *for* loop provides us with numbers from 0 to 25 assigned to the loop variable i. We use the value of i to generate our random number and then use the function randint from the random module, which generates a random integer in the range provided. Because we generate random numbers using the call random.randint(0,25-i), we get a smaller random number range as i gets larger. We could have used the range function `range(len(alphabet)-1,-1,-1)`, but that would look more confusing. Finally, we use an accumulator pattern `key = key + alphabet[ch]` to build up the final key.

```
def keyGen():
    alphabet = "abcdefghijklmnopqrstuvwxyz"
    key = ""
    for i in range(len(alphabet)):
        ch = random.randint(0,25-i)
        key = key + alphabet[ch]
        alphabet = removeChar(alphabet,ch)
    return key
```

Listing 3.7   Generating a random key from the alphabet

Since remembering 26 randomly scrambled letters of the alphabet is probably beyond the capabilities of most people, let's look at another approach to our key-generating problem. Rather than generating a random sequence of 26 letters, let's suppose that we choose a word or short phrase as our password. The question now becomes, how can we use this password as the basis for scrambling up the alphabet? The answer is that we will use two different strings to construct the key, the password, and the alphabet.

The first step is to remove all the letters from the alphabet that are in the password. Next we remove all duplicate letters in the password. We then use the alphabet, in order, starting with the letter after the last letter in the password. When we get to `'z'`, we go to the beginning of the alphabet and use the rest of the characters.

Let's look at an example of how we do this. Suppose our password is "topsecret." Removing the duplicates leaves us with "topsecr." Now if we take the alphabet and remove the letters in our password, we have "abdfghijklmnquvwxyz." The next letter after "r" in our alphabet is "u" so the three strings we will put together to make our final key are "topsecr," "uvwxyz," and "abdfghijklmnq." Putting these all together gives us "topsecruvwxyzabdfghijklmnq."

This may seem like a daunting task, but it is manageable if we break it down into some smaller problems:

1. Remove duplicates from the password.

2. Split the alphabet into parts `beforeLast` and `afterLast`.

3. Remove the letters found in the password from `beforeLast` and `afterLast`.

4. Put together the three parts of the key we need.

We already know how to do Steps 2 and 4, so let's solve the problem of removing duplicate letters from a string. To remove the duplicates from a string we will start by reconstructing the string, one character at a time, using the accumulator pattern. However, we will modify the accumulator pattern by adding one simple rule. If a character is not already part of the reconstructed string, we add it to the new string. Otherwise, if the character has already been added to the reconstructed string, we ignore it.

For example, consider the string "book". We start by creating an empty string, newStr, to build on. Then we iterate through the characters in "book". Since "b" is not already a part of newStr we add it, giving us "b". The next character is "o". Once again "o" is not in newStr so we add it, giving us "bo". Next we have our second "o", but since newStr already has an "o" we ignore this one. The final character, "k" is new, so we add it to newStr giving us "bok".

The key to this approach is asking the question, "Is the current character already a part of the new string we are creating?" To answer this question, we can use the in operator as the condition of an *if* statement. Listing 3.8 shows the Python code we use to create a string with duplicates removed. Notice that although the natural way for you to think about the conditional is to ask the question if ch in newStr: it is awkward to tell Python to do nothing. So, we use the not in operator to ask the opposite question if ch not in newStr:. This allows us to write the *if* statement in a natural way.

```
1    def removeDupes(myString):
2        newStr = ""
3        for ch in myString:
4            if ch not in newStr:
5                newStr = newStr + ch
6        return newStr
```

Listing 3.8   Removing duplicate letters from a string

We are going to use a similar idea to remove the characters from one string that are in another. Once again we begin with an empty string, myString, and apply the accumulator pattern to build up a new string, newStr. If the next character in the original string is not one of the characters in removeString, we add it to newStr. If the next character in myString is in removeString, we will simply ignore it. Listing 3.9 shows the Python code for this process. Let's test the two new functions we have just written. Session 3.11 shows both removeDupes and removeMatches in action.

```
1    def removeMatches(myString,removeString):
2        newStr = ""
3        for ch in myString:
4            if ch not in removeString:
5                newStr = newStr + ch
6        return newStr
```

Listing 3.9   Remove the characters in one string from another

```
>>> removeDupes('topsecret')
'topsecr'
>>> removeMatches('abcdefghijklmnopqrstuvwxyz','topsecr')
'abdfghijklmnquvwxyz'
>>> removeMatches('abcdefghijklmnopqrstuvwxyz',removeDupes('bondjamesbond'))
'cfghiklpqrtuvwxyz'
>>>
```

Session 3.11   Testing removeDupes and removeMatches

Now that we have implemented **removeDupes** and **removeMatches**, the rest of our alphabet scrambling algorithm is fairly easy. Listing 3.10 shows the Python code needed to provide a scrambled version of the alphabet using a password as the starting point.

```
1    def genKeyFromPass(password):
2        key = 'abcdefghijklmnopqrstuvwxyz'
3        password = removeDupes(password)
4        lastChar = password[-1]
5        lastIdx = key.find(lastChar)
6        afterString = removeMatches(key[lastIdx+1:],password)
7        beforeString = removeMatches(key[:lastIdx],password)
8        key = password + afterString + beforeString
9        return key
```

Listing 3.10   Generating a key starting from a password

The **genKeyFromPass** function is a good example of problem solving by top-down design. Look at the code in Listing 3.10. Now imagine how much longer the code would be if we tried to include the code for **removeDupes** and **removeMatches**. The function would be so long it would be much harder to discern what it is doing. Not only do **removeDupes** and `removeMatches` make `genKeyFromPass` more readable, but they can also be used in other functions you write.

To complete this section, let's consider the security of the substitution cipher. Suppose we don't know the key but we want to try to read the secret message anyway. One possibility would be to simply use **brute force**, a method in which we try all possible keys until we get plaintext that makes sense. Since the number of keys is equivalent to the number of different ways we can rearrange the 26 letters of the alphabet, there are 26! or 403×10^{24} possible keys. Suppose that we were able to try 1,000,000 keys every second. To try all possible keys would take us 12,788,288,341,153 years. That is 12 trillion years, roughly a thousand times older than estimates of the age of the universe!

However, as we will see in the chapter on "Cryptanalysis" (Chapter 8), the substitution cipher is quite easy to break by exploiting some simple characteristics of the English language. So easy in fact that the substitution cipher regularly appears in daily newspapers next to the crossword puzzle under the name of "Cryptoquip." The main reason the substitution cipher is easy to break is that there is a one-to-one mapping between letters in the key and letters in the plaintext alphabet. This means that if plaintext "e" maps to ciphertext "k" then it will do so consistently throughout the message. But since "e" is the most common letter in the language, "k" will probably be the most common letter in the ciphertext. This observation gives us a head start in figuring out the rest of the letters.

Exercises

3.23 Write the `removeChar` function using *for* loops rather than slice operators.

3.24 Modify the `removeChar` function so that it works for negative character indexes.

3.25 Modify the `substitutionCipher` function to use the `genKeyFromPass` function.

3.26 Encryption often involves the Caesar cipher—named after Julius Caesar, who used the system to encrypt military messages. Many early Internet users also adopted this cipher. Called `rot13`, the cipher encrypts a message by rotating the plaintext character by 13 positions in the alphabet. For example, "a" becomes "n" and likewise "n" becomes "a". The nice thing about `rot13` is that the same function can be used to encrypt and decrypt a message. Write a function called `rot13` that takes a message as a parameter and rotates all the characters by 13 places.

3.27 Rewrite the Caesar cipher so that it takes the number of places to rotate as a parameter. You will have to write separate encrypt and decrypt functions.

3.7 The Vignère Cipher

The key to cracking a substitution cipher was first discovered by Arab scholars in the ninth century, but it was not widely known in the west until the fifteenth century. Once frequency analysis of ciphers became widespread, the plain substitution cipher became useless. To fix the problems inherent in the simple substitution cipher, Blaise Vignère invented the strategy of using multiple letter mappings [Sin00]. Rather than using one key for the whole message, Vignère's idea was to use a different key for each letter of the message. Using a different key for each letter makes the frequency analysis much more difficult.

The key to the Vignère cipher is the Vignère square. Table 3.3 shows the Vignère square. Each row in the table corresponds to a different key such that we might encode the first letter of our secret message using row 12, the second letter of the message might be encoded with row 7, and so on. The rows that we have chosen here are simple rotations of the alphabet. Each row in the table shifts the letters of the alphabet one place to the left. When a letter shifts past the first column, it moves around to the end of the right side.

Let's now see how to use the Vignère square to encode the message, "the eagle has landed." The first step is to decide on a key. Choosing the word "DAVINCI" as our key, we next align the key across the top of the message, repeating the letters of the key as needed to cover the message. Table 3.4 shows how the letters in "DAVINCI" cover the letters in our message.

To encode the message, we use the row corresponding to the letter in the key, and the column corresponding to the plaintext letter to find the ciphertext letter. For example, the first letter in the message is "t", so we look in column "t" and row "D" and find the letter "w". So, "w" is the first character in the ciphertext. We next look at column "h" and row "A" to find that "h" is the second character. The third character is in column "e" and row "V", which means that "z" is the third character. Notice that the next character in the message is also an "e" but this time we use column "e" and row "I" so this "e" is encoded as an "m". If we continue following this pattern, the entire phrase is encoded as "whz rcooe pnu oailrf".

Although the Vignère cipher was invented in 1562, it went unused for 200 years because the cipher secretaries found it hard to implement. Obviously they did not have Python. Let's write a function to encrypt a message using the Vignère cipher. We will begin by doing a top-down analysis of the procedure needed to encode a message.

Shift	Key
	a b c d e f g h i j k l m n o p q r s t u v w x y z
A	a b c d e f g h i j k l m n o p q r s t u v w x y z
B	b c d e f g h i j k l m n o p q r s t u v w x y z a
C	c d e f g h i j k l m n o p q r s t u v w x y z a b
D	d e f g h i j k l m n o p q r s t u v w x y z a b c
E	e f g h i j k l m n o p q r s t u v w x y z a b c d
F	f g h i j k l m n o p q r s t u v w x y z a b c d e
G	g h i j k l m n o p q r s t u v w x y z a b c d e f
H	h i j k l m n o p q r s t u v w x y z a b c d e f g
I	i j k l m n o p q r s t u v w x y z a b c d e f g h
J	j k l m n o p q r s t u v w x y z a b c d e f g h i
K	k l m n o p q r s t u v w x y z a b c d e f g h i j
L	l m n o p q r s t u v w x y z a b c d e f g h i j k
M	m n o p q r s t u v w x y z a b c d e f g h i j k l
N	n o p q r s t u v w x y z a b c d e f g h i j k l m
O	o p q r s t u v w x y z a b c d e f g h i j k l m n
P	p q r s t u v w x y z a b c d e f g h i j k l m n o
Q	q r s t u v w x y z a b c d e f g h i j k l m n o p
R	r s t u v w x y z a b c d e f g h i j k l m n o p q
S	s t u v w x y z a b c d e f g h i j k l m n o p q r
T	t u v w x y z a b c d e f g h i j k l m n o p q r s
U	u v w x y z a b c d e f g h i j k l m n o p q r s t
V	v w x y z a b c d e f g h i j k l m n o p q r s t u
W	w x y z a b c d e f g h i j k l m n o p q r s t u v
X	x y z a b c d e f g h i j k l m n o p q r s t u v w
Y	y z a b c d e f g h i j k l m n o p q r s t u v w x
Z	z a b c d e f g h i j k l m n o p q r s t u v w x y

Table 3.3 The Vignère square

D	A	V	I	N	C	I	D	A	V	I	N	C	I	D	A	V
t	h	e	e	a	g	l	e	h	a	s	l	a	n	d	e	d

Table 3.4   Matching key letters with message letters

1. Initialize an empty result string.

2. For each letter in the plaintext message

   (a) determine which letter of the key we should use.

   (b) look up the ciphertext letter in the Vignère square, using the key letter row and plaintext character column.

   (c) use the accumulator pattern to add the ciphertext letter to the ciphertext message.

3. Return the result string as the ciphertext message.

At first glance it may seem like looking up a character in Table 3.3 would be the most difficult part of this procedure, but it is not as difficult as it might seem. Let's think about what we know (note that the term ordinal position refers to the position of the letter in the range from 0 to 25. This is mapped using our helper functions developed earlier.):

1. Each row of the table rotates the letters one more position to the left.

2. The row of the table corresponds to the ordinal value of the key letter.

3. The column of the table corresponds to the ordinal value of the plaintext letter.

From the facts outlined previously, the steps we need to follow to find our ciphertext letters are as follows: We start with our plaintext alphabet and then rotate the letters in the alphabet by i positions where i is the ordinal value of the key letter. For example, if the letter is "c", the ordinal value is 2 and the alphabet is modified so that it starts with "c" and the final two letters are "ab". Finally, we find the ciphertext letter at index j of the rotated text, where j is the ordinal value of the plaintext letter.

Before we write the Python code for this procedure, we can make one more simplification. Using modulo arithmetic, we can avoid copying and shifting letters in a string. Without shifting any letters, we can simply use the formula:

```
cipherTextLetter = (plainTextLetterIndex + keyLetterIndex) % 26
```

Suppose we want to encrypt the letter "e" using the key letter "j". The ordinal value for "e" is 4, and the ordinal value for "j" is 9. The ordinal value of the letter "n" comes from applying the formula 9 + 4 % 26 = 13. If you check row "J" and column "e" of Table 3.3, you will see this is exactly right. Let's look at another example. Suppose we want to encrypt the letter "t" using the key letter "s". The ordinal value of "t" is 19, and the ordinal value of "s" is 18. This means that $(18+19)\%26 = 37\%26 = 11$, and 11 is the ordinal value for the letter "l", which you will find in row "s" column "t".

The code for the `vignereIndex` function is shown in Listing 3.11. The `vignereIndex` simply uses our helper functions `letterToIndex` and `indexToLetter` to do the lookups we need.

```
1    def vignereIndex(keyLetter,plainTextLetter):
2        keyIndex = letterToIndex(keyLetter)
3        ptIndex = letterToIndex(plainTextLetter)
4        newIdx = (ptIndex + keyIndex) % 26
5        return indexToLetter(newIdx)
```

Listing 3.11   Looking up a letter in the Vignère square

The final step in implementing the Vignère cipher is to write a function that takes a key and a plaintext message as parameters and returns the ciphertext message. As before, we will take a character-by-character approach to encrypting the message, applying our `vignereIndex` function to each character. The only remaining question is how to decide which letter of the key to use in conjunction with each letter of the message.

One way to solve this problem is to duplicate the key as many times as needed so we can cover all the letters in the message, as we did in Table 3.4. This is easy to do using the string repetition operator as well as some division. If the message is M characters long and our key is K characters long, we need M/K repetitions of the key to cover the message. We can then use a loop such as the following to iterate over the characters in the message and the characters in the duplicated key in parallel:

```
for i in range(len(message)):
    nc = vignereIndex(repeatKey[i],message[i])
```

If our message is long, making another long string by duplicating the key is wasteful. We can avoid duplicating the key by using modulo arithmetic. If our key is K letters long, we want an index counter for our key to repeatedly cycle through the numbers 0 through $K-1$. The modulo operator allows us to do exactly that. Try Session 3.12 for yourself.

(Note that the `end=''` parameter prevents each number from being printed on a separate line.)

```
>>> for i in range(100):
...     print(i % 7, end = '')
...
0 1 2 3 4 5 6 0 1 2 3 4 5 6 0 1 2 3 4 5 6 0 1 2 3 4 5 6
0 1 2 3 4 5 6 0 1 2 3 4 5 6 0 1 2 3 4 5 6 0 1 2 3 4 5 6
0 1 2 3 4 5 6 0 1 2 3 4 5 6 0 1 2 3 4 5 6 0 1 2 3 4 5 6
0 1 2 3 4 5 6 0 1 2 3 4 5 6 0 1 >>>
```

Session 3.12   Demonstrating circular counting with modulo arithmetic

Using the modulo arithmetic demonstrated in the previous session, we can use a counter to keep track of the current character in the message and then use `counter%i` as the index into the key. Listing 3.12 shows the entire function needed to encode a message using the Vignère cipher.

```
1  def encryptVignere(key,plainText):
2      cipherText = ""
3      keyLen = len(key)
4      for i in range(len(plainText)):
5          ch = plainText[i]
6          if ch == ' ':
7              cipherText = cipherText + ch
8          else:
9              cipherText = cipherText + vignereIndex(key[i%keyLen],ch)
10     return cipherText
```

Listing 3.12   Encrypting a message using the Vignère cipher

Exercises

3.28 Write a function `undoVig(keyLetter,ctLetter)` that takes a letter from the key, a ciphertext letter, and returns the plaintext letter.

3.29 Write a function `decryptVignere` that takes a keyword, the ciphtertext for the message, and returns the plaintext message.

3.8   Summary

In this chapter we introduced an important Python data type called strings—sequences of characters that provide a wide range of built-in operators and methods. Strings provide:

- Concatenation
- Repetition
- Indexing
- Slicing
- Length
- Membership

We used string manipulation to implement some basic encryption algorithms. These algorithms allowed us to illustrate iteration over characters in a string as well as the accumulator pattern as it applies to strings. Finally, we used abstraction to build up a collection of small functions that could be used to solve larger problems.

Key Terms

accumulator pattern	cryptography	rail fence cipher
American Standard Code	decryption	repetition
for Information	encryption	sequence
Interchange (ASCII)	index	slice
brute force	key	string
character	length	substitution cipher
ciphertext	plaintext	substring
concatenation	prompt	transposition cipher

Python Keywords

center	find	index	ord
chr	for	input	rjust
count	if	len	str
def	if else	ljust	

Bibliography

[Sin00]   Simon Singh. *The Code Book: The Science of Secrecy from Ancient Egypt to Quantum Cryptography.* Anchor, 2000.

Programming Exercises

3.1 Research the "playfair cipher." Write a program to implement this cipher.

3.2 Research the UPC codes that are used on products of all kinds. Use the `turtle` module to draw a UPC code for a given product name and price.

3.3 Research the US postal bar codes used to encode a zip code. Use the `turtle` module to draw a postal code for a given zip code.

CHAPTER 4

A Nest of Snakes: Introducing the Python Collections

4.1 Objectives

- To understand Python lists
- To use lists as a means of storing data
- To use dictionaries to store associative data
- To implement algorithms to compute elementary statistics

4.2 What Is Data?

Every day there are thousands of earthquakes that occur around the world. Most of them are so mild that they are hardly noticed except by those who have monitoring equipment. If we consider only those earthquakes that you feel, then there may be 35 on a typical day. Some days there may be only 10 but on other days there may be 40 or 50.

What we have just described is a way that earthquake occurrence might be reported through data—an assortment of items, many times numerical, that have been observed, measured, or collected by some means. These data items pertain to some experiment, event, or activity that we are interested in knowing more about. Data, sometimes referred to as "raw data," represents the starting point for analysis that can be done in an attempt to discover underlying characteristics that might be present. These characteristics are typically referred to as **information**. Data can contain information in various forms, and the information can be used in a variety of ways. Sometimes this information allows us to make generalizations about the data items. We may also be able to make predictions of future events based on the data. This analysis is based on the mathematical science of statistics.

This chapter is about data, information, and statistics. We will focus on ways that a programming language like Python can help perform some of the basic data processing tasks common with large amounts of data.

4.3   Storing Data for Processing

Anytime that we work with large amounts of data it is necessary to have some means of organized storage so that processing of the data can take place in an orderly and efficient manner. Computer science provides us with a number of alternatives for accomplishing this task. We will consider two of Python's built-in collections as a means of storing our data values: strings and lists.

4.3.1   Strings Revisited

In the previous chapter we introduced the idea of a string as a sequential collection of characters. Each string is considered to be ordered from left to right, and each individual character can be accessed using the indexing operation. Provided that our data items can be thought of as characters, a string might make the perfect collection mechanism.

As an example, assume that we have just taken a multiple-choice exam where each question has five possible answers labeled A, B, C, D, and E. Our answer sheet might look like this:

```
1.  A
2.  B
3.  E
4.  A
5.  D
6.  B
7.  B
8.  A
9.  C
10. E
```

In order to store our answers for later processing, a simple string of 10 characters could be used. The string will contain the ten data items gathered from the student:

```
>>> myanswers = "ABEADBBACE"
>>> for answer in myanswers:
        print(answer)

A
B
E
A
D
B
B
A
C
E
>>>
```

answer → A
answer → B
,
.

This technique allows easy access to each individual answer. Furthermore, using iteration over strings, we can process the entire exam. However, there are some potential drawbacks. What if the exam we had taken was in math class where we have to solve number problems and write down our final answer? Now the answers are numbers instead of characters. Can a string still be used?

For example, here is our answer sheet now:

```
1.  34
2.  56
3.  2
4.  652
5.  26
6.  1
7.  99
8.  865
9.  22
10. 16
```

If we attempt to use the same string-based storage technique as before, we might get something like this:

```
>>> myanswers = "34562652261998652216"
>>>
```

Of course, it is easy to see that we have a real problem. This organization will not allow us to easily know the correspondence between question and answer. Certainly all of the numeric characters are present but there is no distinction between the individual integer values.

The problem is that we need a way to store collections of integers instead of being restricted to just using characters. Like the string, where there is one character per position, we would like an organization that can provide one integer per position. Fortunately, there is such a collection, the list.

4.3.2   Lists

In addition to the primitive numeric classes, Python has a number of powerful built-in collection classes. We have already seen strings. In this section we introduce the list, a collection that is very similar to strings in general structure but has specific differences that must be understood for them to be used properly. Figure 4.1 shows that strings and lists are examples of sequential collections.

A list is an ordered, sequential collection of zero or more Python data objects. Lists are written as comma-delimited values enclosed in square brackets. We call a list with zero data

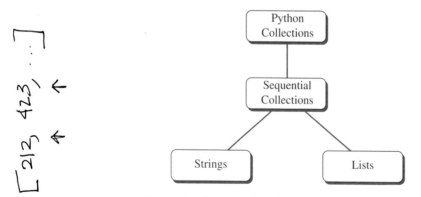

Figure 4.1   Lists and strings as sequential collections

objects the **empty list**, which is represented simply by [ ]. Recall in the previous chapter that strings are homogeneous collections because each item in the collection is the same type of object—a character. Lists, by contrast, are heterogeneous and can be composed of any kind of object. In Session 4.1, the list `mylist` consists of two integers, a floating-point value and a string.

```
>>> [3,"cat",6.5,2]
[3, 'cat', 6.5, 2]
>>> mylist = [3,"cat",6.5,2]
>>> mylist
[3, 'cat', 6.5, 2]
>>>
```

Session 4.1   A Python list

As with other values in Python, asking the interpreter to evaluate a list will simply return the list itself. In order to remember the list for later processing, its reference needs to be assigned to a variable. Evaluating the variable returns the list. Figure 4.2 shows the sequential organization of the items in the example list in Session 4.1.

Since lists are considered to be sequential, they support a number of operations that can be applied to any Python sequence. These are the same operations that we used with strings since both are composed of a sequential collection of items. Table 4.1 reviews these operations and Session 4.2 gives examples of their use.

Figure 4.2   Sequential storage of the elements in a list

Operation Name	Operator	Explanation
Indexing	[ ]	Access an element of a sequence
Concatenation	+	Combine sequences together
Repetition	*	Concatenate a repeated number of times
Membership	in	Ask whether an item is in a sequence
Membership	not in	Ask whether an item is not in a sequence
Length	len	Ask the number of items in the sequence
Slicing	[:]	Extract a part of a sequence

Table 4.1   Operations on any sequence in Python

```
>>> mylist
[1, 3, 'cat', 4.5]
>>> mylist[2]
'cat'
>>> mylist+mylist
[1, 3, 'cat', 4.5, 1, 3, 'cat', 4.5]
>>> mylist*3
[1, 3, 'cat', 4.5, 1, 3, 'cat', 4.5, 1, 3, 'cat', 4.5]
>>> len(mylist)
4           objects?
>>> len(mylist*4)
16
            ← 3-)
>>> mylist[1:3]
[3, 'cat']
>>> 3 in mylist
True
>>> "dog" in mylist
False
>>> del myList[2]
>>> myList
[1, 3, 4.5]
```

Session 4.2   Using sequence operators with lists

Note that the indices for lists, as with strings, start with 0. The slice operation `mylist[1:3]` returns a list of items starting with the item indexed by 1 up to but not including the item indexed by 3.

Strings are **immutable** collections of data where individual items within the string cannot be changed. This is not true for lists. It is possible to change an individual member of a list by using the assignment statement and placing the indexed location on the left-hand side. Thus, lists are **mutable** collections of data that can be modified. Note that the last example in Session 4.2 introduces the **del** operator that allows you to delete an item from a list. This operation is not permitted on strings.

Session 4.3 shows an assignment statement modifying the item at index 2 in the list `changelist`. Figure 4.3 shows that a list is actually a collection of references to Python objects. We call this a **reference diagram**. Changing an item in the list simply changes the reference stored at that position. Note that the same operation does not work when applied to a string variable. The Python interpreter reports an error since strings do not support the ability to change a single character.

```
>>> changelist = [1,2,"buckle my shoe",3,4,"shut the door"]
>>> changelist
[1, 2, 'buckle my shoe', 3, 4, 'shut the door']
>>> changelist[2] = "the sky is blue"
>>> changelist
[1, 2, 'the sky is blue', 3, 4, 'shut the door']
>>>
>>> name = "Monte"
>>> name[2] = "x"        not a list

Traceback (most recent call last):
  File "<pyshell#67>", line 1, in -toplevel-
    name[2] = "x"
TypeError: object does not support item assignment
>>>
```

Session 4.3   Mutating a list

The repetition operator is also impacted by this idea of a collection of references. The result of performing this action is a repetition of references to the data objects in the sequence. This can best be seen by considering the statements in Session 4.4.

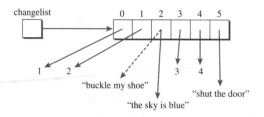

Figure 4.3   The collection of references forming a list

```
>>> mylist = [1,2,3,4]
>>> A = [mylist]*3
>>> A
[[1, 2, 3, 4], [1, 2, 3, 4], [1, 2, 3, 4]]
>>> mylist[2]=45
>>> A
[[1, 2, 45, 4], [1, 2, 45, 4], [1, 2, 45, 4]]
>>>
```

Session 4.4   Mutating a list created with repetition

The variable **A** holds a collection of three references to the original list called **mylist**. Note that a change to one element of **mylist** shows up in all three occurrences in **A**. This is explained, once again, by the fact that the repetition result is actually a list of three references to the same list, as shown in Figure 4.4.

A useful function for creating lists is the **list** function. The **list** function converts other sequences to lists. We have seen two such sequences: strings and ranges. Recall that the

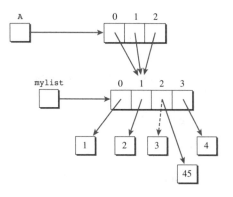

Figure 4.4   The repetition operator copies references

range function returns an object representing a sequence of integers. Session 4.5 demonstrates the use of **list** to create some simple lists from strings and ranges.

```
>>> range(10)
range(10)
>>> list(range(10))
[0, 1, 2, 3, 4, 5, 6, 7, 8, 9]
>>> list(range(10,2,-2))
[10, 8, 6, 4, 2]
>>> list(''the quick fox'')
['t', 'h', 'e', ' ', 'q', 'u', 'i', 'c', 'k', ' ', 'f', 'o', 'x']
>>>
```

Session 4.5   Using the **list** function

Lists support a number of useful methods. Table 4.2 provides a summary. Examples of their use can be seen in Session 4.6.

Method Name	Use	Explanation
append	alist.append(item)	Adds a new item to the end of a list
insert	alist.insert(i,item)	Inserts an item at the **ith** position in a list
pop	alist.pop()	Removes and returns the last item in a list
pop	alist.pop(i)	Removes and returns the **ith** item in a list
sort	alist.sort()	Modifies a list to be sorted
reverse	alist.reverse()	Modifies a list to be in reverse order
index	alist.index(item)	Returns the index of the first occurrence of **item**
count	alist.count(item)	Returns the number of occurrences of **item**
remove	alist.remove(item)	Removes the first occurrence of **item**

Table 4.2   Methods provided by lists in Python

```
>>> mylist
[1024, 3, True, 6.5]
>>> mylist.append(False)
>>> mylist
[1024, 3, True, 6.5, False]
>>> mylist.insert(2,4.5)
>>> mylist
[1024, 3, 4.5, True, 6.5, False]
>>> mylist.pop()
False
>>> mylist
[1024, 3, 4.5, True, 6.5]
>>> mylist.pop(1)
3
>>> mylist
[1024, 4.5, True, 6.5]
>>> mylist.pop(2)
True
>>> mylist
[1024, 4.5, 6.5]
>>> mylist.sort()
>>> mylist
[4.5, 6.5, 1024]
>>> mylist.reverse()
>>> mylist
[1024, 6.5, 4.5]
>>> mylist.count(6.5)
1
>>> mylist.index(4.5)
2
>>> mylist.remove(6.5)
>>> mylist
[1024, 4.5]
>>>
```

Session 4.6   Examples of list methods

You can see that some of the methods, such as **pop**, return a value and also modify the list. Others, such as **reverse**, simply modify the list with no return value. Although **pop** will default to the end of the list, it can also remove and return an item at a specific index location. Note the familiar "dot" notation for asking an object to invoke a method. You can read `mylist.append(False)` as "ask the object **mylist** to perform its **append** method using the value **False** as a parameter." All data objects invoke methods in this way.

Before leaving this section, we will describe one additional string method called **split**, which takes a string as a parameter that indicates the places to break the string into substrings. The substrings are returned in a list. By default, if no parameter is passed to split, it will break the string using one or more spaces as the delimiter. Session 4.7 demonstrates how the **split** method works.

```
>>> a = "minnesota vikings"
>>> a.split()
['minnesota', 'vikings']
>>> a.split('i')
['m', 'nnesota v', 'k', 'ngs']
>>> a.split('nn')
['mi', 'esota vikings']
>>>
```

Session 4.7   Using the **split** method

Exercises

4.1 Create a list with the following five items: 7, 9, 'a', 'cat', False. Assign this list to the variable **myList**.

4.2 Write Python statements to do the following:

   (a) Append 3.14 and 7 to the list.

   (b) Insert the value '_dog_' at position 3.

   (c) Find the index of 'cat'.

   (d) Count the number of 7's in the list.

   (e) Remove the first 7 from the list.

(f) Remove 'dog' from the list using pop and index.

4.3 Split the string "the quick brown fox" into a list of words.

4.4 Split the string "mississippi" into a list using the 'i' as the split point.

4.5 Write a function that takes a sentence as a parameter and returns the number of words in the sentence.

4.6 Although Python provides us with many list methods, it is good practice and very instructive to think about how they are implemented. Implement a Python function that works like the following:

   (a) count

   (b) in — return True if item is in list

   (c) reverse

   (d) index — return -1 if not in the list

   (e) insert

4.7 Write a function shuffle that takes a list and returns a new list with the elements shuffled into a random order.

4.8 Write a function shuffle that takes a list as a parameter and shuffles the list in place.

4.9 Draw a reference diagram to illustrate the differences between the previous two exercises.

4.10 Suppose you initialize the following list: mylist = [[]]*3. Evaluate this expression.

4.11 Evaluate the expression mylist[1].append(2). Explain the result.

4.12 Draw a reference diagram to illustrate what is happening in the previous two exercises.

4.13 Write a code fragment to initialize mylist so that each sublist is independent—that is, so that changes to one list do not affect the others.

4.4 Simple Dispersion

We now turn our attention to the simple idea of **dispersion**—a measure of how spread out the data values are. Throughout the next sections, we analyze data sets using simple statistics and assume that our data is stored in list structures. For example, during one seven-day period last year, there were 20 earthquakes on Monday, 32 on Tuesday, 21 on Wednesday, 26 on Thursday, 33 on Friday, 22 on Saturday, and 18 on Sunday. This data can be stored in the simple list `[20,32,21,26,33,22,18]`.

The easiest way to look at dispersion is to consider the range of values and simply compute the difference between the largest and the smallest value in the data set. In Python, this is very easy to do because there are built-in functions, `max` and `min`, that work on any sequence and return the maximum and minimum values in the collection, as shown in Session 4.8.

```
>>> alist = [20,32,21,26,33,22,18]
>>> max(alist)
33
>>> min(alist)
18
>>>
>>> max("house")
'u'
>>> min("house")
'e'
>>> max(alist) - min(alist)
15
>>>
```

Session 4.8   Using the `min` and `max` functions

Note that these functions work with strings as well as with lists since both are examples of sequences. Characters are "ordered" by their ordinal values. The final example in Session 4.9 shows that the range of the integer list can be computed by subtracting the minimum from the maximum.

To construct a function to return the range of a data set, we will assume that the data values have been placed in a list. The function can then take the list as a parameter and return the range. Listing 4.1 shows such a function and Session 4.9 shows it in use.

```
1  def getRange(alist):
2      return max(alist)-min(alist)
```

Listing 4.1 ✓remember! ✓brackets! A function to return the range of a list

```
>>> getRange([2,4])
2
>>> getRange([20,32,21,26,33,22,18])
15
>>>
```

Session 4.9   Using the getRange function

An interesting question arises if we consider what would happen if we did not have a built-in function to return the maximum value in the list. It would be possible to construct our own getMax function by iterating through the items in the list and keeping track of the largest value seen. The function, shown in Listing 4.2, makes the assumption that there is at least one item in the list (otherwise the idea of a "maximum" makes no sense). The variable maxSoFar does most of the work. We start out by letting maxSoFar be the first item in the list (alist[0]). Then, as we "visit" other items, we check to see if they are greater than maxSoFar. If so, we reassign the maxSoFar variable to the new largest item. After checking the remaining items, maxSoFar holds the maximum of all.

doesn't work! (handwritten)

```
1  def getMax(alist):
2      maxSoFar = alist[0]
3      for pos in range(1,len(alist)):
4          if alist[pos] > maxSoFar:
5              maxSoFar = alist[pos]
6
7      return maxSoFar
```

Listing 4.2   Constructing a function to return the maximum value in a list

Listing 4.3 shows an alternative implementation for the getMax function. This time, the iteration is performed "by item" instead of "by index." In either case, each element of the list is eventually processed and compared against the maximum item seen up to that point. A similar argument can be made to reimplement the getMin function. We would simply keep track of the minimum value seen so far.

```
1   def getMax(alist):
2       maxSoFar = alist[0]
3       for item in alist[1:]:
4           if item > maxSoFar:
5               maxSoFar = item
6
7       return maxSoFar
```

Listing 4.3   Alternative function to return the maximum value in a list

Exercises

4.14 Implement the `getMin` function using iteration by index.

4.15 Implement the `getMin` function using iteration by item.

4.16 Rewrite the `getRange` function using `getMin` and `getMax`.

4.5   Central Tendency

One of the most often used measures of a collection of data is known as **central tendency**—a process that estimates where the "center" of a collection will be found. There are three common ways to compute central tendency: (1) mean, (2) median, and (3) mode.

4.5.1   Mean

The most common measure of central tendency is the **mean** (also called the **average**). To compute the mean, we simply add up the values in a collection and divide by the number of items. Listing 4.4 shows how this is done. Given a list of values, we use the `sum` function to compute a total and the `len` function to compute the number of values. The **mean** is simply the sum divided by the length. Session 4.10 shows the `mean` function in action.

```
1   def mean(alist):
2       mean = sum(alist) / len(alist)
3       return mean
```

Listing 4.4   Computing the mean of a list

```
>>> mean([20,32,21,26,33,22,18])
24.571428571428573
>>>
```

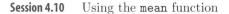

Session 4.10   Using the `mean` function

Exercises

4.17 Create a list of the number of students in each of your classes. Use the `mean` function on that list.

4.18 Replace the call to the `sum` function with an iteration that computes the total of the values in `alist`.

4.5.2 Median

The second measure of central tendency is called the **median**, found by locating the item that occurs in the exact middle of a collection. Another way to determine the median is to find the value located at a point where half of the values lie above it and half of the values lie below.

One way to compute the median is to put the items in order, from lowest to highest, and then find the value that falls in the middle. If there are an odd number of items, this will be a distinct value. However, if there are an even number of items, the average of the two middle values will be used. Figure 4.5 shows the two cases.

It is worth noting that the process of ordering values is often referred to as **sorting**. Sorting is a very important topic in computer science and there are a number of algorithms that

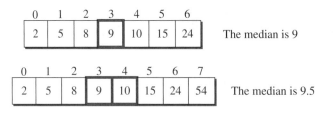

Figure 4.5   Finding the median of a list of values

can be used to take a list of data and place them in order. As you know, the list object has a `sort` method that allows you to put the list in order. Although we will not cover sorting techniques here, you will undoubtedly study them in your algorithms and data structures courses.

The Python statements in Session 4.11 show some of the computation that will be required. Note that with an odd number of values, integer division by 2 will provide the correct index into the list. However, with an even number of items, division by 2 gives the index of the rightmost item of the middle pair.

```
>>> alist = [24,5,8,2,9,15,10]
>>> alist.sort()
>>> alist
[2, 5, 8, 9, 10, 15, 24]
>>> len(alist)
7
>>> len(alist)//2
3
>>> alist[3]
9
>>> alist = [2,5,8,9,10,15,24,54]
>>> len(alist)
8
>>> len(alist)//2
4
>>> alist[4]
10
>>>
```

Session 4.11   Computation required to find the median item

Listing 4.5 shows the complete Python function to compute and return the median value of a list. As noted above, the list items must be in sorted order. To do this, we simply use the `sort` method from the list class. Before sorting, we are careful to make a copy of the original list in case the original order is important for later processing. To make the copy, we use the slice operator (line 2) with beginning index at the start of the list and ending index up to and including the last item.

```
1  def median(alist):
2      copylist = alist[:]    #make a copy using slice operator
3      copylist.sort()
4      if len(copylist)%2 == 0: #even length
5          rightmid = len(copylist)//2
6          leftmid = rightmid - 1
7          median = (copylist[leftmid] + copylist[rightmid])/2
8      else:       #odd length
9          mid = len(copylist)//2
10         median = copylist[mid]
11     return median
```

Listing 4.5   Computing the median of a list

The other important part of the solution is the decision about whether there are an even or odd number of items. To make this choice, we can take advantage of the modulo operator (%) and check the result of dividing by 2. Even numbers will have no remainder. Line 4 in Listing 4.5 shows a simple selection statement to check for a remainder of zero.

Session 4.12 shows the median function in action. Since we have data for seven days, our median number of earthquakes is 22. If there had been an additional day of data, say with 29 quakes, the median would be 24, which is the average of 22 and 26.

```
>>> median([20,32,21,26,33,22,18])
22
>>>
>>> median([20,32,21,26,33,22,18,29])
24
>>>
```

Session 4.12   Using the median function

Exercises

4.19 Draw a reference diagram to illustrate why it is important to make a copy of a list before sorting.

4.20 Find the mean age of ten people near you.

4.21 Find the mean age of ten people near you plus your professor, who is 39 years old.

4.22 Find the median age of ten people near you.

4.23 Find the median age of ten people near you plus your young professor.

4.5.3   Mode

The mode of a data set is the most frequently occurring value. It is possible that there can be more than one mode. For example, in the list [1,5,2,1,1,6,3,1,5], 1 is the mode since it occurs more than any other value. However, if the list contained [1,5,2,1,1,5,5,6,3,1,5], then 1 and 5 would both be considered the mode values since they each occur four times.

In order to compute the mode, we need to process each data item in our list and keep a count of how many times it has occurred thus far. Unfortunately, this is not quite as easy as it might sound. Since we do not know how many different values there are, it is not possible to create individual variables to hold each count. Instead, we need to create a collection of counting variables and try to keep them associated with the correct data value.

Python Dictionaries

In order to solve the mode problem, we need to associate an occurrence count with each individual data value. This unordered, associative collection is called a **dictionary**. Python dictionaries are collections of associated pairs of items where each pair consists of a key and a value. Figure 4.6 shows how Python dictionaries, lists, and strings are related to one another.

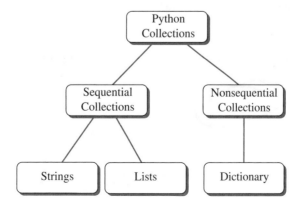

Figure 4.6   Sequential and nonsequential Python collections

In dictionary notation, a key-value pair is written as key:value. Dictionaries are written as comma-delimited key:value pairs enclosed in curly braces. The empty dictionary is written as {}. In the following example, we are creating a dictionary with two entries, each of which is an association between a name (a string) and an age (an integer):

```
>>> ages = {'David':45,'Brenda':46}
>>> ages
{'Brenda': 46, 'David': 45}
>>>
```

We can manipulate a dictionary in a number of ways (see Session 4.13). Accessing a dictionary value by its key looks much like a sequence index operation except that dictionaries are not restricted to numeric indices. To access a value, we use the dictionary key inside the square bracket index operator. To add a new key-value pair to the dictionary, we use the index operator with the new key on the left-hand side of the assignment statement and the new value on the right. In Session 4.13 we add three new values to our **ages** dictionary.

```
>>> ages['David']
45
>>> ages['Kelsey']=19
>>> ages
{'Kelsey': 19, 'Brenda': 46, 'David': 45}
>>> ages['Hannah']=16
>>> ages
{'Hannah': 16, 'Kelsey': 19, 'Brenda': 46, 'David': 45}
>>> ages['Rylea']=7
>>> ages
{'Hannah': 16, 'Kelsey': 19, 'Rylea': 7, 'Brenda': 46, 'David': 45}
>>> len(ages)
5
>>> ages['David'] = ages['David'] + 1
>>> ages['David']
46
>>> ages
{'Hannah': 16, 'Kelsey': 19, 'Rylea': 7, 'Brenda': 46, 'David': 46}
>>>
```

Session 4.13   Examples of adding and modifying values in a dictionary

It is important to note that the dictionary is maintained in no particular order with respect to the keys. The pair `'Rylea': 7` was placed in the middle of the dictionary. In fact, the placement of a key is dependent on some internal storage algorithm designed to make the lookup operation work efficiently. This is one of the real benefits of dictionaries: quick access to data values by key. We also show the `len` function performing the same role it had in previous collections, in this case the number of key-value pairs.

One additional characteristic of dictionaries is that they are mutable—that is, they can be modified. This is similar to the way that lists behave. Recall, however, that strings are immutable and cannot be changed. For example, if `David` has a birthday, then his age needs to be incremented by 1. To do this, we can use the accumulator pattern `ages['David'] = ages['David'] + 1`.

As with lists and strings, dictionaries have a set of common methods. Table 4.3 describes them and Session 4.14 shows them in action. You will see that there are two variations on the `get` method. If the key is not present in the dictionary, `get` will return `None`. `None`, also referred to as the null object, represents an object with no value. A second, optional parameter for the `get` method can specify a return value in the case where the key is not present.

The `keys` method returns a `dict_keys` object. To see the contents of a `dict_keys` object we can convert it to a list using the `list` function. It is possible to iterate over a `dict_keys` object using a *for* loop without first converting it to a list. The `values` and `items` methods work in a similar fashion.

Method Name	Use	Explanation
keys	adict.keys()	Returns a `dict_keys` object
values	adict.values()	Returns a `dict_values` object
items	adict.items()	Returns a `dict_items` object
get	adict.get(k)	Returns the value associated with k; None otherwise
get	adict.get(k,alt)	Returns the value associated with k; alt otherwise
in	key in adict	Returns True if key is in the dictionary; False otherwise
not in	key not in adict	Returns True if key is not in the dictionary; False otherwise
index	adict[key]	Returns the value associated with key
del	del adict[key]	Removes the entry from the dictionary

Table 4.3   Methods provided by dictionaries in Python

The `items` method returns a `dict_items` object. Applying the `list` function to a `dict_items` object returns a list of key value pairs. These pairs are stored as **tuples**. Tuples are very similar to lists in that they are heterogeneous sequences of data. The difference is that a tuple is immutable. Like a string, a tuple element cannot be changed. Tuples are written as comma-delimited values enclosed in parentheses. As sequences, they can use any of the operations that were described earlier for lists and strings.

```
>>> ages.keys()
dict_keys(['Hannah', 'Kelsey', 'Rylea', 'Brenda', 'David'])
>>> list(ages.keys())
['Hannah', 'Kelsey', 'Rylea', 'Brenda', 'David']
>>> ages.values()
dict_values([16, 19, 7, 46, 46])
>>> list(ages.values())
[16, 19, 7, 46, 46]
>>> ages.items()
dict_items([('Hannah', 16), ('Kelsey', 19), ('Rylea', 7), ('Brenda', 46),
            ('David', 46)])
>>> list(ages.items())
[('Hannah', 16), ('Kelsey', 19), ('Rylea', 7), ('Brenda', 46), ('David', 46)]
>>> ages.get('Lena')
>>> print(ages.get('Lena'))
None
>>> ages.get('Lena','No age listed')
'No age listed'
>>> 'Rylea' in ages
True
>>> del ages['David']
>>> ages
{'Hannah': 16, 'Kelsey': 19, 'Rylea': 7, 'Brenda': 46}
>>> for k in ages.keys():
...     print(k)
...
Hannah
Kelsey
Rylea
Brenda
>>> for k in ages:
...     print(k)
...
Hannah
Kelsey
Rylea
Brenda
>>>
```

Session 4.14   Using dictionary methods

Exercises

4.24 You have been given the following lists of students and their test scores:

```
names=['joe','tom','barb','sue','sally']
scores=[10,23,13,18,12]
```

Write a function, `makeDictionary`, that takes the two lists and returns a dictionary with the names as the key and the scores as the values. Assign the result of `makeDictionary` to scoreDict, which will be used in the exercises that follow.

4.25 Using `scoreDict`, find the score for `'barb'`.

4.26 Add a score of 19 for `'john'`.

4.27 Create a sorted list of all the scores in `scoreDict`.

4.28 Calculate the average of all the scores in `scoreDict`.

4.29 Update the score for `'sally'` to be 13.

4.30 Tom has just dropped this class. Delete `'tom'` and his score from `scoreDict`.

4.31 Print out a table of students and their scores with the students listed in alphabetical order.

4.32 Write a function called `getScore` that takes a name and a dictionary as parameters and returns the score for that name if it is in the dictionary. If the name is not in the dictionary, print an error message and return −1.

Computing the Mode

We can now return to our problem of computing the mode of a data set. Using a dictionary of counts, one for each data item, we will be able to track the information necessary to find the mode. We assume that our mode function will receive a list of data values. It will return a list of modes since it is possible that there can be more than one. Listing 4.6 shows the initial implementation of the mode function.

In order to count each occurrence of the data items, we use a dictionary where the key is the data item itself and the associated value is the occurrence count. To process each item, we first check to see if it already exists in the dictionary as a key. If it does, all we need to

```
1    def mode(alist):
2        countdict = {}
3
4        for item in alist:
5            if item in countdict:
6                countdict[item] = countdict[item]+1
7            else:
8                countdict[item] = 1
```

Listing 4.6   Starting the mode function

do is increment the associated count. If it does not, we need to make a new entry in the dictionary for the first occurrence of a new key.

An alternative way to implement this *if* statement would be to use the second form of the **get** method, as described earlier. In this form, if the key is present, its associated value is returned. If the key is not present, the method will allow us to include a default value to be returned. In our case, if the key is not present, we can just return a zero since it has not occurred. Either way, when we add one, the count will be correct. Notice that this is another variation on the accumulator pattern, except that the **get** method allows us to include the initialization of the accumulator variable right in the initialization:

```
countdict[item] = countdict.get(item,0)+1
```

To complete our mode calculation, we need to go through our dictionary, key by key, and find the largest count. The key (or keys) associated with that count will be appended to a list of modes that will be returned at the end of the function. Fortunately, we can rely once again on our collections to provide methods that will do most of the work. Recall that the **values()** method returns a **dict_values** object that behaves much like a list of the values in a dictionary. By using the **max** function, we can then learn the maximum count. It is then just a matter of iterating through the dictionary keys looking for a key with a value that matches the maximum count. When we find such a key, we can place that key in the mode list.

Listing 4.7 shows the complete function. Note that the **modelist** starts out empty. We can iterate through the dictionary keys by using a **for** loop, appending keys to the **modelist** as needed.

Session 4.15 shows the **mode** function in use. The final example in this session uses our earthquake data $[20, 32, 21, 26, 33, 22, 18]$ from the beginning of this chapter. Since each value occurs once, each value is a mode.

```
1   def mode(alist):
2       countdict = {}
3
4       for item in alist:
5           if item in countdict:
6               countdict[item] = countdict[item]+1
7           else:
8               countdict[item] = 1
9
10      countlist = countdict.values()
11      maxcount = max(countlist)
12
13      modelist = [ ]
14      for item in countdict:
15          if countdict[item] == maxcount:
16              modelist.append(item)
17
18      return modelist
```

Listing 4.7 Computing the mode of a list

```
>>> mode([1,1,4,5,6,2,4,7,1,4,6,1])
[1]
>>> mode([1,1,1,2,2,2,3,3,3,4,4,4,4,5,5,5,5,6,6])
[4, 5]
>>> mode([3,6,8,2,6,4,9,2,8,9,4,3,8,3,5,7,1,3,4])
[3]
>>> mode([20,32,21,26,33,22,18])
[32, 33, 18, 20, 21, 22, 26]
>>>
```

Session 4.15 Using the mode function

Exercises

4.33 If you do not have a dictionary to work with, you can still compute the mode by creating a list of integers where the index value into the list is the key. You need a list of size `max(value)` plus one. This will work only when the keys are integers and positive. Note that this is a very inefficient use of memory when the data values are sparse. Implement the mode function using the approach described.

4.6   Frequency Distribution

As we worked through the steps required to compute the mode of a data set, we actually solved the basic statistics problem of finding the **frequency distribution**—a representation of the number of times each value occurs in the data.

4.6.1   Using a Dictionary to Compute a Frequency Table

One way to display a frequency distribution is to show a two-column table. The first column gives the data item, and the second gives the associated count. This appears to be very similar to our count dictionary. In fact, the only difference is that the table will need to show the items in order. Recall that the dictionary does not maintain any obvious order. Our challenge is to order the data.

To write this function, we can start with the mode function from Listing 4.7. Instead of extracting the counts and looking for the maximum, we will extract the keys, convert the `dict_keys` object to a list, and use the built-in `sort` method to provide the ordering. We can then iterate over the sorted list of keys and print a table entry consisting of the key and the associated count from the count dictionary. Listing 4.8 shows the complete function.

Note that we are not ordering the dictionary. We are creating a list of keys using the `keys` method, the list function, and then ordering that list. Once we have the list ordered, we can go back to the dictionary to find the associated counts. Session 4.16 shows the function in action.

```
1  def frequencyTable(alist):
2      countdict = {}
3
4      for item in alist:
5          if item in countdict:
6              countdict[item] = countdict[item]+1
7          else:
8              countdict[item] = 1
9
10     itemlist = list(countdict.keys())
11     itemlist.sort()
12
13     print("ITEM","FREQUENCY")
14
15     for item in itemlist:
16         print(item, "      ",countdict[item])
```

Listing 4.8 Using a dictionary to compute the frequency distribution

```
>>> frequencyTable([3,1,1,5,3,1,2,2,3,5,3,5,4,4,6,7,6,7,5,7,8,
                    3,8,2,3,4,1,5,6,7])
ITEM FREQUENCY
1        4
2        3
3        5
4        3
5        5
6        3
7        4
8        2
>>>
```

Session 4.16 Demonstrating the frequency table function

4.6.2   Computing a Frequency Table Without a Dictionary

It is possible to implement the frequency table function without the use of a dictionary, but doing so requires a bit of ingenuity with respect to list processing. In this section we will work through this alternative approach and introduce a useful pattern for sequential list processing.

Our plan is to start with a sorted copy of the list. Because the list is sorted, all occurrences of distinct counts will be contiguous (next to one another) in the list. As we iterate through the counts, we look for transitions between groups. The difficult part is knowing when these transitions occur.

Figure 4.7 shows how we track the locations of the transitions between groups of equal counts in the list. We use two variables: `current` and `previous`. Both variables will always refer to contiguous pairs of counts. The current count will be compared against the previous count. If they are equal, we know that we are still processing a group of equal counts. However, when the current count no longer matches the previous count (or when we run out of items in the list), we know that we have found the end of a group.

Listing 4.9 shows the complete function. To begin, `previous` will need to be initialized so that the first count in the list is considered to be the start of a new group of equal counts. To do this, we can simply set `previous` to the first item in the list. In addition, an accumulator variable, `groupCount`, will be initialized to 0 since no counts have been processed.

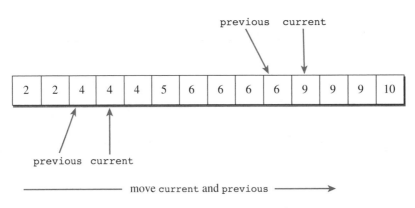

Figure 4.7   Using `previous` and `current` to locate transitions

```
1   def frequencyTableAlt(alist):
2       print("ITEM","FREQUENCY")
3       slist = alist[:]
4       slist.sort()
5
6       countlist = [ ]
7
8       previous = slist[0]
9       groupCount = 0
10      for current in slist:
11          if current == previous:
12              groupCount = groupCount + 1
13              previous = current
14          else:
15              print(previous, "    ", groupCount)
16              previous = current
17              groupCount = 1
18
19      print(current, "    ", groupCount)
```

Listing 4.9   Alternative method for computing a frequency table

We can now process each count in the list. Recall the two possibilities. If the `current` matches the `previous`, then we are still in a group of identical counts. We should increment `groupCount` and move `previous` ahead. On the other hand, if `current` does not match `previous`, we know that we have located a transition. At this point we can print a row in our table consisting of `previous` and `groupCount`. We also need to move `previous` ahead and initialize `groupCount` to 1 so that the next group will be counted correctly.

When all of the counts have been processed, the last row corresponding to the last group will not have been printed, so we can simply print out the value of `current` and `groupCount`.

Exercises

4.34 Modify `frequencyTableAlt` so that it returns a list of key-count tuples.

4.35 Suppose you have a list of key-score values like the following:

[('john',10), ('bob',8), ('john',5), ('bob',17),...]

Write a function that takes such a list as a parameter and prints out a table of average scores for each person.

4.6.3   Visualizing a Frequency Distribution

Frequency distributions can be best visualized through the construction of a graphical representation known as a **histogram** or **bar chart**. To create a histogram, we can use the `Turtle` class to draw one vertical line for each key. The height of the line will represent the frequency with which that key appears in the data set. By comparing the heights of the lines, it is possible to see the relationships that exist between the frequencies.

We use the `frequencyTable` function as a starting point. The frequency dictionary will still be constructed. However, instead of printing out the table, we draw a histogram. As an example, consider the data list $[3, 3, 5, 7, 1, 2, 5, 2, 3, 4, 6, 3, 4, 6, 3, 4, 5, 6, 6]$. Figure 4.8 shows the bar chart that we would like to produce. Note that each vertical line represents the count (previously the second column in the table).

Listing 4.10 shows the complete Python function used to create Figure 4.8. Lines 4–10 should look familiar. They are simply creating our count dictionary as before. The remainder of the function does the work of drawing the bar chart.

In order to create the histogram, we first need to use the `setworldcoordinates` method to scale our turtle window. This will be necessary since the data values can come from a wide range of possibilities. By scaling the window, our histogram will fit nicely within the window.

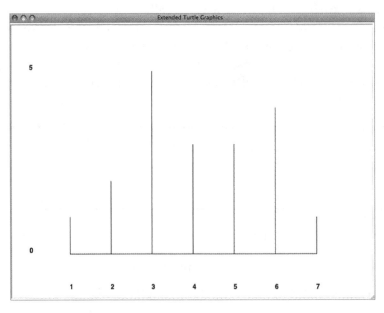

Figure 4.8   A frequency histogram

```
1  import turtle
2  def frequencyChart(alist):
3
4      countdict = {}
5
6      for item in alist:
7          if item in countdict:
8              countdict[item] = countdict[item]+1
9          else:
10             countdict[item] = 1
11
12     itemlist = list(countdict.keys())
13     minitem = 0
14     maxitem = len(itemlist)-1
15
16     countlist = countdict.values()
17     maxcount = max(countlist)
18
19     wn = turtle.Screen()
20     chartT = turtle.Turtle()
21     wn.setworldcoordinates(-1,-1,maxitem+1,maxcount+1)
22     chartT.hideturtle()
23
24     chartT.up()
25     chartT.goto(0,0)
26     chartT.down()
27     chartT.goto(maxitem,0)
28     chartT.up()
29
30     chartT.goto(-1,0)
31     chartT.write("0",font=("Helvetica",16,"bold"))
32     chartT.goto(-1,maxcount)
33     chartT.write(str(maxcount),font=("Helvetica",16,"bold"))
34
35     for index in range(len(itemlist)):
36         chartT.goto(index,-1)
37         chartT.write(str(itemlist[index]),font=("Helvetica",16,"bold"))
38
39         chartT.goto(index,0)
40         chartT.down()
41         chartT.goto(index,countdict[itemlist[index]])
42         chartT.up()
43     wn.exitonclick()
```

Listing 4.10 Creating a histogram

Recall that the `setworldcoordinates` method allows us to reset the coordinates of the lower-left and upper-right corners of the drawing window. In order to find the best set of coordinates, we should look at our data. Line 12 extracts the list of keys from the dictionary. This provides us with the number of individual data items that will directly translate into the number of lines in our histogram. Lines 16–17 perform a similar function, but this time we consider the range of frequency counts. Again, this provides us with information that can be used to scale the heights of the lines.

Lines 19–21 are responsible for creating the drawing turtle and rescaling the window. Note that instead of using (0,0) as the lower-left corner we have chosen to move one unit beyond in both the x and y directions. This will provide us with room later on to draw labels. The upper-right corner will be set slightly larger than the maximum count and value, again to leave some room.

Before drawing the actual bars, it is nice to provide some sort of scale. We can do this by drawing a simple representation of the x and y axes. For our purposes here, we draw a horizontal line to represent the base of the histogram (lines 24–28), and we place minimum and maximum labels on the y axis (lines 30–33).

The actual drawing of each line takes place in lines 39–42. For each key in `itemlist`, we create a label in line 37 and then draw a vertical line from the base of the histogram to the height that represents the count for that key. We are careful to lift the "turtle's tail" as we move the turtle around the histogram so as to not create any additional lines.

Exercises

4.36 Modify the frequency chart function to draw wide bars instead of lines.

4.37 Modify the frequency chart function so that the range of the x axis is not tightly bound to the the number of data items in the list but rather uses some minimum and maximum values.

4.38 Another way to compute the frequency table is to obtain a list of key-value pairs using the `items` method. This list of tuples can be sorted and printed without returning to the original dictionary. Rewrite the frequency table function using this idea.

4.39 A good programming practice is to take a step back and look at your code and to factor out the parts that you have reused into separate functions. This is the case with our `frequencyTable` function. Modify `frequencyTable` so that it returns the dictionary of frequency counts it creates.

4.40 Now write a separate function to print the frequency table using the dictionary created by the `frequencyTable` function in the previous problem.

4.41 Modify `frequencyChart` from Listing 4.10 to use the new `frequencyTable` function.

4.7   Dispersion: Standard Deviation

We now turn to **standard deviation**—an alternative statistical measure of dispersion that shows how much the individual data items of a collection differ from the mean. The larger the spread of the data around the mean, the larger the standard deviation. Data that have a small standard deviation are clustered tightly around the mean. Data that have a large standard deviation are more dispersed.

In mathematics, the equation for computing the standard deviation, usually denoted by s, is given by the following equation:

$$s = \sqrt{\frac{\sum_{i=1}^{n} (x_i - \bar{x})^2}{n - 1}}$$

where $\bar{x}$ is the mean of the data values. Expressed in words this equation says that we should perform the following steps:

1. Find the mean of the data values.

2. For each data value in the collection

   (a) subtract the mean from the data value.
   (b) square this difference.
   (c) add the result to a running sum.

3. Divide the sum by $n - 1$ where n is the number of data values.

4. The square root of the quotient from Step 3 is the standard deviation.

To implement a function to compute the standard deviation, we will again expect a list of values. Since we need to use the square root function, the math library will need to be imported. Finally, Step 1 can be easily accomplished by calling upon the **mean** function we constructed earlier.

Now we can iterate through each value in the data list and perform the subtraction and square operations. The accumulator pattern can be used to keep track of the running sum

```
1  import math
2  def standardDev(alist):
3      theMean = mean(alist)
4
5      total = 0
6      for item in alist:
7          difference = item - theMean
8          diffsq = difference ** 2
9          total = total + diffsq
10
11     sdev = math.sqrt(total/(len(alist)-1))
12     return sdev
```

Listing 4.11   Computing the standard deviation

of these squares (sometimes called the "sum of squares"). Listing 4.11 shows the complete function that returns the computed square root.

Session 4.17 provides two examples of finding the standard deviation. Note that for both data lists the mean is the same—namely, 12.0. However, the standard deviations are different since the values in the first list are much closer to the mean than those of the second. The final example shows the standard deviation for the earthquake count data.

```
>>> datalist = [7,11,9,18,15,12]
>>> mean(datalist)
12.0
>>> standardDev(datalist)
4.0
>>> datalist = [2,10,6,24,18,12]
>>> mean(datalist)
12.0
>>> standardDev(datalist)
8.0
>>> standardDev([20,32,21,26,33,22,18])
5.9401779675119402
>>>
```

Session 4.17   Using the **standardDev** function

Exercises

4.42 Modify the frequency chart function to include a graphical representation of the mean.

4.43 Modify the frequency chart function to draw a line representing plus or minus 1 standard deviation from the mean.

4.44 Using `random.uniform`, generate a list of 1,000 numbers in the range 0–50. Graph the frequency distribution along with the mean and standard deviation.

4.45 Using `random.gauss`, generate a list of 1,000 numbers in the range 0–50. Graph the frequency distribution along with the mean and standard deviation.

4.8 Summary

This chapter introduced three types of Python collections: lists, tuples, and dictionaries. Together with strings, these four data types provide us with a powerful set of tools for solving problems. To investigate the use of these collections, we developed a set of algorithms for performing basic statistical analysis. In particular, we implemented functions to compute the following:

- Dispersion (simple range and standard deviation)
- Central tendency (mean, median, and mode)
- Frequency distribution

We also used the `Turtle` class to create a graphical representation of a frequency histogram.

Key Terms

average	empty list	mean	sequential collection
bar chart	frequency distribution	median	slicing
central tendency	histogram	mode	sorting
concatenation	indexing	mutable	standard deviation
data	key	range	statistics
dictionary	length	reference diagram	tuple
dispersion	list	repetition	

Python Keywords

append	get	list	range
del	insert	max	reverse
dict	items	min	sort
float	keys	None	sum
for	len	pop	values

Bibliography

[qua] U.S. Geological Survey. 2008. Retrieved from http://earthquake.usgs.gov/.

[Wei02] Eric W. Weisstein, *CRC Concise Encyclopedia of Mathematics.* Chapman Hall / CRC, 2002.

Programming Exercises

4.1 `matplotlib` is a powerful graphing package for Python that can draw histograms, bar charts, scatter plots, and many other kinds of graphs. It is particularly useful if you are taking any science course where you may need to graph and analyze data. You can read about and download `matplotlib` for your computer at: http://matplotlib.sourceforge.net/. Read the documentation to learn how to use this module to plot a histogram of the data shown in this chapter.

4.2 Given a list of points of the form $[(x_1, y_1), (x_2, y_2), ..., (x_n, y_n)]$, write a function called `plotRegression` that accepts a list as a parameter and uses a turtle to plot those points and a best-fit line according to the following formulas:

$$y = \bar{y} + m(x - \bar{x})$$

$$m = \frac{\sum x_i y_i - n\bar{x}\bar{y}}{\sum x_i^2 - n\bar{x}^2}$$

Where $\bar{x}$ is the mean of the x-values, $\bar{y}$ is the mean of the y-values, and n is the number of points. The Greek letter $\sum$ represents the sum operation. For example, $\sum x_i$ indicates the addition of all the x values.

Your program should analyze the points and correctly scale the window using `setworldcoordinates` so that each point can be plotted. You should then draw the best-fit line in a different color through the points.

4.3 Have you ever tried to talk like a pirate? Write a function, `toPirate`, that takes an English sentence in the form of a string as a parameter. The `toPirate` function should return a string containing the pirate translation of your sentence. Use the table below to construct a translation dictionary. You can also consult an online website for more pirate phrases.

	English	Pirate Translation
Greetings	hello	avast
	excuse	arrr
People	sir, boy, man	matey
	madam	proud beauty
	officer	foul blaggart
Articles	the	th'
	my	me
	your	yer
	is	be
	are	be
Places	restroom	head
	restaurant	galley
	hotel	fleabag inn

4.4 Now try an even more challenging exercise: Translate two-word phrases into their pirate equivalents. For example, the two-word phrase 'excuse me' would be translated into simply 'arrr.'

CHAPTER 5

Earthquakes, Floods, and Other Natural Disasters

5.1 Objectives

- To use text files to store large data sets
- To access online data sources
- To introduce the *while* loop
- To introduce Boolean expressions

5.2 Using Files for Large Data Sets

All the examples in Chapter 4 used small data sets so that we could concentrate on developing the statistical methods needed to analyze the data. We assumed that our data items were stored in lists, and we constructed our function to process those lists accordingly. Now that we have those functions in place we can turn our attention to using statistical tools to describe larger data sets.

We have already seen that Python provides us with a number of powerful collections to store and manipulate data. However, as the amount of data gets larger, it becomes more and more difficult to fill these collections for later processing. It would certainly be possible to have the user enter the data interactively, but this would require a substantial amount of effort. Instead, large data sets are usually found in data files that are prepared ahead of time. We can then read such data from the file and fill our collections for later processing.

For our purposes here, we will assume that our data files are text files—that is, files filled with characters. The Python programs that we write are stored as text files. We can create

Method Name	Use	Explanation
open	open(filename,'r')	Open a file called **filename** and use it for reading. This will return a reference to a file object.
open	open(filename,'w')	Open a file called **filename** and use it for writing. This will also return a reference to a file object.
close	filevariable.close()	File use is complete.

Table 5.1   Opening and closing files in Python

these files in any number of ways. For example, we can use a text editor to type in and save the data. We can also download the data from a website and then save it in a file. Regardless of how the file is created, Python will allow us to manipulate the contents.

In Python, we must open files before we can use them and close them when we are done with them. As you might expect, once a file has been opened it becomes a Python object just like all other data. Table 5.1 shows the functions that can be used to open and close files.

As an example, suppose we have a text file called **rainfall.txt** that contains the data below representing the total annual rainfall (in inches) for 25 towns in Iowa. The first item on each line is the rain gauge location, usually a town name, and the second is the rainfall amount.

```
Akron 25.81
Albia 37.65
Algona 30.69
Allison 33.64
Alton 27.43
AmesW 34.07
AmesSE 33.95
Anamosa 35.33
Ankeny 33.38
Atlantic 34.77
Audubon 33.41
Beaconsfield 35.27
Bedford 36.35
BellePlaine 35.81
```

```
Bellevue 34.35
Blockton 36.28
Bloomfield 38.02
Boone 36.30
Brighton 33.59
Britt 31.54
Buckeye 33.66
BurlingtonKBUR 37.94
Burlington 36.94
Carroll 33.33
Cascade 33.48
```

Although it would be possible to consider entering this data by hand each time it is used, you can imagine that such a task would be time-consuming and error-prone. In addition, it is likely that there could be data from many more towns.

To open this file, we call the **open** function. The variable **fileref** now holds a reference to the file object returned by **open**. When we are finished with the file, we can close it by using the **close** method. After the file is closed, any further attempts to use **fileref** will result in an error.

```
>>>fileref = open("rainfall.txt","r")
>>>
>>>fileref.close()
>>>
```

5.2.1 Iterating over Lines in a File

We now use this file as input in a program that will do some data processing. In the program, we will read each line of the file and print it with some additional text. Because text files are sequences of lines of text, we can use the *for* loop to iterate through each line of the file.

A line of a file is defined to be a sequence of characters up to and including a special character called the newline character. If you evaluate a string that contains a newline character you will see the character represented as \n. If you print a string that contains a newline character, you will not see the \n; you will see only its effects. When you are typing a Python program and you press the enter or return key on your keyboard, the editor inserts a newline character into your text at that point.

As the *for* loop iterates through each line of the file, the loop variable will contain the current line of the file as a string of characters. The general pattern for processing each line of a text file is as follows:

```
for line in myFile:
    statement1
    statement2
    ...
```

To process all of our rainfall data, we use a *for* loop to iterate over the lines of the file. Using the **split** method, we can break each line into a list containing the city code and the rainfall amount. We can then take these values and construct a simple sentence, as shown in Listing 5.1. The output from the program is shown in Session 5.1.

```python
rainfile = open("rainfall.txt","r")

for aline in rainfile:
    values = aline.split()
    print(values[0], "had",values[1],"inches of rain.")

rainfile.close()
```

Listing 5.1   Simple Python program to read rainfall data from a file

```
Akron had 25.81 inches of rain.
Albia had 37.65 inches of rain.
Algona had 30.69 inches of rain.
Allison had 33.64 inches of rain.
Alton had 27.43 inches of rain.
AmesW had 34.07 inches of rain.
AmesSE had 33.95 inches of rain.
Anamosa had 35.33 inches of rain.
Ankeny had 33.38 inches of rain.
Atlantic had 34.77 inches of rain.
Audubon had 33.41 inches of rain.
```

Session 5.1   Output from the file-reading program (*continues*)

```
Beaconsfield had 35.27 inches of rain.
Bedford had 36.35 inches of rain.
BellePlaine had 35.81 inches of rain.
Bellevue had 34.35 inches of rain.
Blockton had 36.28 inches of rain.
Bloomfield had 38.02 inches of rain.
Boone had 36.30 inches of rain.
Brighton had 33.59 inches of rain.
Britt had 31.54 inches of rain.
Buckeye had 33.66 inches of rain.
BurlingtonKBUR had 37.94 inches of rain.
Burlington had 36.94 inches of rain.
Carroll had 33.33 inches of rain.
Cascade had 33.48 inches of rain.
```

Session 5.1   Output from the file-reading program (*continued*)

5.2.2 Writing a File

Let's think about another example of file processing: converting our file from data about rainfall in inches to data about rainfall in centimeters. This will require that we read the file contents as before, but, instead of printing a message, we will do some computation and then write the results back to another file. The new file will need to be opened for writing.

Listing 5.2 shows the Python program. The new file will be called `rainfallInCM.txt`. A `for` loop will be used to iterate through the input file. This time, each line of the file will be split and the rainfall value in inches will be converted to the equivalent value in centimeters (lines 7–8).

The `write` statement on line 10 does all of the work to create a new line in the output file. Note that it can add only a single string to the file each time it is used. For this reason, we need to use string concatenation to build up the line piece by piece. The first piece, `values[0]`, is the city code. We then add a blank to separate the code from the rainfall amount. Next, the floating point value called `cm` has to be converted to a string using the `str` method. Finally, the entire line is completed by adding a newline character. Session 5.2 shows the contents of the newly created file.

```
1  rainfile = open("rainfall.txt","r")
2  outfile = open("rainfallInCM.txt","w")
3
4  for aline in rainfile:
5      values = aline.split()
6
7      inches = float(values[1])
8      cm = 2.54 * inches
9
10     outfile.write(values[0]+" "+str(cm)+"\n")
11
12 rainfile.close()
13 outfile.close()
```

Listing 5.2   Creating a file with new data

```
$cat rainfallInCM.txt
Akron 65.5574
Albia 95.631
Algona 77.9526
Allison 85.4456
Alton 69.6722
AmesW 86.5378
AmesSE 86.233
Anamosa 89.73819999999999
Ankeny 84.7852
Atlantic 88.31580000000001
Audubon 84.86139999999999
Beaconsfield 89.5858
Bedford 92.32900000000001
BellePlaine 90.9574
Bellevue 87.24900000000001
Blockton 92.1512
Bloomfield 96.5708
Boone 92.202
Brighton 85.3186
Britt 80.1116
Buckeye 85.4964
BurlingtonKBUR 96.3676
Burlington 93.82759999999999
Carroll 84.6582
Cascade 85.0392
```

Session 5.2   Showing the contents of a new text file

5.2.3   String Formatting

As you can see on line 10 of Listing 5.2, converting values to strings and concatenating these strings together can be a tedious process. Fortunately, Python provides us with a better alternative: **formatted strings**—a template in which words or spaces that will remain constant are combined, with room for variables to be inserted into the string. For example, the statement

```
print(values[0], "had",values[1],"inches of rain.")
```

contains the words `had` and `inches of rain` every time, but the city name and the amount is different.

Using a formatted string, we write the previous statement as

```
print("%s had %d inches of rain" % (values[0],values[1]))
```

This simple example illustrates a new string expression. The `%` operator is a string operator called the **format operator**. The left side of the expression holds the template or format string, and the right side holds a collection of values that will be substituted into the format string. Note that the number of values in the collection on the right side corresponds with the number of `%` characters in the format string. Values are taken—in order—from the collection and inserted into the format string.

Let's look at both sides of this formatting expression in more detail. The format string may contain one or more conversion specifications. A conversion character tells the format operator what type of value is going to be inserted into that position in the string. In the example above, the `%s` specifies a string, while the `%d` specifies an integer. Other possible type specifications include `i`, `u`, `f`, `e`, `g`, `c`, or `%`. Table 5.2 summarizes all of the various type specifications.

In addition to the format character, you can also include a format modifier between the `%` and the format character. Format modifiers may be used to left-justify, or right-justify the value with a specified field width. Modifiers can be used to specify the field width and a number of digits after the decimal point. Table 5.3 explains these additional options.

The right side of the format operator is a collection of values that will be inserted into the format string. The collection will be either a tuple or a dictionary. If the collection is a tuple, the values are inserted in order of position. That is, the first element in the tuple corresponds to the first format character in the format string. If the collection is a dictionary, the values are inserted according to their keys. In this case all format characters must use the `(name)` modifier to specify the name of the key.

Character	Output Format
d,i	Integer or long integer
u	Unsigned integer
f	Floating point as m.ddddd
e	Floating point as m.dddde+/-xx
E	Floating point as m.dddddE+/-xx
g	Use %e for exponents less than −4 or greater than +5, otherwise use %f
c	Single character
s	String, or any Python data object that can be converted to a string by using the **str** function.
%	Insert a literal % character

Table 5.2   String Formatting Conversion Characters

Modifier	Example	Description
number	%20d	Put the value in a field width of 20
-	%-20d	Put the value in a field 20 characters wide, left-justified
+	%+20d	Put the value in a field 20 characters wide, right-justified
0	%020d	Put the value in a field 20 characters wide, fill in with leading zeros.
.	%20.2f	Put the value in a field 20 characters wide with 2 characters to the right of the decimal point.
(name)	%(name)d	Get the value from the supplied dictionary using **name** as the key.

Table 5.3   Additional formatting options

Session 5.3 shows some examples of formatted strings in use.

```
>>> a = 10
>>> b = 'apple'
>>> print("The %s costs %d cents" % (b,a))
The apple costs 10 cents
>>> myStr = "The %+15s costs %4.1d cents" % (b,a)
>>> myStr
'The           apple costs   10 cents'
>>> myStr = "The %+15s costs %6.1f cents" % (b,a)
>>> myStr
'The           apple costs   10.0 cents'
>>> myDict = { 'name':'apple', 'cost':10, 'price':15}
>>> print("The %(name)s costs %(price)5.1f cents" % myDict)
The apple costs  15.0 cents
```

Session 5.3   Demonstrating string formatting

Exercises

5.1 Write a program to read the `rainfall.txt` file and then write out a new file called `rainfallfmt.txt`. The new file should format each line so that the city is right-justified in a field that is 25 characters wide, and the rainfall data should be printed in a field that is 5 characters wide with 1 digit to the right of the decimal point.

5.2 Write a function that writes a temperature conversion table called `tempconv.txt`. The table should include temperatures from −300 to 212 degrees Fahrenheit and their Celsius equivalents, presented in two columns with appropriate headings. Each column should be 10 characters wide, and each temperature should have 3 digits to the right of the decimal point.

5.2.4   Alternative File-Reading Methods

In addition to the *for* loop, Python provides three methods to read data from the input file. The **readline** method reads one line from the file and returns it as a string. The string returned by **readline** will contain the newline character at the end. This method returns the empty string when it reaches the end of the file. The `readlines` method returns the contents of the entire file as a list of strings, where each item in the list represents one line of the file. It is also possible to read the entire file into a single string with `read`. Table 5.4 summarizes these methods and Session 5.4 shows them in action.

Note that we need to reopen the file before each read so that we start from the beginning. Each file has a marker that denotes the current read position in the file. Anytime one of the read methods is called, the marker is moved to the character immediately following the last character returned. In the case of `readline`, this moves the marker to the first character of the next line in the file. In the case of `read` or `readlines`, the marker is moved to the end of the file.

Method Name	Use	Explanation
`write`	`filevar.write(astring)`	Adds a string to the end of the file. `filevar` must refer to a file that has been opened for writing.
`read(n)`	`filevar.read()`	Reads and returns a string of n characters, or the entire file as a single string if n is not provided.
`readline(n)`	`filevar.readline()`	Returns the next line of the file with all text up to and including the newline character. If n is provided as a parameter, then only n characters will be returned if the line is longer than n.
`readlines(n)`	`filevar.readlines()`	Returns a list of n strings, each representing a single line of the file. If n is not provided, then all lines of the file are returned.

Table 5.4   Reading and writing methods for files in Python

```
>>> infile = open("rainfall.txt","r")
>>> aline = infile.readline()
>>> aline
'Akron 25.81\n'
>>> infile = open("rainfall.txt","r")
>>> linelist = infile.readlines()
>>> linelist
['Akron 25.81\n', 'Albia 37.65\n', 'Algona 30.69\n', 'Allison 33.64\n',
'Alton 27.43\n', 'AmesW 34.07\n', 'AmesSE 33.95\n', 'Anamosa 35.33\n',
'Ankeny 33.38\n', 'Atlantic 34.77\n', 'Audubon 33.41\n',
'Beaconsfield 35.27\n', 'Bedford 36.35\n', 'BellePlaine 35.81\n',
'Bellevue 34.35\n', 'Blockton 36.28\n', 'Bloomfield 38.02\n',
'Boone 36.30\n', 'Brighton 33.59\n', 'Britt 31.54\n', 'Buckeye 33.66\n',
'BurlingtonKBUR 37.94\n', 'Burlington 36.94\n',
'Carroll 33.33\n', 'Cascade 33.48\n']
>>> infile = open("rainfall.txt","r")
>>> filestring = infile.read()
>>> filestring
'Akron 25.81\nAlbia 37.65\nAlgona 30.69\nAllison 33.64\nAlton
27.43\nAmesW 34.07\nAmesSE 33.95\nAnamosa 35.33\nAnkeny 33.38\n
Atlantic 34.77\nAudubon 33.41\nBeaconsfield 35.27\nBedford 36.35\n
BellePlaine 35.81\nBellevue 34.35\nBlockton 36.28\nBloomfield
38.02\nBoone 36.30\nBrighton 33.59\nBritt 31.54\nBuckeye 33.66\n
BurlingtonKBUR 37.94\nBurlington 36.94\nCarroll 33.33\nCascade 33.48\n'
>>>
```

[handwritten annotations: "← single line", "list of strings", "single string"]

Session 5.4   Using other file-processing methods

Exercises

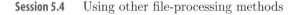

5.3 Open a file during a Python session. Call the **readline** method twice on that file, then call the **readlines** method. What lines does the list returned by **readlines** include?

5.4 Open the file in Exercise 5.3 again, but call **readlines** immediately. Compare the lines returned in this exercise with the previous one.

5.5 Write a program that reads in the contents of a file and writes a new file where all the characters are in uppercase.

5.6 Write a program that reads in a file and then prints out the number of lines, words, and characters in the file.

5.7 Write a program that creates a file with a concordance—an index that tells you which line of the file each word appears on. If a word is on more than one line, the concordance will show you all of the lines containing that word. *Hint:* Use a dictionary keyed by each word to solve this problem.

5.2.5   Statistics with Real Data

We complete this section by using our statistical functions from "A Nest of Snakes" (Chapter 4) on a large data set. When working with real data, it is often necessary to perform some basic data processing to get the data into a format that works for our purposes. We will use a large data file that contains detailed data pertaining to earthquake occurrences around the world. This file was also the source of the simple count data used in "A Nest of Snakes" (Chapter 4).

Earthquakes

The U.S. Geological Survey (USGS) maintains a log of all significant earthquakes that occur around the world. This log covers a seven-day period and includes data pertaining to the magnitude, date and time, location, and depth of the quake. In its raw form, a portion of the log (a text file) looks as follows:

```
2.8 2006/10/19 02:02:10 62.391 -149.751 15.0 CENTRAL ALASKA
2.5 2006/10/19 00:31:15 20.119 -156.213 1.5 MAUI REGION, HAWAII
5.0 2006/10/18 21:15:51 4.823 -82.592 37.3 SOUTH OF PANAMA
2.6 2006/10/18 21:12:25 59.934 -147.904 30.0 GULF OF ALASKA
3.4 2006/10/18 20:59:21 36.540 -89.640 7.7 SOUTHEASTERN MISSOURI
2.7 2006/10/18 20:11:22 61.023 -151.418 60.0 SOUTHERN ALASKA
3.1 2006/10/18 16:40:15 20.282 -156.611 4.7 MAUI REGION, HAWAII
2.7 2006/10/18 14:12:19 59.808 -152.538 50.0 SOUTHERN ALASKA
2.8 2006/10/18 14:02:12 60.686 -151.871 90.0 KENAI PENINSULA, ALASKA
4.9 2006/10/18 12:10:01 1.758 127.488 127.0 HALMAHERA, INDONESIA
6.2 2006/10/18 10:45:36 -15.081 167.243 138.5 VANUATU
2.8 2006/10/18 10:45:17 32.162 -115.895 6.3 BAJA CALIFORNIA, MEXICO
3.3 2006/10/18 10:08:45 32.165 -115.891 7.3 BAJA CALIFORNIA, MEXICO
```

```
2.8 2006/10/18 08:22:27 32.263 -115.297 3.4 BAJA CALIFORNIA, MEXICO
3.7 2006/10/18 05:34:15 62.326 -151.224 85.9 CENTRAL ALASKA
4.6 2006/10/18 03:25:03 -21.538 -66.593 201.7 POTOSI, BOLIVIA
3.7 2006/10/18 02:32:26 57.560 -137.186 1.0 OFF THE COAST OF SOUTHEASTERN ALASKA
4.9 2006/10/18 02:01:27 1.355 97.157 25.8 NIAS REGION, INDONESIA
2.5 2006/10/18 00:18:42 19.801 -155.391 10.6 ISLAND OF HAWAII, HAWAII
3.1 2006/10/17 22:59:01 61.444 -150.523 60.0 SOUTHERN ALASKA
...
```

Note that the "columns" of the data file are separated by spaces. The last column is actually a sequence of words denoting a location.

Earthquake Statistics

For this example, we will focus on the first column of earthquake data, which represents the severity of each earthquake. Seismologists measure severity in units of magnitude. The larger the magnitude, the greater the severity of the earthquake.

Our first task in analyzing this real data source is to process the data file by extracting the pertinent data from the file and storing it in an appropriate collection. For our purposes here, we need to process the file and create a list of magnitudes so that our statistics functions can do their work.

Assume our data file is called `earthquakes.txt`. We can use a combination of file processing, string processing, and list manipulation to construct our list. We write a small function (Listing 5.3) that will return the list of magnitudes. Line 2 opens the file so that we can read the data line by line using a *for* loop (line 5). Note that line 7 converts the magnitude string to a `float`, which means that this will be a list of floating point numbers representing the magnitudes of earthquakes that have occurred.

```
1   def makeMagnitudeList():                          def function
2       quakefile = open("earthquakes.txt","r")       open txt
3
4       maglist = [ ]                                 empty list
5       for aline in quakefile:                       iteration
6           vlist = aline.split()                     split txt columns @ space
7           maglist.append(float(vlist[0]))           empty list add 1st column
8       return maglist                                          values @ end
```

Listing 5.3 Processing the earthquake data file

We can now use our basic statistics functions to learn about the earthquakes that have occurred during this seven-day period of time. Session 5.5 first calls the `makeMagnitudeList` function and then uses statistical functions to compute values for the range, mean, median, mode, and standard deviation. We can see that the range of earthquake magnitudes is 4.2 units, from a maximum of 6.7 to a minimum of 2.5. The three measures of central tendency seem to show some inconsistency. The mean of 3.76 and the median of 3.5 are fairly similar. However, the mode of 2.5 is quite small.

```
>>> magList = makeMagnitudeList()
>>> getRange(magList)
4.2
>>> max(magList)
6.7
>>> min(magList)
2.5
>>> mean(magList)
3.7671641791044794
>>> median(magList)
3.5
>>> mode(magList)
[2.5]
>>> standardDev(magList)
1.0650429183420023
```

Session 5.5   Statistics from the earthquake data

The reason for this difference between mean and mode becomes apparent when we look at our frequency table (Session 5.6). Although most of the earthquakes reported during the past week were relatively small in magnitude—as we would expect—it happens that there were some very strong ones with magnitudes of 6 and higher. For this period of time the mean is thus shifted up by these infrequent but strong events.

```
>>> frequencyTable(magList)
ITEM FREQUENCY
2.5         18
2.6         15
```

Session 5.6   Frequency table for earthquake magnitude data (*continues*)

```
2.7        14
2.8        12
2.9        11
3.0         4
3.1        10
3.2         6
3.3         7
3.4         3
3.5         3
3.6         1
3.7         7
3.9         1
4.0         3
4.1         3
4.2         5
4.3         6
4.4         6
4.5         6
4.6         8
4.7         6
4.8         9
4.9         9
5.0         4
5.1         6
5.2         3
5.3         4
5.4         1
5.5         1
5.7         2
5.8         1
6.0         1
6.2         1
6.3         1
6.4         1
6.6         1
6.7         1
>>>
```

Session 5.6   Frequency table for earthquake magnitude data (*continued*)

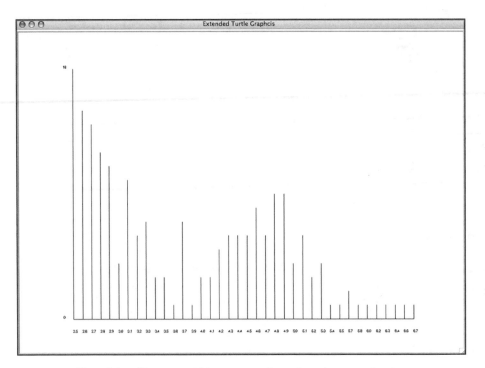

Figure 5.1   Frequency histogram of earthquake magnitudes

Finally, we can use our histogram generator from "A Nest of Snakes" (Chapter 4) to construct a visual representation of the magnitude frequency. When we look at the distribution of earthquake magnitudes, it is visually apparent that the majority of them were minor. Although the frequency table provides the same information, it is often preferable to "see" the relationships (Figure 5.1).

Exercises

5.8 Frequency tables are often created by placing data items in a range. Implement a function that will group the earthquake data by the following criteria: Micro (0–3), Minor (3–3.9), Light (4–4.9), Moderate (5–5.9), Major (6–6.9), Strong (7–7.9), and Great (>=8)

5.9   Using the criteria from the previous exercise, use the `frequency chart` function from Chapter 4 to draw a visual representation of the data.

5.10   Write a function to process the earthquake data file and create lists of earthquake magnitudes, one for each date. Your function should return a list of lists that looks something like this:

```
[[date1, magnitude1, magnitude2, magnitude3,...],
 [date2, magnitude1, magnitude2 ],
 ...]
```

5.11   Modify the function in the previous exercise to return a dictionary of key-value pairs where the key is the date and the value is a list of magnitudes for the earthquakes that occurred on that date.

5.3   Reading Data from the Internet

Although reading data from files is useful, in today's world accessing data on the Internet is becoming even more meaningful. Fortunately, Python makes it easy to get online data using the `urllib.request` module. The name of the module comes from the fact that the "web address" of your favorite website is also known as a **Uniform Resource Locator** or URL.

Using the `urllib.request` module, we can read data from web pages just as easily as we can read data from a file. In fact, iteration and all of the methods described in Table B.7 in "Python Quick Reference" (Appendix B) work on web pages as well as files. We could also use a *for* loop to iterate through each line of a web page, as we did in Section 5.2. However, in this section we explore the use of the **read**, **readline**, and **readlines** methods. Session 5.7 illustrates the use of the **read** method, which reads an entire web page into a string variable called `pageText`.

Rather than using the **open** function as we did for files, we can create a URL object for reading by calling `urllib.request.urlopen`. The **urlopen** function hides all of the networking details needed to communicate with the website and returns an object that acts just like a file.

```
>>> import urllib.request
>>> page = urllib.request.urlopen("http://knuth.luther.edu/~david/helloworld.html")
>>> pageText = page.read()
>>> pageText
b'<html>\n<head>\n    <title>Hello Everyone</title>\n</head>\n<body>\n
<h1>Hello Python</h1>\n</body>\n</html>\n'
>>> decodedPageText = pageText.decode("utf-8")
>>> decodedPageText
'<html>\n<head>\n    <title>Hello Everyone</title>\n</head>\n<body>\n
<h1>Hello Python</h1>\n</body>\n</html>\n'
>>> print(decodedPageText)
<html>
<head>
    <title>Hello Everyone</title>
</head>
<body>
    <h1>Hello Python</h1>
</body>
</html>

>>> page = urllib.request.urlopen("http://knuth.luther.edu/~david/helloworld.html")
>>> pageText = page.readline()
>>> pageText
b'<html>\n'
>>>
>>> page = urllib.request.urlopen("http://knuth.luther.edu/~david/helloworld.html")
>>> pageText = page.readlines()
>>> pageText
[b'<html>\n', b'<head>\n', b'    <title>Hello Everyone</title>\n',
b'</head>\n', b'<body>\n', b'    <h1>Hello Python</h1>\n', b'</body>\n',
b'</html>\n']
>>>
```

Session 5.7   Capturing the contents of a web page with `urllib.request`

Notice that when we evaluate **pageText**, we get one long string that is not formatted very well. However, if you look closer, you will see that this is not really a string at all. It is actually what Python calls a byte array. Byte arrays look like strings but closer inspection reveals that there is a small b preceding the quote delimited contents. Unlike text files, which are simple collections of characters, web pages can be encoded in many different ways. To be sure that they are read properly, Python returns the contents as encoded bytes of data.

If we know how the data has been encoded, then it is easy to decode it (turn it back into a string) by using the `decode` method. Note that the line

```
>>>decodedPageText = pageText.decode("utf-8")
```

assumes that the text is encoded using `utf-8`. The variable `decodedPageText` is now a standard string that can be manipulated using any string methods and functions described earlier.

When we evaluate `decodedPageText`, we get one long string that is still not formatted very well. However, it does contain newline characters (`\n`). As was mentioned in Section 5.2, when evaluating a string we can see the `\n` characters embedded in the sequence of characters, but when printing the string, it appears as it would if we were editing the file.

The `readline` method makes use of the new line character to return only one line of the web page at a time. Note that it actually returns a byte array as before. Similarly, the `readlines` method returns a list of byte arrays, one for each line of the web page.

5.3.1   Using a *while* Loop to Process Data

Often you will want to process data from a website or a file but you may not know how much data you want to read at the start. One approach you can take is to read a small amount of data and ask a question. The answer to this question may determine how much more data to read or whether to read any more data at all. This approach requires a more general way of iterating over the characters or lines in a file.

Python provides us with a general loop mechanism called a *while* loop. Its structure is as follows:

```
while <condition>:
    statement 1
    statement 2
    ...
```

As you may guess from the template shown above, the *while* loop continues to perform the statements in the body of the loop as long as the condition remains true. Once the condition evaluates to false the *while* loop stops performing the statements in the body. A condition can be any Python Boolean expression. Recall that Boolean expressions evaluate to `True` or `False`. Although we introduce the *while* loop in this section, you will find more details and examples of its use in Section 7.4.4.

Suppose that we want to count the number of lines in the heading of a web page and then print those parts of the web page that are in the body section. The heading is the part of the web page that starts with the string <head> and ends with the string </head>. The body is the part that begins with the string <body> and ends with the string </body>. Those strings that begin with < and end with > are called **hypertext markup language** (HTML) tags.

Before we can start counting the lines in the heading of a web page, we must read all of the lines before the line containing the <head> tag. In Listing 5.4 we do this on lines 7–9. Notice that before we enter the *while* loop we do an initial **readline** called a **priming read**, a process that allows the condition of the *while* loop to be evaluated for the first time. Without this call to **readline**, **line** would have no value.

Now that we have read the line that contains the <head> tag, we can start counting lines. Since the number of lines in the heading of a web page is different for each page, we can use a *while* loop to read lines until we encounter the </head> tag. As we read each line, we can simply increment a counter variable **numHeadLines** (see lines 11–14 in Listing 5.4).

It is important to remember that the last thing you will do in the body of the *while* loop is to read the next line. If you do not read the next line, you will continue to process the same line over and over again in an **infinite loop**. Infinite loops are almost never good, and it is your responsibility to make sure that something changes in the body of your *while* loop so that the condition will eventually fail.

After we have read the line containing the </head>, we continue to read lines until we find the <body> tag (see lines 16–18). We then read and print the lines of the body (see lines 20–23). Notice that when we print the line read by **readline** we use the statement **print line[:-1]**. Recall that the slice operation **[:-1]** returns the entire sequence except for the last item. Since the last item in the line is a newline character, we remove it or else we get two newlines due to the fact that **print** automatically adds a newline for us.

The statement on line 21 of Listing 5.4 also demonstrates compound Boolean expressions. Recall that in a compound Boolean expression we can combine multiple Boolean expressions using the logical operators **and**, **or**, and **not**. The first part of the compound Boolean expression **line != ""** checks for the end of file condition. Recall that **readline** returns an empty string when it encounters the end of a file. The second part of the expression checks for the end of the body section, denoted by the tag </body>. The **and** operator allows us to exit the loop whenever we reach the end of the file or the end of the body section.

```
1  import urllib.request
2
3  def countHead(url):
4      page = urllib.request.urlopen(url)
5      numHeadLines = 0
6
7      line = page.readline().decode('utf-8')
8      while '<head>' not in line:
9          line = page.readline().decode('utf-8')
10
11     line = page.readline().decode('utf-8')
12     while '</head>' not in line:
13         numHeadLines = numHeadLines + 1
14         line = page.readline().decode('utf-8')
15
16     line = page.readline().decode('utf-8')
17     while "<body>" not in line:
18         line = page.readline().decode('utf-8')
19
20     line = page.readline().decode('utf-8')
21     while line != "" and "</body>" not in line:
22         print (line[:-1])
23         line = page.readline().decode('utf-8')
24
25     print ("number of lines in header = ", numHeadLines)
26
27     page.close()
```

Listing 5.4   Counting lines in the head and the body

Exercises

5.12 Start up a Python session and use `urllib.request` to read the source for your favorite web page.

5.13 Write a function called `savePage` that takes a string representing a URL, and a file name as a parameter and then saves the contents of the web page to the file.

5.14 Using the `read` method, write your own `readline` function that takes an opened URL object as a parameter and returns a single line as a string. *Hint:* You will want to make use of the optional parameter of the `read` method.

5.15 Using the `readline` method, write your own `readlines` function that takes an opened URL object as a parameter and returns a list of the lines.

5.16 Write a function that opens a web page and returns a dictionary of all the links and their text on that page. A link is defined by an HTML tag that looks like

```
<a href="http://my.computer.com/some/file.html">link text</a>
```

The link is everything in quotes after the `href=`, and the text is everything between the `>` and the `</a>`.

5.17 Write a Python function that can generate an outline for a web page. Your function should print the title of the web page and the text between any `<h1>`, `<h2>`, `<h3>`, or `<h4>` tags. Each level of heading tag should be indented properly so that all `<h2>` tags are indented under their `<h1>` tag, etc.

5.18 Use a *while* loop to implement the *for* loop `for i in range(10)`.

5.19 Use a *while* loop to implement the *for* loop `for i in range(10,-1,-1)`.

5.3.2   Stock Market Data

Let's return to Internet data sources and statistics. For as long as there has been a stock market, investors have tried to analyze the price of stocks in many different ways in order to predict whether the market will go up or down. Lots of seemingly crazy indicators have been discovered over the years that supposedly predict stock market trends: A Democrat in the White House means bad news for stocks; short skirts indicate that the market will go up, and long skirts indicate a downward trend; if an NFC team wins the Super Bowl, it will be a bull market, but an AFC team indicates a bear market [Mal03].

These indicators were not just made up. They come from years of observation. In fact, for some of these indicators there really is a mathematical correlation. However, the relationship is not causal, just coincidence. In this section we look at one algorithm for determining correlation and apply it to stock market data that is readily available on the Internet.

Accessing Stock Data

There are many sources of stock market data on the Internet. For purposes of this section and the exercises that follow, we will use `http://finance.yahoo.com`. Session 5.8 shows how easy it is to get some stock information for Target corporation. First we use `urllib.request` to open the data source, then we use the `readlines` method and the slice operator to get the first ten lines of data.

```
>>> url1 = urllib.request.urlopen('http://ichart.yahoo.com/table.csv?s=TGT')
>>> data = url1.readlines()[:10]
>>> data
[b'Date,Open,High,Low,Close,Volume,Adj Close\n',
 b'2012-05-31,58.20,58.46,57.84,57.91,6856500,57.91\n',
 b'2012-05-30,57.80,57.84,57.00,57.79,7232100,57.79\n',
 b'2012-05-29,57.90,58.17,57.39,58.13,4792600,58.13\n',
 b'2012-05-25,57.43,57.71,57.17,57.62,4293900,57.62\n',
 b'2012-05-24,56.86,57.39,56.65,57.25,4460600,57.25\n',
 b'2012-05-23,56.24,56.89,55.94,56.78,3956300,56.78\n',
 b'2012-05-22,55.89,56.90,55.81,56.67,5777400,56.67\n',
 b'2012-05-21,55.43,55.90,54.93,55.83,4779400,55.83\n',
 b'2012-05-18,55.07,56.00,54.91,55.46,7144300,55.46\n']
>>>
```

Session 5.8   Example data for Target (TGT)

Before we go any further, it is important to understand a bit more about the structure of a URL. There is a lot of information packed into a URL, and if you want to get the most out of the `urllib.request` module it is important for you to understand the components of a URL. Figure 5.2 illustrates the four components of a URL: (1) protocol, (2) host name, (3) resource, and (4) parameters.

The protocol—`http` in this case—tells the program that an attempt is being made to load a web page. Other possible values for protocol include `ftp` for file transfer protocol, or `file` for a file on your hard drive. The host name tells the program the name of the web server. This is probably the part you are most familiar with. The resource may indicate a particular HTML file to load. It may also be a program that you want the web server to run. If the resource is a program, the web server will run the program and the results of the program will be sent back to the web browser. The parameters are the last components, similar to the parameters you pass to a function call. In this case, the parameters are passed

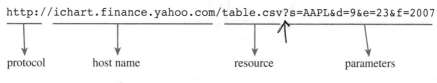

Figure 5.2   The components of a URL

along to the program on the web server. Notice that the first parameter is separated from the resource by a ?.

Parameters are always specified as key-value pairs. The first parameter in Figure 5.2 is s=AAPL. This is important because it is the parameter that corresponds to the stock ticker for which we want a price quote. Any additional key-value pairs are separated by an &. In this case, the keys d, e, and f indicate the ending month, day, and year for the quote. Keys a, b, and c can also be used to specify a starting month, day, and year. You may want to experiment with these parameters by simply typing this URL into your web browser to see what data you receive.

Correlating Stock Data

Correlation measures the strength and direction of the relationship between two variables. Expressed another way, correlation measures the tendency of two variables to increase or decrease at the same time. This measure is often called the correlation coefficient. Returning to the examples cited earlier in this section, we decide that one variable may be the value of the Dow Jones Industrial Average and the other the length of women's skirts, or the winner of the Super Bowl.

In addition, we will look at variables representing the stock prices for two companies. So we will ask the following question: "Is the stock price for company A correlated with the stock price for company B?" For example, if the prices are correlated and one company is on an upward trend, does that indicate that it is also a good time to invest in the other company?

Although there are several algorithms for calculating a correlation coefficient, we will use the **Pearson correlation coefficient**. The formula for calculating this coefficient is

$$r = \frac{\sum_{i=1}^{n}(x_i - \bar{x})(y_i - \bar{y})}{(n-1)S_x S_y}$$

where $\bar{x}$ and $\bar{y}$ are the means of the two variables x and y, and S_x, S_y are the standard deviations.

Figure 5.3 illustrates some different correlational values between two variables. The values from one variable are used as the x coordinate and the values from the other variable are used as the y coordinate. Each of the four examples shows 1,000 pairs of values of the x, y variables. When the variables are highly correlated, they nearly form a line. When they are not correlated, the points form a cloud or wide band. It is important to remember that a value of 1.0 indicates that the two variables are positively correlated, while a value of -1.0 indicates that the two variables are negatively correlated. A value of 0.0 indicates that there is no correlation between the two values.

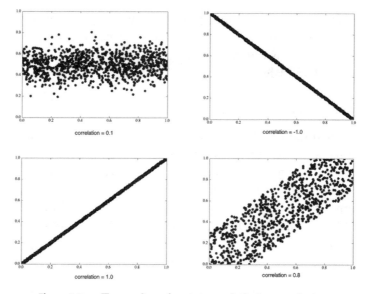

Figure 5.3   Examples of points and their correlation

Listing 5.5 implements the Pearson correlation formula. We use the mean and standard deviation functions from "A Nest of Snakes" (Chapter 4). The two parameters `xlist` and `ylist` represent the values that we want to correlate. The two lists have the same length, and they are parallel, which means that the x value at a particular position in the list and a y value at the same position represent a single x, y data point. For example, using our stock data, the values at a particular index in `xlist` and `ylist` represent the stock price for a particular day.

```python
def correlation(xlist, ylist):
    xbar = mean(xlist)
    ybar = mean(ylist)
    xstd = standardDev(xlist)
    ystd = standardDev(ylist)
    num = 0.0
    for i in range(len(xlist)):
        num = num + (xlist[i]-xbar) * (ylist[i]-ybar)
    corr = num / ((len(xlist)-1) * xstd * ystd)
    return corr
```

Listing 5.5   The Pearson correlation function

Let's use this function to compute the correlation between the stock prices for Apple Computer (AAPL) and for Coca Cola (Coke). To do this, we need to access the stock data for each corporation and extract the closing price for each day. Using `urllib.request`, we can open and read the results into one big list using the `readlines` method. At this point the data is a list of strings. In order to process the list, we need to split each string into the components Date, Open, High, Low, Close, Volume, and Adj Close. Since each of these components is separated by a comma, we can use the `split` method to create a list using the `','` as the parameter for the split character.

When working with real data, it is a good idea to make use of Python's interactive capabilities to learn a bit more about your data. You can also practice your list manipulation skills at the same time. Session 5.9 shows how to read the stock data for AAPL, and how we can use the split method to turn a list of strings into a list of lists. Notice that after we have split the list into its component parts, the individual items in the list are still strings. In order to use the data in our correlation function, we will need to convert the strings into floating-point numbers.

```
>>> url1 = urllib.request.urlopen('http://ichart.yahoo.com/table.csv?s=AAPL')
>>> t1Data = url1.readlines()
>>> t1Data[:10]
[b'Date,Open,High,Low,Close,Volume,Adj Close\n',
b'2012-05-31,580.74,581.50,571.46,577.73,17559800,577.73\n',
b'2012-05-30,569.20,579.99,566.56,579.17,18891600,579.17\n',
b'2012-05-29,570.90,574.00,565.31,572.27,13576100,572.27\n',
b'2012-05-25,564.59,565.85,558.47,562.29,11732400,562.29\n',
b'2012-05-24,575.87,576.50,561.23,565.32,17722500,565.32\n',
b'2012-05-23,557.50,572.80,553.23,570.56,20889200,570.56\n',
b'2012-05-22,569.55,573.88,552.58,556.97,24816800,556.97\n',
b'2012-05-21,534.50,561.54,534.05,561.28,22539500,561.28\n',
b'2012-05-18,533.96,543.41,522.18,530.38,26153300,530.38\n']
>>> t1Data[0].decode("utf-8").split(',')
['Date', 'Open', 'High', 'Low', 'Close', 'Volume', 'Adj Close\n']
>>> t1DataAlt = [line.decode("utf-8").split(',') for line in t1Data[1:] ]
>>> t1DataAlt[:3]
[['2012-05-31', '580.74', '581.50', '571.46', '577.73', '17559800', '577.73\n'],
['2012-05-30', '569.20', '579.99', '566.56', '579.17', '18891600', '579.17\n'],
['2012-05-29', '570.90', '574.00', '565.31', '572.27', '13576100', '572.27\n']]
>>>
```

Session 5.9   Investigating data interactively

Session 5.9 contains another new Python programming trick for creating lists. The line

```
t1Data = [line.decode("utf-8").split(',') for line in t1Data[1:] ]
```

uses a **list comprehension** to construct a list of lists. We will come back to this but first let's look at the general form of a list comprehension and some simpler examples of its use.

The general form of a list comprehension is

```
[<expression> for <item1> in <sequence1>
              for <item2> in <sequence2>
              ...
              if <condition> ]
```

Any of the items that correspond to a loop variable in one of the *for* loops can be used in the expression. You need to have only one *for* loop in the list comprehension, and the `if` is optional.

List comprehensions allow you to easily create one list based on doing some processing or selection criteria applied to another list. For example, suppose we want to create a list of the cubes of the first 10 numbers. One way to do this would be as follows:

```
>>> cubes = []
>>> for x in range(1,11):
        cubes.append(x*x*x)

>>> cubes
[1, 8, 27, 64, 125, 216, 343, 512, 729, 1000]
```

Using list comprehensions, we can do this in a single step:

```
>>> cubes = [x*x*x for x in range(1,11)]
>>> cubes
[1, 8, 27, 64, 125, 216, 343, 512, 729, 1000]
>>>
```

The variable x takes on the values 1 through 10 as you might expect from the `for x in range(1,11)` clause in the list comprehension. Each time through the loop, the expression `x*x*x` is computed and added to the list that is being constructed.

List comprehensions can also be used with the *if* statement to create a shorter list by keeping only those values from a longer list that meet a certain criteria. This operation is often referred to as "filtering." For example, suppose you wanted to create a list of all the even cubes, starting from the list of cubes we created previously:

```
>>> evenCubes = [x for x in cubes if x % 2 == 0]
>>> evenCubes
[8, 64, 216, 512, 1000]
```

With a better understanding of list comprehensions, we can now return to preparing the data for use with the correlation algorithm. Once the data has been split into the list of lists format, we can extract the closing price for each day. To make sure the data is compatible, we want to extract only the closing prices for each day that both stocks were traded. For example, suppose we were comparing a relatively new Internet stock such as Amazon (AMZN) against an old stock such as AT&T (T). We would have data on Amazon going back only to 1997 whereas AT&T has been traded since the early 1900s.

The stockCorrelate function is shown in Listing 5.6. Most of the work in stockCorrelate involves processing the stock data from the Internet to get it into a form we can use with the correlate function. Lines 3–7 read the data from the Yahoo website. Lines 8–9 move the

```
1  def stockCorrelate(ticker1, ticker2):
2      url1 = urllib.request.urlopen(
3          'http://ichart.yahoo.com/table.csv?s=%s'%ticker1)
4      url2 = urllib.request.urlopen(
5          'http://ichart.yahoo.com/table.csv?s=%s'%ticker2)
6      t1Data = url1.readlines()
7      t2Data = url2.readlines()
8      t1Data = [line[0:-1].decode("utf-8").split(',') for line in t1Data[1:] ]
9      t2Data = [line[0:-1].decode("utf-8").split(',') for line in t2Data[1:] ]
10     t1Close = []
11     t2Close = []
12     for i in range(min(len(t1Data), len(t2Data))):
13         if t1Data[i][0] == t2Data[i][0]:
14             t1Close.append(float(t1Data[i][4]))
15             t2Close.append(float(t2Data[i][4]))
16
17     return correlation(t1Close, t2Close)
```

Listing 5.6   Correlating data retrieved from Yahoo

raw data into a list of lists format. Notice that the expression used in the list comprehension is `line[0:-1].decode("utf-8").split(',')`. This expression constructs a new list for each line of data. Finally, the two lists of closing stock prices are constructed in the loop on lines 12–15. Now that the two lists of closing prices have been created, all that is left is to return the result of calling the correlation function on the two lists.

Exercises

5.20 Use the `stockCorrelate` function to find out if there is a correlation between your two favorite companies.

5.21 Write a function that will graph the closing prices for a stock. Your function should accept a beginning date and an ending date along with the ticker symbol for a stock.

5.22 Write a function that will graph the high, low, and closing prices for a stock. Your function should accept a beginning date and an ending date along with the ticker symbol for a stock.

5.23 Write a function that accepts a company name as a parameter and returns the ticker symbol for the company. You will need to look at the Yahoo website.

5.24 Find out if there is a correlation between volume and price for a company of your choice.

5.25 Write a function that will determine the correlation between two stocks for a given date range.

5.26 Write a function that will accept a list of stocks as a parameter and will return the two stocks from the list that are most highly correlated.

5.4 Summary

This chapter used external data sources as input into Python programs. These data sources, called text files, can reside on a local machine or may be available via the Internet. We also showed how to create formatted output by using format strings. This allows for structured output as well as formatted numeric values, columns of data, and justification. We used our statistical functions to analyze real earthquake data. Finally, using stock market data, we developed another statistical function called correlation.

Key Terms

File Transfer Protocol (FTP)

format operator

formatted string

hostname

hypertext markup language (HTML)

Hypertext Transfer Protocol (HTTP)

infinite loop

list comprehension

Pearson correlation coefficient

priming read

protocol

text file

Uniform Resource Locator (URL)

Python Keywords

and	not	readline	while
close	open	readlines	write
float	or	urllib	
for	read	urlopen	

Bibliography

[Mal03] Burton G. Malkiel. *A Random Walk Down Wall Street.* W. W. Norton & Company, 2003.

Programming Exercise

5.1 Imagine that you have removed the stock listing pages from the current issue of the *Wall Street Journal* and then pinned them to a wall in your room. Now imagine that you take a step back and throw 20 darts at the wall. You invest $10,000 in the stock of whichever ticker symbol your darts land on. The question is how wealthy will you become? Will you do better or worse than investing in the stocks listed on the Dow Jones Industrial Average? Will you do better or worse than professional money managers who carefully research all of their trades? Write a program to investigate these questions. You can find lists of stocks at the following URL: http://www.dbc.com/cgi-bin/htx.exe/SYMBOLS/ASTOCK.html?SOURCE=core/dbc.

CHAPTER 6

Pycture Perfect Programs

6.1 Objectives

- To understand pixel-based image processing
- To use nested iteration
- To use and understand tuples
- To implement a number of image processing algorithms
- To understand passing functions as parameters

6.2 What Is Digital Image Processing?

Digital photography is a very common way to produce photographs today. It seems that almost everyone has a digital camera as well as software that can organize and manipulate photographs. In this chapter we consider digital images and many of the techniques that can be used to modify them.

Digital image processing refers to the process of using algorithms to edit and manipulate digital images. A digital image is a finite collection of small, discrete picture elements called pixels. These pixels are organized in a two-dimensional grid and represent the smallest amount of picture information that is available. If you look closely at an image, pixels can sometimes appear as small "dots." More pixels in your image mean more detail or resolution.

Digital cameras are often rated according to how much resolution they provide. Typically resolution is expressed as a number of megapixels. One megapixel means that the picture you take is composed of 1 million pixels. An 8 megapixel camera is capable of taking a picture with up to 8 million pixels.

6.2.1   The RGB Color Model

Each pixel in the digital image is limited to having a single color. The specific color depends on a formula that mixes various amounts of the primary colors red, green, and blue. Viewing colors as a combination of red, green, and blue is often referred to as the **RGB color model**.

The amount of each primary color component is referred to as its intensity. Intensities will range from a minimum of 0 to a maximum of 255. For example, a color with 255 red intensity, 0 green intensity, and 255 blue intensity will be purple (or magenta). Black will have zero intensity for all primary color components and white will have full color intensity, 255, for all. Table 6.1 shows some common combinations.

An interesting question arises when you consider how many colors there might be using the RGB color model. Since each of the three colors has 256 intensity levels, there are $256^3 = 16,777,216$ different combinations of red, green, and blue intensities. All of these colors make up the color palette for the RGB color model.

6.2.2   The cImage Module

In order to manipulate images we will use a group of objects found in our cImage module. (See "Installing the Required Software" (Appendix A) for instructions on downloading and installing cImage.py). This module contains objects that allow us to construct and manipulate pixels. We can also construct an image from a file or create a blank image that we can fill in later. In addition, we can create windows where images can be displayed.

Color	Red	Green	Blue
Red	255	0	0
Green	0	255	0
Blue	0	0	255
Magenta	255	0	255
Yellow	255	255	0
Cyan	0	255	255
White	255	255	255
Black	0	0	0

Table 6.1   Red, green, and blue intensities for some common colors

Method Name	Example Use	Explanation
`Pixel(r, g, b)`	`p = Pixel(25, 200, 143)`	Create a pixel with 25 red, 200 green, and 143 blue.
`getRed()`	`r = p.getRed()`	Return the red component intensity.
`getGreen()`	`g = p.getGreen()`	Return the green component intensity.
`getBlue()`	`g = p.getBlue()`	Return the blue component intensity.
`setRed()`	`p.setRed(100)`	Set the red component intensity to 100.
`setGreen()`	`p.setGreen(45)`	Set the green component intensity to 45.
`setBlue()`	`p.setBlue(87)`	Set the blue component intensity to 87.

Table 6.2 Pixel object

The `Pixel` Object

Images are collections of pixels. In order to represent a pixel, we need a way to collect together the red, green, and blue components. The `Pixel` object provides a constructor and methods that allow us to create and manipulate the color components of pixels. Table 6.2 shows the constructor and methods provided by pixel objects. Session 6.1 shows them in action. The constructor will require the three color components. It will return a reference to a `Pixel` object that can be accessed or modified. We can extract the color intensities using the `getRed`, `getGreen`, and `getBlue` methods. Similarly, we can modify the individual components within a pixel using `setRed`, `setGreen`, and `setBlue`.

```
>>> from cImage import *
>>> p = Pixel(200,100,150)
>>> p
(200, 100, 150)
>>> p.getRed()
200
>>> p.setBlue(20)
>>> p
(200, 100, 20)
>>>
```

Session 6.1 Creating and using a pixel

The `ImageWin` Object

Before creating images, we will create a window that can be used to display our images. The `ImageWin` object provides a constructor that produces a window with a title, width, and height. When a window is constructed, it is immediately shown. The code below produces an empty window that is 600 pixels wide and 400 pixels high. Table 6.3 shows additional methods for the `ImageWin` object. Note that the `getMouse` method returns a coordinate position within the window itself and is not related to any particular image that might be displayed within the window.

```
>>> from cImage import *
>>> myWin = ImageWin("Image Processing",600,400)
>>>
```

Method Name	Example Use	Explanation
`ImageWin(title,width,height)`	`ImageWin("Pictures",800,600)`	Create a window to display images that are 800 pixels wide and 600 pixels high.
`exitOnClick()`	`myWin.exitOnClick()`	Close the image window and exit when the mouse is clicked.
`getMouse()`	`pos = myWin.getMouse()`	Return an (x, y) tuple representing the position of the mouse click in the window.

Table 6.3   The `ImageWin` object

Method Name	Example Use	Explanation
`FileImage(filename)`	`im = FileImage(` `"pic.gif")`	Create an image object from a file named pic.gif.
`EmptyImage(width,` `height)`	`im = EmptyImage(300,` `200)`	Create an empty image that is 300 pixels wide and 200 pixels high.
`getWidth()`	`w = im.getWidth()`	Return the width of the image in pixels.
`getHeight()`	`h = im.getHeight()`	Return the height of the image in pixels.
`getPixel(col,row)`	`p = im.getPixel(150,` `100)`	Return the `Pixel` from row 100, column 150.
`setPixel(col,row,` `newp)`	`im.setPixel(150,100,` `Pixel(255,255,255))`	Set the pixel at row 100, column 150 to be white.
`setPosition(col,` `row)`	`im.setPosition(20,20)`	Position the top-left corner of the image at (col, row) in the window.
`draw(imagewin)`	`im.draw(myWin)`	Draw the image `im` in the `myWin` image window. It will default to the upper-left corner.
`save(fileName)`	`im.save(fileName)`	Save the image to a file. Use `gif` or `ppm` as the extension.

Table 6.4   `FileImage` and `EmptyImage` Objects

Now that we have a window, we need to create images to display. The `cImage` module provides two kinds of image objects: `FileImage` and `EmptyImage`. These objects allow us to create and manipulate images, and they give us simple access to the pixels in each image. Table 6.4 shows the two constructors for creating images as well as other methods that are provided by both objects.

The `FileImage` Object

The `FileImage` object is an image that is constructed from files such as those that are created by digital cameras or that reside on web pages. For example, the file `lutherBell.gif` was taken with an ordinary digital camera. Session 6.2 shows that the `FileImage` constructor needs only the name of the image file. It converts the image stored in that file to an image object. In this case, `bell` is the reference to that object. Finally, we can use the `draw` method to ask the image object to show itself in an image window. The default positioning is to place the image in the upper-left corner of the window. Figure 6.1 shows the result.

```
>>> from cImage import *
>>> myWin = ImageWin("Luther Bell",300,200)
>>> bell = FileImage("lutherBell.gif")
>>> bell.draw(myWin)
>>>
```

Session 6.2 Creating and showing a file image

Figure 6.1 Drawing an image in a window

As we said earlier, an image is a two-dimensional grid of pixel values. Each small square in Figure 6.2 represents a pixel that can take on any one of the millions of colors in the RGB color model. We can access information about our specific image by using the `getWidth` and `getHeight` methods (see Session 6.3). This image is 300 pixels across and 200 pixels top to bottom. Rows are numbered from 0 to 1 less than the height of the image. Columns are numbered from 0 to 1 less than the width.

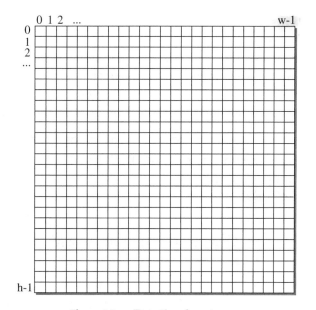

Figure 6.2   Details of an image

```
>>> bell.getWidth()
300
>>> bell.getHeight()
200
>>> bell.getPixel(124,165)
(117, 123, 123)
>>>
```

Session 6.3   Accessing information about an image

We can access a particular pixel by using the `getPixel` method. To use `getPixel`, we need to provide the location for the pixel of interest. The location will be a pair of values, one specifying the column and one specifying the row. Each unique column-row pair will provide access to a single pixel.

In the example, we are accessing the pixel located at column 124, row 165. In other words, it is the pixel that is 125 pixels from the left and 166 pixels from the top. It is important to remember that we start counting at 0. The value that is returned in our example shows the red, green, and blue components of the `Pixel` at that location in our image.

The `EmptyImage` Object

We often want to build a new image pixel by pixel starting with a "blank" image. Using the `EmptyImage` constructor, we can create an image that has a specific width and height but where each pixel is void of color. This means that each `Pixel` has the value (0,0,0) or "black." The statements in Session 6.4 create an empty image with all black pixels.

```
>>> myImWin = ImageWin("Empty Image", 300, 300)
>>> emptyIm = EmptyImage(300,300)
>>> emptyIm.draw(myImWin)
>>>
```

Session 6.4   Creating and displaying an empty image

As an example to show the basic use of the image methods, we will construct an image that starts out empty and is filled with white pixels at specific locations. Session 6.5 starts by creating a window and an empty image that is sized to fit within the window. In order to create a line of white pixels, we use a loop variable `i` and iterate over the range from 0 to 299. The `setPixel` method can be called using the value of `i` for both column and row with a pixel called `whitePixel` that has been created with a combination of red, green, and blue corresponding to the color `white`. We draw the image in the window as shown in Figure 6.3. Finally, we save the image to a file using the `save` method.

```
>>> from cImage import *
>>> myImWin = ImageWin("Line Image",300,300)
>>> lineImage = EmptyImage(300,300)
>>> whitePixel = Pixel(255,255,255)
>>> for i in range(300):
        lineImage.setPixel(i,i,whitePixel)

>>> lineImage.draw(myImWin)
>>> lineImage.save("lineImage.gif")
>>>
```

Session 6.5   Using <code>EmptyImage</code>

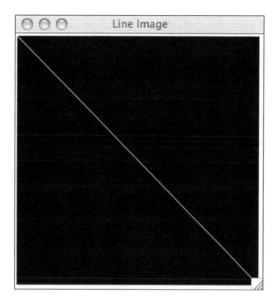

Figure 6.3   Creating a white diagonal line

Exercises

6.1 Modify Session 6.5 to create a line with random pixel colors.

6.2 Write a function to create an image of a rectangle. Start with an `EmptyImage`. *Challenge*: Create a filled rectangle.

6.3 Write a function to create an image of a circle.

6.4 Download an image from the Web or your personal image collection and display it in a window. Note the image must be in gif format.

6.5 Modify some pixels in the image from the previous question and save it.

6.6 Why is the number of color intensities limited to the range 0–255? Do some research to find the answer to this question.

6.3   Basic Image Processing

We now have all of the tools necessary to do some simple image processing. Our first examples will perform color manipulations on an image. In other words, we want to take the existing pixels and modify them in some way to change the appearance of the original image. The basic idea will be to systematically process each pixel one at a time and perform the following operations:

1. Extract the color components.

2. Build a new pixel.

3. Place that pixel in a new image at the same location as the original.

Once we see the general pattern, the options are endless. Note that all of the newly constructed images in this section will be the same dimensions as the image they are based on.

6.3.1   Negative Images

When images are placed on film and then developed, a set of **negatives** is produced. A negative image is also known as a color-reversed image. In a negative image, red becomes cyan where cyan is the mixture of green and blue. Likewise, yellow becomes blue and blue becomes yellow. Regions that are white turn black, black turns white, light turns dark and dark turns light. This continues for all possible color combinations.

At the pixel level, the negative operation is just a matter of "reversing" the red, green, and blue components in that pixel. Since color intensity ranges from 0 to 255, a pixel with a large amount of a specific color—say, red—will have a small amount in the negative. At the maximum, a pixel with a red intensity of 255 will have a red intensity of 0 in the negative. This suggests that the way to create a negative pixel is to subtract each of the red, green, and blue intensity values from 255. The results can then be placed in a new pixel.

Listing 6.1 shows a function that will take a `Pixel` as a parameter and return the negative pixel using the suggested process from above. Note that the function expects to receive an entire `Pixel` and will decompose the color components, perform the subtractions, and then build and return a new `Pixel`. We can easily test this function as shown in Session 6.6.

```
1   def  negativePixel(oldPixel):
2       newred = 255 - oldPixel.getRed()
3       newgreen = 255 - oldPixel.getGreen()
4       newblue = 255 - oldPixel.getBlue()
5       newPixel = Pixel(newred, newgreen, newblue)
6       return newPixel
```

Listing 6.1   Constructing a negative pixel

```
>>> apixel = Pixel(155,23,230)
>>> negativePixel(apixel)
(100, 232, 25)
>>>
```

Session 6.6 Testing the `negativePixel` function

In order to create the negative image, we call the **negativePixel** function on each pixel. We need to come up with a pattern that will allow us to process each pixel. To do this, we can think of the image as having a specific number of rows equal to the height of the image. Each row in turn has a number of columns equal to the width of the image. With this in mind, we can build an iteration that will systematically move through all of the rows and within each, will move through all of the columns. This gives rise to the notion of **nested iteration**—the placement of an iteration as the process inside of another iteration. In other words, for each pass of the "outer" iteration, the "inner" iteration will run to completion. The inner iteration will run from start to finish for each pass of the outer iteration.

As an example, consider the code fragment in Session 6.7 using *for* statements. The outer iteration is moving over the list [0,1,2], which was produced by **range(3)**. For each item in that list, the inner loop will iterate over the characters 'c', 'a', 't'. This means that the **print** function will be called for each character in the string "cat" for each number in the list [0,1,2].

```
>>> for num in range(3):
        for ch in "cat":
            print(num,ch)


0 c
0 a
0 t
1 c
1 a
1 t
2 c
2 a
2 t
>>>
```

Session 6.7 Showing nested iteration with lists and strings

The resulting output shows nine lines. Each group of three represents one pass of the outer loop. Within each group, the value of num stays the same. For each value of num, the entire inner loop completes, and therefore each of the three characters of the string appears.

We can now apply this idea to the construction of a function to compute the negative of each pixel in an image (see Listing 6.2). The function will take a single parameter that gives the name of a file containing an image. The function will not return anything but will simply display both the original and the negative image.

The first step (lines 2–8), is to create an image window, open an original image, and draw it in the window. We then need to create an empty image that has the same width and height as the original. Note that width and height are the width and height of both the original and new image.

Using the idea of nested iteration, we will first iterate over the rows, starting with row 0 and extending down to height-1. For each row, we will process all of the columns within the row.

```
for row in range(height):
    for col in range(width):
```

Each pixel is accessed by row and col. We can get the original color tuple at that location using the getPixel method (line 12). Once we have the original pixel, we can use the negativePixel function to transform it into the negative. Finally, using the same row and col, we can place the new negative pixel in the new image (line 14) using the setPixel method. Once the iteration is complete for all pixels, the new image is drawn in the window. Note that we use the setPosition method to place the new image next to the original. Figure 6.4 shows the resulting images.

Figure 6.4   A negative image

```
1  def makeNegative(imageFile):
2      myimagewindow = ImageWin("Image Processing",600,200)
3      oldimage = FileImage(imageFile)
4      oldimage.draw(myimagewindow)
5
6      width = oldimage.getWidth()
7      height = oldimage.getHeight()
8      newim = EmptyImage(width,height)
9
10     for row in range(height):
11         for col in range(width):
12             originalPixel = oldimage.getPixel(col,row)
13             newPixel = negativePixel(originalPixel)
14             newim.setPixel(col,row,newPixel)
15
16     newim.setPosition(width+1,0)
17     newim.draw(myimagewindow)
18     myimagewindow.exitOnClick()
```

Listing 6.2   Constructing a negative image

6.3.2   Grayscale

Another very common color manipulation is to convert an image to grayscale, where each pixel will be a shade of gray, ranging from very dark (black) to very light (white). With grayscale, each of the red, green, and blue color components will take on the same value. In other words there are 256 different grayscale color values ranging from darkest (0, 0, 0) to lightest (255, 255, 255). The standard color known as "gray" is typically coded as (128, 128, 128).

Our task then is to take each color pixel and convert it into a gray pixel. The easiest way to do this is to consider that the intensity of each red, green, and blue component needs to play a part in the intensity of the gray. If all of the color intensities are close to zero, the resulting color is very dark, which should in turn show as a dark shade of gray. On the other hand, if all of the color intensities are closer to 255, the resulting color is very light and the resulting gray should be light as well.

This analysis gives rise to a simple but accurate formula for grayscale. We will simply take the average intensity of the red, green, and blue components. This average can then be used for all three color components in a new pixel that will be a shade of gray. Listing 6.3 shows a function, similar to the **negativePixel** function described previously, that takes a **Pixel** and returns the grayscale equivalent. Session 6.8 shows the function in use.

```
1  def  grayPixel(oldpixel):
2      intensitySum = oldpixel.getRed() + oldpixel.getGreen() + \
3                     oldpixel.getBlue()
4      aveRGB = intensitySum // 3
5
6      newPixel = Pixel(aveRGB,aveRGB,aveRGB)
7      return  newPixel
```

Listing 6.3   Constructing a grayscale pixel

```
>>> grayPixel( Pixel(34,128,74) )
(78, 78, 78)
>>> grayPixel( Pixel(200,234,165) )
(199, 199, 199)
>>> grayPixel( Pixel(23,56,77) )
(52, 52, 52)
>>>
```

Session 6.8   Testing the `grayPixel` function

Now the process of creating a grayscale image can proceed in the same way as described for creating the negative (see Listing 6.4). After opening and drawing the original image, we create a new, empty image. Using nested iteration, process each pixel, this time converting each to the corresponding grayscale value (line 13). The final image is shown in Figure 6.5.

We developed the previous examples by continually building upon a framework of simple ideas. We started with the pixel, then created a function to transform the color components

Figure 6.5   A grayscale image

```
1  def makeGrayScale(imageFile):
2      myimagewindow = ImageWin("Image Processing",600,200)
3      oldimage = FileImage(imageFile)
4      oldimage.draw(myimagewindow)
5
6      width = oldimage.getWidth()
7      height = oldimage.getHeight()
8      newim = EmptyImage(width,height)
9
10     for row in range(height):
11         for col in range(width):
12             originalPixel = oldimage.getPixel(col,row)
13             newPixel = grayPixel(originalPixel)
14             newim.setPixel(col,row,newPixel)
15
16     newim.setPosition(width+1,0)
17     newim.draw(myimagewindow)
18     myimagewindow.exitOnClick()
```

Listing 6.4 Constructing a grayscale image

of a pixel, and finally applied that function to all of the pixels in the image. This stepwise construction is a very common methodology used in writing computer programs. Building upon those functions that already work in order to provide more complex functionality that can again be used as a foundation allows programmers to be very efficient. We take this one step further in the next section.

Exercises

6.7 Write a function that removes all red from an image.

6.8 Write a function that enhances the red intensity of each pixel in an image.

6.9 Write a function that diminishes the blue intensity of each pixel in an image.

6.10 Write a function that manipulates all three color intensities in a pixel using a strategy of your own choice.

6.11 Write a function that takes a color image and displays a black and white image next to it. *Hint:* You may want to start by converting the image to grayscale. Any pixel with a gray value less than some threshold will become black. All other pixels will be white.

6.3.3   A General Solution: The Pixel Mapper

If you compare the Python listings for the `makeGrayScale` and `makeNegative` functions, you will note that there is quite a bit of redundancy. In fact, the same steps were followed with only one exception—namely, the function that was called to map each original pixel into a new pixel. This similarity causes us to think that we could factor out the code that is the same and create a more general Python function. This is another example of using abstraction to solve problems.

Figure 6.6 shows how such a function might be constructed. We will create a function called `pixelMapper` that will take two parameters, an original image and an RGB function. The `pixelMapper` function transforms the original image into a new image using the RGB function. After applying the RGB function to every pixel, the transformed image is returned. In this way we have a single function that is capable of transforming an image given any function that manipulates the color intensities of a single pixel.

In order to implement this general pixel mapper, we need to be able to pass a function as a parameter. Up to this point, all of our parameters have been data objects such as integers, floating point numbers, lists, tuples, and images. The question to consider is whether there is any difference between a function and a typical data object.

The answer to this question is that there is no difference. To understand why, we will first look at a simple example. The function `squareIt` takes a number and returns the square.

```
def squareIt(n):
    return n * n
```

We can invoke the `squareIt` function with the usual syntax (see Session 6.9), placing the actual value to be squared as a parameter. However, if we evaluate the name of the function without invoking it (without the parameters in parentheses), we can see that the result is a function definition. The name of a Python function is a reference to a data object—in particular, a function definition (see Figure 6.7). Note that the strange looking "number," 0x1021730, is actually the address where the function is stored in memory.

Figure 6.6   A general pixel mapping function

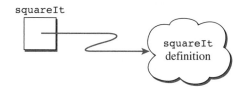

Figure 6.7   A function is a data object

Since a function is simply another data type, you might wonder what kinds of operators you can use with it. In fact there are only two operators that you can use with a function. The parentheses are actually an operator that tells Python to apply the function to the supplied parameters. In addition, since a function is an object, you can use the assignment operator to give a function another name, as shown in Session 6.9. Note that now the variable z is a reference to the same data object as squareIt and can be used with the parenthesis operator.

```
>>> squareIt(3)
9
>>> squareIt(squareIt(3))
81
>>> squareIt
<function squareIt at 0x1021730>
>>> z = squareIt
>>> z(3)
9
>>> z
<function squareIt at 0x1021730>
```

Session 6.9   Evaluating the squareIt function

Since any Python object can be passed as a parameter, it is certainly possible to pass the function definition object. We just need to be careful not to invoke the function prior to passing it. To show this (Session 6.10), we create a simple function called test that expects two parameters, a function object and a number. The body of test will invoke the function object using the number as a parameter and return the result.

```
>>> def test(funParm, n):
        return funParm(n)
>>>
>>> test(squareIt,3)
9
>>> test(squareIt,5)
25
>>> test(squareIt(3),5)
Traceback (most recent call last):
  File "<stdin>", line 1, in <module>
  File "<stdin>", line 2, in test
TypeError: 'int' object is not callable
```

Session 6.10   Using a function passed as a parameter

We can then use our **test** function by passing the **squareIt** function definition. In addition, we will pass the integer 3. Remember, when we pass the function definition object, we do not include the parentheses pair. Figure 6.8 shows the references immediately after **test** has been called and the parameters have been received. A copy of the reference to the actual parameter **squareIt** is received by **funParm** and **n** contains a reference to the object 3.

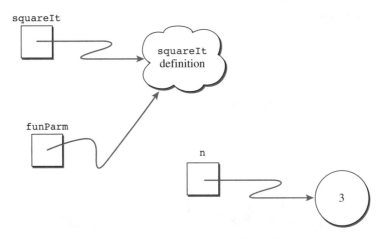

Figure 6.8   Passing the method and an integer

The statement `return funParm(n)` will cause the function referred to by `funParm` to be invoked on the value of `n`. In this case, since `funParm` is a reference to `squareIt`, the `squareIt` function will be invoked with the value of 3. The next example shows the result of passing 5 instead of 3. Note the error message at the end of the session when we call the `squareIt` function instead of passing the definition.

With these mechanics in place, it is now possible to create an implementation for our general `pixelMapper` function (see Listing 6.5). Recall that this function will take two parameters, an image and an RGB function. Lines 3–5 construct a new empty image that is the same size as the original. Line 10, which is inside of our nested iteration, does most of the work. The `rgbFunction` parameter is applied to each pixel from the original image and the resulting pixel is placed in the new image. Once the nested iteration is complete, we will return the new image.

```
1  def pixelMapper(oldimage,rgbFunction):
2
3      width = oldimage.getWidth()
4      height = oldimage.getHeight()
5      newim = EmptyImage(width,height)
6
7      for row in range(height):
8          for col in range(width):
9              originalPixel = oldimage.getPixel(col,row)
10             newPixel = rgbFunction(originalPixel)
11             newim.setPixel(col,row,newPixel)
12
13      return newim
```

Listing 6.5   *A general pixel mapping method*

We can complete our example by calling the `pixelMapper` function using one of our RGB functions from the previous sections. Listing 6.6 shows a main function, `generalTransform`, that sets up the image window and loads the original image. Line 6 invokes `pixelMapper` using the `grayPixel` function. The result is identical to that shown in Figure 6.5.

```
1  def generalTransform(imageFile):
2      myimagewindow = ImageWin("Image Processing",600,200)
3      oldimage = FileImage(imageFile)
4      oldimage.draw(myimagewindow)
5
6      newimage = pixelMapper(oldimage,grayPixel)
7      newimage.setPosition(oldimage.getWidth()+1,0)
8      newimage.draw(myimagewindow)
9      myimagewindow.exitOnClick()
```

Listing 6.6   Calling the general pixel mapping function

Exercises

6.12 Use a reference diagram to explain the error message in Session 6.10.

6.13 Use the `generalTransform` and `pixelMapper` functions to create a negative image using the `negativePixel` function developed earlier.

6.14 Write an RGB function to remove the red from a pixel. Test this function with `pixelMapper`.

6.15 Write an RGB function to convert a pixel to black and white. Test this function with `pixelMapper`.

6.16 Write an RGB function of your choice. Test this function with `pixelMapper`.

6.17 Sepia tone is a brownish color that was used for photographs in times past. The formula for creating a sepia tone is as follows:

$$newR = (R \times 0.393 + G \times 0.769 + B \times 0.189)$$
$$newG = (R \times 0.349 + G \times 0.686 + B \times 0.168)$$
$$newB = (R \times 0.272 + G \times 0.534 + B \times 0.131)$$

Write an RGB function to convert a pixel to sepia tone. *Hint:* Remember that RGB values must be integers between 0 and 255.

6.4 Parameters, Parameter Passing, and Scope

Throughout many of the previous chapters, we have used functions to implement abstraction. We have broken problems down into smaller, more manageable pieces and have implemented functions that we can call over and over again. In the previous section we pushed this idea one step further by passing functions as parameters to other functions. In this section we explore in more detail the underlying mechanics of how functions and parameter passing work.

Consider the function shown in Listing 6.7, which computes the hypotenuse of a right triangle. Using the **Pythagorean theorem**, $a^2 + b^2 = c^2$, this function needs the lengths of the two sides, called a and b, and computes and returns the length of the long side, called c. Session 6.11 shows the function in use.

```
1  import math
2  def hypotenuse(a,b):
3      c = math.sqrt(a**2 + b**2)
4      return c
```

Listing 6.7   A simple function to compute the hypotenuse of a triangle

```
>>> hypotenuse(3,4)
5.0
>>>
>>> side1 = 3
>>> side2 = 4
>>> hypotenuse(side1,side2)
5.0
>>>
>>> hypotenuse(side1*2, side2*2)
10.0
>>>
>>> hypotenuse
<function hypotenuse at 0x42b70>
```

Session 6.11   A simple method

In the first example, references to the objects 3 and 4 are passed to the function. These are known as the **actual parameters** as they represent the "actual" data that the function will receive. As we have seen before, the parameter list (a,b) receives these object references one at a time, in order, from left to right. So, a receives a reference to the object 3 and b receives a reference to the object 4. These parameters, defined in the function itself, are known as the **formal parameters**.

In the second example shown, the actual parameters are not literal numbers but are instead names that are referring to the objects 3 and 4. Prior to the function call, Python evaluates the two names `side1` and `side2` in order to find the objects. Once again, a receives a reference to the object 3 and b receives a reference to the object 4.

6.4.1   Call by Assignment Parameter Passing

In general, the process by which a function's formal parameter receives an actual parameter value is known as **parameter passing**. There are many different ways to pass parameters and different programming languages have chosen to use a variety of them. In Python, however, all parameters are passed using a single mechanism known as **call by assignment** parameter passing.

Call by assignment parameter passing uses a simple two-step process to pass data when the function is called. Calling a function is also known as **invocation**. The first thing that happens is that the actual parameters are evaluated. This evaluation results in an object reference to the result. In the first case from Session 6.11, evaluating a literal number simply returns a reference to the number itself. In the second example, evaluating a variable name returns the object reference named by that variable.

Once the evaluation of the actual parameters is complete, the object references are passed to and received by the formal parameters in the function. The formal parameter becomes a new name for the reference that is passed. In a sense it is as if we executed the assignment statement `formal parameter = actual parameter`.

As a final example, consider the third invocation shown in Session 6.11. Here the actual parameters are expressions that double the lengths of the original sides. Call by assignment parameter passing evaluates these expressions first and then assigns the references to the resulting objects to the formal parameters a and b. The `hypotenuse` function has no idea where the references came from or how complicated the original expression might have been. The references that are received are simply the results of the evaluation.

Call by assignment parameter passing has some important ramifications that may not be obvious to you at first. Changes to the formal parameter may or may not result in changes to the actual parameter depending on whether the actual parameter is mutable or immutable. If the actual parameter is immutable, then changes to the formal parameter will have no effect outside the function. If the actual parameter is mutable, then changes to the object referenced by the formal parameter will be visible outside the function.

For example, if the actual parameter is a reference to the integer 3, then assigning a reference to the integer 5 to the formal parameter would not be visible outside the function. If the actual parameter is a reference to a list, then any changes to the contents of the list including additions or deletions will be visible outside the function. However, if the formal parameter is assigned to a different list, the behavior is consistent with the behavior for integers.

6.4.2 Namespaces

In Python, all of the names defined in a program, whether for data or for functions, are organized into **namespaces**—collections of all names that are available to be accessed at a particular point in time during the execution of a Python program. When we start Python, we create two namespaces. The first is called the **built-in namespace** (see Figure 6.9), and it includes all of the system-defined names of functions and data types that we regularly use in Python. Names such as **range, str**, and **float** are included in this namespace. The second is called the **main namespace**, and it is initially empty. Python calls these two namespaces **__builtin__** and **__main__**.

As we begin to create our own names in a Python session, they are added to the main namespace. As shown in the example in Session 6.11, the variable names **side1** and **side2** are now added to the main namespace. The function name **hypotenuse** is also added to the main namespace. Note that the names are added as a result of an assignment statement or a method definition. The objects referred to by the names are shown as well. Figure 6.10 shows the location of the names and the objects they reference. Note that the objects exist outside the namespace.

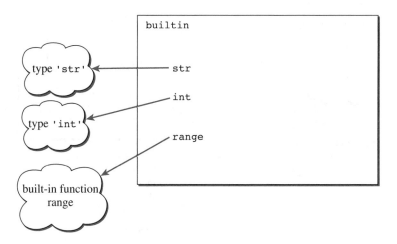

Figure 6.9 The builtin namespace

At this point it is instructive to investigate the namespace idea interactively. Python provides us with the function **dir** that allows us to see a list of the names in any namespace. Session 6.12 shows what happens when we invoke the **dir** function after defining the **hypotenuse** function and assigning values to the **side1** and **side2** variables.

In addition to the three names that we just created, there are four other names of interest defined in our namespace. The **__builtins__** refers to the built-in namespace we referred to earlier. It is possible for you to find out the names of the objects in the built-in namespace by calling the function **dir(__builtins__)**. The **__doc__** name is always available to hold a reference to a string that describes the namespace. The **__main__** namespace does not have documentation but other namespaces such as math may. **__name__** holds the name of the current namespace. In Session 6.12 you can see that we evaluated **__name__** to find that we are in the **__main__** namespace.

The final name in the list from **dir** that we have yet to discuss is **math**. This name appears because we imported the math module on line 1 of the session. As you can see, the name **math** refers to an object that is a module. It is important to note that a module defines its own namespace. Just as with the built-in namespace, you can find out the names in the math namespace by evaluating **dir(math)**. Note that the math namespace also has its own **__name__** and **__doc__** entries.

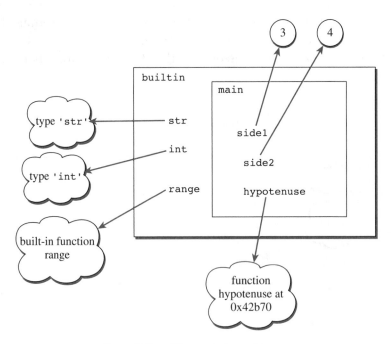

Figure 6.10   The **main** namespace

```
>>> import math

>>> def hypotenuse(a,b):

...     c= math.sqrt(a**2+b**2)

...     return c

...

>>> side1 = 3

>>> side2 = 4

>>> dir()

['__builtins__', '__doc__', '__name__', '__package__', 'hypotenuse', 'math',
'side1', 'side2']

>>> __name__

'__main__'

>>> math

<module 'math' from '.../lib/python3.0/lib-dynload/math.so'>

>>> dir(math)

['__doc__', '__file__', '__name__', '__package__', 'acos', 'asin', 'atan',
'atan2', 'ceil', 'copysign', 'cos', 'cosh', 'degrees', 'e', 'exp', 'fabs',
'floor', 'fmod', 'frexp', 'hypot', 'isinf', 'isnan', 'ldexp', 'log', 'log10',
'modf', 'pi', 'pow', 'radians', 'sin', 'sinh', 'sqrt', 'tan', 'tanh', 'trunc']

>>> math.__doc__

'This module is always available.  It provides access to the\nmathematical
functions defined by the C standard.'

>>>
```

Session 6.12   Exploring the __main__ namespace

We now have all the tools needed to understand the difference between the statements `import math` and `from math import *`. Session 6.13 shows the result of calling the `dir` function after importing the math module using the statement `from math import *`. Notice that all the names from the math module now appear as part of the main namespace. This allows us to call functions such as `sqrt` directly without prefacing the function name with the module name.

```
>>> from math import *

>>> dir()

['__builtins__', '__doc__', '__name__', '__package__', 'acos', 'asin', 'atan',
'atan2', 'ceil', 'copysign', 'cos', 'cosh', 'degrees', 'e', 'exp', 'fabs',
'floor', 'fmod', 'frexp', 'hypot', 'isinf', 'isnan', 'ldexp', 'log', 'log10',
'modf', 'pi', 'pow', 'radians', 'sin', 'sinh', 'sqrt', 'tan', 'tanh', 'trunc']

>>>
```

Session 6.13   Importing the math names into the `__main__` namespace

Exercises

6.18 Try calling the `dir` function on the `__builtins__` object.

6.19 Import the `turtle` module and find out the names defined.

6.20 Look at the `__doc__` string for the `turtle` module.

6.21 If you put a string at the beginning of any Python file, that string becomes the `__doc__` string for that module. Try adding a string to the beginning of one of your Python files. Can you import that file and see the string you added? The `help` function also returns this string as part of the documentation for a module.

6.4.3   Calling Functions and Finding Names

When a function is invoked, a new namespace known as the local namespace is created corresponding to the function itself. This namespace includes those names that are created inside the function. This includes the formal parameters as well as any names that are used on the left-hand side of an assignment statement in the body of the function. These names are referred to as local variables since they have been created within the function and are part of the local namespace. When the function is completed, either due to a `return` statement or simply due to running out of code statements, the local namespace is destroyed. This means that all of the locally defined names are no longer available for use.

It is important to note the placement of these namespaces with respect to one another. The main namespace is placed inside the built-in namespace. Likewise, local namespaces are placed inside the namespace of the module where they are defined. For programs that you write, the namespaces for your functions will be placed in the main namespace. The namespaces for functions from modules that you import will be placed in the namespace of the imported module. Figure 6.11 shows the placement of the local namespace for the `hypotenuse` function when it is called. This figure also provides an illustration of the call by assignment mechanism. Note that the formal parameters a and b are referring to the same objects as the actual parameters side1 and side2.

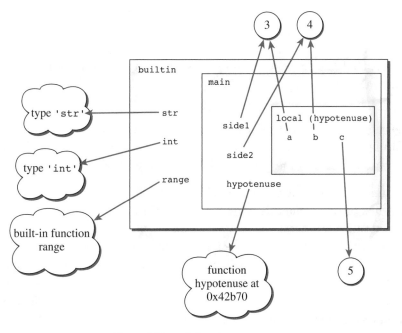

Figure 6.11   A local namespace

When a name is used in a statement, Python needs a way to locate the particular occurrence of that name among all of the names that have been introduced up to that point. In order to find the name, Python uses the following simple rules:

1. Whenever a name is used, except on the left-hand side of an assignment statement, Python searches through the namespaces in the following order:

   (a) The current local namespace, if one exists

   (b) The main or module namespace

   (c) The built-in namespace

   When Python finds the first occurrence of the name, the search ends. Looking again at Figure 6.11, you may find it helpful to think of this as searching from the "inside out." If the name is not found, an error is reported.

2. When you use a name on the left-hand side of an assignment statement, Python searches only the current namespace.

   (a) If the name is not found, a new name is created in the current namespace.

   (b) If the name is found, then the old reference will be replaced with the object from the right-hand side of the assignment statement.

   This means that the same name may exist in many different namespaces but Python will always use the name as governed by rule 1.

To show these rules in action, consider the code shown in Session 6.14. Here, function `test1` defines one formal parameter value called `a`. It adds 5 to `a` and prints the result. Since `a` is a formal parameter, it becomes part of the local namespace for the function `test1`.

Next, an assignment statement creates a variable called `a` and sets it to refer to the object 6. This occurrence of the name `a` is added to the main namespace. When we invoke `test1` using `a` as the actual parameter, call by assignment parameter passing will first evaluate `a`. The result is a reference to the object 6, which is passed and received by the formal parameter `a` in the local namespace. When the assignment statement is performed in the function `test1`, Python must search for the name `a`. The result of the search is that the `a` from the local namespace is used in the statement `a = a + 5`. The `a` in the main namespace is unaffected and still refers to the object 6.

```
>>> def test1(a):
...     a = a + 5
...     print(a)
...
>>> a = 6
>>> test1(a)
11
>>> a
6

>>> def test2(b):
...     print(b)
...     print(a)
...
>>> test2(14)
14
6
>>> a
6
>>> b
Traceback (most recent call last):
  File "<stdin>", line 1, in ?
NameError: name 'b' is not defined
>>>
```

Session 6.14   Showing `name` lookup rules at work

In the second example in Session 6.14, `test2` is defined with a formal parameter called `b`. This function prints `b` and then prints `a`. However, the name `a` is not defined in the local namespace for `test2`. When the print statements are executed, we will use the previous rules to locate the names. The result of the search is that `b` is found in the local namespace but `a` is found in the main namespace.

In this example, the reference to the object 14 is assigned to the formal parameter `b` in `test2` so that the first `print` statement simply prints the value 14. The second `print` statement tries to find a variable called `a`. Since it cannot be found in the local scope, the search proceeds outward to the main namespace where `a` is found with a value of 6. Therefore, 6 is printed.

Note that after the call to `test2` completes, `a` still has the value 6 since it is part of the main namespace. Once the function `test2` completes, the namespace is destroyed and `b` is no longer present. Since `b` does not exist in the main namespace, an error is reported that `b` is not defined.

6.4.4   Modules and Namespaces

The `hypotenuse` function defined earlier uses the `sqrt` function from the math library. In order to access that function, we needed to import the math module. In Python, the statement `import math` creates a name in the current namespace with a reference to a new namespace for the module itself. In this case, the name `math` is added to the main namespace. The new namespace for the math module is placed in the built-in namespace, as is shown in Figure 6.12. The math namespace contains names of functions such as `sqrt`. Note that the name `sqrt` refers to a function definition.

It is important to note that the namespace for the math module was placed in the built-in namespace, not in the main namespace. The namespaces for all imported modules will be placed at the same level within the built-in namespace. The only thing that will be placed

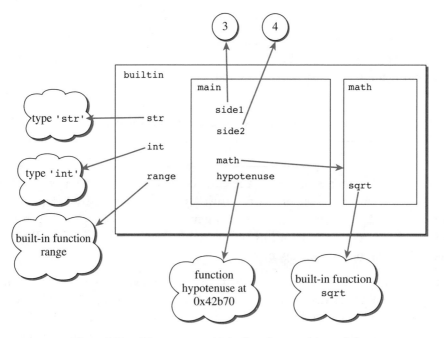

Figure 6.12   Namespaces including imported module

directly in the main namespace is the name of the module with the corresponding reference to the module namespace.

To take this one step further, consider the `hypotenuse` function at the point where the `sqrt` function has been invoked. As before, the namespace for `hypotenuse` has been placed as a local namespace in the main namespace. When the `hypotenuse` function calls the `sqrt` function, a new local namespace for `sqrt` is created. Even though the call to `sqrt` was made from the `hypotenuse` namespace, the `sqrt` namespace is placed in the math namespace since that is where the `sqrt` function was defined.

The local namespace created when a function is called is always created in the namespace for the module in which the function was defined. In our example, this is true regardless of how the `math` module is imported. Even if we had imported `math` using `from math import *` the namespace for `sqrt` would be placed in the math namespace.

Figure 6.13 shows all of the namespaces up to this point. According to the name lookup rules defined earlier, searches for names used in the `sqrt` function will start in the local `sqrt` namespace, proceed outward to the math namespace, and finally to the built-in namespace.

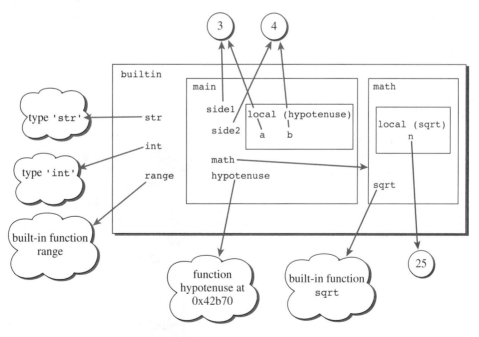

Figure 6.13   Invocation of `sqrt` function from `math`

6.5   Advanced Image Processing

We now turn our attention to some image processing algorithms that require the manipulation of more than one pixel either in the original or in the new image. These techniques will require that we look for additional patterns in the way that we process the pixels of the image.

6.5.1   Resizing

One of the most common manipulations performed on images is **resizing**—the process of increasing or decreasing the dimensions (width and height) of an image. In this section we focus on enlarging an image. In particular, we consider the process of creating a new image that is twice the size of the original.

Figure 6.14 shows the basic idea. The original image is three pixels wide by four pixels high. When we enlarge the image by a factor of 2, the new image will be 6 pixels wide by 8 pixels high. This presents a problem with respect to the individual pixels within the image.

The original image has 12 individual pixels. No matter what we do, we will not be able to create any new detail in the image. This means that when we increase the number of pixels to 48 in the new image, 36 of the pixels must use information that is already present in the original. Our problem is to decide systematically how to "spread" the original detail over the pixels of the new image.

Figure 6.15 shows one possible solution to this problem. Each pixel of the original will be mapped into 4 pixels in the new image. Every 1-by-1 block of pixels in the original image

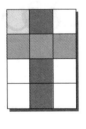
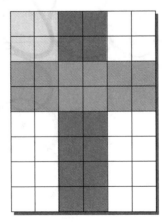

Figure 6.14   Enlarging an image by a factor of 2

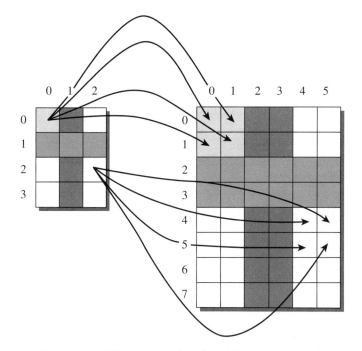

Figure 6.15 Mapping each old pixel to 4 new pixels

is mapped into a 2-by-2 block in the new image. This results in a one-to-four mapping that will be carried out for all of the original pixels. Our task is to discover a pattern for mapping a pixel from the original image onto the new image.

An example of this mapping process shows that pixel $(0, 0)$ will be mapped to pixels $(0, 0)$, $(1, 0)$, $(0, 1)$, $(1, 1)$. Likewise, pixel $(2, 2)$ maps to pixels $(4, 4)$, $(5, 4)$, $(4, 5)$, $(5, 5)$. Extending this pattern to the general case of a pixel with location (`col`, `row`) gives the four pixels (2 × col, 2 × row), (2 × col + 1, 2 × row), (2 × col, 2 × row + 1), (2 × col + 1, 2 × row + 1). Figure 6.16 illustrates the mapping equations for a particular pixel. You should check your understanding by considering other pixels in the original image.

Listing 6.8 shows the complete function for doubling the size of an image. Since the new image will be twice the size of the old, it will be necessary to create an empty image with dimensions that are double those of the original (see lines 2–5).

Now we can use nested iteration to process each original pixel. As before, two *for* loops, one for the columns and one for the rows, will allow us to systematically process each pixel. Using the color components from each old pixel, we copy them to the new image. Lines 11–14 use the pattern discussed above to assign each pixel in the new image. Note that each of the four pixels receives the same color tuple. The result can be seen in Figure 6.17.

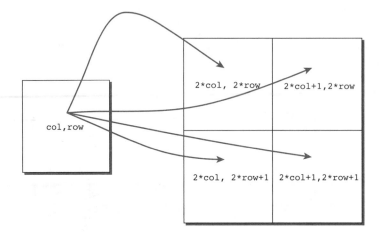

Figure 6.16   Mapping for a pixel at location (col, row)

```
 1 | def double(oldimage):
 2 |     oldw = oldimage.getWidth()
 3 |     oldh = oldimage.getHeight()
 4 |
 5 |     newim = EmptyImage(oldw*2,oldh*2)
 6 |
 7 |     for row in range(oldh):
 8 |         for col in range(oldw):
 9 |             oldpixel = oldimage.getPixel(col,row)
10 |
11 |             newim.setPixel(2*col,2*row,oldpixel)
12 |             newim.setPixel(2*col+1,2*row,oldpixel)
13 |             newim.setPixel(2*col,2*row+1,oldpixel)
14 |             newim.setPixel(2*col+1,2*row+1,oldpixel)
15 |
16 |     return newim
```

Listing 6.8   Doubling the size of an image

Figure 6.17 Enlarged image

6.5.2 Stretching: A Different Perspective

In the previous section we developed an algorithm for enlarging an image. That solution required us to map each pixel in the original image to 4 pixels in the new image. In this section we consider an alternative solution: constructing a new image by mapping pixels from the new image to the original. Viewing problems from many different perspectives can often provide valuable insight. Our alternative solution takes advantage of this insight and leads to a simpler solution.

Figure 6.18 shows the same image as before. However, this time the pixel mapping is drawn in the reverse direction. More specifically, instead of looking at the problem from the perspective of the original image, we are turning our focus to the pixels of the new image. As we process the pixels of the new image, we need to figure out which pixel in the original image should be used.

Listing 6.9 shows the completed code for our new function, which will take an original image as a parameter and return the new, enlarged image. Again, we will need a new empty image that is twice the size of the original. This time we write our iteration to process each pixel in the new image. The nested iteration idea will still work but the bounds will need to be in terms of the new image, as can be seen in lines 7–8.

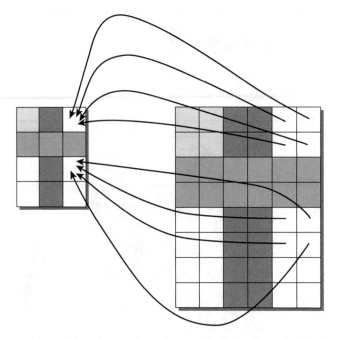

Figure 6.18   Mapping each of 4 new pixels back to 1 old pixel

```
1  def double(oldimage):
2      oldw = oldimage.getWidth()
3      oldh = oldimage.getHeight()
4
5      newim = EmptyImage(oldw*2,oldh*2)
6
7      for row in range(newim.getHeight()):
8          for col in range(newim.getWidth()):
9
10             originalCol = col//2
11             originalRow = row//2
12             oldpixel = oldimage.getPixel(originalCol,originalRow)
13
14             newim.setPixel(col,row,oldpixel)
15
16     return newim
```

Listing 6.9   Doubling the size of an image: Mapping new back to old

We now need to perform the pixel mapping. As we saw in the last section, the pixels at locations $(4,4)$, $(5,4)$, $(4,5)$, $(5,5)$ will all map back to pixel $(2,2)$ in the original. As another example (see again Figure 6.18, pixels $(4,0)$, $(5,0)$, $(4,1)$, $(5,1)$ will all map back to pixel $(2,0)$). Our task is to find the mapping pattern that will allow us to locate the appropriate pixel in the general case.

Once again, it may appear that there are four cases since four pixels in the new image associate to a single pixel in the original. However, upon further examination, that is not true. Since we are considering the problem from the perspective of the new image, there is only **one** pixel that is of interest in the original. This suggests that there may be a single operation that will map each of the new pixels back to the original. Looking at the example pixels, we can see that integer division will perform the operation that we need (see Figure 6.19).

More specifically, in the examples given above, we need an operation that can be done to both 4 and 5 where the result will be 2. Also, the same operation on 0 and 1 will need to yield 0. Recall that both `4//2` and `5//2` give a result of 2 since the `//` operator when working on integers gives an integer result while discarding the remainder. Likewise, `0//2` and `1//2` both give 0 as their result.

We can now use this operation to complete the function. Lines 10–11 extract the correct pixel from the original image by using the integer division operator to compute the corresponding column and row. Once the pixel has been chosen, we can assign it to the location in the new image. Of course, the result is the same as seen in the last section (see again Figure 6.17).

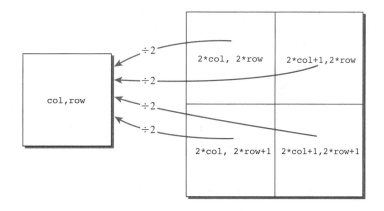

Figure 6.19   Mapping back using integer division

As we stated earlier, enlarging an image provides no new detail. The result can therefore look "grainy" or "blocky" due to the fact that we are mapping one pixel to many locations in the new image. Although we cannot create any new detail to add to the image, it is possible to "smooth" out some of the hard edges by processing each pixel with respect to those around it.

Exercises

6.22 Write a function to quadruple the size of an image.

6.23 Write a general function for enlarging an image that accepts a scale parameter for enlarging in the x direction and another parameter for enlarging in the y direction.

6.24 Write a function for reducing the size of an image.

6.25 Write a function that will smooth the enlarged image. *Hint:* You will want to replace each pixel in the enlarged image with the average of itself and its neighbors.

6.26 Write a function to remove noise from an image. You can do this by replacing each pixel with the median of itself and its neighbors.

6.5.3   Flipping an Image

We now consider manipulations that physically transform an image by moving pixels to new locations. In particular, we consider a process known as **flipping**. Creating a **flip image** requires that we decide where the flip will occur. For our purposes in this section, we will assume that flipping happens with respect to a line that we will call the **flip axis**. The basic idea is to place pixels that appear on one side of the flip axis in a new location on the opposite side of that axis, keeping the distance from the axis the same.

As an example, consider the simple image with 16 pixels in Figure 6.20 and a flip axis placed vertically at the center of the image. Because we are flipping on the vertical axis, each row will maintain its position relative to every other row. However, within each row, the pixels will move to the opposite side of the axis, as shown by the arrows. The first pixel will be last and the last pixel will be first.

The structure of this function is similar to those we have written thus far. We build our nested iteration such that the outer iteration will process the rows and the inner iteration will process each pixel within the row. Listing 6.10 shows the completed function. Note that the new image is the same height and width as the original.

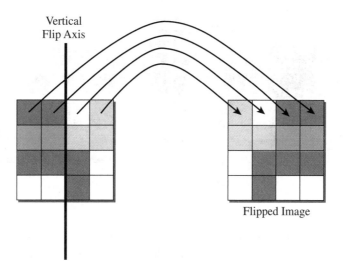

Vertical
Flip Axis

Flipped Image

Figure 6.20   Flipping an image on the vertical axis

```
1  def verticalFlip(oldimage):
2      oldw = oldimage.getWidth()
3      oldh = oldimage.getHeight()
4
5      newim = EmptyImage(oldw,oldh)
6
7      maxp = oldw-1
8      for row in range(oldh):
9          for col in range(oldw):
10
11             oldpixel = oldimage.getPixel(maxp-col,row)
12
13             newim.setPixel(col,row,oldpixel)
14
15     return newim
```

Listing 6.10   Creating the vertical flip of an image

We need to discover a pattern to map each pixel from its original location into a new location with respect to the flip axis. Referring to Figure 6.20 we can see that the following associations are needed in an image that is 4 pixels wide: column 0 will map to column 3, column 1 will map to column 2, column 2 will map to column 1, and column 3 will map to column 0. In general, small values map to large values and large values map to small.

Figure 6.21   A flipped image

The first thing we might try is to use the width and simply subtract the original column to get the new column. If we try this with column 0, we immediately see that there is a problem since $4 - 0$ is 4, which is outside the range of valid column values. The cause of this error is that we start counting the columns (as well as the rows) with zero.

To fix this, we can base the subtraction on the actual maximum pixel position instead of the width. Since the pixels in this example are named with column 0 though column 3 (width of 4), we can use 3 as our base for the subtraction. In this case, the general mapping equation will be `(width-1) - column`. Note that `width-1` is a constant, which means that we can perform this calculation just once, outside the loop as we do on line 7.

Since we are performing a flip using a vertical flip axis, the pixels stay in the same row. Line 11 uses the calculation above to extract the proper pixel from the original image and line 13 places it in its new position in the new image. Note that `row` is used in both `getPixel` and `setPixel`. Figure 6.21 shows the resulting image.

Exercises

6.27 Write the function `horizontalFlip` to flip an image on the horizontal axis.

6.28 Rewrite the `verticalFlip` function so that it flips an image in place.

6.29 *Mirroring* is a manipulation similar to flipping. When producing a mirror, the pixels on one side of the mirror axis are reflected back on the other side. In a mirror operation half of the pixels are lost. Implement a mirror on the vertical axis.

6.30 Implement a mirror on the horizontal axis.

6.31 Implement a mirror at a specific column or row. *Note:* This operation will change the image size.

6.32 Write a function `rotateImage90` that takes an image as a parameter and rotates the image by 90 degrees.

6.33 Write a function `rotateImage180` that takes an image as a parameter and rotates it by 180 degrees.

6.34 Write a function `rotate` that takes an image and a number of degrees to rotate the image. Note that this rotation may leave some empty pixels. You will also need to size the new image so it can hold the entire rotated image.

6.5.4   Edge Detection

Our final image processing algorithm in this chapter is called **edge detection**—an image processing technique that tries to extract feature information from an image by finding places in the image that have very dramatic changes in color intensity values. For example, assume that we have an image containing two apples, one red and one green, that are placed next to one another. The border between a block of red pixels from the red apple and a block of green pixels from the green apple might constitute an edge representing the distinction between the two objects.

As another example, consider the grayscale image (actually black and white) shown in Figure 6.22. In the left image there are three objects: a white square, a cloud, and a star. The right image shows the edges that exist. Each black pixel in the edge image denotes a point where there is a distinct difference in the intensity of the original grayscale pixels. Finding these edges helps to differentiate between any features that may exist in the original image.

Edge detection has been studied in great detail. There are many different approaches that can be used to find edges within an image. In this section we describe one of the classic algorithms for producing the edges. The mathematics used to derive the algorithm are beyond the scope of this book. However, we can easily develop the ideas and techniques necessary to implement the algorithm.

In order to find an edge, it is necessary to evaluate each pixel in relation to those that appear around it. Since we are looking for places where intensity on one side of the pixel is greatly different from the intensity on the other, it will help us to simplify the pixel values. Our first step in discovering edges will be to convert the image to grayscale. This means that the intensity of the pixel can be thought of as the common color component intensity.

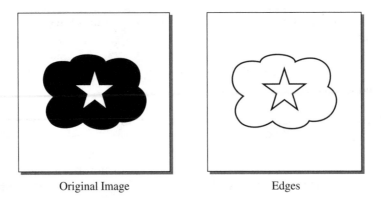

Original Image   Edges

Figure 6.22   A simple edge detection

(Recall that shades of gray are made from pixels with equal quantities of red, green, and blue.) Each pixel can then be thought to have one of 256 intensity values.

As a means of looking for these intensity differences, we use the idea of a **kernel**, also known as a *filter* or a *mask*. These kernels will be used to weight the intensities of the surrounding pixels. For example, consider the 3 by 3 kernels shown in Figure 6.23. These "grids" of integer weights are known as the **Sobel operators**, named after Irwin Sobel who developed them for use in edge detection.

The left mask, labeled `XMask`, will be used to look for intensity differences in the left to right direction of the image. You can see that the leftmost column of values is negative and the rightmost column is positive. Likewise, the `YMask` will look for intensity differences in the up and down direction as can be seen by the location of the positive and negative weights.

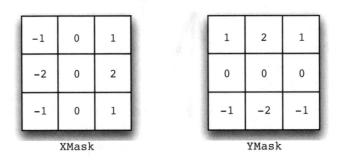

XMask   YMask

Figure 6.23   Kernel masks for convolving pixels

The kernels will be used during **convolution**—a process in which pixels in the original image will be mathematically combined with each mask. The result will then be used to decide whether that pixel represents an edge.

Convolution will require a mask and a specific pixel. The mask will be "centered" on the pixel of interest, as shown in Figure 6.24. Each weight value in the mask now associates with one of the nine pixel intensities "under" the mask. The convolution process will simply compute the sum of nine products where each product is the weight multiplied by the intensity of the associated pixel. If you have a large intensity on the left side and a small intensity on the right (indicating an edge), you will get a weighted sum with a large negative value. If you have a small intensity on the left and a large intensity on the right, you will get a large positive weighted sum. Either way, a large absolute value of the weighted sum will indicate an edge. This same argument applies for the top-to-bottom split of the YMask.

To implement convolution, we will first need to consider a way to store the kernels. Since kernels look very similar to images, rows and columns of weights, it makes sense to take advantage of this structure. We will use a **list of lists** implementation for the kernel. For example, the XMask discussed earlier will be implemented as the list [[-1,0,1],[-2,0,2], [-1,0,1]]. The outer list contains three items, each of which represents a row in the kernel. Each row has three items, one for each column. Similarly, the YMask will be [[1,2,1],[0,0,0],[-1,-2,-1]].

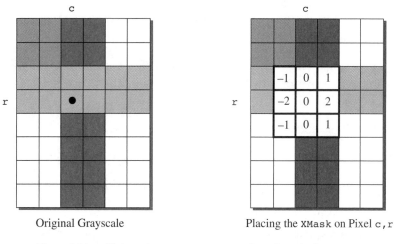

Original Grayscale   Placing the XMask on Pixel c,r

Figure 6.24 Using the XMask to convolve the pixel at c,r

Accessing a specific weight within a kernel will require two index values, one for the outer list and one for the inner list. Since we are implementing the outer list to be a list of three rows, the first index will be the row value. Once we select a row list, the second index will be used to get the specific column.

For example, XMask[1][2] will access the item in XMask indexed by 1, which is the middle row of the XMask. The 2 indexes the last item in the list that corresponds to the last column. This access is for the weight stored in the middle row and last column of XMask.

We can now construct the convolve function. We said earlier that this process requires an image, a specific pixel within the image, and a kernel. The tricky part of this function is to align the kernel and the underlying image. An easy way to do this is to think about a mapping. The kernel row indices will run from 0 to 2. Likewise for the column indices. For a pixel in the image with index (column,row), the row indices for the underlying pixels will run from row-1 to row+1 and for the columns it will be column-1 to column+1.

We will define the *base index* to be the starting index for the 3×3 grid of underlying image pixels. The base index for the columns will be column-1 and the base index for the rows will be row-1. As we process the pixels of the image, the difference between the current image row value and the base index for the rows will be equal to the row index needed to access the correct row in the kernel. Likewise, we can do the same thing for the columns.

Once we have computed the index into the kernel we can use it to compute the product of the weight and the pixel intensity. We will first access the pixel and then extract the red component that will be its grayscale intensity. Since we have already converted the image to grayscale, we can use any one of the red, green, or blue components for the intensity. Finally, that product can be added to a running sum of products for all underlying pixels. The complete convolve function is shown in Listing 6.11. Note that the final step is to return the value of the sum.

Now that we can perform the convolution operation for a specific pixel with a kernel, we can complete the edge detection algorithm. The steps of the process are as follows:

1. Convert the original image to grayscale.

2. Create an empty image with the same dimension as the original.

3. Process each inner pixel of the original image by performing the following:

   (a) Convolve the pixel with the XMask; call the result gX.

   (b) Convolve the pixel with the YMask; call the result gY.

   (c) Compute the square root of the sum of squares of gX and gY; call the result g.

```
1  def convolve(anImage,pixelRow,pixelCol,kernel):
2      kernelColumnBase = pixelCol - 1
3      kernelRowBase = pixelRow - 1
4
5      sum = 0
6      for row in range(kernelRowBase,kernelRowBase+3):
7          for col in range(kernelColumnBase,kernelColumnBase+3):
8              kColIndex = col-kernelColumnBase
9              kRowIndex = row-kernelRowBase
10
11             apixel = anImage.getPixel(col,row)
12             intensity = apixel.getRed()
13
14             sum = sum + intensity * kernel[kRowIndex][kColIndex]
15
16     return sum
```

Listing 6.11   Convolution for a specific pixel

(d) Based on the value of **g**, assign the corresponding pixel in the new image to be either black or white.

Listing 6.12 shows the Python code that implements the steps outlined previously. We begin by converting the original image to grayscale using the **pixelMapper()** function developed earlier in the chapter. This will allow for simple intensity levels within each pixel. We will also need an empty image that is the same size as the original. It will also be useful to define a few data objects for use later. Since each pixel in the edge detection result will be either black or white, we will create black and white tuples that can be assigned later in the process. Also, we will need the list of lists implementation of the two kernels. These initializations are done on lines 3–8.

Now it is time to process the original pixels looking for an edge. Since each pixel is required to have eight surrounding pixels for the convolution operation, we will not process the first and last pixel on each row and column. This means that our nested iteration will start at one, not zero, and it will continue through **height-2** and **width-2** as shown on lines 10–11.

Each pixel will now participate in the convolution process using both kernels. The resulting sums will be squared and summed together, and in the final step we will take the square root (see lines 12–14).

The value of this square root, called **g**, represents a measure of how much difference exists between the pixel and those around it. The decision as to whether the pixel should be

```
1   import math
2   def edgeDetect(theImage):
3       grayImage = pixelMapper(theImage,grayPixel)
4       newim = EmptyImage(grayImage.getWidth(), grayImage.getHeight())
5       black = Pixel(0,0,0)
6       white = Pixel(255,255,255)
7       XMask = [ [-1,-2,-1],[0,0,0],[1,2,1] ]
8       YMask = [ [1,0,-1],[2,0,-2],[1,0,-1] ]
9
10      for row in range(1,grayImage.getHeight()-1):
11          for col in range(1,grayImage.getWidth()-1):
12              gx = convolve(grayImage,row,col,XMask)
13              gy = convolve(grayImage,row,col,YMask)
14              g = math.sqrt(gx**2 + gy**2)
15
16              if g > 175:
17                  newim.setPixel(col,row,black)
18              else:
19                  newim.setPixel(col,row,white)
20
21      return newim
```

Listing 6.12   The edge detection method

labeled as an edge is made by comparing g to a threshold value. It turns out that when
using these kernels, 175 is a good threshold value for considering whether you have found
an edge. Using simple selection, we will just check to see if the value is greater than 175. If
it is, we will color the pixel black; otherwise we will make it white. Figure 6.25 shows the
result of executing this function.

Figure 6.25   Running the edge detection algorithm

Exercises

6.35 Try several different threshold values in `edgeDetect`. What effect does changing the threshold have on the image? Does 175 work best for all images? What would be a way to automatically select a good threshold for an image?

6.36 Modify the convolve function so that it applies the kernel to the red, green, and blue components separately and returns a tuple of values as a result.

6.37 Convolution has many uses. For example, a simple convolution kernel is the blurring kernel, which looks like this:

$$\begin{bmatrix} 1 & 2 & 1 \\ 2 & 1 & 2 \\ 1 & 2 & 1 \end{bmatrix}$$

In this case we simply apply the kernel and return the weighted average without doing any thresholding. Write a blur function that uses the new convolve function to blur an image.

6.38 The sharpen kernel looks like this:

$$\begin{bmatrix} -1 & -1 & -1 \\ -1 & 9 & -1 \\ -1 & -1 & -1 \end{bmatrix}$$

You can sharpen a pixel by emphasizing its value and deemphasizing the pixels around it. Sharpening is the opposite of blurring. Use the sharpen kernel to sharpen an image.

6.39 Write a general function that can take an image and a kernel and then return an image with the convolution kernel applied to each pixel.

6.40 Research convolution kernels and find a new one to try.

6.6 Summary

In this chapter we focused on `cImage`—a new module that contains a number of data types that can be used to manipulate digital images. In particular, `cImage` includes the following:

- `ImageWin`
- `EmptyImage`

- `FileImage`
- `Pixel`

To process the pixels of an image, we used a pattern called nested iteration—that is, iteration inside iteration. Nested iteration allowed us to process all of the pixels in a given row, column by column, before moving on to the next row. We also introduced the notion of namespaces—collections of names available at a particular point in time. These namespaces are organized to allow us to look up names when they are used, thereby making sure that there are no ambiguities. This chapter concluded with a more detailed consideration of the mechanics of parameter passing.

Key Terms

actual parameter	flip image	list of lists	pixel
built-in namespace	flipping	local namespace	Pythagorean theorem
call by assignment	formal parameter	main namespace	resizing
convolution	grayscale	namespace	RGB color model
digital image	image processing	negative	Sobel operators
edge detection	invocation	nested iteration	
flip axis	kernel	parameter passing	

Python Keywords

`dir`	`for`	`math`	`return`
`EmptyImage`	`ImageWin`	`Pixel`	
`FileImage`	`import`	`range`	

Bibliography

[Par96] J. R. Parker. *Algorithms for Image Processing and Computer Vision*. Wiley, 1996.

Programming Exercises

6.1 Write a program to create a collage. Your program should combine several images with different effects applied to the images.

6.2 Write a program to blend one image with another. You can try different techniques for combining the RGB values for two pixels, each from a different image.

6.3 Take a picture of yourself against a white background. Use the fact that you can "filter" out all the white pixels to place your picture in an interesting scene. This same process is used all the time by weather forecasters on television. The only difference is that they stand in front of a solid blue or solid green background called a *chromakey*.

6.4 Another way to put yourself in an interesting picture is to take a picture of yourself against a relatively plain background, then take another picture of exactly the same background (use a tripod here with autofocus off) without you in it. Now you can compare the two images and remove the pixels that are exactly the same, or close to the same. Once you have removed those pixels, you can superimpose yourself on any background.

6.5 Using `getMouse` to get the coordinates of a pixel in an image, devise a way to remove the red-eye effect from the area of the image you click on.

6.6 Using `getMouse`, write a program that will allow you to "cut" a rectangular region out of an image and place it somewhere in a new image.

CHAPTER 7

Data Mining: Cluster Analysis

7.1 Objectives

- To use Python lists as a means of storing data
- To implement a nontrivial data mining application
- To understand and implement cluster analysis
- To use visualization as a means of displaying patterns

7.2 What Is Data Mining?

We have already considered ways that statistical techniques can help us to process and summarize large amounts of data. By computing statistical measures such as the range, mean, standard deviation, and frequency, we can begin to make statements about our data. In this chapter we will explore this idea further.

Large amounts of data can be overwhelming. Consider once again the data set from "Earthquakes, Floods, and Other Natural Disasters" (Chapter 5) that represents all of the earthquakes that took place around the world in a two-week period. A portion of this large data file is again shown here:

```
2.8 2006/10/19 02:02:10 62.391 -149.751 15.0 CENTRAL ALASKA
2.5 2006/10/19 00:31:15 20.119 -156.213 1.5 MAUI REGION, HAWAII
5.0 2006/10/18 21:15:51 4.823 -82.592 37.3 SOUTH OF PANAMA
2.6 2006/10/18 21:12:25 59.934 -147.904 30.0 GULF OF ALASKA
3.4 2006/10/18 20:59:21 36.540 -89.640 7.7 SOUTHEASTERN MISSOURI
```

```
2.7 2006/10/18 20:11:22 61.023 -151.418 60.0 SOUTHERN ALASKA
3.1 2006/10/18 16:40:15 20.282 -156.611 4.7 MAUI REGION, HAWAII
2.7 2006/10/18 14:12:19 59.808 -152.538 50.0 SOUTHERN ALASKA
2.8 2006/10/18 14:02:12 60.686 -151.871 90.0 KENAI PENINSULA, ALASKA
4.9 2006/10/18 12:10:01 1.758 127.488 127.0 HALMAHERA, INDONESIA
6.2 2006/10/18 10:45:36 -15.081 167.243 138.5 VANUATU
2.8 2006/10/18 10:45:17 32.162 -115.895 6.3 BAJA CALIFORNIA, MEXICO
3.3 2006/10/18 10:08:45 32.165 -115.891 7.3 BAJA CALIFORNIA, MEXICO
2.8 2006/10/18 08:22:27 32.263 -115.297 3.4 BAJA CALIFORNIA, MEXICO
3.7 2006/10/18 05:34:15 62.326 -151.224 85.9 CENTRAL ALASKA
4.6 2006/10/18 03:25:03 -21.538 -66.593 201.7 POTOSI, BOLIVIA
3.7 2006/10/18 02:32:26 57.560 -137.186 1.0 OFF THE COAST OF SOUTHEASTERN ALASKA
4.9 2006/10/18 02:01:27 1.355 97.157 25.8 NIAS REGION, INDONESIA
2.5 2006/10/18 00:18:42 19.801 -155.391 10.6 ISLAND OF HAWAII, HAWAII
3.1 2006/10/17 22:59:01 61.444 -150.523 60.0 SOUTHERN ALASKA
...
```

Recall that each line of data represents one earthquake. Each line consists of seven fields. Each of the seven fields describes a significant attribute related to that earthquake. These attributes are, in order from left to right, magnitude, date, time of day, latitude, longitude, depth, and location.

Although it may not seem possible, it is very likely that there are important pieces of information hidden away within this data that are not obvious from the simple types of descriptive statistics used in "A Nest of Snakes" (Chapter 4). This is where we can use **data mining**—the application of automated techniques that attempt to discover underlying patterns. These techniques can be applied to any number of data domains. For example, in business, data mining is often used for marketing purposes to find patterns exhibited by consumers. Once these patterns are identified, they can be used to recommend the products that a customer might purchase. In addition, there are many applications in science and medicine where finding patterns in large amounts of data is required.

Cluster analysis is a data mining technique that attempts to divide the data into meaningful groups called **clusters**. These clusters represent data values that show some kind of similarity to each other while exhibiting a dissimilar relationship to data values outside of the cluster.

In this chapter we focus our attention on cluster analysis as a way to find hidden information in a collection of data. Our goal is to implement one version of cluster analysis along with tools that allow us to see the results.

7.3   Cluster Analysis: A Simple Example

As a simple example of what can be learned through cluster analysis, consider the data shown in Figure 7.1. This data represents the performance of a class of mathematics students. The x-axis gives the homework total for the semester as a percentage of total points available; the y-axis shows the performance on exams, again as a percentage of total points.

At first glance it may not be apparent that there are patterns within the data. In fact, if we were looking at the raw data scores and there were hundreds of students in the class, it is very unlikely that we would notice anything. However, if we run the data through a cluster analysis routine, we may discover that some of the points tend to group together as shown in Figure 7.2. Our analysis technique has identified three clusters, labeled A, B, and C. All of the data points in cluster A are said to have some underlying characteristic in common with each other based on some measure of similarity. The same can be said for clusters B and C. The points that appear in different clusters have characteristics that make them similar to each other but distinguish them from other clusters.

It is important to note that some of the points do not appear in any of the three clusters. These points have characteristics that are different from the characteristics that define the other clusters. In addition, these points do not have enough similarity to form their own cluster. Some cluster analysis techniques will allow for this and some will require that all points eventually be placed in a cluster.

If we analyze our results further, we might be able to infer that these clusters are actually identifying performance clues for our students. For example, cluster A would seem to suggest that there are a number of students who do well on both exams and homework. This could

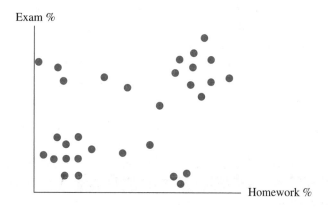

Figure 7.1   Data representing exam scores and homework totals

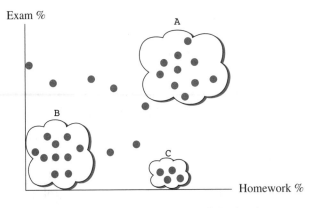

Figure 7.2   Possible clusters within the data

suggest a causal relationship and it is supported by cluster B where students did poorly on both measures. Cluster C could lead us to think that these are the students who have "test anxiety" since they did well with the homework but still could not perform on the exams.

In any case, it is clear that there are some natural relationships that appear within our data set. Finding these relationships can be critical to understanding underlying processes that are inherent in the data. Using these clusters to describe, predict, or otherwise quantify relationships within data can be a very powerful tool.

7.4   Implementing Cluster Analysis on Simple Data

We now turn our attention to developing the fundamental steps of the cluster analysis technique. In order to concentrate on the algorithm we use a very simple data set. Later, we will apply these same ideas to our more complex earthquake data. Our example data in this section consists of exam scores for a group of 21 students taking an introduction to computer science course. These scores represent the percentage of correct answers. The range of scores is between 0 and 100.

A simple listing of the scores is shown in Table 7.1. Our initial observation does not reveal any patterns. We could certainly use our previous work to compute descriptive statistics that might yield a bit more information, but in this case we are interested in knowing if there are any patterns of similarity among the student scores. Cluster analysis could help us to answer that question.

34	56	12	44	87	45	76
98	25	34	76	12	78	98
78	90	89	45	77	22	11

Table 7.1   Table of scores

7.4.1   Distance Between Two Points

One of the most important steps in the cluster analysis algorithm is to classify data points as to their similarity to other data points. In order to measure this similarity, we need some way to suggest that two points are "close" to one another. This can be done by computing a value that we will call the "distance" between two data points.

There are many ways to measure the distance between two data points. For our purposes here, we use a simple measure of distance known as **Euclidean distance**. Consider the two data points, A and B, shown in Figure 7.3. If we assume that point A has location X_1 and point B has location X_2, then the distance between them, d, will be the simple difference between the two location values $d = X_2 - X_1$. However, since we do not know whether this difference will be positive or negative, the absolute value should be used.

An alternative way to eliminate negative values is to square them since the squaring operation will always result in a positive number. To get the original value back, we can then take the square root. Using this approach yields the equation $d = \sqrt{(X_2 - X_1)^2}$.

Although this may seem like extra work, the benefit can be seen if we extend our example to computing the distance between two points in more than one dimension. Figure 7.4 shows our two points. This time the location of point A is given by the pair (X_1, Y_1). Likewise, point B has location (X_2, Y_2). To compute the distance d between the two points now requires that we use the two-dimensional version of the previous equation, which is also known as the Pythagorean theorem: $d = \sqrt{(X_2 - X_1)^2 + (Y_2 - Y_1)^2}$.

In general, this can be extended to handle any number of dimensions. The distance between two data points in n dimensions, can be computed as the square root of the squares of the differences between each of the n coordinates. For example, consider a point A in five-

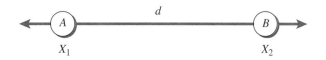

Figure 7.3   Simple distance between two points

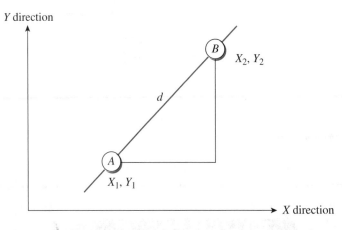

Figure 7.4   Two-dimensional distance between two points

dimensional space with location (23, 44, 12, 76, 34). If point B has location (67, 55, 85, 23, 24), the distance between point A and point B is given by

$$d = \sqrt{(67 - 23)^2 + (55 - 44)^2 + (85 - 12)^2 + (23 - 76)^2 + (24 - 34)^2}$$

Listing 7.1 shows a function to compute the distance between two points. Each point is defined as a list of n coordinate values. Starting with **sum** initialized to 0, we iterate through the coordinate list. If we assume that each point has the same dimensionality, the index range for **point1** will be the same as the index range for **point2**. Line 4 computes the square of the difference and line 5 adds that value to the running **total**. Finally, the square root is computed and returned.

```
1  def euclidD(point1, point2):
2      total = 0
3      for index in range(len(point1)):
4          diff = (point1[index]-point2[index]) ** 2
5          total = total + diff
6
7      euclidDistance = math.sqrt(total)
8      return euclidDistance
```

Listing 7.1   Computing the Euclidean distance between two points

7.4.2 Clusters and Centroids

Clusters of data points exhibit the characteristic that all of the points in the cluster are similar to one another. Another way to think about this similarity is to suggest that all of the data points in the cluster are associated with some notion of a center point. This center point can be used to identify a particular cluster.

A **centroid** is defined as the mean of a collection of data points. Each cluster will have a centroid that represents the center of the cluster. It is important to note that the centroid does not need to be an actual point in the cluster. It is simply the "point" that tends to be in the center of all others.

To compute the centroid for a set of points, we calculate the mean value for each dimension. For example, if we have two points, in two dimensions, $(3, 7)$ and $(1, 5)$, the centroid will be $\left(\dfrac{3+1}{2}, \dfrac{7+5}{2} \right)$ or $(2, 6)$. This can be extended to include any number of points with any number of dimensions.

Figure 7.5 shows three points, $(2, 4), (5, 8), (8, 6)$, each with two dimensions. The centroid $(5, 6)$, shown by the star, represents the notion of center with respect to the three points. If these points were considered to be a cluster, we could use the centroid as its identity.

7.4.3 The K-Means Cluster Analysis Algorithm

There are many different clustering algorithms. We present here one of the oldest and easiest to understand techniques—the **K-means algorithm**. The basic steps of this simple

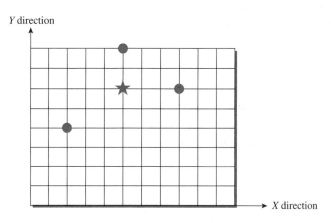

Figure 7.5 The centroid of three points in two dimensions

to describe and implement algorithm are as follows:

1. Decide how many clusters you would like to create; call that number k.

2. Randomly choose k of the data points to serve as the initial centroids for the k clusters.

3. Repeat the following steps:

    (a) Assign each data point to a cluster corresponding to the centroid it is closest to.

    (b) Recompute the centroids for each of the k clusters.

4. Show the clusters.

The number of iterations performed in Step 3 can vary. Sometimes, a simple maximum iteration value is used. Alternatively, the step can be repeated until the clusters become stable. Clusters are considered to be stable when the centroids no longer change from iteration to iteration. Under some circumstances, this may never occur as the points will tend to oscillate back and forth between different clusters.

We should also note that choosing the initial centroids randomly can lead to empty clusters and results that differ from run to run. We will mention more about some of the shortcomings in Section 7.6.

7.4.4   Implementation of K-Means

We now implement the cluster analysis algorithm on the exam data set and assume that the data is stored in a file named `cs150exams.txt` with one score per line. There is no order or additional identifying information in the data file. We need to process the file line by line and extract the exam scores.

Since we need to keep the individual scores separate, we assign an identification key to each score starting with 1 and proceeding through n, where n is the number of scores. In other words, we can identify each score by using the line number from the file. In this way we can then associate the key with any additional information that may be present in the data file. (This will be very useful in later examples.)

Listing 7.2 shows a function that takes a file name as a parameter and returns the dictionary as described above. We first open the file, create an empty dictionary, and then start accessing each line of the file. Since the only data on the line is the test score, we can simply use the `int` function to convert it to an integer. Line 10 enters the score in the dictionary associated with the key. It is important to note that the score is placed in a list before it is added to the dictionary. Recall that each data point can be multidimensional. Even though it is not the case here, the `euclidD` function will expect all data points to be lists of values.

```
1   def  readFile(filename):
2       datafile = open(filename, "r")
3       datadict = {}
4
5       key = 0
6       for aline in datafile:
7           key = key + 1
8           score = int(aline)
9
10          datadict[key] = [score]
11
12      return datadict
```

Listing 7.2   Processing the exam score data file

The next step is to choose the number of clusters, referred to as k on the previous page. Often the number of clusters may be based on some preconceived notion about the data values. In this case, we create five clusters, assuming that one possible reason for clustering the data is to look for groupings that represent one of five grading categories, say A, B, C, D, or F.

Now we need to pick k random data values to be our initial centroids. To implement this, we use the `randint` function from the `random` module. This random number generator will pick an integer in the range `[a,b]` including the endpoints. For example, `randint(2,5)` will return a random integer between 2 and 5 inclusive.

It is important that we choose k random values that are unique. If we were to simply iterate k times, there is no guarantee that the k values will not contain a duplicate. In order to satisfy this requirement, we need to use a *while* loop.

Indefinite Iteration

Most of the iteration performed up to this point has used the *for* loop. Recall that the *for* loop allows a group of statements to be repeated, once for each value in a sequence. For example, in the Python statement

```
for num in [1,2,3,4,5]:
    print("hello")
```

the `print` function, which makes up the body, will be executed (repeated) five times. Each time through the loop, the loop variable `num` will take on a subsequent value from the list. The total number of iterations is strictly given by the number of items in the sequence provided.

This type of iteration is often referred to as **definite iteration** since the number of repetitions is (*definitely*) known based on the size of the iteration sequence. Whenever we know the number of times we want to iterate, the *for* loop is the appropriate construct to use. However, in many cases, we do not know how many iterations will be necessary. We know that we want to repeat a process, and we know that we want to eventually stop the repetition, but the actual number of repetitions is uncertain. In these cases, we need to turn to a form of iteration known as **indefinite iteration**, a process where we state a condition that will be used to decide whether to continue with the iteration process. If the condition is satisfied, we will perform the process again and then recheck the condition. When the condition no longer holds, the process will no longer be repeated.

The `while` loop

In order to implement indefinite iteration in Python, we use the *while* loop, which is similar to the *for* loop and the *if* statement in that it will control a body of statements (see Listing 7.3). As with other structured statements, the statements in the body will be indented.

```
1  while <condition>:
2      statement1
3      statement2
4      ...
5      statementn
```

Listing 7.3   The `while` loop template

Figure 7.6 shows the logical flow of control created by the *while* loop. The condition can be any Boolean expression—that is, any expression that evaluates to `True` or `False`. The statements in the body will be executed repeatedly until the condition evaluates to `False`. It is important to note that if the Boolean expression is `False` initially, the statements will never be executed. In other words, the statements in the body will be executed zero or more times, depending on the value of the condition.

As an example, consider the familiar code fragment shown in Listing 7.4. Here we are using a *for* loop to compute the sum of the first 10 integers. Line 1 initializes an accumulator variable, `total`, that will be used to keep the running sum. The *for* loop (line 2) will automatically iterate through the sequence produced by the **range** function, [1, 2, 3, 4, 5,

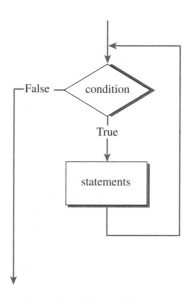

Figure 7.6 The *while* loop

```
1  total = 0
2  for anum in range(1,11):
3      total = total + anum
4  print(total)
```

Listing 7.4 Summation from 1 to 10 using a *for* loop

6, 7, 8, 9, 10], assigning each subsequent value to the loop variable **anum**. The body of the iteration (line 3) adds the value of **anum** to the accumulator. Finally, the value of the **total** is printed.

We can rewrite the summation fragment using a *while* loop, as shown in Listing 7.5. The algorithm remains the same. We will iterate over the values from 1 to 10 and add each to an accumulator variable called **total**. As before, line 1 initializes the accumulator variable and line 4 performs the addition to compute the running sum. Lines 2, 3, and 5 taken together form the iteration control.

It is important to note that the iteration process is not simply the **while <condition>:** but includes a number of other statements as well. In order to write a correct iterative process using a *while* loop, it is necessary to include three parts: the **initialization**, the **condition**, and the **change of state.** All of these parts must work together for the iteration to succeed.

```
1  total = 0
2  anum = 1                    #initialization
3  while anum <= 10:           #condition
4      total = total + anum
5      anum = anum + 1         #change of state
6  print(total)
```

Listing 7.5   Summation from 1 to 10 using a *while* loop

Line 3 provides the condition upon which the iteration will continue. In this example, as long as the value of the variable **anum** is less than or equal to 10, the body statements will be executed. In order to evaluate this condition, it is necessary to provide an initial value for **anum**. Recall that the **while** loop evaluates the condition first, before performing the body. Any variables being used in the condition must have their initial values prior to entering the **while** loop. Since the goal of this iteration is to count from 1 to 10, it makes sense to start the value of **anum** at 1.

If the condition succeeds, control proceeds to the body. After completion of the body, the condition will be rechecked. The only way for the iteration to stop is for the condition to fail. This requires that a change occur inside the body that will directly impact the result of the condition. This change of state is a critical part of the iteration. Without it, the condition that was **True** originally would remain **True** and therefore the **while** statement would never stop. In this example, line 5 provides this change of state. Each time through the body, the value of **anum** is incremented by 1. Eventually, the value of **anum** will reach 11, which will cause the condition to fail.

It is common for beginning programmers to forget one of these three parts or to include them but have inconsistencies. For example, consider Listing 7.6. Here, the initialization and condition are correct but the change of state is missing. This means that once the condition is found to be **True**, nothing exists in the body to change the condition to **False**. The result will be a **while** loop that never stops. This is known as an **infinite loop**. The result will be a **while** loop that never stops.

```
1  total = 0
2  anum = 1
3  while anum <= 10:
4      total = total + anum
5  print(total)
```

Listing 7.6   Infinite loop

Listing 7.7 shows a function that will process the data file using an indefinite iteration. Line 7 uses the **readline** method to get the next line of the file. This method will return the empty string, "", when there are no more lines in the file. The condition will check for the empty string and allow execution of the body only if there was a line of data present in the file.

After the line has been processed, it is necessary to recheck the condition. Before this can happen, a change of state must occur. For this example, the change of state is to read the next line of data from the file. Either a valid line or the empty string will be returned and the condition can be reevaluated.

```
1  def readFile(filename):
2      datafile = open(filename, "r")
3
4      datadict = {}
5
6      key = 0
7      aline = datafile.readline()
8      while aline != "":
9          key = key + 1
10         score = int(aline)
11         datadict[key] = [score]
12
13         aline = datafile.readline()
14
15     return datadict
```

Listing 7.7   Processing the exam score data file using indefinite iteration

Exercises

7.1 Write a function that prints the numbers from 0 to 50 counting by 5. This function must use a *while* loop.

7.2 Write a function that takes a string as a parameter and returns the number of spaces in the string. This function must use a *while* loop.

7.3 Write a function that asks the user to enter exam scores one at a time until the word **stop** is entered. When **stop** is entered, the program should compute the average of the scores.

7.4 Write a function that takes a string as a parameter and returns **True** if the string is a palindrome, and **False** otherwise. This function should use a *while* loop. *Hint:* A palindrome is a word that is spelled the same forward and backward.

7.4.5   Implementation of K-Means Continued

The function shown in Listing 7.8 implements the centroid selection process. It takes the number of centroids (called **k**) and the data dictionary as parameters. Line 2 creates an empty list of centroids. Our task is to fill this list with **k** randomly selected data points. Since we do not want to use a specific key twice, we will store a list of the selected keys and check each randomly selected key against this list. If the key is already in the list, we do not include its data point as a centroid and instead continue on to pick another key randomly. This process will continue until **k** centroids have been selected. Since we do not know how many random selections will be required, a *while* loop is used.

```
1  def createCentroids(k, datadict):
2      centroids=[]
3      centroidCount = 0
4      centroidKeys = []
5
6      while centroidCount < k:
7          rkey = random.randint(1,len(datadict))
8          if rkey not in centroidKeys:
9              centroids.append(datadict[rkey])
10             centroidKeys.append(rkey)
11             centroidCount = centroidCount + 1
12
13     return centroids
```

Listing 7.8   Choosing k random centroids

We keep track of the number of valid centroids that have been found with `centroidCount`. As long as that number is less than **k**, we continue to generate random keys. If an unused key is found, it is added to the list in line 10 and the count is incremented (line 11).

Listing 7.9 implements a function to actually create the clusters. `createClusters` takes the number of clusters (again called **k**), the previously created centroids, the data dictionary, and the number of repetitions as parameters and returns a list of the clusters. Each cluster will be represented by a list. Since we have a collection of clusters, a list of those cluster lists will be the appropriate way to store them. Lines 4–6 create this list of **k** empty clusters.

```python
def createClusters(k, centroids, datadict, repeats):
    for apass in range(repeats):
        print("****PASS",apass,"****")
        clusters = []
        for i in range(k):
            clusters.append([])

        for akey in datadict:
            distances = []
            for clusterIndex in range(k):
                dist = euclidD(datadict[akey],centroids[clusterIndex])
                distances.append(dist)

            mindist = min(distances)
            index = distances.index(mindist)

            clusters[index].append(akey)

        dimensions = len(datadict[1])
        for clusterIndex in range(k):
            sums = [0]*dimensions
            for akey in clusters[clusterIndex]:
                datapoints = datadict[akey]
                for ind in range(len(datapoints)):
                    sums[ind] = sums[ind] + datapoints[ind]
            for ind in range(len(sums)):
                clusterLen = len(clusters[clusterIndex])
                if clusterLen != 0:
                    sums[ind] = sums[ind]/clusterLen

            centroids[clusterIndex] = sums

        for c in clusters:
            print ("CLUSTER")
            for key in c:
                print(datadict[key], end=" ")
            print()

    return clusters
```

Listing 7.9   Creating the clusters

We now go through each item in our data dictionary and assign it to the proper cluster. Recall that we have a list of centroids, one for each cluster. We want to assign each data point to the cluster with the closest centroid. We can do this by using our distance function, `euclidD`, described earlier.

Since there are **k** clusters, each data point will have **k** distances associated with it, one from each centroid. Line 9 creates an empty list of distances, and lines 10–12 compute the distance between the data point and each centroid. These distances are placed in the distance list. The `distances`, `centroids`, and `clusters` lists are parallel to each other. This means that for any particular index number **i**, **i** will refer to data for the same cluster in both lists. Figure 7.7 shows the three parallel lists and the relationship between them.

Once we have all of the distances computed, we can look for the closest centroid. Recall that Python provides a function called `min` that returns the smallest value in a list (line 14). Once we know the smallest value, we can use the list method `index` to find where the minimum occurred in the distance list (line 15). The index of the minimum tells us which cluster the data point should belong to. By using that index, we can access the list of

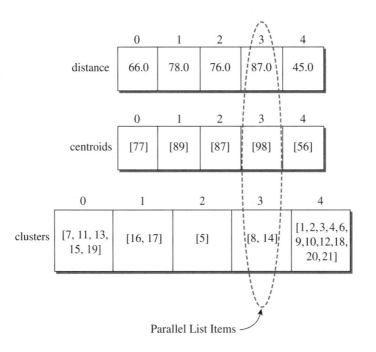

Figure 7.7   Parallel lists

clusters and append the key to the proper cluster (line 17). Again, it is important to remember that we are storing the keys instead of the actual data points.

The final step in the K-means algorithm requires that we recompute the centroids for each cluster. Since the centroid of a cluster is simply the average of all data points in the cluster, we can iterate through the points, create a running sum, and then divide by the number of points.

Lines 19–20 implement the centroid recalculation. Line 19 is important since our data points can be multidimensional. **dimensions** is the number of dimensions within the data point. For our exam score example, this will be one. Recall that to compute the new centroid we must take the average of the coordinate value in each dimension.

A list of running sums, represented by **sums** will include a sum for each dimension of the data point. Each sum component is initialized to 0. Lines 24–25 calculate the running sums of the components and lines 26–29 compute the average. The last statement (line 31) assigns the average to the proper position in the centroids list.

Recall that the clustering process is repeated a number of times. In this function, the parameter **repeats** will allow the user to decide how many iterations to perform. Listing 7.9 also includes a small fragment of code (lines 33–37) that prints out the contents of the clusters after each pass. Finally, Listing 7.10 shows a function that will perform the cluster analysis on the **cs150exams.txt** data file. It will make three passes through the data in order to produce five clusters.

```
1  def clusterAnalysis(dataFile):
2      examDict = readFile(dataFile)
3      examCentroids = createCentroids(5, examDict)
4      examClusters = createClusters(5, examCentroids, examDict, 3)
5
6  clusterAnalysis("cs150exams.txt")
```

Listing 7.10   Cluster analysis for the exam data set

When we run the program, the output in Session 7.1 is produced. In the first pass (pass 0), the exam scores are spread over the five clusters. Pass 1 shows that some of the scores have moved due to the new centroid values that were computed after pass 0. Finally, the last pass shows a final modification of the clusters. If we were using this analysis to assign grades, we might suggest that the first cluster would be the "A"s, the second would be the "F"s, and so on. It is important to note that running the program again could give different results due to the random selection of initial centroids.

```
****PASS 0 ****
CLUSTER
[98] [98] [90] [89]
CLUSTER
[34] [12] [44] [45] [25] [34] [12] [45] [22] [11]
CLUSTER
[56] [76] [76] [77]
CLUSTER
[87]
CLUSTER
[78] [78]
****PASS 1 ****
CLUSTER
[98] [98]
CLUSTER
[34] [12] [44] [45] [25] [34] [12] [45] [22] [11]
CLUSTER
[56]
CLUSTER
[87] [90] [89]
CLUSTER
[76] [76] [78] [78] [77]
****PASS 2 ****
CLUSTER
[98] [98]
CLUSTER
[34] [12] [25] [34] [12] [22] [11]
CLUSTER
[56] [44] [45] [45]
CLUSTER
[87] [90] [89]
CLUSTER
[76] [76] [78] [78] [77]
```

Session 7.1 Clusters of exam scores

Exercises

7.5 Load and run the `clusterAnalysis` function using the exam score data. Compare your clusters with those shown in Session 7.1.

7.6 Run `clusterAnalysis` again but try to use different numbers of clusters and passes.

7.7 Modify `createClusters` so that the outer loop uses indefinite iteration. The loop should exit when the clusters no longer change.

7.8 The previous exercise could create an infinite loop if the clusters are oscillating. Add another condition to the loop to make sure that no more than `maxRepeats` number of iterations occur.

7.9 Implement a different distance method and use it to cluster the exam data. Do you see any changes in the clusters?

7.5   Implementing Cluster Analysis: Earthquakes

We started this chapter by considering real data describing earthquakes that occurred during a two-week period. Given the raw data, it might be difficult to see any type of pattern or similarity. However, if we extend our cluster analysis technique from the previous section, we might discover some interesting results.

7.5.1   File Processing

Our first problem will be to find a way to process and store the data contained in the data file so that we can use it in our clustering algorithm. Recall that each line of the file looks like the following:

```
3.7 2006/10/18 05:34:15 62.326 -151.224 85.9 CENTRAL ALASKA
```

This entry describes an earthquake of magnitude 3.7 that occurred at a depth of 85.9 kilometers in the general region of Central Alaska. The exact longitude and latitude as well as time are also provided.

For this example we deploy our cluster analysis algorithm using the location data. In other words, we would like to see if there are clusters of earthquakes that occur in close proximity to one another. To do this, we need to understand how the location data is stored in the file and what it means.

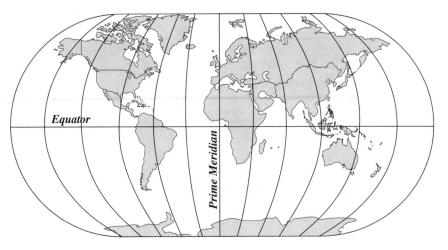

Figure 7.8 Longitude and latitude measurements on the globe

Each earthquake is described by providing its exact location as a pair of values called the longitude and latitude. Figure 7.8 shows how these values map to locations on the globe. The latitude values run north–south with zero latitude located at the equator. The north pole of the globe is +90 and the south pole is −90.

Likewise, the longitude values run west–east, with the zero being the prime meridian, an imaginary line that runs north–south through Greenwich, England. For latitudes in the far west the measurement is −180 and the far east measurement is +180 since the globe is assumed to be a full 360 degree circle on the equator.

Note that our data points now have two dimensions—namely, a latitude and a longitude. Recall however that our previous description of the algorithm will still work since we went to the trouble of making the `euclidD` function work with multidimensional data points.

We can now work on extracting the necessary data from the file. Looking at the example line again shows us that there are seven distinct pieces of data for each earthquake. Also, after looking closer, we can see that each item is separated by a blank with the exception of the name, which can have many words. We can easily extract the data values we want by splitting the input line into a list of items and then index the items appropriately, as shown in Session 7.2.

```
>>> aline
' 3.7 2006/10/18 05:34:15 62.326 -151.224 85.9 CENTRAL ALASKA'
>>> items = aline.split()
>>> items
['3.7', '2006/10/18', '05:34:15', '62.326', '-151.224', '85.9',
 'CENTRAL', 'ALASKA']
>>> items[3]
'62.326'
>>> items[4]
'-151.224'
>>> items[6:]
['CENTRAL', 'ALASKA']
>>>
```

Session 7.2 File processing for earthquake data

We can build the Python code using the framework from Session 7.2. After opening the file, we iterate through the lines, split each one, and then extract the data. Listing 7.11 shows a new implementation of `readFile`, which creates a data dictionary of two-dimensional data points.

```
1  def readFile(filename):
2      datafile = open(filename, "r")
3      datadict = {}
4      key = 0
5
6      for aline in datafile:
7          items = aline.split()
8          key = key + 1
9          lat = float(items[3])
10         lon = float(items[4])
11         datadict[key] = [lon,lat]
12
13     return datadict
```

Listing 7.11 Processing the earthquake data file

We are still using the key as a way to refer uniquely to each line of the file. In this case, the `datadict` dictionary associates the key with the longitude–latitude data point. Lines 9–10 extract the longitude and latitude data. Note that we need to convert these values into floating-point numbers.

Once we have our data points, we can use our `clusterAnalysis` function as follows: `clusterAnalysis("earthquakes.txt")`. Remember that we need to make decisions about how many clusters we want to create and how many iterations should be used. Unfortunately, when we run our program, the output, a fragment of which is shown below, is difficult to understand. The reason for this is that our simple output mechanism displays the contents of each cluster by showing the data points.

```
CLUSTER
[-177.81800000000001, -30.312999999999999]
[-178.768, -20.655999999999999]
[-177.83099999999999, -20.097999999999999]
[-176.92599999999999, -22.847000000000001]
[-121.491, -56.020000000000003]
[-176.048, -19.716000000000001]
[-175.98599999999999, -23.420000000000002]
[-175.851, -23.574999999999999]
[-175.869, -23.436]
[-176.03999999999999, -23.495000000000001]
. . .
```

7.5.2 Visualization

There is one more modification that will make our results much more interesting. Instead of printing the longitudes and latitudes in long lists, we will use **visualization** to plot the positions of the earthquakes on a map of the world and show the clusters as points on that map. This process of "visualizing" the data can be quite useful, especially if we are looking for hard-to-see relationships that may not be readily apparent from long lists of data. It is common to try to find some way to visualize the clusters.

As an example of what we are describing, consider Figure 7.9, where the earthquake data has been processed using six clusters. Each earthquake is shown as a point on the map. In addition, the clusters are colored to distinguish one from the other. It can be readily seen that there are definite relationships as to where these earthquakes are taking place (although you likely knew this already).

We can easily build this visualization by using the `turtle` module. The basic idea is to use the turtle to plot a colored "dot" at each earthquake location given by the longitude and latitude. The color will be dependent on the cluster to which the earthquake belongs. The challenging part is setting up the drawing window so that the map and the coordinates are consistent with our longitude and latitude values.

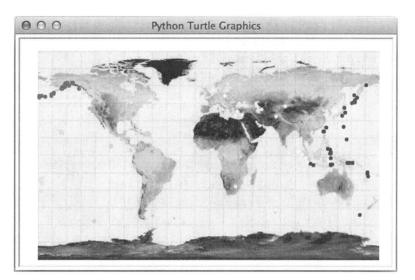

Figure 7.9 Plotting earthquakes to show clusters. Courtesy of Scientific Visualization Studio/NASA.

Listing 7.12 shows a function to generate clusters and visualize them. To start, we make use of the `readFile`, `createCentroids`, and `createClusters` functions as we did previously. Once the clusters have been computed we create a Turtle called `quakeT` using the `turtle` constructor. Looking again at Figure 7.9, you can see that the background of the turtle drawing window contains an image of the world. This image, stored in a file named `worldmap.gif`, is 448 pixels wide by 266 pixels high. By using the `bgpic` method (line 8), we can set the image to be the background picture for the drawing window. Since we want the drawing window to include only the area of the map, we can then use the `screensize` method (line 9) to reset the width and height of the drawing window.

From our previous discussion about longitude and latitude, we know that the lower-left corner of the map should be location $(-180, -90)$ and the upper-right corner should be $(180, 90)$. We can "remap" our plotting by realizing that the current lower-left corner is $(-224, -133)$ and the upper-right corner is $(224, 133)$. That means we simply need to compute multiplication factors for the width and the height (`wFactor` and `hFactor` in lines 11 and 12) and use them when we plot the longitude and latitude (line 24).

The next lines turn off the locational marker for the turtle and raise the tail so that lines are not drawn as the turtle is moved from location to location. Finally, line 17 creates a list of colors that will be used to distinguish each cluster—**red** for the first cluster, **green** for the second, and so on.

We can now show the contents of each cluster by iterating through the clusters and processing each earthquake in the cluster. Line 20 sets the tail color by using `clusterIndex` as

```
1  def visualizeQuakes(dataFile):
2      datadict = readFile(dataFile)
3      quakeCentroids = createCentroids(6, datadict)
4      clusters = createClusters(6, quakeCentroids, datadict, 7)
5
6      quakeT = turtle.Turtle()
7      quakeWin = turtle.Screen()
8      quakeWin.bgpic("worldmap.gif")
9      quakeWin.screensize(448,266)
10
11     wFactor = (quakeWin.screensize()[0]/2)/180
12     hFactor = (quakeWin.screensize()[1]/2)/90
13
14     quakeT.hideturtle()
15     quakeT.up()
16
17     colorlist = ["red","green","blue","orange","cyan","yellow"]
18
19     for clusterIndex in range(6):
20         quakeT.color(colorlist[clusterIndex])
21         for akey in clusters[clusterIndex]:
22             lon = datadict[akey][0]
23             lat = datadict[akey][1]
24             quakeT.goto(lon*wFactor,lat*hFactor)
25             quakeT.dot()
26     quakeWin.exitonclick()
```

Listing 7.12   Visualizing earthquake clusters

an index into the `colorlist`. For each earthquake in the cluster, we extract the longitude and latitude data from the `datadict` and use those two values as coordinates for the turtle. Once the turtle has been directed to the proper location, the `dot` method will plot a point using the current tail color. It should be noted that the number of colors in the `colorlist` must be at least as big as the number of clusters being created so that each cluster gets a unique color.

Exercises

7.10 Load and run the code for the `visualizeQuakes` function. How do your results compare with those in the book?

7.11 Try to change the number of clusters. Be sure to add more colors if you add more clusters.

7.12 Go to `http://earthquake.usgs.gov` and copy the latest 7 days of earthquake data. You may have to edit what you copy slightly in order to run `visualizeQuakes` or change the `readData` function to match.

7.13 Using the earthquake data, try to cluster the quakes by their depth instead of latitude and longitude. Now visualize the data on the map using this new clustering.

7.6   Cluster Analysis Shortcomings and Solutions

The basic K-means cluster analysis algorithm is easy to implement. However, there can be a number of problems that occur. We briefly describe a few of these here and leave the solutions for you as exercises.

Step 2 of our algorithm required that we pick k data points to serve as the initial centroids. Our solution to this was to use a random selection. This meant that two runs of the program could produce different results. It seems likely that by choosing the centroids in a more intentional manner we can impact the way that the clusters are ultimately constructed. This could be based either on user input or on data analysis.

It is possible that clusters can become empty as the iteration process continues. In our implementation, once a cluster becomes empty there is no way for it to be repopulated since it no longer has a centroid. When a cluster becomes empty, some method might be employed to create a new centroid so that data points can be added in the next iteration. Of course, it is always possible to leave the cluster empty and produce fewer clusters than originally specified as would happen in our implementation.

Sometimes a cluster can get too large or can encompass data points that are seemingly not related. This can happen when there are data points in the data set that are clearly different from the rest (sometimes referred to as *outliers*). When an outlier is found, it may be possible to provide some special processing so as to create an additional cluster, or to exclude it from any cluster thereby nullifying the impact the outlier might have on the centroid calculations.

Exercises

7.14 Implement a solution to the empty cluster problem.

7.15 Implement a solution for duplicate data values. This could happen if you have two exam scores that are identical but belong to different people.

7.16 Implement an alternative to random centroid selection where the user has some say in the process.

7.17 Implement an alternative to random centroid selection where some simple data analysis is done to try and pick the "best" centroid values.

7.18 Implement a function to find and eliminate outliers in the data set.

7.7   Summary

In this chapter we implemented the K-means algorithm—a simple and easy to implement cluster analysis technique that is vulnerable to problems in some cases. It can be applied to a wide variety of application domains and performs in a fairly efficient manner. There do exist other techniques for cluster analysis, and we urge you to consider some of them for comparison purposes.

As part of the implementation, we revisited the notion of iteration and presented a much more detailed view of the `while` statement. We utilized lists—more specifically parallel lists—and dictionaries as a means of organizing our data. Finally, we created a visualization for our cluster analysis results.

Key Terms

centroid	condition	indefinite iteration	visualization
change of state	data mining	infinite loop	
cluster analysis	definite iteration	initialization	
clusters	Euclidian distance	K-means algorithm	

Python Keywords

for	range	while
open	readline	

Bibliography

[qua]   U.S. Geological Survey. 2008. Retrieved from: http://earthquake.usgs.gov/.

[TSK06] Pang-Ning Tan, Michael Steinbach, and Vipin Kumar. *Introduction to Data Mining.* Addison-Wesley, 2006.

Programming Exercises

7.1 Find another data set that interests you and try to use the clustering techniques described in this chapter on that data. Possibilities include sports statistics, weather data, and medical data.

7.2 Research other cluster analysis algorithms and implement them on the data from this chapter. How do the results differ?

CHAPTER 8

Cryptanalysis

8.1 Objectives

- To understand more advanced examples of using a dictionary in Python
- To understand more advanced examples of using lists in Python
- To use pattern matching with regular expressions
- To learn how simple programs can help you solve more advanced problems

8.2 Introduction

In "Codes and Other Secrets" (Chapter 3) we studied several algorithms for encrypting secret messages. One of the most secure algorithms for encryption today is called RSA, named after the authors Ron Rivest, Adi Shamir, and Leonard Adleman. RSA is used by your web browser when you make a secure connection to your bank and when you shop online at your favorite store. Obviously, any encryption technique that is widely used for such sensitive data will be the target of many attacks. If someone learned how to break RSA, they could easily steal many bank account numbers and passwords.

In this chapter we look at the topic of **cryptanalysis**—the field of code breaking. Of course, the study of breaking codes is as old as the field of making codes. In fact, some of the first computer scientists were deeply involved in cryptanalysis. Charles Babbage, the designer of the difference engine, was working on breaking the Vignère cipher we coded in

"Codes and Other Secrets" (Chapter 3). Alan Turing, creator of the Turing Test for artificial intelligence and the Turing Machine, is responsible for breaking the German Enigma cipher during World War II.

Breaking advanced codes by brute force is an interesting exercise for people with access to supercomputers or who want to investigate distributed computing. The rail fence cipher introduced in "Codes and Other Secrets" (Chapter 3) can be easily broken using a brute force approach on any computer. **Brute force** simply means to try all possibilities. However, many beginning computer science students are reluctant to try a brute force approach to anything, convincing themselves that "there must be a better way." In fact, many times a brute force solution is appropriate simply because it takes advantage of the computer's ability to make millions of calculations very quickly.

As a problem-solving challenge, we will see that there are more interesting ways to attack the codes we developed in "Codes and Other Secrets" (Chapter 3). In particular, we will see in this chapter some examples of short Python programs that can enhance our human abilities for problem solving. Just as we use a calculator to solve complex math problems, short Python programs can help us solve other complex problems.

We start this chapter with a simple brute force attack on the rail fence cipher. Next we show how to use frequency analysis to crack the substitution cipher. Finally, we see that frequency analysis can also be used to crack the Vignère cipher.

8.3   Cracking the Rail Fence

One of the programming problems in "Codes and Other Secrets" (Chapter 3) was to write a generalized version of the transposition cipher we described in Section 3.4, called the **rail fence cipher**. In this section we will look at a brute force technique to break this cipher. Let's begin by reviewing the procedure for the rail fence.

The key to the rail fence cipher is the number of rails used. When you know the number of rails, you encrypt the message by filling the rails top to bottom and left to right. For example, let's suppose we want to encrypt the message "new ipod coming tomorrow" using three rails.

rail 1	n		o	c	i		m	r
rail 2	e	i	d	o	n	t	o	o
rail 3	w	p		m	g	o	r	w

Once we have constructed the rails, we create a new string for each rail by concatenating the letters in the rail from left to right, then we concatenate the rails from top to bottom. This gives us the message "n oci mreidontoowp mgorw".

Cryptanalysts intercepting this message may know that the message was encrypted using the rail fence cipher, but they will not know how many rails were used. A brute force way to decrypt this message is to try decrypting the message using 2 rails, 3 rails, 4 rails and so on until we find a message that makes sense.

Assuming that we have written the function `railDecrypt` (see section 8.3.3), we might use a simple *for* loop to try all possible different numbers of rails. Session 8.1 shows our first attempt at a brute force decryption.

```
for i in range(1,len(cipherText)+1):
    print(railDecrypt(cipherText,i))

['n', 'oci', 'mreidontoowp', 'mgorw']
['nn', 'toocoiw', 'pm', 'rmegiodrow']
['new', 'ipod', 'coming', 'tomorrow']
['nmn', 'rtmoeogciooidwr', 'opw']
['nienw', 'itpomdo', 'croom']
['nienwg', 'itpoomdo', 'rcroomw']
['ncmino', 'irdtwmo', 'eoopg']
['ncmino', 'o', 'irdtwmro', 'eoopgw']
['noimednow', 'c', 'riotop']
['noimednow', 'c', 'riotopm']
['noimednow', 'g', 'c', 'riotopmo']
['noimednow', 'gr', 'c', 'riotopmow']
['n', 'oci', 'mreidon']
['n', 'oci', 'mreidont']
['n', 'oci', 'mreidonto']
['n', 'oci', 'mreidontoo']
```

Session 8.1   Brute force decryptions of the rail fence cipher (*continues*)

```
['n', 'oci', 'mreidontoow']
['n', 'oci', 'mreidontoowp']
['n', 'oci', 'mreidontoowp']
['n', 'oci', 'mreidontoowp', 'm']
['n', 'oci', 'mreidontoowp', 'mg']
['n', 'oci', 'mreidontoowp', 'mgo']
['n', 'oci', 'mreidontoowp', 'mgor']
['n', 'oci', 'mreidontoowp', 'mgorw']
```

Session 8.1   Brute force decryptions of the rail fence cipher (*continued*)

8.3.1   Checking Our Work with a Dictionary

As you can see from Session 8.1 the problem with the brute force approach is that if the ciphertext is quite long there may be many lines of gibberish to scan through before finding the one message that is correct. One way we can improve this situation is to use a `dictionary` both literally and in the Python sense. You can see that our `railDecrypt` function returns a list of strings. Suppose that we checked each string against a dictionary to see if it was gibberish or a real word. A list of strings with a high percentage that appear in the dictionary is more likely to represent a real message than a list of strings with a low percentage.

In our case we do not need a dictionary that includes definitions. All we need is a file that contains numerous real words. Many of these lists of words are freely available on the Internet. We will refer to one such list stored in a file called `wordlist.txt`.

The wordlist file contains 41,238 English words, with one word on each line. To make looking up words easy, we will load this file into a Python dictionary. Listing 8.1 is an example of a function that reads a file of words and returns a Python dictionary containing all the words in the file.

Since we are not storing a useful value along with the key, one question you might ask is "why use a dictionary?" The answer is speed. Suppose you rewrote the `createWordDict` function to be `createWordList`, so that `createWordList` returned a list of words rather than a dictionary. We can still check whether a word was in our wordlist with the Python statement `if w in wordList:`. If you checked the amount of time Python needed to decide whether a word was in the list, you would see that, on average, using a dictionary is 2,500

```
1  def createWordDict(dname):
2      myDict = {}
3      myFile = open(dname, 'r')
4      for line in myFile:
5          myDict[line[:-1]] = True
6      return myDict
```

Listing 8.1   Loading words from a file into a dictionary

times faster than using a list. One disadvantage to using the dictionary is that there is some wasted space since we do not have any use for the value that goes with each key. Python actually provides a data type called a **set** that behaves like a dictionary but stores only the keys.

Exercises

8.1 Write a createWordList function to create a list of words from the wordlist file.

8.2 Write a createWordSet function to create a set of words from the wordlist file.

8.3 Devise an experiment to measure performance of createWordList, createWordSet, and createWordDictionary. You can use the time module with the function time.time to get the current clock time, which may be accurate to several milliseconds. Getting the clock time before you start a task and after you complete a task allows you to estimate how long the task takes.

8.3.2   A Brute Force Solution

Let's return to the main theme of using brute force to crack the rail fence cipher. We can now count the number of decrypted words that are found in the dictionary. We can improve our algorithm by remembering which rail size had the largest number of recognizable words. After we have tried out all possible rail sizes, we can simply look at the message with the most correct words. Note that we should recognize that no list of words is likely to contain every word in our message.

Listing 8.2 shows a complete solution for breaking the rail fence cipher. On line 9 we begin a loop that iterates over all the words returned by **railDecrypt**. If a word is in the dictionary of known words, we increment the **goodCount** by one. By now you will recognize this pattern as the accumulator pattern. On lines 12–14 we use another common pattern. We might call this the **minmax pattern**. When the current decrypted word list contains more known words than any of the previous decryptions, we remember it by setting `maxGoodSoFar` to the number of real words. The `if` statement on line 12 checks to see if the latest `goodCount` is greater than the largest known `goodCount`, called `maxGoodSoFar`. In addition, we remember the best version of the message so far by assigning it the name `bestGuess`.

The assignment statement on line 14 is a good one to look at closely. The expression `" ".join(words)` is a very useful combination of strings and lists. In fact, you can think of it as the opposite of the split function. In this example, the `join` method glues together all of the strings in the list `words` separating them using the space character. Note that you can join the words together using any (and as many) characters as you want. If you wanted to separate the words with two dashes, you would simply change the call to `"--".join(words)`.

```
1  def railBreak(cipherText):
2      wordDict = createWordDict('wordlist.txt')
3      cipherLen = len(cipherText)
4      maxGoodSoFar = 0
5      bestGuess = "No words found in dictionary"
6      for i in range(1,cipherLen+1):
7          words = railDecrypt(cipherText,i)
8          goodCount = 0
9          for w in words:
10             if w in wordDict:
11                 goodCount = goodCount + 1
12         if goodCount > maxGoodSoFar:
13             maxGoodSoFar = goodCount
14             bestGuess = " ".join(words)
15     return bestGuess
```

Listing 8.2   A brute force algorithm for breaking the rail fence cipher

Exercises

8.4 Given the list of words `['the', 'quick', 'brown', 'fox']` use the `join` method on the following separator strings: `" "`, `':'`, `","`, `"--"`.

8.5 Using the `railDecrypt` function from Listing 8.3, run the `railBreak` function from Listing 8.2 on the cipher text "n oci mreidontoowp mgorw".

8.6 Use the rail fence encryption function to encrypt your own message. Give the cipher-text to a partner to decrypt.

8.7 Find a different word list on the Internet to use with the `railBreak` function. Compare the values of `maxGoodSoFar` for different word lists on the same ciphertext message.

8.3.3   A Rail Fence Decryption Algorithm

It is now time to write the `railDecrypt` function we have been using in the previous sections. The key to the rail decrypt algorithm is to remember how the message was put together in the first place. With that set of steps in mind, the `railDecrypt` function will simply undo the original operation. Let's go back to our original example and examine the encrypted string ("n oci mreidontoowp mgorw") a bit more carefully. We know that in this case we used three rails. We also know that because the string is 24 characters long each rail was 24 ÷ 3 or 8 characters. Using the fact that we have three rails and each rail is 8 characters long, we know that characters 0, 0+8, and 0 + 2*8 are the first characters of each row and therefore are the first three letters of the decrypted message. As you can see in Table 8.1, Character 0 is `'n'`, character 8 is `'e'`, and character 16 is `'w'`. To determine the next three characters of the message we shift each of those three positions 1 to the right. Shifting to the right gives us 1, 1 + 8, and 1 + 2 * 8. This gives us the next three characters of `' '`, `'i'`, and `'p'`.

0	1	2	3	4	5	6	7	8	9	10	11	12	13	14	15	16	17	18	19	20	21	22	23	24
n		o	c	i		m	r	e	i	d	o	n	t	o	o	w	p		m	g	o	r	w	

Table 8.1   Cipher text with character indices.

The method we used for finding the first six characters in the decrypted message is an example of something the computer does for us all the time. That is, it translates the coordinates for data stored in tabular form into linear form. The memory in the computer is a one-dimensional structure. So, if we want to store a two-dimensional table in the computer's memory, we need to map from the row, column coordinates corresponding to a cell in the table to a location in memory. In fact there are two ways to do the mapping. One way is called **row major storage** and the second is called **column major storage**. Row major storage is most often used.

Table 8.2 illustrates how 18 contiguous memory locations would be organized using both row major and column major storage.

Row major storage takes the first row of the table and stores all the values on that row one after the other, followed by the second row and the third and so on. Column major

1	2	3	4	5	6
7	8	9	10	11	12
13	14	15	16	17	18

Row major storage

1	4	7	10	13	16
2	5	8	11	14	17
3	6	9	12	15	18

Column major storage

Table 8.2   Examples of row and column major storage

storage takes the first column and stores all the values in that column one after another, followed by the second column and the third column and so on. The question is how do you compute the position in memory for any one row–column value?

For row major storage, the answer is a generalization of the pattern we started when figuring out how to decode our secret message. For a given row and column, we find the value by using the formula

$$position = column + row \cdot rowLength$$

In Listing 8.3 you can see this formula in use on line 6 as part of the **railDecrypt** function.

Let's look at the entire **railDecrypt** function. The first thing to notice is that the ciphertext and the number of rails are both parameters passed to the **railDecrypt** function. The nested *for* loops in lines 4–7 act as if you are accessing the characters of the message in the original two-dimensional table format. The calculation on line 7 allows us to figure out the index into the one-dimensional string.

```
1  def railDecrypt(cipherText,numRails):
2      railLen = len(cipherText) // numRails
3      solution = ''
4      for col in range(railLen):
5          for rail in range(numRails):
6              nextLetter = (col + rail * railLen)
7              solution = solution + cipherText[nextLetter]
8      return solution.split()
```

Listing 8.3   Decrypting the rail fence cipher

As a final note, if you have not already written the **railEncrypt** function as described in "Codes and Other Secrets" (Chapter 3), you might think of the rail encrypt function as a transformation of the original plaintext string, using a column major storage scheme. The equation for finding the memory location in a column major storage scheme is

$$position = row + column \cdot numRows$$

The column major calculation allows you to treat the plaintext string as if it were a table of characters stored in column major format. Iterating over the string column by column and using the accumulator pattern gives you the ciphertext string you have just decoded.

Exercises

8.8 Write the `railEncrypt` function using the column major access pattern just described.

8.9 Now that you have seen the details of the `railDecrypt` function you can make it smarter in two ways:

(a) You do not need to check cases where the number of rails is greater than the message length divided by two. Can you explain why?

(b) You only need to check cases where the number of rails evenly divides the total message length. Can you explain why?

8.4   Cracking the Substitution Cipher

The substitution cipher is much harder to crack than the rail fence cipher. As we mentioned previously, there are 26! or roughly 4×10^{26} different possible arrangements of the alphabet that could be used as a key. Clearly the brute force strategy for finding the key would take an extremely long time. However, the substitution cipher does have a fatal flaw that we can exploit.

The flaw is that the substitution cipher allows us to take advantage of patterns in the English language that help us deduce letters in the key. The first pattern we will exploit is that some letters in the English language are much more popular than others. If we count the number of times each letter occurs in a document such as this book, or any other English language book, we would find that the letters *e, t, a, o,* and *i* are much more common than many other letters in the alphabet.

8.4.1   Letter Frequency

We can write our own program to calculate the frequency of letters. There are two ways we could report on letter frequency. One simple way would be to count the total number of occurrences of each letter. However, the total would change depending on the size of the document. A better way is to report the percentage. That is the total count for each letter divided by the total number of letters. In "A Nest of Snakes" (Chapter 4), you used Python

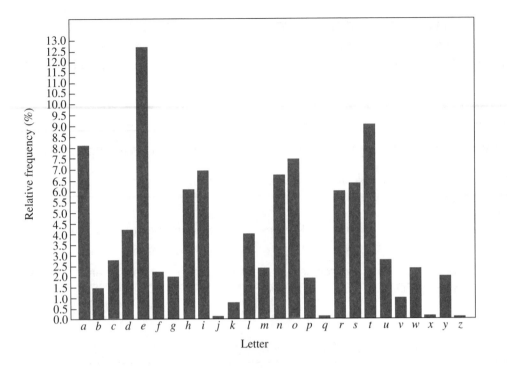

Figure 8.1   Relative letter frequencies

to explore other interesting statistics in detail. We will keep our analysis very simple in this chapter. Figure 8.1 shows a graph of the results we are looking for in our letter frequency program.

To generate the data for the graph in Figure 8.1, we will write a Python function that takes a string, `text`, as a parameter. For each letter in the alphabet, the function prints out the number of times each letter occurred in `text` and the percentage of the total characters in `text` that the count represents. Counting the letters is easy since we can use the `count` method of the string class. The trickier part of this exercise is that in order to get an accurate percentage we need to ignore nonletter characters like spaces, and punctuation marks and numbers.

One effective way to ignore nonletter characters is to remove them from the string before we start counting. We need a way to remove all the nonletter characters from `text`. Earlier, we wrote a function that can remove characters from a string called `removeMatches`. The problem is we do not have a handy string full of all the nonletter characters, but we can create one. Session 8.2 shows how we can make a string of *nonLetters* by first removing all the *letters* from the string we want to count. The text string at the end of the session is ready for analysis by our counting function.

```
>>> text = 'Are there 25, 26, or 27 non-letters to remove?'
>>> text = text.lower()
>>> text
'are there 25, 26, or 27 non-letters to remove?'
>>> nonLetters = removeMatches(text,'abcdefghijklmnopqrstuvwxyz')
>>> nonLetters
'   25, 26,27 - ?'
>>> text = removeMatches(text,nonLetters)
>>> text
'arethereornonletterstoremove'
>>>
```

Session 8.2   Demonstrating `removeMatches`

To count all the letters of the alphabet, we will use the dictionary technique we introduced in "A Nest of Snakes" (Chapter 4) to keep track of the frequency of numbers. The key for each entry in the dictionary is the letter. To build our dictionary, we will simply iterate over all the characters in a string. The dictionary will initially keep track of the number of times each character occurs in the string. After all the counts have been accumulated, we will make a second pass through the dictionary and convert the counts into percentages. Listing 8.4 shows the Python code for the letter-counting function.

```
1  def letterFrequency(text):
2      text = text.lower()
3      nonletters = removeMatches(text,'abcdefghijklmnopqrstuvwxyz')
4      nonletters = removeDupes(nonletters)
5      text = removeMatches(text,nonletters)
6      lcount = {}
7      total = len(text)
8      for ch in text:
9          lcount[ch] = lcount.get(ch,0) + 1
10     for ch in lcount:
11         lcount[ch] = lcount[ch] / total
12     return lcount
```

Listing 8.4   Counting the frequency of each letter in the alphabet

Let's look at a session where we calculate the text frequencies of the letters in H. G. Wells's *War of the Worlds*, a novel that is free from copyright and freely downloadable from project Gutenberg (`http://www.gutenberg.org`). We will use the `read` method to read in the entire file from disk as one string, then use our `letterFrequency` function to compute the relative frequencies of each letter. Session 8.3 demonstrates the use of `letterFrequency`.

```
>>> wells = open('wells.txt')
>>> text = wells.read()
>>> lf = letterFrequency(text)
>>> lf
{'a': 0.083323852323795439,
 'b': 0.015227686444052563,
 'c': 0.024048580692872176,
 'd': 0.047549633084930883,
 'e': 0.12521332271460264,
 'f': 0.02288241651971102,
 'g': 0.024187240457363899,
 'h': 0.060299220661015986,
 'i': 0.067993059901018255,
 'j': 0.00097417373001877237,
 'k': 0.0076582854542351668,
 'l': 0.037996330849308833,
 'm': 0.025634279538085215,
 'n': 0.072031969964161779,
 'o': 0.070976022526878665,
 'p': 0.018196427555606121,
 'q': 0.00067552192957506113,
 'r': 0.059904573639001084,
 's': 0.060178337789407815,
 't': 0.096688520393651514,
 'u': 0.026789777757551624,
 'v': 0.0087817850844757947,
 'w': 0.022974856362705499,
 'x': 0.0013865976449172308,
 'y': 0.018047101655384264,
 'z': 0.00038042550770806075}
```

Session 8.3   Unsorted letter frequency for *War of the Worlds*

Of course, it would be much more interesting to see the information sorted from most frequent letter to least frequent. Unfortunately, dictionaries are not guaranteed to be ordered in any particular way, so we will have to extract the information from the dictionary into a list and then sort the list. We can extract all the key value pairs from a dictionary using the `items` method along with the `list` function. For example, the first three elements in the list returned by `items` on our letter frequency dictionary are as follows:

```
>>> list(lf.items()) [:3]
[('a', 0.083323852323795439),
 ('b', 0.015227686444052563),
 ('c', 0.024048580692872176)]
```

The sort function provided by Python is extremely powerful. Let's see how we can use it to sort this list from the most frequently used letter to the least. The first question you might ask is how does the sort function know what value to use when it sorts this list? Remember, a list can contain *any* Python object, and so the sort function must be able to sort any kind of object. In this case the elements on our list are tuples, so the `sort` function defaults to using the first element of the tuple. Fortunately, the `sort` function takes some optional parameters that make it more flexible.

There are two optional parameters for the `sort` method: *key* and *reverse*. If we call `sort` with the optional parameter reverse set to `True`, the `sort` function will sort the list from largest to smallest instead of the other way around. You should try this for yourself on a simple list of integers such as x = `[3,7,4,9]`. Then call x.`sort(reverse = True)`. You will see that x is now sorted from highest to lowest.

The second optional parameter, `key` will allow us to write a function that takes one object as a parameter and returns a value from that object that we should use as the sort key for that object. For example, suppose we had a list of turtles and we wanted to sort the list according to the x coordinate of each turtle. In the case of our dictionary, we just want to write a function that can return the frequency number from a tuple. This is a very short two-line function, as shown in Listing 8.5.

```
1   def getFreq(t):
2       return t[1]
```

Listing 8.5   Returning the second value in a tuple

Using the `getFreq` method along with the *key* and *reverse* parameters, we can now sort our letter frequency dictionary just how we want it (see Session 8.4). It is worth repeating here that the `sort` method undergoes an **in-place sort**—that is, it modifies the list it is sorting. It does not create a new list, nor does the `sort` function return any value. A common mistake is to write a statement such as `myList = myList.sort()`. Try this for yourself, and you will see that unfortunately `myList` has been set to `None` rather than sorted.

```
>>> lfList = lf.items()
>>> lfList.sort(key=getFreq,reverse=True)
>>> for entry in lfList:
...         print("%s %5.3f" % entry)
e 0.125
t 0.097
a 0.083
n 0.072
o 0.071
i 0.068
h 0.060
s 0.060
r 0.060
d 0.048
l 0.038
u 0.027
m 0.026
g 0.024
c 0.024
w 0.023
f 0.023
p 0.018
y 0.018
b 0.015
v 0.009
k 0.008
x 0.001
j 0.001
q 0.001
z 0.000
```

Session 8.4   Sorted letter frequency from *War of the Worlds*

Exercises

8.10 Evaluate the following statements:

```
l1 = [4,5,3,9,1,6,7]
l1 = l1.sort()
```

What is the value of `l1` when you are done?

8.11 Write a function called `extractLetters` that simply keeps all the letter characters in a string. This function could be used in place of the two calls to `removeMatches`.

8.4.2 Ciphertext Frequency Analysis

Letter popularity is critical for breaking a substitution cipher. Because a substitution cipher makes a one-for-one letter substitution from the plaintext to the ciphertext, the most popular letter in the plaintext will also be the most popular letter in the ciphertext. This small amount of information is enough to begin breaking the encryption through **frequency analysis**.

Let's do a bit of cryptanalysis on the following paragraph.

> ul ilahvble jkhbevbt hk kul letl cs kul dvk kuhk kul kuvbt uhe ahel sci vkjlzs
> jkhivbt hk vkj jkihbtl hddlhihbwl hjkcbvjule wuvlszq hk vkj mbmjmhz juhdl hbe
> wczcmi hbe evazq dliwlvnvbt lnlb kulb jcal lnvelbwl cs eljvtb vb vkj hiivnhz kul
> lhizq acibvbt ohj ocbelismzzq jkvzz hbe kul jmb xmjk wzlhivbt kul dvbl killj
> kcohiej olqgivetl ohj hzilheq ohia ul eve bck ilalagli ulhivbt hbq gviej kuhk
> acibvbt kulil ohj wlikhvbzq bc gillrl jkviivbt hbe kul cbzq jcmbej olil kul shvbk
> acnlalbkj sica ovkuvb kul wvbeliq wqzvbeli ul ohj hzz hzcbl cb kul wcaacb

The first step in breaking this code is to apply our letter frequency analysis to the encrypted text. The results of this are shown in Table 8.3.

One approach would be to hope that there is an exact match in the frequencies of letters between the plaintext sample and the ciphertext. If this were the case, we could figure out the key by matching the letters in order of their popularity: $e \leftrightarrow l$, $t \leftrightarrow b$, $a \leftrightarrow k$, $n \leftrightarrow h$,

Frequency	Letter	Frequency	Letter
0.134	l	0.024	q
0.095	b	0.022	w
0.086	k	0.022	o
0.086	h	0.018	s
0.077	v	0.018	m
0.070	i	0.013	d
0.059	j	0.011	n
0.053	u	0.009	g
0.051	e	0.002	x
0.046	c	0.002	r
0.042	z	0.000	y
0.031	a	0.000	p
0.029	t	0.000	f

Table 8.3   Relative frequency of letters in the ciphertext

and so on. Using these letter substitutions, the first line of ciphertext would be decrypted as follows: "se ieunoter hantrotm na ase erme df ase yoa asna ase asotm snr unre fdi oahelf haniotm na oah haintme." Clearly a blind mapping is not the answer.

8.4.3   Letter Pair Analysis

Because there is bound to be some variation in the frequency of letters—particularly in smaller samples—we have to try to match the letters with a bit more flexibility. Let's begin by assuming that the four most popular plaintext letters will match the four most popular ciphertext letters in some order. For example, a ciphertext 'l' will be either 'e', 't', 'n', or 'a'. Likewise the ciphertext letters 'b', 'k', and 'h' will match one of 'e', 't', 'n', or 'a'.

Notice that of the four letters we are trying to identify, two are vowels and two are consonants. One way that we can statistically tell the difference between a vowel and a consonant is to notice that vowels frequently appear before or after almost any other letter in the alphabet. Consonants typically have a small number of letters that they appear next to.

This suggests that we can write a variation of our letter frequency function to figure out how frequently each letter appears next to another.

Although this may seem like a daunting task, it is important to understand that if we start with our basic letter frequency function, we are already a long way toward our goal. Let's look at the additional problems we need to solve:

1. Rather than count the number of times each letter occurs, we want to keep a list of neighboring letters. The list will contain all the letters that appear before or after the letter in question.

2. The output of the function will be a dictionary that contains a key for each letter of the alphabet and a list of neighboring letters.

3. We need to be careful about how we account for nonletters in our counting. If we simply delete nonletters as we did previously, we will end up creating false neighbors.

Once again we want to keep track of some information that is indexed by a letter. This suggests that we will use a dictionary again. The difference is that we need to keep track of something more complicated than a simple number. The good news is that dictionaries can store any Python object as a value. To keep track of a character's neighbors, we use that character as the key and store a list of neighboring characters as the value. For example, if our dictionary is called `myNeighbors`, then `myNeighbors['q']` will evaluate to the list of letters that occur next to `'q'`. For example in one large text the letter `'q'` appears next to the letters `['u', 'e', 'o', 's', 'n', 'd', 'i', 'h', 'a', 'c']`.

Once we know that we will use a list for keeping track of the neighbors, the next problem is easy to solve. We can use the `len` function to find the length of our list of neighbors after we have processed all the characters in the string.

An outline of our new function is as follows:

1. Create an empty dictionary `nbDict`.

2. Loop over all the characters in a string.

   (a) If the current character is not in `nbDict`, add an empty list. Otherwise, retrieve the list of neighbors already stored.

   (b) Add the next character as a neighbor of the current character.

(c) If the next character is not in **nbDict**, add an empty list. Otherwise retrieve the list of neighbors already stored.

(d) Add the current character as a neighbor of the next character.

3. Loop over all the keys of the dictionary and replace the list with the length of the list.

4. Return the dictionary

There are a couple of ideas in the overview worth considering. First, notice that when we are looking at the character at index **i** in the character string we add the character at index **i + 1** as a neighbor. At the same time, we add the character at index **i** as a neighbor of the character at index **i + 1**. In this way we can ensure that as we move through the list we are getting the neighboring characters that occur both before and after each character.

Second, we need to be careful about which characters we add to the list of neighbors. If a letter is already on the neighbor list, we do not want to add it again. In addition, since we do not wish to count spaces, punctuation marks, numbers, or any other nonletter as neighbors, we will ignore those characters. The easiest way to make sure that we are counting only letters is to check if the character is one of the 26 letters of the alphabet. To do this, we write a little function that takes two parameters: a character and a list. Let's call this function **maybeAdd**. Listing 8.6 shows the complete function to add a character to a list under the conditions described above.

```
def maybeAdd(ch,toList):
    if ch in 'abcdefghijklmnopqrstuvwxyz' and ch not in toList:
        toList.append(ch)
```

Listing 8.6   Conditionally adding a character to a list

The **maybeAdd** function is a good example of a function that modifies one of its parameters. Notice that we are passing a list as a parameter but we are not returning a list. Session 8.5 shows the **maybeAdd** function in action.

```
>>> myList = []
>>> maybeAdd('a',myList)
>>> myList
 ['a']
>>> maybeAdd('-',myList)
>>> myList
 ['a']
>>> maybeAdd('b',myList)
>>> myList
 ['a', 'b']
>>> maybeAdd('a',myList)
>>> myList
 ['a', 'b']
```

Session 8.5   Testing the `maybeAdd` function

```
1    def neighborCount(text):
2        nbDict = {}
3        text = text.lower()
4        for i in range(len(text)-1):
5            nbList = nbDict.setdefault(text[i],[])
6            maybeAdd(text[i+1],nbList)
7            nbList = nbDict.setdefault(text[i+1],[])
8            maybeAdd(text[i],nbList)
9        for key in nbDict:
10           nbDict[key] = len(nbDict[key])
11       return nbDict
```

Listing 8.7   Creating a dictionary of neighbors

Listing 8.7 shows the complete `neighborCount` function. There are several interesting things to think about in the `neighborCount` function. First, we use the statement `for i in range(len(text)-1)` rather than iterating over each character in the string because we need to index the current character as well as the next character. We use `len(text)-1` because we consider the current character and the next character. If we simply used `len(text)`, we would eventually get an index out of range error.

Another statement to look at carefully is `nbList = nbDict.setdefault(text[i],[])`. The `setdefault` method first checks to see if the key is in the dictionary. If it is not, it adds a default value and returns a reference to the default value. This statement is a shortcut for the Python code shown in Listing 8.8.

```
1    nbList = nbDict.get(text[i])
2    if nbList == None:
3        nbDict[text[i]] = []
4        nbList = nbDict[text[i]]
```

Listing 8.8   Adding a new default value to a dictionary

This pattern is quite common when using dictionaries. Using the `setdefault` method is a good idea because it reduces the amount of code you need to write and reduces your chances of making an error.

Now we will use the `neighborCount` function to continue our analysis of the ciphertext. Session 8.6 shows the `neighborCount` function in action. After building the dictionary `freqDict` we will print the number of neighbors for the common letters "e," "n," and "t."

```
>>> freqDict = neighborCount(text)

>>> for i in 'ent':
....        print(i, freqDict[i])
....
e 26
n 25
t 21
```

Session 8.6   Number of neighbors for e, n, and t

This session shows us that *e* appears next to 26 different letters, *n* appears next to 25 different letters, and *t* appears next to 21 different letters. We were hoping for a result that would allow us to easily differentiate between vowels and consonants. Unfortunately, this is not it.

In order for these counts to be more useful, we need a bit more detail. For example *e* probably appears frequently next to many different letters, whereas *n* or *t* appear next to some letters very frequently and other letters infrequently. We need to see the frequency with which different letters appear next to each other. What we need to build is a table like that shown in Table 8.4.

Let's improve `neighborCount` so we can produce a table of letter pair frequency counts. This may allow us to learn enough to make better guesses about which letters are vowels and which are consonants. The most important change we will make is to replace the list

	a	b	c	d	e	f	g	h	i	j	k	l	m	n	o	p	q	r	s	t	u	v	w	x	y	z
a	0	0	0	3	5	1	0	4	3	0	0	5	2	8	0	2	0	10	5	8	1	1	6	0	0	0
b	0	0	0	0	1	0	0	0	1	0	0	0	1	0	0	0	0	2	0	0	0	0	0	0	1	0
c	0	0	0	0	4	0	0	1	1	0	0	1	0	2	2	0	0	1	0	0	0	0	0	0	1	0
d	3	0	0	0	9	0	2	0	6	0	0	0	0	9	0	0	0	2	3	0	0	0	0	0	1	0
e	5	1	4	9	4	1	3	17	2	0	0	2	7	7	0	3	0	15	3	0	0	4	2	0	1	2
f	1	0	0	0	1	0	0	0	0	0	0	2	0	0	3	0	0	2	0	0	1	0	0	0	0	0
g	0	0	0	2	3	0	0	0	1	0	0	0	0	11	0	0	0	0	0	0	0	0	0	0	0	0
h	4	0	1	0	17	0	0	0	3	0	0	0	0	0	0	0	0	0	2	16	0	0	0	0	0	0
i	3	1	1	6	2	0	1	3	0	0	0	2	1	20	0	2	0	8	2	8	0	4	1	0	0	0
j	0	0	0	0	0	0	0	0	0	0	0	0	0	0	0	0	0	0	0	0	1	0	0	0	0	0
k	0	0	0	0	0	0	0	0	0	0	0	0	0	0	0	0	0	0	0	0	0	0	0	0	0	0
l	5	0	1	0	2	2	0	0	2	0	0	6	1	2	3	0	0	2	0	0	1	0	0	0	7	0
m	2	1	0	0	7	0	0	0	1	0	0	1	2	0	7	0	0	1	0	0	0	0	0	0	0	0
n	8	0	2	9	7	0	11	0	20	0	0	2	0	0	8	0	0	2	0	2	4	0	0	0	1	0
o	0	0	2	0	0	3	0	0	0	0	0	3	7	8	0	0	0	4	2	3	2	1	2	0	0	0
p	2	0	0	0	3	0	0	0	2	0	0	0	0	0	2	0	0	0	0	0	0	0	0	0	0	0
q	0	0	0	0	0	0	0	0	0	0	0	0	0	0	0	0	0	0	0	0	0	0	0	0	0	0
r	10	2	1	2	15	2	0	0	8	0	0	2	1	2	4	0	0	4	0	3	1	0	0	0	1	0
s	5	0	0	3	3	0	0	2	2	0	0	0	0	0	2	0	0	0	0	12	4	0	0	0	0	0
t	8	0	0	0	0	0	0	16	8	0	0	0	0	2	3	0	0	3	12	0	0	0	0	0	0	0
u	1	0	0	0	0	1	0	0	0	1	0	1	0	4	2	0	0	1	4	0	0	0	0	0	0	0
v	1	0	0	0	4	0	0	0	4	0	0	0	0	0	1	0	0	0	0	0	0	0	0	0	0	0
w	6	0	0	0	2	0	0	0	1	0	0	0	0	0	2	0	0	0	0	0	0	0	0	0	0	0
x	0	0	0	0	0	0	0	0	0	0	0	0	0	0	0	0	0	0	0	0	0	0	0	0	0	0
y	0	1	1	1	1	0	0	0	0	0	0	7	0	1	0	0	0	1	0	0	0	0	0	0	0	0
z	0	0	0	0	2	0	0	0	0	0	0	0	0	0	0	0	0	0	0	0	0	0	0	0	0	0

Table 8.4 Letter pair frequency analysis for one paragraph

of letters with a dictionary so that we can keep a count for each neighboring letter. This will create a dictionary of dictionaries. For example d['a']['x'] tells us the number of times the letters 'a' and 'x' appear next to each other.

The necessary modifications are actually quite simple. In the neighborCount function we need to change only the calls to setdefault to create a dictionary instead of an empty list.

We do this by changing [] to { }

The change occurs in the `maybeAdd` function. This function is different because it is now updating a count of each neighboring letter in a dictionary rather than simply appending a letter to a list. Listing 8.9 shows the new version of `maybeAdd`. It is worth noting that line 3 is another example of the accumulator pattern that you have seen in so many different places already. Once again the `setdefault` function simplifies the implementation of this pattern.

```
1    def maybeAdd(ch,toDict):
2        if ch in 'abcdefghijklmnopqrstuvwxyz':
3            toDict[ch] = toDict.setdefault(ch,0) + 1
```

Listing 8.9   New `addMaybe` function for a dictionary of dictionaries

Session 8.7 shows the result of calling the `neighborCount` function on the entire text. Let's look at what we can learn about the letters *e*, *n*, and *t*. This data shows us that *e* appears more frequently next to a very large number of letters. In addition, although both *n* and *t* appear next to many different letters, they do so much less frequently. Also note that *e* appears least frequently next to other vowels and a couple of consonants like *z* and *j*.

```
>>> d = neighborCount(text)
>>> print d['e']
{'a': 1924, 'c': 1655, 'b': 1261, 'e': 2616, 'd': 4815, 'g': 1007, 'f': 656,
 'i': 903, 'h': 8586, 'k': 704, 'j': 143, 'm': 2552, 'l': 2898, 'o': 230,
 'n': 4547, 'q': 26, 'p': 1328, 's': 4134, 'r': 8258, 'u': 167, 't': 3149,
 'w': 1436, 'v': 2094, 'y': 798, 'x': 331, 'z': 70}

>>> print d['n']
{'a': 5198, 'c': 577, 'b': 108, 'e': 4547, 'd': 4030, 'g': 3181, 'f': 100,
 'i': 6671, 'h': 32, 'k': 341, 'j': 10, 'm': 33, 'l': 225, 'o': 3995,
 'n': 278, 'q': 7, 'p': 12, 's': 912, 'r': 375, 'u': 1246, 't': 1739,
 'w': 291, 'v': 65, 'y': 204, 'x': 6}

>>> print d['t']
{'a': 3821, 'c': 697, 'b': 34, 'e': 3149, 'd': 2, 'g': 29, 'f': 281,
 'i': 4506, 'h': 10393, 'm': 80, 'l': 587, 'o': 3144, 'n': 1739, 'p': 228,
 's': 3082, 'r': 1877, 'u': 1705, 't': 880, 'w': 217, 'y': 298, 'x': 84}
```

Session 8.7   Testing the `neighborCount` function

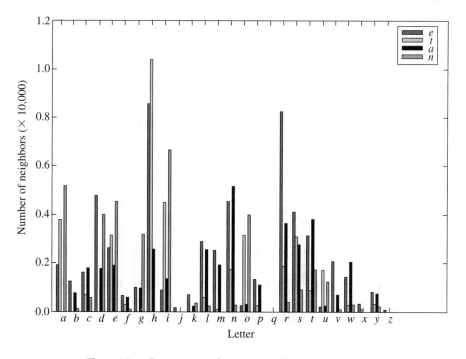

Figure 8.2   Letter pair frequencies for *a*, *e*, *n*, and *t*.

The data, as we have shown it in Session 8.7, is difficult to interpret. Although we can present the data as shown in Table 8.4, a better way to get an idea of how the letter pairs work out is to create a histogram. Figure 8.2 shows a histogram that compares the frequencies with which letters *a*, *e*, *n*, and *t* occur with all the other letters of the alphabet. This plot was produced with the `matplotlib` module of Python (see Exercise 1 in Chapter 4).

Compared with the output from Session 8.5, the histogram in Figure 8.2 shows us that *e* and *a* appear more frequently with more other letters. (Exercise 8.13 will ask you to create your own dictionary for the ciphertext paragraph. When you do, you will get frequency pairs for the letters *l*, *b*, *k*, and *h* that are the same as those shown in Table 8.5.)

The histogram in Figure 8.3 corresponds to Table 8.5. You can see that *l* and *h* are vowels since they appear more frequently with more letters. The letters *k* and *b* are consonants. But which of these ciphertext characters is *a* and which is *e*?

We have three pieces of evidence to make a good guess about the letter *l*. First, it was the most common letter in the ciphertext paragraph. Second, our pair analysis indicates that *l* is a vowel because it appears relatively frequently with many other letters. Finally, we can

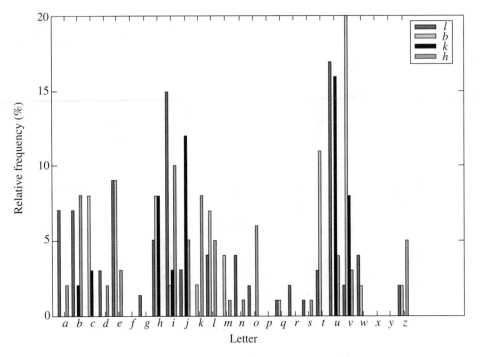

Figure 8.3   Letter frequency in the ciphertext

see that the letter l appears next to itself four times but the letter h never appears next to itself. Since it is much more common for e to appear next to itself than the letter a (unless you are writing a thesis about aardvarks), we can probably conclude that l maps to the e and h maps to a.

Now that we have two letter mappings in place let's plug them into the ciphertext and see if that gives us any clues that will help decrypt the letters b and k. We can use the Python string `replace` method to help us replace the ciphertext letters with the plaintext letters we have figured out. Session 8.8 shows how to replace the ciphertext l with E and h with A. From now on we will use uppercase for the decoded plaintext letters to make it clear which letters we have decoded and which we still need to work on.

	a	b	c	d	e	f	g	h	i	j	k	l	m	n	o	p	q	r	s	t	u	v	w	x	y	z
b	0	0	8	0	9	0	0	8	2	0	2	7	4	0	0	0	1	0	0	11	0	20	2	0	0	2
k	0	2	3	0	0	0	0	8	3	12	0	0	0	0	0	0	0	0	0	0	16	8	0	0	0	0
l	7	7	0	3	9	0	1	5	15	3	0	4	0	4	2	0	1	2	1	3	17	2	4	0	0	2
h	2	8	0	2	3	0	0	0	10	5	8	5	1	1	6	0	0	0	1	0	4	3	0	0	0	5

Table 8.5   Frequency pairs for the four most common ciphertext letters

```
>>> ciphertext = ciphertext.replace('l','E')

>>> ciphertext = ciphertext.replace('h','A')

>>> ciphertext
'uE iEaAvbEe jkAbevbt Ak kuE EetE cs kuE dvk kuAk kuE kuvbt
uAe aAeE sci vkjEzs jkAivbt Ak vkj jkiAbtE AddEAiAbwE AjkcbvjuEe
wuvEszq Ak vkj mbmjmAz juAdE Abe wczcmi Abe evazq dEiwEvnvbt EnEb kuEb
jcaE EnveEbwE cs eEjvtb vb vkj AiivnAz kuE EAizq acibvbt oAj
ocbeEismzzq jkvzz Abe kuE jmb xmjk wzEAivbt kuE dvbE kiEEj kcoAiej
oEqgivetE oAj AziEAeq oAiauE eve bck iEaEagEi uEAivbt Abq gviej kuAk
acibvbt kuEiE oAj wEikAvbzq bc giEErE jkviivbt Abe kuE cbzq jcmbej
oEiE kuE sAvbk acnEaEbkj sica ovkuvb kuE wvbeEiq wqzvbeEi uE oAj Azz
AzcbE cb kuE wcaacb'
```

Session 8.8   First character replacement

Exercises

8.12 Create a frequency histogram for the ciphertext paragraph.

8.13 Produce a table similar to Table 8.4.

8.4.4   Word Frequency Analysis

We have made some progress, but we still have a long way to go. Let's employ another cryptanalysis technique to help with the next step. This technique will look at the short words—namely, the words that are one, two, or three letters long.

An easy way to do this is to reorder the words in the ciphertext and sort them by their length. Remember that we said the `sort` function can accept a key function as a parameter. Listing 8.10 shows a Python function that accepts one word as a parameter and returns the length of the word. Session 8.9 shows how to use our `sortByLen` function and provides us with some interesting new clues.

```
1    def sortByLen (w)
2        return len(w)
```

Listing 8.10   Comparing two words by length

```
>>> cipherwords.sort(key=sortByLen)
>>> cipherWords
['uE', 'Ak', 'cs', 'Ak', 'Ak', 'cs', 'vb', 'uE', 'bc', 'uE', 'cb',
 'kuE', 'kuE', 'dvk', 'kuE', 'uAe', 'sci', 'vkj', 'vkj', 'Abe', 'Abe',
 'vkj', 'kuE', 'oAj', 'Abe', 'kuE', 'jmb', 'kuE', 'oAj', 'eve', 'bck',
 'Abq', 'oAj', 'Abe', 'kuE', 'kuE', 'kuE', 'oAj', 'Azz', 'kuE']
```

Session 8.9   Sorting cipher text words by length

The new clues from Session 8.9 are that the word *Ak* appears three times, *uE* appears twice, *Abe* appears four times, and *kuE* appears 10. So we might ask these questions:

1. What are some popular three-letter words?

2. What three-letter words end in "e"?

3. What three-letter words begin with "a"?

Exercise 8.15 at the end of this section asks you to write a function that reads a string and prints out a list of words that are of a given length, ordered from most popular to least. If you run such a function on the text of *War of the Worlds* you would produce Table 8.6. Now the choices for the letters *k* and *u* become clear. Since the most popular three-letter word is *the* and it is the only one in the top 10 that ends in *e*, it is a pretty safe assumption that *kuE* corresponds to the word *THE*. In addition, since *and* is the second most popular three-letter word, we can also make the assumption that *b* maps to *N* and *e* maps to *D*. Session 8.10 shows what happens when we make these four additional substitutions.

Word	Count
the	4959
and	2555
was	851
had	579
for	369
but	295
his	250
out	231
all	225
not	212

Table 8.6   Three-letter word frequency counts

```
>>> ciphertext = ciphertext.replace('b','N')

>>> ciphertext = ciphertext.replace('e','D')

>>> ciphertext = ciphertext.replace('k','T')

>>> ciphertext = ciphertext.replace('u','H')

>>> ciphertext
'HE iEaAvNED jTANDvNt AT THE EDtE cs THE dvT THAT
THE THvNt HAD aADE sci vTjEzs jTAivNt AT vTj jTiANtE AddEAiANwE
AjTcNvjHED wHvEszq AT vTj mNmjmAz jHAdE AND wczcmi AND Dvazq
dEiwEvnvNt EnEN THEN jcaE EnvDENwE cs DEjvtN vN vTj AiivNz  THE
EAizq aciNvNt oAj ocNDEismzzq jTvzz AND THE jmN xmjT wzEAivNt THE
dvNE TiEEj TcoAiDj oEqgivDtE oAj AziEADq oAiaHE DvD NcT iEaEagEi
HEAivNt ANq gviDj THAT aciNvNt THEiE oAj wEiTAvNzq Nc giEErE
jTviivNt AND THE cNzq jcmNDj oEiE THE sAvNT acnEaENTj sica ovTHvN
THE wvNDEiq wqzvNDEi HE oAj Azz AzcNE cN THE wcaacN'
```

Session 8.10   Second replacement, using word frequency

In addition to *and* and *the* other words such as *that, at, had,* and *then* also appear. Considering that we have mapped only six letters, this result is very promising. In fact you can probably make some additional guesses yourself based on what you see.

Referring back to Table 8.6, let's try to decrypt a few more letters. First, we might notice that another popular three-letter word appearing in the partially decrypted ciphertext is the word *oAj*. Looking at our list of popular three-letter words, we see that *was* is the third most popular word. In addition *was* has an *a* in the middle position. Scanning through the rest of the ciphertext, we can see that there are many words that end in *j*. Of course, *s* is a very popular letter at the end of words because it makes a word plural. Once again you can write a function to find out what letters appear most frequently at the end of a word. It is very likely you would find out it is *s*. If we use the mappings, *o* maps to *W* and *j* maps to *S*, we now find that our ciphertext looks like the following:

> HE iEaAvNED STANDvNt AT THE EDtE cs THE dvT THAT THE THvNt
> HAD aADE sci vTSEzs STAivNt AT vTS STiANtE AddEAiANwE ASTcN-
> vSHED wHvEszq AT vTS mNmSmAz SHAdE AND wczcmi AND Dvazq dEi-
> wEvnvNt EnEN THEN ScaE EnvDENwE cs DESvtN vN vTS AiivnAz THE
> EAizq aciNvNt WAS WcNDEismzzq STvzz AND THE SmN xmST wzEAivNt
> THE dvNE TiEES TcWAiDS WEqgivDtE WAS AziEADq WAiaHE DvD NcT
> iEaEagEi HEAivNt ANq gviDS THAT aciNvNt THEiE WAS wEiTAvNzq Nc
> giEErE STviivNt AND THE cNzq ScmNDS WEiE THE sAvNT acnEaENTS
> sica WvTHvN THE wvNDEiq wqzvNDEi HE WAS Azz AzcNE cN THE wcaacN

We can get two more letters with another observation. Look at the last three letters of each word and notice that there are several that end in *vNt*. There are nine words that end in the pattern *vNt*. A common English language suffix for words is *ing*. This gives us the vowel *i*, which means that we now know the mappings for the vowels *a, e,* and *i*.

At this point we can also make an educated guess that the word *cs* in the ciphertext is probably *of*. The pair frequency profile of *c* fits that of a vowel, and the word *of* makes the most sense in the context of the phrase "STANDING AT THE EDGE cs THE dIT."

Finally, let's make one more substitution before looking at the whole text again. There is another common letter in the ciphertext that we have not decoded yet: it is "z". Notice that we have the partially decoded three-letter word *Azz*. The only three-letter word in our top ten that has a double letter is the word *all*, so it is a good bet that *z* maps to *L*.

> 'HE iEaAINED STANDING AT THE EDGE OF THE dIT THAT THE THING
> HAD aADE FOi ITSELF STAiING AT ITS STiANGE AddEAiANwE ASTON-
> ISHED wHIEFLq AT ITS mNmSmAL SHAdE AND wOLOmi AND DIaLq

dEiwEInING EnEN THEN SOaE EnIDENwE OF DESIGN IN ITS AiiInAL THE EAiLq aOiNING WAS WONDEiFmLLq STILL AND THE SmN xmST wLEAiING THE dINE TiEES TOWAiDS WEqgiIDGE WAS ALiEADq WA- iaHE DID NOT iEaEagEi HEAiING ANq gIiDS THAT aOiNING THEiE WAS wEiTAINLq NO giEErE STIiiING AND THE ONLq SOmNDS WEiE THE FAINT aOnEaENTS FiOa WITHIN THE wINDEiq wqLINDEi HE WAS ALL ALONE ON THE wOaaON

We have made good progress, finding the mappings for 12 letters with only 14 more letters to fill in. Table 8.7 shows the letters we have identified and those that we have yet to figure out. We could continue to make some deductions about what letters go where. But let's look at another way we can use Python to help us by doing some automated pattern matching—a very common application for computers.

Plaintext	A	B	C	D	E	F	G	H	I	J	K	L	M	N	O	P	Q	R	S	T	U	V	W	X	Y	Z
Ciphertext	h			e	l	s	t	u	v			z		b	c			j	k							

Table 8.7 Progress on mapping the letters

Exercises

8.14 Write a function `wordPop` that accepts a text and a length N and returns the list of all the words that are N letters long, sorted by their length.

8.15 Write a function that returns the most popular ending letter for words.

8.16 Write a function that finds the most popular suffixes for words. You may want to try this function for two- and three-letter suffixes.

8.4.5 Pattern Matching with Partial Words

What we would like to do is select a word from the partially decoded ciphertext and ask the program to find a word from the dictionary that is the same length and matches the letters that we have decoded so far. It turns out that humans are pretty good at the task of **pattern matching**. For example, given *aADE* you can probably come up with the words *MADE*, *FADE*, and *WADE*. Some of those would work for us but others would not. For example, *FADE* would not work for us because *F* has already been decoded. Ideally we would like to give the function the set of letters that are legal to use when matching the coded parts of the words. If the computer comes back with only one match, we can then be pretty sure that we have decoded some additional letters.

Most modern programming languages today provide a pattern-matching library that uses **regular expressions**. In Python, regular expressions are available through the `re` module. Regular expressions are extremely useful and powerful programming tools. We just barely scratch the surface in this section, but we will see how even a simple use of regular expressions can make the final decryption step easier.

Regular expressions allow us to see if two strings match, much like the `==`, except that in regular expressions we can use wild card characters as part of the match. For example, we can test to see if the string `.ADE` matched `FADE`. When using regular expressions, the `.` character is a `wildcard` that matches any character. The regular expression function that we use to test if two strings match is called `match`. The `match` function takes two parameters: a regular expression and the string we want to match against. Session 8.11 illustrates the use of the match function as well as some simple pattern matching.

```
>>> re.match('.ADE','FADE')
<_sre.SRE_Match object at 0x5d6e3a0>

>>> re.match('.ADE','FADER')
<_sre.SRE_Match object at 0x5d6e218>

>>> re.match('.ADE','ADE')

>>> re.match('.ADE','FUDE')
```

Session 8.11   Trying regular expression matches

If two strings match, the `match` function returns a match object. At this point we can just think of the match object as being our indication of success. As you learn to use more advanced regular expressions, you will use the match object for more interesting purposes. If the two strings do not match, the function returns `None`. This allows us to use `re.match` as a condition in an `if` statement.

Now since we want to be more specific in our matches, let's learn some additional regular expression syntax. Within a regular expression, the square brackets (`[]`) allow us to define a set of characters, any one of which may match. For example, `[abc]` will match *a* or *b* or *c*, but not any other character. In addition, we can use the `+` character to match multiple instances of a character. For example, `[abc]+` will match *a* or *b* or *c* or *abc* or *aaaaaaa* or *bbbb* or *aaabbbccc* or any other combination of the letters *abc*. You read the + character to mean "one or more," so we say that the regular expression [abc]+ means "match one or more instances of the characters *a*, *b*, or *c*."

You may also have noticed that '.ADE' matched 'FADER'. This is because the regular expression matcher starts at the beginning and tries to match the whole regular expression. Once the end of the expression is found the matcher does not care what comes after. If we want to indicate to the matcher that we do not want anything to come after the pattern we provide, we must end our pattern with a $.

Table 8.7 showed that we have not decoded *B, C, J, K, M, P, Q, R, U, V, W, X, Y*, or *Z*. When we check for matches in the dictionary, we can use the regular expression [BCJKMPQRUVWXYZ] to limit our choices for a particular letter position to match only those characters. The call to match for the example we have been using would be re.match('[BCJKMPQRUVWXYZ]ADE','FADE'). Since *F* is not one of the characters inside the square brackets, this call would fail and return None. However, re.match('[BCJKMPQRUVWXYZ]ADE', 'MADE') would be successful and return a match object since *M* is one of the characters in the brackets.

Let's write a Python function that uses the regular expression module to create a list of all the words in the dictionary file that match a given regular expression. The basic form of our function is really quite simple. We use a loop to read through all the words in the dictionary, trying to match each word against the regular expression. If a word matches, we add it to the list. If the word does not match, we ignore it. When we have tested all the words, we return the list that we constructed. The code for this matching function, called checkWord, is shown in Listing 8.11.

```
1   def checkWord(regex):
2       resList = []
3       wordFile = open('wordlist.txt')
4       for line in wordFile:
5           if re.match(regex,line[:-1]):
6               resList.append(line[:-1])
7       return resList
```

Listing 8.11   Matching words from the dictionary against patterns

Session 8.12 uses the checkWord function to see if we can identify some more letters. In our partially decoded message we have the string *aOiNING*. Using the pattern '.o.ning' the checkWord function matches the word *morning* from the dictionary. The second example uses a pattern that explicitly restricts the possible matches to our list of unmapped characters. The rest of Session 8.12 finds matches for some additional words.

```
>>> checkWord('.o.ning')
['morning']

>>> checkWord('[bcjkmpqruvwxyz]o[bcjkmpqruvwxyz]ning')
['morning']

>>> checkWord('a..i.al')

['admiral',
 'admiralty',
 'ambivalence',
 'ambivalent',
 'ambivalently',
 'antimalarial',
 'arrival']

>>> checkWord('a..i.al$')
['admiral', 'arrival']

>>> checkWord('a[bcjkmpqruvwxyz][bcjkmpqruvwxyz]i[bcjkmpqruvwxyz]al$')
['arrival']
```

Session 8.12   Using `checkWord` to find matches

Constructing the pattern string for the `checkWord` parameter is quite tedious. We can reduce the amount of work we must do by making the `checkWord` function more intelligent. To do so, let's pass two parameters to the `checkWord` function: a string of unused letters and the word from the partially decoded ciphertext. This means that letters to keep in place will (initially) be capitalized and letters that we can match from the unused group will be in lowercase.

We can use the `re` module's replace function (called `re.sub`) to substitute all of the lowercase characters with the group of letters we want to match. Line 5 of Listing 8.12 shows the use of the `re.sub` function. Notice that we can use a simplified pattern to represent all of the lowercase characters. The pattern `[a-z]` is the same as typing `[abcdefghijklmnopqrstuvwxyz]`.

The syntax for the `re.sub` function is as follows `re.sub(`*pattern, replacement string, target string*`)`. The `re.sub` function finds each instance of the *pattern* in the *target string* and replaces it with *replacement string*. We have added a print statement to the `checkWord` function so that you can see the final version of the regular expression constructed by `checkWord`.

```
1    def checkWord(unused,pattern):
2        resList = []
3        wordFile = open('wordlist.txt')
4        rePat = '['+unused+']'
5        regex = re.sub('[a-z]',rePat,pattern) + '$'
6        regex = regex.lower()
7        print('matching ', regex)
8        for line in wordFile:
9            if re.match(regex,line[:-1]):
10               resList.append(line[:-1])
11       return resList
```

Listing 8.12   `checkWord` construction of a regular expression

```
>>> checkWord('bcjkmpqruvwxyz','WONDEiFmLLq')
matching  wonde[bcjkmpqruvwxyz]f[bcjkmpqruvwxyz]ll[bcjkmpqruvwxyz]$
['wonderfully']
>>> checkWord('bcjkmpqruvwxyz','AiiInAL')
matching  a[bcjkmpqruvwxyz][bcjkmpqruvwxyz]i[bcjkmpqruvwxyz]al$
['arrival']
>>> checkWord('bcjkmpqruvwxyz','mNmSmAL')
matching  [bcjkmpqruvwxyz]n[bcjkmpqruvwxyz]s[bcjkmpqruvwxyz]al$
['unusual']
```

Session 8.13   Using the new `checkWord` to find matches

Session 8.13 illustrates the new `checkWord` function in action. But as you can see, there is one more improvement we could make. It would be nice if `checkWord` could tell us the ciphertext to plaintext mapping for the letters that complete the match. In fact, regular expressions allow us to do this very nicely by using match objects and **capture groups**, which allow us to find out what characters in the target word matched letters in different parts of our pattern. You create a capture group by surrounding some part of the regular expression with left and right parentheses. Here is a simple example: `'F(..)L(..)$'`. This regular expression will match any word that starts with an F followed by any two letters, followed by an L followed by two more letters. So, words like *fueled* or *foiled* or *fooler* would all match.

Session 8.14 illustrates the use of capture groups in regular expressions. Let's suppose that we matched the word FOILED. The first capture group corresponds to the first set of parentheses, so the letters in the capture group would be *OI*. The second capture group would contain the letters *ED*. The match object allows us to get capture groups by number, using the **group** method, or to get all the capture groups as a list using the **groups** method.

```
>>> cg = re.match('F(..)L(..)','FOILED')

>>> cg
<_sre.SRE_Match object at 0x5d7dda0>

>>> cg.group(1)
'OI'

>>> cg.group(2)
'ED'

>>> cg = re.match('F(..)L(..)','FOOLER')

>>> cg.groups()
('OO', 'ER')
```

Session 8.14   *Demonstrating capture groups*

Now that you have some idea of how capture groups work with regular expressions we will use them to create a list of character maps that show us which characters we can substitute for which. We begin with the **checkWord** function and add this new feature. There are three key differences between the new version and the old one:

1. We need to create a list of the lowercase ciphertext letters in our original pattern.

2. We need to add capture groups to the regular expression.

3. When we get a matching word, we must save the matching letters from the capture groups along with their ciphertext equivalents.

Listing 8.13 shows the entire new version of `checkWord` now called `findLetters`. Let's look at the lines where there are significant differences from the old `checkWord` function. The first thing we want to do is create a list of all the lowercase ciphertext letters in the partially decrypted word (`pattern`). You could write a loop to do this and build this list yourself by checking one letter at a time. However, the `re` module has a function called `findall` that does exactly this job for us. It returns all the substrings of a string that match a particular regular expression. Session 8.15 demonstrates the `findall` function in action. Line 4 uses the `findall` function to create the list of ciphertext letters.

```
>>> re.findall('[123]','1,234')
['1', '2', '3']

>>> re.findall('[1234]+','1,234')
['1', '234']

>>> re.findall('[A-Z]','Hello World')
['H', 'W']
```

Session 8.15   Finding all occurrences of a regular expression

We next make a very minor change to line 6 to add parentheses around our regular expression that matches the undecoded ciphertext letters. This ensures that each instance of a lowercase letter in the pattern will end up in its own capture group.

Finally, lines 11–17 make use of the match object and the `groups` function. When a match is made against a word from the word list file, the call `myMatch.groups()` gives us the letters that were used to make the matching word. At this point we have two lists that contain important information. The `ctLetters` list contains the original ciphertext letters and the `matchingLetters` list contains the plaintext letters that complete the word.

We must now match the letters from `ctLetters` with the corresponding letters from `matchingLetters`. It is easy to know which letter from `ctLetters` corresponds to a letter in `matchingLetters` because they are parallel lists. The first letter in `ctLetters` corresponds to the first letter in `matchingLetters` and so on. We could write our own function that accepts two lists and puts the letters together into a new list moving through the lists one item at a time, but Python has a handy function that does this for us. It is the `zip` function, which takes two lists and "zips" them together, matching the first item from `list1` with the first item from `list2` and so on. Session 8.16 illustrates how zip works.

```
1   def findLetters(unused,pattern):
2       resList = []
3       wordFile = open('wordlist.txt')
4       ctLetters = re.findall('[a-z]',pattern)
5       print(ctLetters)
6       rePat = '(['+unused+'])'
7       regex = re.sub('[a-z]',rePat,pattern) + '$'
8       regex = regex.lower()
9       for line in wordFile:
10          myMatch = re.match(regex,line[:-1])
11          if myMatch:
12              matchingLetters = myMatch.groups()
13              matchList = []
14              for l in matchingLetters:
15                  matchList.append(l.upper())
16              resList.append(line[:-1])
17              resList.append(zip(ctLetters,matchList))
18      return resList
```

Listing 8.13   Showing the matching letters

```
>>> zip([1,2,3],[4,5,6])
[(1, 4), (2, 5), (3, 6)]

>>> zip(['a','b','c'],['Z','Y','X'])
[('a', 'Z'), ('b', 'Y'), ('c', 'X')]

>>> zip(['a','b','c'],['Z','Y','X'],[1,2,3])
[('a', 'Z', 1), ('b', 'Y', 2), ('c', 'X', 3)]
```

Session 8.16   Using the zip function to create a list of tuples

Session 8.17 shows how the **findLetters** function can help us finish decoding the ciphertext. On the first line **findLetter** searches for the mappings that use the partially decrypted word 'AiiInAL'. We discover that 'AiiInAL' is a good match for the word 'arrival'. The third line of the session shows us that the ciphertext letter i maps to the plaintext letter R and n maps to the plaintext letter V.

Additional calls to **findLetters** give us the mappings for m, g, i, r, q, and n. Now a message is really starting to show. With just a few more substitutions we will have the entire message decoded.

```
>>> findLetters('bcjkmpqruvwxyz','AiiInAL')
['i', 'i', 'n']
['arrival', [('i', 'R'), ('i', 'R'), ('n', 'V')]]

>>> findLetters('bcjkmpqruvwxyz','ALiEADq')
['i', 'q']
['already', [('i', 'R'), ('q', 'Y')]]

>>> findLetters('bcjkmpqruvwxyz','giEErE')
['g', 'i', 'r']
['breeze', [('g', 'B'), ('i', 'R'), ('r', 'Z')]]

>>> findLetters('bcjkmpqruvwxyz','mNmSmAL')
['m', 'm', 'm']
['unusual', [('m', 'U'), ('m', 'U'), ('m', 'U')]]

>>> ciphertext = ciphertext.replace('m','U')

>>> ciphertext = ciphertext.replace('g','B')

>>> ciphertext = ciphertext.replace('i','R')

>>> ciphertext = ciphertext.replace('r','Z')

>>> ciphertext = ciphertext.replace('q','Y')

>>> ciphertext = ciphertext.replace('n','V')
```

Session 8.17   Demonstrating the `findLetters` function

HE REaAINED STANDING AT THE EDGE OF THE dIT THAT THE THING HAD aADE FOR ITSELF STARING AT ITS STRANGE AddEARANwE AS-TONISHED wHIEFLY AT ITS UNUSUAL SHAdE AND wOLOUR AND DI-aLY dERwEIVING EVEN THEN SOaE EVIDENwE OF DESIGN IN ITS AR-RIVAL THE EARLY aORNING WAS WONDERFULLY STILL AND THE SUN xUST wLEARING THE dINE TREES TOWARDS WEYBRIDGE WAS ALREADY WARaHE DID NOT REaEaBER HEARING ANY BIRDS THAT

aORNING THERE WAS wERTAINLY NO BREEZE STIRRING AND THE
ONLY SOUNDS WERE THE FAINT aOVEaENTS FROa WITHIN THE wINDERY
wYLINDER HE WAS ALL ALONE ON THE wOaaON

From here we need only a couple more substitutions to complete the message, as shown in
Session 8.18.

```
>>> findLetters('cjkmpqwx','wOaaON')
['w', 'a', 'a']

['common',
 [('w', 'C'), ('a', 'M'), ('a', 'M')],
 'pompon',
 [('w', 'P'), ('a', 'M'), ('a', 'P')]]
>>> ciphertext = ciphertext.replace('w','C')

>>> ciphertext = ciphertext.replace('a','M')
>>> findLetters('jkpqwx','dIT')
['d']

['kit',
 [('d', 'K')],
 'pit',
 [('d', 'P')],
 'wit',
 [('d', 'W')]]

>>> findLetters('jkpqwx','AddEARANCE')
['d', 'd']
['appearance', [('d', 'P'), ('d', 'P')]]

>>> ciphertext = ciphertext.replace('d','P')
 findLetters('jkpqwx','xUST')
['x']
['just', [('x', 'J')]]
```

Session 8.18   The last substitutions

| Plaintext | A B C D E F G H I J K L M N O P Q R S T U V W X Y Z |
| Ciphertext | h g w e l s t u v x y z a b c d f i j k m n o p q r |

Table 8.8   Final mapping of the letters

HE REMAINED STANDING AT THE EDGE OF THE PIT THAT THE
THING HAD MADE FOR ITSELF STARING AT ITS STRANGE APPEAR-
ANCE ASTONISHED CHIEFLY AT ITS UNUSUAL SHAPE AND COLOUR
AND DIMLY PERCEIVING EVEN THEN SOME EVIDENCE OF DESIGN
IN ITS ARRIVAL THE EARLY MORNING WAS WONDERFULLY STILL
AND THE SUN JUST CLEARING THE PINE TREES TOWARDS WEY-
BRIDGE WAS ALREADY WARM HE DID NOT REMEMBER HEARING
ANY BIRDS THAT MORNING THERE WAS CERTAINLY NO BREEZE
STIRRING AND THE ONLY SOUNDS WERE THE FAINT MOVEMENTS
FROM WITHIN THE CINDERY CYLINDER HE WAS ALL ALONE ON THE
COMMON

Table 8.8 shows the final key that maps the ciphertext letters to the plaintext letters. Notice that the `keyGen` function we wrote earlier was used to create the key from the password `hgwells`.

8.4.6   Regular Expression Summary

We conclude this section with a summary of the regular expression syntax and the functions we have used from the `re` module. These are summarized in Tables 8.9 and 8.10.

`.`	Match any character.
`[abc]`	Match *a* or *b* or *c*.
`[^abc]`	Match any characters other than *a* or *b* or *c*.
`[abc]+`	Match one or more occurrences of the characters *abc*—for example, *b* or *aba* or *ccba*.
`[abc]*`	Match zero or more occurrences of the characters *abc*—for example, *b* or *aba* or *ccba*.
(regex)	Create a capture group.

Table 8.9   Simple regular expression syntax

Method	Use	Explanation
match	re.match('[abc]XY.')	Matches any string that starts with a, b, or c followed by XY followed by any character. Returns a match object on success or None.
sub	re.sub('[tv]','X','vxyzbgtt')	Returns 'XxyzbgXX'. Like replace except to use regular expression matching.
findall	re.findall('[bc]+','abcdefedcba')	Returns ['bc','cb']. Returns a list of all substrings matching the regular expression.
groups	matchObj.groups()	Returns a list of all capture groups matched. matchObj is created by a call to match.
group	matchObj.group(2)	Returns a single capture group. matchObj is created by a call to match.

Table 8.10   Regular expression module functions

Exercises

8.17 Write a regular expression pattern to match all words ending in *s*.

8.18 Write a regular expression pattern to match all words ending in *ing*.

8.19 Write a regular expression pattern to match all words with *ss* anywhere in the string.

8.20 Write a regular expression pattern to match all words beginning and ending with the letter *a*.

8.21 Write a regular expression pattern to match all the words that start with *st*.

8.22 Write a regular expression to match all the four-letter words where the middle two letters are vowels.

8.23 Write a function that can extract the host name from a URL. The host name is the part of the URL that comes after `http://` but before the next /.

8.24 Write a function that can take a file name and return the name and the suffix as two separate strings. *Note:* In order to match the . character in a regular expression, you must use \..

8.5 Summary

In this chapter we explored cryptanalysis by implementing techniques for reading encrypted text. We utilized many past features of Python, including lists and dictionaries. However, in this chapter we extended these ideas by using lists and dictionaries as containers for other lists and dictionaries. We used a brute force solution to systematically solve a hard problem. Part of that solution introduced a pattern called "minmax" for systematically finding a "better" answer given a "best" answer so far. Finally, we introduced the notion of a regular expression and showed how this powerful pattern matching tool can help us to locate missing letters in partially decrypted text.

Key Terms

brute force method	cryptanalysis	pattern matching	row major storage
capture group	frequency analysis	rail fence cipher	substitution cipher
column major storage	"minmax" pattern	regular expression	

Python Keywords

cmp	join
for	None
if	sort

Bibliography

[Sch94] Bruce Schneier. *Applied Cryptography: Protocols, Algorithms, and Source Code in C.* Wiley, 1994.

[Sin00] Simon Singh. *The Code Book: The Science of Secrecy from Ancient Egypt to Quantum Cryptography.* Anchor, 2000.

[wor] Translatum. Retrieved from http://www.translatum.gr/dictionaries/download-english.htm.

Programming Exercises

8.1 Decode the following paragraph:

```
 jyn fg jggtwj djtfcn stf sjyn edcyjnc ia zy stes fjqtye z
wzdn owcff gstf gsq sjyn edcyjnc gsjg mtgs tg gszi xjqcfg
owzm gstyc cycxtcf gz gtyq otgf ty gsq xcdhq jyn gsc wzdn
ntn edty jyn aczawc ntn lcjfg iazy gsc wjxof jyn fwzgsf jyn
hjda jyn jyhszktcf jyn zdjyeigjyf jyn odcjvljfg hcdcjwf jyn
lditg ojgf jyn gsc wzdn fajvc fjqtye ltdfg fsjwg gszi gjvc
zig gsc szwq aty gscy fsjwg gszi hziyg gz gsdcc yz xzdc yz
wcff gsdcc fsjwg oc gsc yixocd gszi fsjwg hziyg jyn gsc
yixocd zl gsc hziygtye fsjwg oc gsdcc lzid fsjwg gszi yzg
hziyg yctgscd hziyg gszi gmz cphcagtye gsjg gszi gscy
adzhccn gz gsdcc ltkc tf dtesg zig zyhc gsc yixocd gsdcc
octye gsc gstdn yixocd oc dcjhscn gscy wzoocfg gszi gsq szwq
sjyn edcyjnc zl jygtzhs gzmjdnf gszi lzc msz octye yjiesgq
ty xq ftesg fsjww fyill tg
```

8.2 Working with a partner, pick two paragraphs of text from a current newspaper. Encrypt the paragraphs separately and trade the resulting ciphertext. Use the techniques in this chapter to decode the message from your partner.

CHAPTER 9

Fractals: The Geometry of Nature

9.1 Objectives

- To introduce functional programming style
- To practice writing recursive functions
- To introduce grammars and production rules

9.2 Introduction

Take a look at the tree in Figure 9.1. Notice that you could choose any of the major branches of that tree, cut it off, and it would bear a strong resemblance to the entire tree. Furthermore, you could cut one of the branches off of that branch and it would resemble the entire tree. In fact, you could continue to prune the tree down to the size of some small twigs and you would see that even the twigs have the same basic shape and structure as the entire tree. This self-similarity at smaller and smaller scales is the essence of a **fractal**.

Now take a look at the tree in Figure 9.2. Not only is it reminiscent of the real tree, but it is even more obviously self-similar. In fact, this tree was drawn using a `turtle` tree drawing program that uses the following simple instructions:

1. Draw a trunk that is **n** units long.

2. Turn to the right 30 degrees and draw another tree with a trunk that is $n - 15$ units long.

3. Turn to the left 60 degrees and draw another tree with a trunk that is $n - 15$ units long.

Figure 9.1 A tree

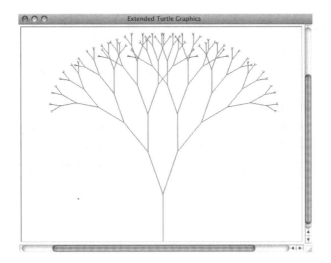

Figure 9.2 A fractal tree drawn with `turtle`

At first glance you may think that all this would do is draw a Y. But remember that each time we draw a tree we follow the same set of steps. Those steps include drawing a trunk and then a smaller tree to the right and a smaller tree to the left. What we have just described is a **recursive** process for drawing a tree.

9.3   Recursive Programs

Before we look at the program used to draw the tree we must first learn a little more about recursion. In computer science and mathematics a recursive function is a function that calls itself. A very simple, but **erroneous**, illustration of a recursive function is shown in Listing 9.1.

```
1   def hello():
2       print("Hello World")
3       hello()
```

Listing 9.1   An erroneous recursive function

The `hello` function prints the message "Hello World" and then calls itself again. If you ran this function in Python, the program would continue to call itself and print "Hello World" until Python simply crashed. A more useful way of thinking about recursive functions is as follows:

1. Are we done yet? Have we found a problem that is small enough to solve trivially? If so, solve it without any further work and return the answer.

2. If not, simplify the problem, and solve the simpler problem. Combine the result of solving the simplified problem with what you know to solve the original. Return the combined result.

The first step is called the **base case**. Every recursive program must have a base case in order to know when to stop. This is precisely the thing that is missing from the program in Listing 9.1.

The second step is often called the **recursive step**. The recursive step involves simplifying the problem in a way that moves it closer to the base case. Sometimes you will need to combine the result returned by the recursive call with some data you saved when you simplified the problem. In other cases the problem is solved just by making the simplifying step.

9.3.1   Recursive Squares

Let's look at a problem of drawing the nested boxes shown in Figure 9.3.

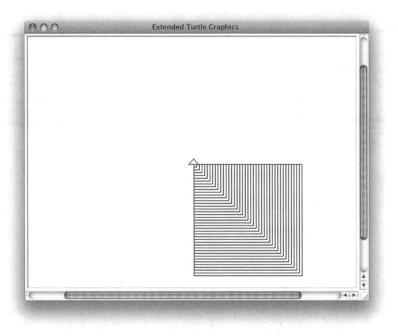

Figure 9.3   Nested boxes

(handwritten in left margin: When to stop bc problem is @ simplest)

In this case we need to draw a series of squares. We know how to draw a single square. But how do we draw the entire picture? Let's start by identifying the base case. Since drawing a square that has a side length of 1 unit is the smallest possible square, we will identify that as the base case. The simplification step is to recursively draw smaller and smaller squares until we get to the point where the side length is 1.

Listing 9.2 shows the code for the nested boxes. The `drawSquare` function should look familiar to you. The nested box function is a recursive process that follows the two important steps outlined previously. First, line 7 checks for the base case. The expression `side >= 1` will evaluate to `False` as soon as the side parameter is less than 1. Because there is no `else` clause, notice that as soon as the side is less than 1, the `nestedBox` simply returns without doing anything.

When the value of `side` is greater than 1, we draw a square that has a side length of `side`. After the square is drawn, the next step is to call `nestedBox` recursively, reducing the side length by 5. By reducing the value of `side` by 5 we are moving toward the base case.

```
1   def  drawSquare(aTurtle,side):
2       for  i  in  range(4):
3           aTurtle.forward(side)
4           aTurtle.right(90)
5
6   def  nestedBox(aTurtle,side):
7       if  side  >=  1:
8           drawSquare(aTurtle,side)
9           nestedBox(aTurtle,side-5)
```

Listing 9.2   Recursively drawing boxes

Exercises

9.1 Run the **nestedBox** function with an initial side of 200, then modify **nestedBox** by reversing lines 8 and 9. Can you explain the different behavior? *gets bigger*

9.2 Write a recursive function to draw concentric nested boxes where each box is centered around the same point. You may find it helpful to write a helper function called **drawCenteredSquare** that accepts parameters for a turtle, the center x and y positions, and the length of the side.

9.3.2   Classic Recursive Functions

It is also often possible to use recursion to express mathematical functions in an elegant way. The following exercises allow you to explore simple recursion by writing some nongraphical functions.

Exercises

9.3 The factorial function is defined as follows:

$$fact(n) = \begin{cases} n \cdot fact(n-1) & n > 0 \\ 1 & otherwise \end{cases}$$

Write a recursive function **fact** that computes the factorial of any positive integer.

9.4 Write a recursive function to compute the sum of all the numbers in a list.

9.5 Write a recursive function to find the minimum number in a list.

9.6 Write a recursive function to find the maximum number in a list.

9.7 Write a recursive function to reverse the characters in a string.

9.8 Write a recursive function to decide if a given string is a palindrome.

9.3.3   Drawing a Recursive Tree

Let's return to the problem of drawing the tree in Figure 9.1. Recall that the instructions for drawing the tree are as follows:

1. Draw a trunk that is **n** units long.

2. Turn to the right 30 degrees and draw another tree with a trunk that is $n - 15$ units long.

3. Turn to the left 60 degrees and draw another tree with a trunk that is $n - 15$ units long.

Now let's apply the rules for recursion to implement a program that follows the tree drawing instructions.

First, we must identify the base case. When drawing a tree, the base case is a tree where the trunk is less than some predefined value. We could say that a trunk length of 1 is the smallest possible tree we could draw, but in fact we can pick any number to use as the smallest trunk length. If the trunk length is less than or equal to our predefined minimum, we can simply stop drawing new trees and return.

We have already seen the recursive step in drawing the tree. In fact, there are two of them. Steps 2 and 3 both specify that we need to "draw another tree." It is also important to notice that not only are we drawing another tree (recursively), but we are also making progress toward the base case by drawing a trunk that is smaller than the current trunk length. Listing 9.3 shows our recursive Python function.

The amazing thing about the **tree** function is its length. You will see that recursion often offers us the capability of elegantly capturing a complex process. Let's look at the code carefully and see how it compares with the rules we defined. First, notice that we check for the base case on line 2. We have written the program slightly longer than necessary to make it clear that we are checking for the base case. The explicit return and the **else** clause could be removed if the conditional was changed to **trunkLength >= 5**.

```
1  def tree(t,trunkLength):
2      if trunkLength < 5:
3          return
4      else:
5          t.forward(trunkLength)
6          t.right(30)
7          tree(t, trunkLength-15)
8          t.left(60)
9          tree(t, trunkLength-15)
10         t.right(30)
11         t.backward(trunkLength)
```

base

Listing 9.3   A recursive tree function

If we have not reached the base case, the turtle moves forward and turns to the right 30 degrees. Then on line 7 we make the first recursive call to draw a smaller tree on the right side of the trunk. When this side of the trunk is done, then the function returns and turns 60 degrees to the left, and the left side of the trunk is drawn. Run this program and carefully watch the order that the branches are drawn in. You will notice that no left side branches are drawn until we have reached our first instance of a base case. You will also notice that the turtle needs to be turned 90 degrees to the left before making the initial call to the function since we want the tree to grow up.

Exercises

9.9 Rewrite the **tree** function using the conditional **trunkLength >= 5** to check for the base case.

9.10 Swap the rules for the tree so that it draws the left side of the tree before the right.

9.11 You can create a more interesting and realistic looking tree by randomizing the angle the turtle turns. Rather than always using a 30 degree angle, select an angle between 15 and 45 degrees.

9.12 You can add additional realism by randomizing how much the branches shrink each time you make a recursive call. Instead of always subtracting 15, try subtracting a random amount between 5 and 25.

9.13 Finally, you can add color to the tree by making the large branches brown, and the small branches green. Choose a threshold value for the length of the trunk and set the color accordingly.

9.3.4   The Sierpinski Triangle

Let's look at another simple fractal called the Sierpinski triangle. Imagine that you have three triangles that are all the same size. If you take the first two triangles and put them side by side and then balance the third triangle on the peaks of the first two triangles, you will get a new, larger triangle composed of those three triangles. Further suppose that you constructed each of the three original triangles from three smaller triangles, and each of the three smaller triangles with three smaller triangles still. Figure 9.4 gives you an idea about what is involved. The idea of self-similarity at smaller and smaller scales is key to the concept of a fractal, and it is key to understanding recursion.

Writing a program to draw the Sierpinski triangle is more complex than the fractal tree, but it is still surprisingly simple. We will invent a simple base case for this program called the *depth*, which represents the number of times we subdivide the original triangle. When we reach a sufficient depth, we then draw a triangle of the appropriate size for that depth. In fact, we start the depth with a positive number, and each time we recursively divide a triangle we subtract one from the depth. When we reach a depth of 0, we then finally draw a very small triangle.

The Sierpinski triangle shown in Figure 9.4 shows a triangle of depth 2. Notice that there are nine shaded triangles, which represent the triangles drawn by the base case. The triangles numbered 1, 5, and 9 were not drawn but are artifacts of the three surrounding triangles. Figure 9.5 shows a Sierpinski triangle of depth 5.

The `sierpinski` function will accept three points as parameters. These points define the three corners of the triangle. To subdivide a large triangle into three smaller triangles, we

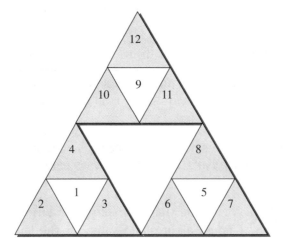

Figure 9.4   The Sierpinski triangle

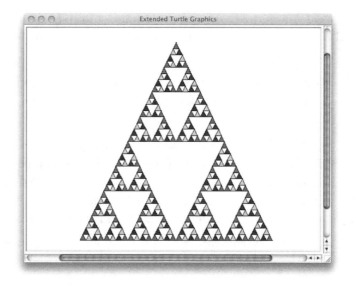

Figure 9.5   A Sierpinski triangle of depth 5

use the following rule: For each corner of the large triangle, create a small triangle using the given corner and the points that are halfway between the given corner and the other two corners. For example, consider triangle ABC in Figure 9.6. The three new triangles we can construct are triangles A13, B21, and C32.

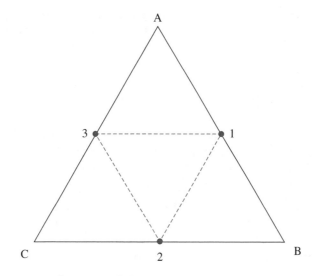

Figure 9.6   Splitting a triangle equally

Points 1, 2, and 3 are calculated by finding the midpoint of line segments AB, BC, and CA, respectively. Recall that we can calculate the midpoint of a line segment (m_x, m_y) using the equation $m_x = \frac{x_1+x_2}{2}$ and $m_y = \frac{y_1+y_2}{2}$.

Drawing the smaller triangles is the recursive step in our function and will involve three recursive calls to the sierpinski function using the vertices calculated by the method just described.

The function we will write requires two simple helper functions: a draw triangle function and a function to calculate the coordinates of a point halfway between two other points. The drawTriangle function takes a turtle and three points as parameters. The goto method is used to simply connect the three points. The midPoint function simply encodes the equation from above and returns a tuple giving the x and y coordinates of the midpoint.

```
1  def drawTriangle(t,p1,p2,p3):
2      t.up()
3      t.goto(p1)
4      t.down()
5      t.goto(p2)
6      t.goto(p3)
7      t.goto(p1)
8
9  def midPoint(p1,p2):
10     return ((p1[0]+p2[0])/2.0,(p1[1]+p2[1])/2.0)
11
12 def sierpinski(myTurtle,p1,p2,p3,depth):
13     if depth > 0:
14         sierpinski(myTurtle,p1,midPoint(p1,p2),midPoint(p1,p3),depth-1)
15         sierpinski(myTurtle,p2,midPoint(p2,p3),midPoint(p2,p1),depth-1)
16         sierpinski(myTurtle,p3,midPoint(p3,p1),midPoint(p3,p2),depth-1)
17     else:
18         drawTriangle(myTurtle,p1,p2,p3)
```

Listing 9.4   Drawing a Sierpinski triangle

The sierpinski function and the two helper functions are shown in Listing 9.4. Note that the final version of the function has a parameter for the turtle as well as a parameter for the depth. The first line of sierpinski checks to see whether the depth is greater than zero. If that is the case, we make three recursive calls to sierpinski. Each recursive call represents one of the three subtriangles. When we make the recursive call, we subtract 1 from the depth to move toward the base case. When the function reaches a depth of zero, no more recursion is required. At this point a triangle is drawn and the function simply returns. Note that the larger the depth specified originally, the smaller this triangle will be.

Exercises

9.14 Try calling `sierpinski` with different shaped triangles.

9.15 Modify the `sierpinski` and `drawTriangle` functions to add color. *Hint:* Make each recursive call draw in a different color.

9.16 Modify the `sierpinski` function so that it unconditionally draws a triangle at each depth rather than just at a depth of 0.

9.17 Change the order of the recursive calls inside the `sierpinski` function.

9.3.5   Call Tree for a Sierpinski Triangle

Hopefully by now you have tried to run the `sierpinski` function on your own a few times, and it should now be clear that the triangle is drawn in thirds. After a third of the larger triangle has been completed, then the next third will be drawn and finally the last third will be drawn. Within each smaller third, the same behavior holds true.

We can graph this behavior using a **call tree**, which enables us to order the recursive calls to the `sierpinski` function to explain why the triangle is drawn in the order it is. The call tree for a Sierpinski triangle of depth 2 is shown in Figure 9.7. Notice that the labels on the arrows on the call tree match the triangle numbers shown in Figure 9.4.

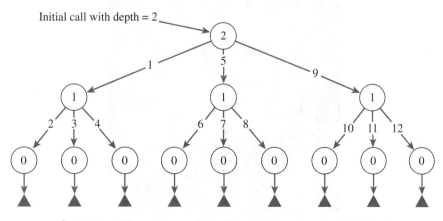

Figure 9.7   The call tree for a Sierpinski triangle of depth 2

Exercises

9.18 Make a call tree for a Sierpinski triangle of depth 3.

9.19 You can generate a Sierpinski square by subdividing a square recursively. Take a square, divide it into 3 by 3 squares. Apply the division algorithm to every square except the center one. When you get to a sufficiently small square, stop subdividing and draw the square.

9.4   Snowflakes, Lindenmayer, and Grammars

Here in northern Iowa we get a lot of snow. It is said that no two snowflakes are exactly alike. Snowflakes are another item in nature that can be reproduced by using fractal techniques. The photo in Figure 9.8 is of a snowflake. The snowflake in Figure 9.9 was produced using the **Koch curve**, a fractal algorithm developed by Helge von Koch in 1904.

A Koch snowflake is constructed from several Koch curves. Let's look at Koch's algorithm for drawing a curve in more detail. The simplest possible curve is actually a straight line of

Figure 9.8   Photo of a snowflake. Courtesy of NOAA.

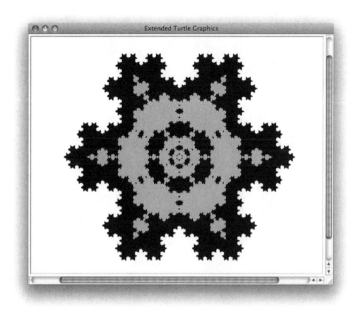

Figure 9.9 A snowflake produced using a fractal algorithm developed by Helge von Koch in 1904.

length n, the base case. The next easiest curve can be described in terms of the following set of turtle instructions:

```
forward(n)
left(60)
forward(n)
right(60)
right(60)
forward(n)
left(60)
forward(n)
```

If you think recursively about the curve, you can imagine that each straight line can be replaced by a set of shorter lines following the instructions above. Figure 9.10 illustrates the Koch curve at several levels of detail.

At this point you could write a simple recursive function to plot a Koch curve. (In fact, Exercise 9.23 asks you to do so.) But let's look at a different way of thinking about fractals and recursion.

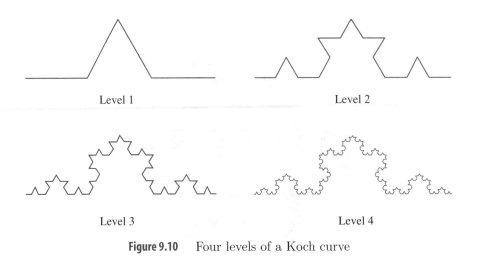

Level 1   Level 2

Level 3   Level 4

Figure 9.10   Four levels of a Koch curve

9.4.1   L-Systems

In 1968 Astrid Lindenmayer, a biologist, invented the **L-system**, a formal mathematical theory designed to model the growth of biological systems. You can think of L-systems as containing the instructions for how a simple cell can grow into a complex organism. L-systems can be used to specify the rules for all kinds of fractals.

As it turns out, L-systems are based on a formal idea from computer science called a **grammar**, which may be used for many purposes, including the specification of programming languages. A grammar consists of a set of **symbols** and one or more **production rules**. These rules specify how one symbol can be replaced by one or more other symbols. A production rule has two parts: (1) the left side, which specifies a symbol, and (2) the right side, which specifies the symbols that can replace the one on the left. Let's look at a simple example of a grammar:

Axiom   A
Rules   A $\rightarrow$ B
            B $\rightarrow$ AB

We can interpret this grammar as follows, beginning with the **axiom**, the starting point. Axiom A is the simplest string you can produce in the grammar. You may also think of the axiom in terms of a base case for the grammar. The rules tell us how we can construct more complicated strings that are part of the grammar. For example, rule 1 tells us that we can substitute the string B for A, and rule 2 tells us that we can change the string B into the string AB.

When you apply the rules to a string, you must work from left to right, applying the rule where the left side matches the current symbol. If a rule matches, then you *must* apply the rule. Let's look at an example:

A	Axiom
B	(apply rule 1 to A)
AB	(apply rule 2 to B)
BAB	(apply rule 1 to A, then apply rule 2 to B)
ABBAB	(apply rule 2 to B, then rule 1 to A, then rule 2 to B)
BABABBAB	(rules applied: 1, 2, 2, 1, 2)

Try to apply the rules and produce a few more lines on your own. If you are applying the rules correctly, you will notice that the length of each string follows the Fibonacci sequence of numbers: 1, 1, 2, 3, 5, 8, 13, 21, ...

To make the transition from these simple L-systems to an L-system that a turtle can use to draw pictures, consider the interpretation of the symbols used to define the L-system. Suppose that rather than using the symbols A and B we used the symbols F, B, +, and −. F indicates that the turtle should move forward and draw a line. B indicates the turtle should move backward while drawing a line. The "+" symbol indicates that the turtle should turn right and "−" indicates that the turtle should turn left.

Let's return to the Koch curve and consider the set of steps we outlined to draw a simple curve. We can specify the following set of actions as an L-system:

Axiom   F
Rule   F → F − F + + F − F

Notice that the axiom gives us a straight line, which is the simplest Koch curve. But if we apply the production rule one time, we get the string F−F++F−F. This gives us the next simplest Koch curve. Applying the production rule to the string F−F++F−F gives us the string F−F++F−F−F−F++F−F++F−F++F−F−F−F++F−F.

Given a string of instructions, it is straightforward to write a Python function that could interpret the string and make the appropriate calls to turtle methods. To successfully draw a Koch curve, we would need to know the distance to have the turtle go forward, along with the angle for the turtle to turn.

Listing 9.5 shows the code for the function `drawLS`. The `drawLS` function simply iterates over each character in the instruction string. When an "F" or "B" is encountered, the turtle is instructed to move forward or backward `distance` units. When a "+" or "−" is encountered, the turtle is instructed to turn right or left by **angle** degrees. If any other character is encountered, an error message is printed.

```
def drawLS(aTurtle,instructions,angle,distance):
    for cmd in instructions:
        if cmd == 'F':
            aTurtle.forward(distance)
        elif cmd == 'B':
            aTurtle.backward(distance)
        elif cmd == '+':
            aTurtle.right(angle)
        elif cmd == '-':
            aTurtle.left(angle)
        else:
            print('Error: %s is an unknown command'%cmd)
```

Listing 9.5　A simple function to follow an L-system string

Exercises

9.20 Use the `drawLS` function to draw the string F-F++F-F-F-F++F-F++F-F++F-F-F-F++F-F. Use an angle of 60 degrees and a distance of 20.

9.21 Apply the production rule for the Koch curve one more time and draw the results using `drawLS`.

9.22 Experiment with the `drawLS` function using different angles and distances.

9.23 Write a simple recursive function to draw a Koch curve.

9.24 Using the function for a Koch curve, draw a snowflake with six sides.

9.25 One of Lindenmayer's very first L-systems was a set of rules to model the growth of algae. The rules are as follows:

Axiom　A
Rules　A → AB
　　　　　B → A

Apply these rules to construct five new strings. The length of each string represents the number of algae cells.

9.26 Here is another simple set of rules that generate `cantor dust`.

Axiom   A

Rules   A → ABA

B → BBB

Apply the rules to produce five new strings.

9.4.2 Automatically Expanding Production Rules

Applying the production rules in an L-system can be very tedious, so let's write a function to automate the process. We first need to determine "how production rules can be represented in Python." In fact, this problem is similar to the translation problem in Chapter 4. The solution is to use a Python dictionary.

A dictionary can represent any number of production rules where the left side of the rule is the key and the right side of the rule is the value. For example, the set of production rules that generates the Fibonacci numbers is as follows:

Axiom   A

Rules   A → B

B → AB

The Python dictionary that corresponds to these rules can be stored as

```
productionRules = {'A': 'B',
                   'B': 'AB'}
```

Now let's write a Python function to take an initial string and apply a set of production rules a specified number of times. Listing 9.6 shows the Python function `applyProduction`.

```
def applyProduction(axiom,rules,n):
    for i in range(n):
        newString = ""
        for ch in axiom:
            newString = newString + rules.get(ch,ch)
        axiom = newString
    return axiom
```

Listing 9.6   Automatically applying production rules

Everything in the `applyProduction` function should look familiar. The outer loop allows us to apply the production rules to the string n times. The inner loop is a simple accumulator pattern that allows us to construct a new string by applying the production rules one character at a time. Notice the statement `rules.get(ch,ch)` shown on line 5. This statement elegantly handles the case where there is a character but no production rule for expanding the character further. Recall that the **get** method allows us to specify a default value for the case that a key is not found in the dictionary. In this instance when character ch has no production rule, we simply leave the character in place.

Session 9.1 shows the `applyProduction` function in action using the Fibonacci production rules.

```
>>> axiom = 'A'
>>> myRules = {'A': 'B', 'B': 'AB'}
>>> for i in range(10):
        res = applyProduction(axiom,myRules,i)
        print("%3d %s" % (len(res),res))

 1 A
 1 B
 2 AB
 3 BAB
 5 ABBAB
 8 BABABBAB
13 ABBABBABABBAB
21 BABABBABABBABBABABBAB
34 ABBABBABABBABBABABBABABBABBABABBAB
55 BABABBABABBABBABABBABBABABBABABBABBABABBABABBABBABABBAB
>>>
```

Session 9.1   Using the production rule expander

Exercises

9.27 Use the `applyProduction` and `drawLS` functions to draw a Koch curve of level 5.

9.28 We can easily draw a Koch snowflake using L-system rules by starting with a more complex axiom. Use the `applyProduction` and `drawLS` functions to draw a fractal using the axiom F++F++F and the production rule F → F-F++F-F.

9.29 Using an angle of 90 degrees and the following L-system, draw the resulting figure for several different levels of expansion.

Axiom   F-F-F-F

Rules   F → F − F + F + FF − F − F + F

This figure is known as the quadric Koch island.

9.4.3   More Advanced L-Systems

In order to use L-systems to model plant growth we need to add one more feature to the L-systems grammar: the characters "[" and "]". The left square bracket and right square bracket characters represent operations to save and restore the state of the turtle. That is whenever a "[" is encountered in the string, the position and heading of the turtle is saved. When a "]" is encountered, the position and heading from the last save are restored.

Using these new characters, we can now use an L-system to specify the tree we drew using Listing 9.3. The grammar for this new L-system is as follows:

Axiom   X

Rules   X → F[−X]+X

F → FF

Starting with the axiom "X" and applying the production rules twice gives us the string "F F [− F [− X] + X] + F [− X] + X". Suppose that we use an angle of 60 degrees and a distance of 20 units. This string instructs the turtle to take the following actions:

1. Go forward a total of 40 units.

2. Save the position and heading; call this state W.

3. Turn left 60 degrees.

4. Go forward 20 units.

5. Save the position and heading; call this state Z.

6. Turn left 60 degrees.

7. Do nothing. X is not a recognized command.

8. Restore the turtle position to the saved state called Z.

9. Turn right 60 degrees.

10. Do nothing.

11. Restore the position and heading to the saved state called W.

12. Turn right 60 degrees.

13. Go forward 20 units.

At this point we have succeeded in simply drawing a Y. But notice that the difference between this approach and the code we used in Listing 9.3 is that we no longer need to have the turtle back up. By using the save and restore operations, we can simply jump the turtle back to any previous position.

Let's modify the **drawLS** function to support the save and restore operations. Listing 9.7 shows the new function. Notice that in this version we have removed the final **else** statement with the corresponding error message. This allows the function to silently ignore any commands it does not recognize. The **stateSaver** list allows us to append new states that we want to save to the end of the list. Using the **pop** method allows us to restore the most recently saved state.

Finally, let's write a simple function that combines all of our work into a single function that applies the production rules and draws the resulting L-system. The **lsystem** function takes seven parameters:

axiom	The initial axiom
rules	A dictionary specifying the production rules
depth	The number of times to expand the production rules
initialPosition	The initial position for the turtle
heading	The initial heading for the turtle
angle	The angle to turn for the "+" or "−" operations
length	The distance to move forward or backward for an "F" or "B."

```
1  def drawLS(aTurtle,instructions,angle,distance):
2      stateSaver = []
3      for cmd in instructions:
4          if cmd == 'F':
5              aTurtle.forward(distance)
6          elif cmd == 'B':
7              aTurtle.backward(distance)
8          elif cmd == '+':
9              aTurtle.right(angle)
10         elif cmd == '-':
11             aTurtle.left(angle)
12         elif cmd == '[':
13             pos = aTurtle.position()
14             head = aTurtle.heading()
15             stateSaver.append((pos,head))
16         elif cmd == ']':
17             pos,head = stateSaver.pop()
18             aTurtle.up()
19             aTurtle.setposition(pos)
20             aTurtle.setheading(head)
21             aTurtle.down()
```

Listing 9.7   An improved L-system drawing function

The code for the `lsystem` function is shown in Listing 9.8.

```
1  def lsystem(axiom,rules,depth,initialPosition,heading,angle,length):
2      aTurtle = turtle.Turtle()
3      win = turtle.Screen()
4      aTurtle.up()
5      aTurtle.setposition(initialPosition)
6      aTurtle.down()
7      aTurtle.setheading(heading)
8      newRules = applyProduction(axiom,rules,depth)
9      drawLS(aTurtle,newRules,angle,length)
10     win.exitonclick()
```

Listing 9.8   A function to expand and draw an L-system

Session 9.2 shows the use of this function to draw a simple tree.

```
>>> myRules = {'X' : 'F[-X]+X', 'F':'FF'}
>>> axiom = 'X'
>>> lsystem(axiom,myRules,7,(0,-200),90,30,2)
```

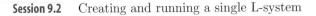

Session 9.2 Creating and running a single L-system

Here are the rules for drawing something that looks like a sprig of rosemary.

Axiom H
Rules $H \rightarrow HFX[+H][-H]$
$\qquad\quad X \rightarrow X[-FFF][+FFF]FX$

Using an angle of 25.7 degrees, we get the image shown in Figure 9.11.

From here on you are on your own to explore the world of L-systems. The following exercises have some examples to get you started, but there are many more available if you do some research.

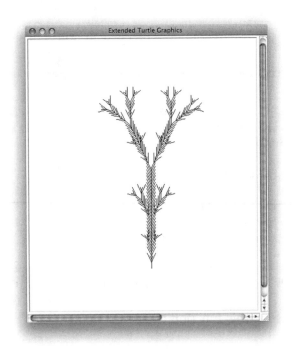

Figure 9.11 A sprig of rosemary drawn by a turtle

Exercises

9.30 Modify the `drawLS` function to support the "G" operation, which allows the turtle to go forward without drawing a line.

9.31 Using your modified `drawLS` function, try the following L-system:

Axiom F – F – F
Rules F → F – F – F – GG
G → GG

9.32 Implement the following L-system using an angle of 25:

Axiom F
Rules F → F [– F] F [+ F] F

9.33 Implement the following L-system using an angle of 25:

Axiom F
Rules F → F F + [+ F – F – F] – [– F + F + F]

9.34 Implement the following L-system using an angle of 45:

Axiom FX
Rules F →
Y → + F X – F Y +
X → – F X + + F Y –

9.5 Summary

In this chapter we introduced recursion, a powerful programming technique that allows us to elegantly solve problems by taking advantage of "self-reference." Fractals are graphically self-referential—that is, they contain smaller versions of themselves. We can implement recursion by simply letting a Python function call itself. Identification of the nonrecursive case, called the base case, is important to make sure that the recursive calls work correctly. Finally, we implement the notion of L-systems, which formally denote fractal behavior using a set of grammar rules. A string of symbols can be produced by applying these rules over and over. By interpreting this result string as turtle commands, the fractal can be drawn.

Key Terms

axiom	erroneous	Koch curve	recursion
base case	fractal	L-system	recursive step
call tree	grammar	production rule	symbol

Python Keywords

```
def    elif    for    if
```

Bibliography

[Fla02] Gary William Flake. *The Computational Beauty of Nature*. MIT Press, 2002.

[Lin68] A. Lindenmayer. Mathematical models for cellular interactions in development. *Journal of Theoretical Biology*, 18:280–315, 1968.

[Man82] Benoit B. Mandelbrot. *The Fractal Geometry of Nature*. Freeman, 1982.

Programming Exercises

9.1 Modify the `L-system` function so that it recursively expands the rules. This will allow you to add a vertical bar (`"|"`) operator that means go forward but the distance to go forward is scaled according to the depth of the recursion.

9.2 Research L-systems and find a different set of production rules to implement.

CHAPTER 10

Astronomy

10.1 Objectives

- To explore classes and objects further
- To understand how to construct a class
- To write constructors, accessor methods, and mutator methods
- To understand the concept of `self`
- To explore instance data
- To implement a graphical simulation using objects

10.2 Introduction

Have you ever witnessed a lunar eclipse? The resulting images of a shadowed moon with changes in color and brightness cause us to ask questions as to the details of this uncommon occurrence. We learned in science class that this fascinating celestial event is caused by the relative motion of the earth, sun, and moon as they orbit around one another. Early astronomers such as Ptolemy and Copernicus built elaborate models of the planets to show their relative positions or sizes. These models were constructed so that the motion of the planets in the model matched the motion of the planets in the night sky.

In this chapter we take up the task of building a different type of planetary model, a software model. Our model will consist of planets, suns, and moons and it will also be capable of showing relative movement. We examine ways that modern programming languages and techniques allow real situations to be represented and manipulated as programming constructs.

10.2.1   Programming

Many people assume that computer science is all about programming. As we have seen thus far, computer science is much more. It is the study of problems, the problem-solving process, and the solutions to those problems. These solutions, also known as algorithms, provide a starting point for programming.

Programming is the process of taking an algorithm and encoding it into a notation that the computer can understand and execute. These notations are referred to as programming languages. As you are already aware, in this text we are using the programming language Python to represent our solutions.

Programming is an important part of what a computer scientist does. It is through programming that we create a representation of our solution. However, the solutions that we achieve are often impacted by the process and language that we choose.

Algorithms describe the solution to a problem in terms of the data needed to represent the problem instance and a set of steps necessary to produce the intended result. Programming languages must provide a way to represent both the process and the data required by the solution. In other words, programming languages like Python must provide control structures and data types.

We have already seen some of these basic requirements in action. We know that our programs process statements in sequence. In addition, special statements such as `if` and `for` enable the flow of control mechanisms to allow selection and iteration of groups of statements. We can also use abstraction to bundle statements together into functions that when invoked can be passed parameters to allow them to do their work. In some cases, a result is returned.

In this chapter, we focus on data. Of course we will still need control structures to represent our algorithms. However, we learn that specific requirements for solving a problem can often be included as part of the **data model** that we build.

10.2.2   Object-Oriented Programming

Python supports the **object-oriented programming** paradigm. This means that Python considers data to be very important in the problem-solving process. In fact, in many ways data becomes the focus of what we do when confronted with a new problem to solve. Object-oriented programming is about **objects**—the individual data items that are manipulated to solve a problem. In Python, every data item is an object.

In order to understand objects, you must also understand the idea of a **class**. Each object must be an instance of a class. Classes are used in object-oriented programming to describe what an object will "look" like, what an object knows about itself (its **instance data**), and what an object can do (its **methods**). Classes are often described as templates for objects in that each object that belongs to a specific class will have the same instance data and methods. However, since the specific values of these instance data items will be different, the objects will likely behave differently when asked to perform their methods.

You are already familiar with some of these ideas from your work with the `Turtle` class. When we create a turtle using the statement `t = Turtle()`, we are creating an instance of the `Turtle` class. You can create more than one turtle, and each turtle has its own instance data. For example, each turtle has a position, a heading, a color, and so on. Each turtle has a number of methods—for example, `forward`, `left`, and `up`. The behavior of a specific turtle is dependent upon the values of its own instance data. So if one turtle has a red tail, it will draw a red line when the `forward` method is called, but a turtle with a blue tail will draw a blue line when its `forward` method is called.

10.2.3   Python Classes

We have already explored a number of classes that are provided by Python. Some of these, such as `int`, `bool`, and `float`, are called primitive classes because they represent only a single value. For example, the integer (object) 5 is an instance of the class `int`. Likewise, the object `True` is an instance of the class `bool`.

Similarly, we have explored classes such as `str` and `list` that describe string and list objects. These so-called collection classes provide a structure that allows objects to be grouped together. For example, Session 10.1 shows that the list `[23, 66, True]` is a collection of three objects: two integers and a Boolean. The list structure provides a number of methods that we can use to manipulate these collections. Indexing allows us to "ask" the list for one of its objects using the linear position, also known as the index. The `reverse` method reverses the order of the items in the list. Note that we used the familiar dot operator to have the list object invoke the `reverse` method.

```
>>> mylist = [23,66,True]
>>> mylist[1]
66
>>> mylist.reverse()
>>> mylist
[True, 66, 23]
```

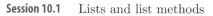

Session 10.1   Lists and list methods

Although it may not be obvious, even integers use methods to perform basic arithmetic. Session 10.2 shows an integer variable called `count` with an initial value of 1. The next statement performs an addition using the accumulator pattern that we have seen many times before. As we would expect, the value of `count` is now 2. The next statement looks a bit strange. This is the accumulator pattern once again. However, the right side of the assignment is actually using a special method called `__add__()` to perform the addition. This method is defined in the `int` class and returns the result of adding the value of the object to the value of the parameter, in this case 1. It is worth noting that the **indexing operator** shown above is also a special method called `__getitem__()`. Notice that `myList.__getitem__(1)` is equivalent to `myList[1]`.

```
>>> count = 1
>>> count = count + 1
>>> count
2
>>> count = count.__add__(1)
>>> count
3
>>>
>>>
>>> mylist.__getitem__(1)
66
>>>
```

Session 10.2   Addition and indexing methods

10.3   Designing and Implementing a Planet Class

We now turn our attention to solving the problem of building a model of the solar system. To do so will require that we consider the data that will be present. However, even with the rich set of built-in classes provided by Python, it is often preferable to describe our problem and solution in terms of classes that are specifically designed to represent the objects present in the problem. We begin by building a simple representation of a planet and then we will design and implement a `Planet` class.

To design a class to represent the idea of a planet, it is necessary to consider the data the planet objects will need to know about themselves. The values of the instance data will help to differentiate the individual planet objects. We assume that each planet has a name.

Each planet also has size information such as the radius and the mass. We also want each planet to know how far it is from the sun.

In addition to data, the class will provide methods that a planet can perform. Some of these might be simple, such as returning the name of the planet. Other methods may require more computation. In Python, the general format for defining a class begins with the keyword `class` followed by the name of the class and a colon. The methods for the class are indented under the class heading, and look just like function definitions.

```
class classname:

    def method1()
        . . .

    def method2()
        . . .
    . . .
```

10.3.1   Constructor Method

The first method that all classes should provide is the **constructor**, which can be defined as the way data objects are created. To create a `Planet` object, we will need the four pieces of information listed previously as parameters: (1) name, (2) radius, (3) mass, and (4) distance. The constructor will then create **instance variables** to hold these values. Each instance variable holds a reference to an object.

In Python, the constructor is always called `__init__`. (Note that there are two underscores before and after `init`.) Methods in class definitions are written in the same way as other functions seen thus far. We provide the name of the method and then a collection of parameters that describe the initial state of the new object. These parameters will be filled in with values when the method is invoked.

Listing 10.1 shows the constructor for the `Planet` class. Notice that even though we stated that four pieces of information would be necessary to construct a planet, there are five formal parameters. The extra parameter, `self`, is a special parameter that will always refer to the object that is being constructed. It must always be the first parameter in the list. Python automatically adds an actual parameter corresponding to `self` when you call the constructor. This means you should not explicitly pass a parameter corresponding to `self`.

Line 3 defines an instance variable called name, which is attached to the special parameter self by a dot. This notation, self.name, appearing on the left side of an assignment statement in the constructor defines an instance variable. Since self refers to the object being constructed, self.name refers to a variable in the object. We call these variables instance variables. Lines 4–6 introduce the other three instance variables described previously.

```
1   class Planet:
2       def __init__(self, iname, irad, im, idist):
3           self.name = iname
4           self.radius = irad
5           self.mass = im
6           self.distance = idist
```

Listing 10.1   Planet class with a constructor

We use the constructor to create an instance of the class by using the name of the class (we do not call __init__ directly). Just as __add__ is called automatically when the + operator is used, __init__ is called automatically when the class name is followed by the () function call operator. Session 10.3 shows the familiar assignment statement (similar to creating an instance of the Turtle class). As stated above, the call to the Planet constructor requires only four parameters even though it is defined to have five. The first parameter, self, never receives an explicit value as it always refers implicitly back to the object being constructed. Note that evaluating the reference myplanet shows that it is an instance of the Planet class. The value 0x58530 is the actual address in memory where the object is stored.

```
>>> myplanet = Planet("X25", 45, 198, 1000)
>>> myplanet
<__main__.Planet instance at 0x58530>
>>>
```

Session 10.3   Using the constructor

The newly created object myplanet is an instance of the Planet class with a name of "X25", a radius of 45, a mass of 198, and a distance of 1000. Figure 10.1 shows a logical view of this object. Note that we have separated the object into two distinct layers. The inner layer, which we call the state, contains the instance variable names. The outer layer contains the names of the methods. In both cases the names are simply references to the actual objects.

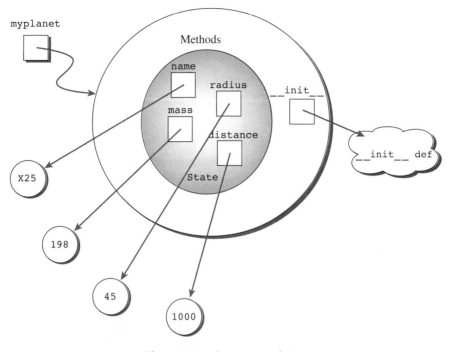

Figure 10.1 A Planet object

We draw objects in this fashion to suggest that there is a strong relationship between the methods of an object and its instance data.

10.3.2 Accessor Methods

The next methods that we will write are commonly called **accessor methods** as they allow us to access the instance variables of the object. These are sometimes also referred to as "getter" methods since the word "get" often appears in the name. It is typical that each instance variable might have an associated accessor method. For example, Listing 10.2 shows the four accessor methods associated with the instance variables **name**, **radius**, **mass**, and **distance** from the **Planet** class.

Session 10.4 shows a few of these methods being used with the **Planet** object named **myplanet** created earlier. The getName method returns the string referenced by the **name** instance variable.

In the getName method we referred to the **name** instance variable as **self.name**, where self is a synonym for **myplanet** (**self** and **myplanet** both reference the same object). In order

```
1  def getName(self):
2      return self.name
3
4  def getRadius(self):
5      return self.radius
6
7  def getMass(self):
8      return self.mass
9
10 def getDistance(self):
11     return self.distance
```

Listing 10.2   Simple accessor methods in the Planet class

to see this more clearly, you can access the instance variable directly using an expression such as myplanet.name.

Although either of these two techniques will allow us to access instance variables within the object, at this point it is preferable to use the accessor methods. Using the accessor methods provides a more formal and controlled access to the object. On a large software project, it is common for the internal representation of an instance variable to change. An accessor method hides those internal changes from the user. The common term for this practice is **information hiding**.

```
>>> myplanet.getName()
'X25'
>>> myplanet.getMass()
198
>>> myplanet.name
'X25'
```

Session 10.4   Using accessor methods

It is also possible to create accessor methods that return computed results based upon values of instance variables. For example, if we assume that a planet is a sphere, we can write an accessor method that will return the volume of the planet since the radius is already an instance variable. We can also include methods that return the surface area as well as the density of the planet. Listing 10.3 shows these methods. Each of these attributes (volume, surface, and density) are quantities, not instance variables, that can be ascertained through some computation or manipulation involving instance data. Session 10.5 shows these methods in action.

```
1  def getVolume(self):
2      v = 4/3 * math.pi * self.radius**3
3      return v
4
5  def getSurfaceArea(self):
6      sa = 4 * math.pi * self.radius**2
7      return sa
8
9  def getDensity(self):
10     d = self.mass / self.getVolume()
11     return d
```

Listing 10.3   Additional accessor methods in the `Planet` class

```
>>> myplanet.getVolume()
381703.50741115981
>>> myplanet.getSurfaceArea()
25446.900494077323
>>> myplanet.getDensity()
0.0005187272219291404
>>>
```

Session 10.5   Using other accessor methods

There are two additional details that we should look at before moving on. In the methods to compute volume and surface area, we used the value of `pi` from the math module. This requires that we import `math` at the start of the `Planet` class (before the class definition itself). Also, the computation for density, the result of dividing the mass by the volume, uses the `getVolume` method. To call the `getVolume` method, we must use `self.getVolume` since `self` is a reference to the `Planet` object. Note that `self` is a reference to the object invoking the `getDensity` method, which in turn can be asked to invoke the `getVolume` method. If we had simply tried to call `getVolume` directly, we would get an error since there is no method to return volume other than the method defined in the `Planet` class.

Exercises

10.1 Modify the `Planet` class constructor to add a new instance variable called `numMoons`.

10.2 Write a new accessor method to return the number of moons that references the `numMoons` instance variable created in Exercise 10.1.

10.3 Write a new accessor method for `Planet` called `getCircumference`.

10.4 Create a new class called `Sentence`. The constructor should accept a single parameter that is a string. Create an instance variable that stores the sentence as a string. Assume the sentence has no punctuation.

10.5 Write the following accessor methods for the sentence class created in Exercise 10.4

    (a) `getSentence`: Return the sentence as a string.

    (b) `getWords`: Return the list of words in the sentence.

    (c) `getLength`: Return the number of characters in the sentence.

    (d) `getNumWords`: Return the number of words in the sentence.

10.6 Create a variation of the `Sentence` class, again called `Sentence`. The constructor should accept a single parameter that is a string. This time create an instance variable that stores the sentence as a list of words.

10.7 Write the following accessor methods for the new class created in Exercise 10.6

    (a) `getSentence`: Return the sentence as a string.

    (b) `getWords`: Return the list of words in the sentence.

    (c) `getLength`: Return the number of characters in the sentence.

    (d) `getNumWords`: Return the number of words in the sentence.

10.3.3　Mutator Methods

Mutator methods are procedures that mutate or change an object in some way. Changes to the object involve changes to one or more of the instance variables. Recall that each object from a particular class has the same instance variables but the values of those variables are different, therefore allowing the object to "behave" differently when asked to perform methods. In order to change those variable values, we provide methods.

A mutator method will allow us to change the name of a planet in our example. Instead of using a cryptic name, such as "X25," we can change the name to something more meaningful. To do this, we need a method that takes the new name as a parameter and modifies the value of the **name** instance variable. Listing 10.4 shows the **setName** method. As before, the first parameter is **self**. In addition, a second parameter that will receive the new name (**newname**) is defined. The value of **newname** is then assigned to the instance variable **name** in the body of the method. It is important to note that nothing is returned from this method. In fact, that is a typical pattern to recognize. Mutator methods modify the state of an object but do not return any value to the caller.

```
1  def setName(self, newname):
2      self.name = newname
```

Listing 10.4 Mutator methods in the **Planet** class

When we use this method, as shown in Session 10.6, we provide one parameter value. Although the method definition has two parameters, the first, **self**, will receive a reference to the object implicitly. Since the state of the object has now changed, it responds differently when asked to perform the **getName** method.

```
>>> myplanet.getName()
'X25'
>>> myplanet.setName("Gamma Hydra")
>>> myplanet.getName()
'Gamma Hydra'
>>>
```

Session 10.6 Using a mutator method

Exercises

10.8 Write a mutator method called **setMoons** that changes the number of moons around our planet.

10.9 Add an instance variable **moonList** and a corresponding mutator method called **addMoon** that adds the name of a moon to the **moonList**.

10.10 Write a mutator method for the **Sentence** class that allows you to capitalize all the words in a sentence.

10.11 Write a mutator method for the **Sentence** class that allows you to add a punctuation mark to the end of the sentence.

10.12 Write an accessor method that allows you to translate a sentence into piratese or any other language. Note you could add a dictionary as an instance variable of the class. Refer to Chapter 4 for details on translating English to pirate.

10.3.4   Special Methods

We mentioned earlier the existence of special methods that were related to system functionality such as integer addition and item selection in a list. There are a number of other special methods that we can define within a class. One of these, **__str__**, is used to provide a string representation for an object.

Session 10.7 shows the result of printing a **Planet** object. The **print** function automatically tries to convert the object into a string representation. Unfortunately, the **Planet** object does not know how to respond to this request. The result is the default representation, which is certainly not very helpful.

```
>>> print(myplanet)
<__main__.Planet object at 0x58fd0>
>>>
```

Session 10.7   Printing a **Planet** object

There are two ways that we can provide better printing capability for the **Planet** class. One is to define a method called **show** that will allow any **Planet** object to show itself in a form by printing the individual instance variable items. For this example, we will simply print the name of the planet. We can implement this method as shown in Listing 10.5.

```
1  def show(self):
2      print(self.name)
```

Listing 10.5   The **show()** method

Now if we create a **Planet** object, we can ask it to show itself. The object will respond by printing its name (see Session 10.8). However, we still cannot print the object directly. In order to provide a better solution, we need to implement a method that allows the object to convert itself to a string. This is what the **print** function needs to do its job.

```
>>> myhome = Planet("Earth",6371,5.97e24,152097701)
>>> myhome.show()
Earth
>>> print(myhome)
<__main__.Planet object at 0x590d0>
>>>
```

Session 10.8   Using the `show()` method

In Python, the special method `__str__` provides this functionality. We have already seen that the default implementation for `__str__` returns the string with the class name and instance address. What we need to do is provide an alternative implementation for the `__str__` method that provides more user-friendly information. In this case, `__str__` will simply return the name of the planet.

To do this, we define a method with the name `__str__` and give a new implementation, as shown in Listing 10.6. The method does not require any other additional information other than the `self` parameter. The method in turn returns the string that we have chosen to represent the object. Session 10.9 shows the result of printing the object. It also demonstrates that when you call the `str` function on an object it automatically invokes the `__str__` method for that object. Figure 10.2 shows the complete reference diagram for the `myhome` planet object.

```
1  def __str__(self):
2      return self.name
```

Listing 10.6   The `__str__` Method

```
>>> myhome = Planet("Earth",6371,5.97e24,152097701)
>>> print(myhome)
Earth
>>> myhome.__str__()
'Earth'
>>> str(myhome)
'Earth'
```

Session 10.9   Using the `__str__` method

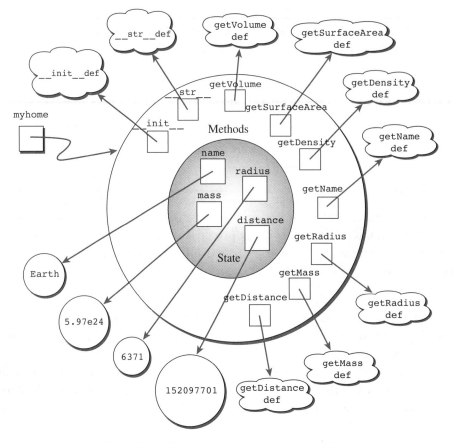

Figure 10.2   Logical view of a `Planet` object

Exercises

10.13 Add a `__str__` method to the `Sentence` class you started in Exercise 10.4 or 10.6.

10.14 Implement the `__getitem__` method for the `Sentence` class. This method should allow you to use the index operator notation to access a word in the sentence.

10.15 Implement the `__len__` method so that you can use the `len` operator.

10.16 Implement the `__contains__` method so that you can ask if a word is `in` a sentence.

10.17 Implement the `__add__` method to allow you to concatenate two sentences together. Make sure your `__add__` method returns a new instance of **Sentence**.

10.18 Design a class to represent a die. The constructor should allow you to specify how many sides the die has. Add a roll method that simulates rolling a die. Implement the `__str__` method.

10.19 Implement the `__ge__`, `__gt__`, `__le__`, `__lt__`, `__eq__`, and `__ne__` methods for the **Die** class. These methods allow you to compare the values of the current roll of two dice.

10.20 Design a class to implement a playing card. The card should remember its rank and suit. Implement the `__ge__`, `__gt__`, `__le__`, `__lt__`, `__eq__`, and `__ne__` methods for the card using the rule that the 2 is the lowest card in a suit and the ace is the highest. When comparing cards with equal rank from two different suits, use the rule that spades are the lowest suit followed by clubs, diamonds, and hearts.

10.21 Design a class to represent a deck of cards. The **Deck** class should provide methods for shuffling and drawing.

10.22 Using the **Deck** class, implement a simple blackjack game.

10.23 Design a class to represent a bank account. Provide methods for checking the balance, and for depositing and withdrawing money. The constructor should allow you to provide a customer ID for the account. The beginning balance should be initialized to 0.

10.24 Extend the bank account class in the previous exercise so that it has a transfer method. The transfer method should take an amount and an instance of an account to transfer the money to.

10.25 Design a class to represent a fraction. The constructor should accept two parameters: a numerator and a denominator. Implement the special methods for addition, subtraction, multiplication, division, comparison, and conversion to string format.

10.26 Extend the **Fraction** class so that fractions are always simplified to their lowest terms.

10.3.5   Methods and `self`

When methods are invoked, they will create local namespaces in the namespace where they are defined. The difference between functions and methods is that each local namespace will also have a reference to the object that invoked the method. The name we have been using for this reference is `self`.

Consider again the `Planet` class described earlier. When we create a new instance (see Session 10.10), we are adding the variable `myplanet` to the main namespace with a reference to the object being constructed. Now when we invoke a method such as `getName`, a local namespace is created and placed in the main namespace. The formal parameter, `self`, implicitly receives a reference to the object that made the invocation (in this case `myplanet`). The result can be seen in Figure 10.3. Although it is not a requirement that the first formal parameter be called `self`, that is a common convention that we will continue to use.

```
>>> myplanet = Planet("X25", 45, 198, 1000)
>>> myplanet
<__main__.Planet object at 0x58530>
>>>
>>> myplanet.getName()
'X25'
```

Session 10.10   Showing scope with methods

When we look at the `getName` method, the only statement is `return self.name`. When Python evaluates `self.name`, it first evaluates the name `self`, which returns a reference to the object that invoked the method. Once we have the reference to the object, we continue to search for `name` in the instance variables of the object. Since `self` refers to the `myplanet` object, it is the value of the `name` instance variable in `myplanet` that is returned. It is for this reason that each object, when invoking the `getName` method, will behave differently since these objects will likely have a different value for the `name` instance variable.

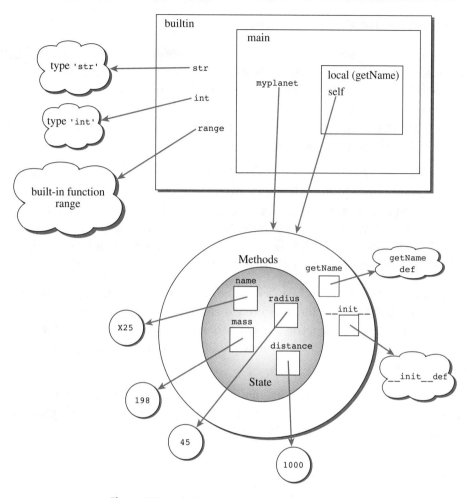

Figure 10.3   A local namespace for a method

Exercises

10.27 Turtles have many instance variables including x, y, color, and heading. Draw a reference diagram showing the namespaces for the following session at the point immediately after the forward method has been invoked.

```
>>> import turtle
>>> myTurtle = turtle.Turtle()
>>> myTurtle.forward(10)
```

10.3.6   Details of Method Storage and Lookup

Before moving on, it is important to understand the difference between the descriptive view of objects that we are using and the actual storage and lookup mechanism that Python uses. We have been representing objects as containing both instance variables and methods. This is an accurate representation for the instance variables since each object needs its own copies. However, it turns out that methods are stored in a slightly different fashion since they are shared by all instances of a class.

In order to see this, consider Figure 10.4. When a class is defined, the name of the class is added to the current namespace with a reference to a **class definition object**. In this case, we have added the name `Planet` to the `main` namespace with a reference to a corresponding class definition object. Class definition objects store method names that refer to method definitions that are implemented by the class. In this case we are showing only two of the many methods that have been implemented by `Planet`.

When an instance of the `Planet` class is created, as was done using `myplanet = Planet( "X25", 45, 198, 1000)`, the Planet reference is followed to gain access to the `__init__` method definition. This constructor is executed and an object is created with the given instance variable values. This object is referenced from the `main` namespace using the name `myplanet`.

You should note that there is one additional instance variable being shown in Figure 10.4. The `__class__` instance variable is used to provide each object with a reference to the class definition object to which it belongs. Now, when a method is called,

```
myplanet.getName()
```

the lookup sequence can proceed a follows. First, `myplanet` is dereferenced to gain access to the object. Next, the `__class__` reference is followed to find the class definition object, then the method name, `getName`, is used to access the method definition. When this method is invoked, a namespace is created and placed following the same steps as explained in the previous sections.

It is important to note that only one copy of the method definition is needed—no matter how many objects exist for a particular class. Since each object will have have a `__class__` reference, the method definitions can always be located from the object. Furthermore, since each method has a formal parameter, `self`, that will reference back to the object making the invocation, there can be no confusion when different objects call the same method. Each will get its own local namespace with an appropriate value for `self`.

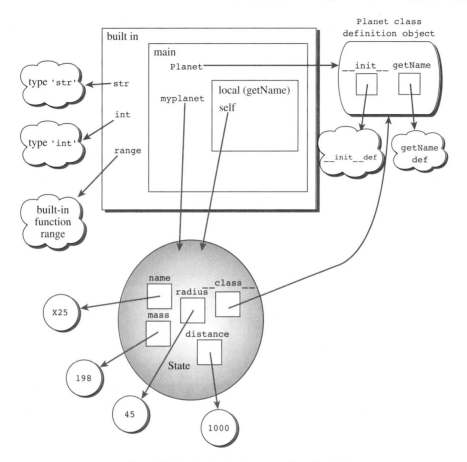

Figure 10.4   Actual storage of methods

10.4   Designing and Implementing a Sun Class

Our task in this chapter is to construct a software model of a planetary system. This means that we need to consider not only the planets that might be present but also the most important member, the sun. For this example we will consider the sun to be similar to a planet, in that it is a large, round, celestial body. It will certainly have some of the same characteristics as planets, including name, mass, and radius. However, since the sun is at the center of the solar system, it will not have any distance measure. In addition, the sun provides heat and light that can be characterized by the temperature on the surface.

Given that description, we can create a Sun class using the same patterns that we followed for the Planet class. Our constructor will require values for the name, mass, radius, and temperature. Listing 10.7 shows a partial implementation of the class, which includes the __init__, getMass, and __str__ methods. We leave the rest of the methods as an exercise.

```
import math
class Sun:
    def __init__(self, iname, irad, im, itemp):
        self.name = iname
        self.radius = irad
        self.mass = im
        self.temp = itemp

    def getMass(self):
        return self.mass

    def __str__(self):
        return self.name
```

Listing 10.7   The Sun class

Exercises

10.28 Complete the implementation of the Sun class by writing the following methods:

(a) getRadius

(b) getTemperature

(c) getVolume

(d) getSurfaceArea

(e) getDensity

(f) setName

(g) setRadius

10.29 Write a function to print a table of radius, volume, and surface area for values of radius between 10 and 500 using increments of 10.

10.5   Designing and Implementing a Solar System

Now we are ready to build our solar system, which will consist of a sun and a collection of planets, each defined to be some distance away from the sun. We will assume that the sun resides at the center of the solar system. The SolarSystem class will be implemented in the same way as the other classes seen so far. We need to provide a constructor that will be responsible for defining the instance variables. We also define appropriate accessor and mutator methods.

The complete SolarSystem class is shown in Listing 10.8. Our constructor (lines 2–4) will assume that a basic SolarSystem object must have a Sun object at its center. This means that the constructor will expect to receive a Sun object as a parameter but will assume an empty collection of planets. We will implement the planet collection as a list.

```
1  class SolarSystem:
2      def __init__(self, asun):
3          self.thesun = asun
4          self.planets = []
5
6      def addPlanet(self, aplanet):
7          self.planets.append(aplanet)
8
9      def showPlanets(self):
10         for aplanet in self.planets:
11             print(aplanet)
```

Listing 10.8   The SolarSystem class

In order to add a Planet to the SolarSystem, we include a mutator method called addPlanet that can modify the collection of planets. This method (lines 6–7) receives a Planet object as a parameter and adds the object to the collection of planets. Since the collection is a list, the modification will simply use the append method.

Finally, a simple accessor method called showPlanets (lines 9–11) will show all of the planets in the solar system. This can be implemented by iterating through the list of planets and printing each one of them. Recall that the Planet class implements the __str__ method that returns the name of the planet.

In order to use the three classes we have implemented, we must save them as Python files. The classes Sun, Planet, and SolarSystem will be saved in the files sun.py, planet.py, and solarsystem.py. When we store a class in a file like this, we have created a module that can be used by other programs. This is no different than turtle, math, or cImage. To use our `Planet`, `Sun`, or `SolarSystem` classes, we simply import the module that contains them.

Session 10.11 shows statements that import the modules, and it creates a solar system with four planets. Note that the module name is the same as the file name but without the `.py`. After importing the modules, we create a `Sun` object called `sun` and a `SolarSystem` object called `ss` using `sun` as its center. Next we create a new `Planet` object p with planet name "MERCURY" and add it as the first planet in the solar system. Similarly, three other planets are created and added. Finally, we call the `showPlanets` method, which prints the names of the planets as described above. Figure 10.5 shows all of the objects and references present at this point.

```
>>>from sun import *
>>>from planet import *
>>>from solarsystem import *
>>>
>>>sun = Sun("SUN", 5000, 1000, 5800)
>>>ss = SolarSystem(sun)
>>>
>>>p = Planet("MERCURY", 19, 10, 25)
>>>ss.addPlanet(p)
>>>
>>>p = Planet("EARTH", 50, 60, 30)
>>>ss.addPlanet(p)
>>>
>>>p = Planet("MARS", 47, 50, 35)
>>>ss.addPlanet(p)
>>>
>>>m = Planet("JUPITER", 75, 100, 50)
>>>ss.addPlanet(p)
>>>
>>>ss.showPlanets()
MERCURY
EARTH
MARS
JUPITER
>>>
```

Session 10.11   Creating and showing a solar system with four planets

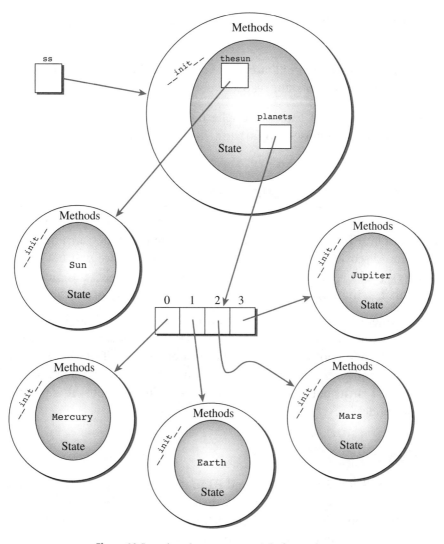

Figure 10.5   A solar system with four planets

Exercises

10.30 Write a method `numPlanets` that returns the number of planets in the solar system.

10.31 Write a method `totalMass` that returns the total mass of the solar system. The total mass should include all the planets, including the sun.

10.32 Given the recent controversy over Pluto, write a `removePlanet` method for the `SolarSystem` class.

10.33 Write two methods, called `getNearest` and `getFarthest`, that will return the planet closest or farthest from the sun respectively.

10.34 Write a `__str__` method that prints the name of the sun and the names of all the planets, in order, from closest to farthest from the sun.

10.6   Animating the Solar System

Now that we can create a solar system, it is a natural next step to consider whether we can draw it and then place it in motion. In this section we construct an animation based on the laws of motion discovered by Sir Isaac Newton. Although we will not attempt to take into account every possible variable that exists in nature's complex interaction of planetary objects, the resulting simulation will still rely on the basic laws of physics.

Understanding planetary movement requires an understanding of the basic laws of motion as described by Newton. In particular, it is necessary to understand how objects that are in motion interact with one another and how those interactions affect the movements. Since this is not a course in physics, we will resist the temptation to describe all of the derivation required. However, it turns out that by using a few simple equations, it is possible to create a fairly accurate model.

10.6.1   Using Turtles

In order to draw our `SolarSystem`, `Sun`, and `Planet` objects, we will use our `Turtle` class. Recall that a `Turtle` is a graphical object that has a number of instance variables, including position and color. In addition, a turtle can define a coordinate system. The turtle can be moved to any position within that coordinate window, and if its tail is in the down position, a line will be drawn. In this application, we will also take advantage of the fact that our `turtle` module allows many such turtles to exist simultaneously in the same window. This means that we can provide each planet with a `Turtle` object that can be used to graphically represent the planet.

Our first modification will be to the `SolarSystem` class. Since the solar system represents the bounds of our animation, we will use a `Turtle` to provide a user-defined planetary coordinate system. When a solar system is created, we will provide a width and a height that can in turn be used to define the upper and lower bounds on the x and y axes within that coordinate system.

Listing 10.9 shows the new `SolarSystem` class. The constructor now has two parameters, `width` and `height`. Note however that the sun is no longer a parameter as it will be added later. Instead, the instance variable `thesun` will be initially set to `None`. By doing things in this order, we allow the planets and sun to take advantage of the graphics setup work that will be done by the `SolarSystem`.

```
class SolarSystem:
    def __init__(self, width, height):
        self.thesun = None
        self.planets = []
        self.ssturtle = turtle.Turtle()
        self.ssturtle.hideturtle()
        self.ssscreen = turtle.Screen()
        self.ssscreen.setworldcoordinates(-width/2.0,-height/2.0,
                                          width/2.0,height/2.0)

    def addPlanet(self, aplanet):
        self.planets.append(aplanet)

    def addSun(self, asun):
        self.thesun = asun

    def showPlanets(self):
        for aplanet in self.planets:
            print(aplanet)

    def freeze(self):
        self.ssscreen.exitonclick()
```

Listing 10.9   The `SolarSystem` class with a hidden `turtle`

Lines 5–8 create instance variables called `ssturtle` and `ssscreen` that will provide graphical functionality to the solar system. Since the turtle will not actually draw anything, we will hide it so that the shape cannot be seen. Using the `width` and `height`, we use the `setworldcoordinates` method to create a coordinate system that is equally distributed around the position $(0, 0)$.

Two additional methods have been added to the `SolarSystem` class. Lines 14–15 define a method called `addSun` that will allow us to add a sun to the solar system. The `freeze` method (lines 21–22) simply lets the user "freeze" the screen after the animation has been completed. This keeps the window from automatically closing.

We next modify the Sun class (shown in Listing 10.10) by creating two new instance variables, self.x and self.y, which will keep track of the coordinate position for the sun. Since we assume that the sun is at the center of the solar system, initializing these values to zero provides a good starting point.

```
class Sun:
    def __init__(self, iname, irad, im, itemp):
        self.name = iname
        self.radius = irad
        self.mass = im
        self.temp = itemp
        self.x = 0
        self.y = 0

        self.sturtle = turtle.Turtle()
        self.sturtle.shape("circle")
        self.sturtle.color("yellow")

    #other methods as before

    def getXPos(self):
        return self.x

    def getYPos(self):
        return self.y
```

Listing 10.10   The Sun class with visualization

By adding self.sturtle as a third instance variable of the Sun class, each Sun object will contain a Turtle object to do the graphical work. Since the color of the Turtle can be user defined, we set it to "yellow". In addition, we change the shape of the turtle from the default triangle to a circle. The majority of the Sun class methods remain unchanged in this new implementation. Two new accessor methods, getXPos and getYPos, will allow us to retrieve the x and y coordinates of the sun.

Finally, the Planet class will also be modified so that each instance of Planet will contain a Turtle (see Listing 10.11). Like the Sun class, each planet will need to keep track of its position using an x and a y coordinate value. The initial x value will be the distance from the sun. The initial y value will simply be 0. This means that all of the planets are initially lined up on the x-axis. We use the color of the turtle to individualize each Planet. When a Planet is created, a color will be provided through the constructor. The shape of the turtle will also be set to circle.

Lines 16–18 move the planet into its initial position. Note that in order to move the planet, the tail of the turtle is raised before invoking the goto method so as not to leave a line. Of course, we need to lower it again once the planet arrives at its destination.

```python
class Planet:
    def __init__(self, iname, irad, im, idist, ic):
        self.name = iname
        self.radius = irad
        self.mass = im
        self.distance = idist
        self.x = idist
        self.y = 0
        self.color = ic

        self.pturtle = turtle.Turtle()

        self.pturtle.color(self.color)
        self.pturtle.shape("circle")

        self.pturtle.up()
        self.pturtle.goto(self.x, self.y)
        self.pturtle.down()


    #other methods as before

    def getXPos(self):
        return self.x

    def getYPos(self):
        return self.y
```

Listing 10.11   The Planet class with visualization

Session 10.12 shows how these classes can be used to create an initial visual representation of a solar system. First, an instance of **SolarSystem** is created with a width and height of two units. Next a **Sun** object is created and added to the solar system. Finally, four planets with different names, colors, and distances from the sun are added. Since the sun and the planets have associated **Turtles** in their constructors, they are automatically shown when the objects are created. The resulting image is shown in Figure 10.6.

```
>>> ss = SolarSystem(2,2)
>>>
>>> sun = Sun("SUN", 5000, 10, 5800)
>>> ss.addSun(sun)
>>>
>>> m = Planet("MERCURY", 19.5, 1000, .25, "blue")
>>> ss.addPlanet(m)
>>>
>>> m = Planet("EARTH", 47.5, 5000, 0.3, "green")
>>> ss.addPlanet(m)
>>>
>>> m = Planet("MARS", 50, 9000, 0.5, "red")
>>> ss.addPlanet(m)
>>>
>>> m = Planet("JUPITER", 100, 49000, 0.7, "black")
>>> ss.addPlanet(m)
>>>
>>> ss.freeze()
```

Session 10.12   Creating and showing a sun and four planets

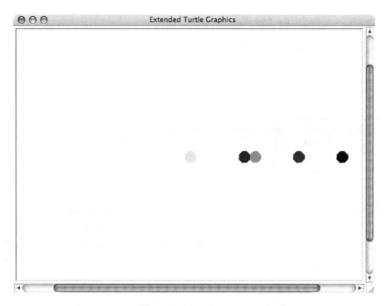

Figure 10.6   Visualizing the sun and planets

Exercises

10.35 Load and run the code shown in Session 10.12.

10.36 Add a planet called SATURN to the solar system created in Exercise 10.36.

10.37 Modify the `Planet` class so that each planet can be a different size. *Hint:* You will want to look up the `resizemode` and `shapesize` methods in the `turtle` documentation.

10.6.2 Planetary Orbits

Planetary orbits are shaped by a number of variables and related equations. We begin by defining some of the necessary vocabulary and then move on to describe the equations that will be used to calculate the actual orbits. To simplify our work, we will continue to assume that our universe exists in only two dimensions. However, you should note, as we go through the explanations, that extending to three dimensions would not be difficult.

Distance Between Objects

To start, assume that a planet is located at some position in the solar system, call it (x, y). The behavior of the planet is dependent upon its distance from other objects in the solar system. Since we are working in two dimensions, the distance will once again be computed using the notion of Euclidian distance, as was described in Chapter 7.

To review, for an object located at position (a, b), the distance between it and the planet described above would be $\sqrt{(x - a)^2 + (y - b)^2}$. If we assume that the sun is at position $(0, 0)$, then the distance between the planet and the sun is simply $\sqrt{x^2 + y^2}$. This distance is often referred to as **r**. For planet interaction, the closer two objects are to one another (smaller **r**), the more they interact. Two objects that are separated by a large distance will have very little interaction with each other.

Velocity

Our planet is not stationary in the solar system. It is moving. The basic description of how it moves is given by its **velocity**. Velocity is defined as the change in distance divided by the change in time. For example, if we are walking in a straight line with a constant velocity of 5 km per hour, we can say that 1 hour from now we will be 5 km from our current location, and after 2 hours we will be 10 km from here, and so on.

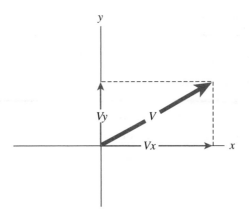

Figure 10.7   Understanding velocity in two dimensions

Velocity in two dimensions is slightly more complex than walking in a straight line. Figure 10.7 shows that velocity, V, is actually a combination of two components. The x-component, called Vx, is the change in the x direction for that given amount of time. Similarly, the y-component, called Vy, is the change in the y direction. This idea, known as a vector in physics, will be important to us for calculating planetary movement in two dimensions.

Acceleration

The velocity of our planet will not be constant. This means that the velocity is being changed over some period of time. This change is known as **acceleration**. Acceleration in two dimensions, like velocity, is defined by a vector with two components, Ax and Ay. Acceleration can cause an object to change direction by altering one or both of the velocity components.

For this example, the acceleration of the planet will be changing due to interactions with other objects in the solar system. This will in turn cause the velocity to change, therefore moving the planet to a new position in the two-dimensional space. We describe these interactions in a later section.

Calculating Distance from Velocity and Velocity from Acceleration

The two previous sections provide relationships for velocity and acceleration that use time in the denominator. If we know that a certain amount of time has elapsed, then a bit of algebra allows us to calculate important values related to the movement of an object. For example, since velocity is the distance traveled divided by the time, it follows that the distance traveled can be computed from the velocity and the time ($v = \frac{d}{t}$ becomes $d = v \cdot t$). If an object is traveling at a certain velocity for a period of time, this allows us to know how far it has moved.

We said earlier that the velocity is actually a vector with both an x-component and a y-component. This simply means that the calculation above must be done twice, once for each component. So, the distance moved in the x direction, Dx, is the x-component of the velocity, Vx, multiplied by the time. Likewise for the movement in the y direction.

Since acceleration is the change in velocity over a given period of time $a = \frac{v}{t}$, the same analysis can be done to compute the velocity components—$Vx = Ax \cdot t$ and $Vy = Ay \cdot t$.

Mass and Gravity

We said earlier that the distance between two objects affects the amount of interaction that occurs between them. In addition to distance, there are other factors that need to be considered. First, the mass of the planet will dictate how much effect it has on other objects in its vicinity. The mass of an object describes a basic notion of how much matter is present in the object. A planet with a large mass will exert more force on other planets of smaller mass at the same distance.

Gravity is an idea that we are all familiar with—the "pull" that keeps us on the earth, what causes us to come back down if we jump in the air. In general, gravity is a force that very massive objects exert on other objects. The gravity that the earth exerts on a person standing on the surface is what we usually consider to be our weight. Since objects with more mass will be "pulled" to a greater extent given the same gravity, the idea of weight and mass can be thought of as similar ideas.

Interaction of the Planets

In order to write a program that will plot the path of planets, we need to use some basic equations that compute the affect of planet interaction. The first important equation, known as Newton's law of universal gravitation, states that the force or attraction, F, between two objects can be computed as $F = G\frac{m_1 m_2}{r^2}$ where G is a constant, m_1 and m_2 are the masses of the two objects, and r is the distance between the two objects. G is often referred to as the **gravitational constant**.

Another famous equation is $F = ma$, where F is the force exerted by an object, m is its mass, and a is its acceleration. By setting these two equations equal to one another and solving for acceleration, it is possible to create an equation to calculate the acceleration of one object as a result of the force exerted on it by another, $a_1 = G\frac{m_2}{r^2}$. In other words, the acceleration experienced by the first object due to the force of gravity from the second object can be calculated by multiplying the gravitational constant by the mass of the second object and dividing by the square of the distance between the two objects.

Figure 10.8 can be used to compute the individual acceleration components for a planet that is experiencing an interaction with the sun. Notice that there are two similar triangles. The large one has sides x, y, and r. The smaller, representing the force that is "pulling" on the planet has sides Fx, Fy, and F. Since the two triangles are so-called similar triangles, the ratios of corresponding sides must be equal. From this we can derive the following sequence of equations for the x-component of acceleration:

1. $\dfrac{Fx}{F} = \dfrac{x}{r}.$

2. Multiplying by F gives $Fx = \dfrac{F \cdot x}{r}.$

3. $Fx = \dfrac{G \cdot m_s \cdot m_p \cdot x}{r^3}$ since $F = G \cdot \dfrac{m_1 m_2}{r^2}.$

4. $Ax = \dfrac{G \cdot m_s \cdot x}{r^3}$ since $Fx = m_p \cdot Ax.$

A similar derivation can be used to get the y-component.

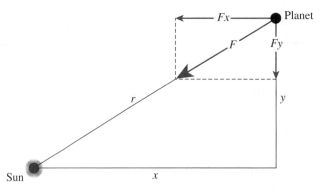

Figure 10.8   Using similar triangles to compute the acceleration components

10.6.3　Implementation

It is now time to implement these equations so that we can compute the positions of the planets as they revolve around the sun. The basic algorithm calculates the amount of planet movement that takes place over a fixed period of time. It also calculates the planet's change in velocity over that same period of time. Each time the planet moves, the gravitational force changes since the distance between it and the sun will have changed. The change in force will cause a new velocity, which in turn will cause the next change in distance. These steps will be repeated for some number of time periods.

For each time step, do the following (assume that the value of the time period and the value of the gravitational constant have been set):

1. Using the current velocity and elapsed time, move the planet to a new location by computing the x distance and the y distance from the velocity components.

2. Compute the new distance from the planet to the sun.

3. Use Newton's gravitational equations to compute the new acceleration components for the planet.

4. Use this new acceleration to adjust the velocity components.

In order to implement these steps, we first need to modify our `Planet` class so that each planet can remember additional information that will be required. Each planet will now need to know its current velocity and to be given an initial velocity as part of the constructor. Since velocity is a vector, we will keep track of the x-component and the y-component separately. Listing 10.12 shows the modifications that need to be made to the `Planet` class. The only parameters that have been added are for the two velocity components.

```
1  class Planet:
2      def __init__(self, iname, irad, im, idist, ivx, ivy, ic):
3
4          #other instance variables as before
5
6          self.velx = ivx
7          self.vely = ivy
```

Listing 10.12　The `Planet` class with animation

Since we have added some additional velocity attributes, we will need to provide corresponding accessor and mutator methods (see Listing 10.13). In addition, we have added a moveto method that will modify the x and y location of the planet. It will also move the turtle to that location leaving a line behind (tracing out the orbit).

```
1      def moveTo(self , newx , newy):
2          self.x = newx
3          self.y = newy
4          self.pturtle.goto(newx , newy)
5
6      def getXVel(self):
7          return self.velx
8
9      def getYVel(self):
10          return self.vely
11
12      def setXVel(self , newvx):
13          self.velx = newvx
14
15      def setYVel(self , newvy):
16          self.vely = newvy
```

Listing 10.13   Animation methods in the Planet class

Most of the animation will occur as part of the SolarSystem class. Recall that a SolarSystem consists of a sun and a collection of planets. Each instance of Planet now has the information necessary to allow the SolarSystem object to compute its movement and position according to the equations described earlier. Listing 10.14 shows the specific method, called movePlanets, that is used to move each planet in the solar system one time step. Each time this method is called, all of the planets will move to their next position.

Let's take a look at each line of this method so that we can understand how the equations have been implemented in Python. First, lines 3–4 set the two important constants that are needed to run the animation. G is Newton's gravitational constant. For simplicity in our example, we will use .1, but in the exercises at the end of the section you will explore using the actual value. We use dt for the time step, and in this case we will compute the movement that takes place in .001 seconds.

Line 6 sets up the iteration that will process each planet in the solar system. The steps that need to be performed to compute the movement for each planet have already been described. Lines 7–8 move the planet based on its current velocity. Note that the new x location is computed from the x-component of the velocity and the new y location is computed from the y-component. Once the planet has been moved to a new location, it is necessary to recompute the distance between the planet and the sun (lines 10–12).

```
1  def movePlanets(self):
2
3      G = .1
4      dt = .001
5
6      for p in self.planets:
7          p.moveTo(p.getXPos() + dt * p.getXVel(),
8                   p.getYPos() + dt * p.getYVel())
9
10         rx = self.thesun.getXPos() - p.getXPos()
11         ry = self.thesun.getYPos() - p.getYPos()
12         r = math.sqrt(rx**2 + ry**2)
13
14         accx = G * self.thesun.getMass()*rx/r**3
15         accy = G * self.thesun.getMass()*ry/r**3
16
17         p.setXVel(p.getXVel() + dt * accx)
18         p.setYVel(p.getYVel() + dt * accy)
```

Listing 10.14   Animation method in the `SolarSystem` class

Lines 14–15 can now compute the new acceleration components based on this new distance. The acceleration is not stored as part of the `Planet` object. It is simply computed and then used to modify the velocity (lines 17–18). The two velocity components are set individually based on the old velocity and the change due to the acceleration. Be sure to go back to the earlier equations and make sure that you understand how each calculation is done.

Now we can finish the animation by creating a solar system and allowing it to move the planets. Listing 10.15 shows a function that creates a simple solar system with a sun and four planets. Although we have used the names of real planets, the values for mass, distance, and initial velocities are not accurate. However, they will work nicely to create a stable system of planetary orbits.

As each planet is created, it is given an initial velocity, all in the y-component, and then added to the solar system. The real work of the animation is done by lines 19–21. The `numTimePeriods` constant simply sets the number of individual positions that will be calculated for each planet. Recall that each time period will actually represent .001 of a second.

Figure 10.9 shows the result of executing this function. Note that each planet travels through an elliptical orbit. The specific shape is dictated by the starting position, the mass, and the initial velocity of the planet. Notice that the time interval is sufficient to allow the inner two planets to make complete orbits. However, the outer two planets would need more time to complete a single orbit. It is also important to note that this animation

```
1  def createSSandAnimate():
2      ss = SolarSystem(2,2)
3
4      sun = Sun("SUN", 5000, 10, 5800)
5      ss.addSun(sun)
6
7      m = Planet("MERCURY", 19.5, 1000, .25, 0, 2, "blue")
8      ss.addPlanet(m)
9
10     m = Planet("EARTH", 47.5, 5000, 0.3, 0, 2.0, "green")
11     ss.addPlanet(m)
12
13     m = Planet("MARS", 50, 9000, 0.5, 0, 1.63, "red")
14     ss.addPlanet(m)
15
16     m = Planet("JUPITER", 100, 49000, 0.7, 0, 1, "black")
17     ss.addPlanet(m)
18
19     numTimePeriods = 2000
20     for amove in range(numTimePeriods):
21         ss.movePlanets()
22
23     ss.freeze()
24
25 createSSandAnimate()
```

Listing 10.15   Creating and moving a solar system with four planets

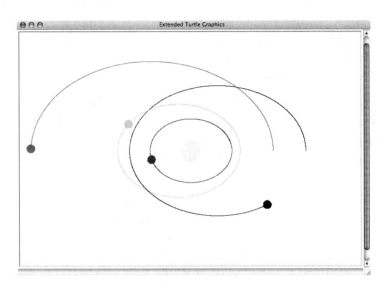

Figure 10.9   Running the animation for two seconds

model takes into account only the interaction between a planet and the sun. It does not model the interaction of planets with each other. In reality, the accelerations must be computed by taking into account all of the other planets. We leave this modification as an exercise.

Exercises

10.38 Load the `Sun`, `Planet`, and `SolarSystem` classes, as well as the `createSSandAnimate` function. Run the solar system simulation.

10.39 Modify the `numTimePeriods` variable of `createSSandAnimate` to make the simulation run longer.

10.40 Modify the initial velocity of one planet and observe the change in its orbit.

10.41 Modify the mass of the sun and observe the change in the orbit of each planet. Make sure you try increasing and decreasing the mass.

10.42 Create a new planet and add it to the solar system. *Hint:* Make sure that your planet is located inside the initial boundaries of the solar system, or change the initial boundaries.

10.43 The real value for Newton's gravitational constant is `G = 6.673e-11`. Using this value for `G` and a time step of 1800, look up the real values for the mass, distance, and velocity of the sun and one or more planets, and create a real model of the solar system.

10.44 Modify the `movePlanets` method so that planets interact with each other. *Hint:* The `accx` and `accy` variables will accumulate for the sun and all other planets. Try running the initial set of planets with this improved model. You may need to change their masses or initial velocities.

10.45 Add a moon to the earth or any of the other planets.

10.7 Summary

In this chapter we explored the implementation of our own data types by creating classes. This ability allows the programmer to create solutions using a data model that closely resembles the problem domain. Classes provide a description of objects (instances of classes) by defining data and methods. Objects are created by calling the constructor method.

Other methods, both accessor and mutator, allow the programmer to communicate with individual objects. We also introduced a number of special methods that are defined by Python, in some cases bound to operators. Finally, we use the `Turtle` to implement a graphical simulation of planetary movement.

Key Terms

acceleration	gravitational constant	method
accessor method	gravity	mutator method
class	index operator	object
class definition object	information hiding	object-oriented programming
constructor	instance data	state
data model	instance variable	velocity
dot operator	mass	

Python Keywords

`__init__`	`class`	`list`
`__str__`	`float`	`self`
`bool`	`int`	`str`

Bibliography

[Fey70] Richard Feynman. *Feynman Lectures on Physics*. Addison Wesley, 1970.

[TM04] Paul A. Tipler and Gene Mosca. *Physics for Scientists and Engineers*. W. H. Freeman, 5th edition, 2004.

Programming Exercises

10.1 Modify the `SolarSystem` class to support more than one Sun.

10.2 Modify the `Planet` class so that the planet does not have the instance variables for `x` and `y` but simply uses the `x` and `y` location stored in the turtle.

10.3 Research *n*-body simulations. Using the ideas from this chapter, implement your own simple *n*-body simulation.

CHAPTER 11

Bears, Fish, and Plants, Oh My!

11.1 Objectives

- To explore classes and objects further
- To design a large multiclass application
- To implement a graphical simulation using objects

11.2 Bears and Fish

Yellowstone National Park is one of the most famous natural places in the United States. People have been visiting the park for many years hoping to see the Old Faithful geyser, the Yellowstone River waterfalls, and, of course, the bears.

For years it was common to see bears along roads and in park campgrounds. Unfortunately, many tourists failed to realize that these great creatures were actually wild and therefore certainly dangerous. Even with new laws to prevent curious humans from feeding the bears, many of the bears had to be relocated. The hope was to reacquaint bears with their natural food sources and at the same time reduce the number of injuries to humans.

One important food source for bears is fish, which bears like to eat. Bears depend on fish to provide a staple part of their diet, especially in the spring and summer when bears are leaving hibernation and beginning to care for young cubs. However, it turns out that the relationship between bears and fish can be much more complicated.

Consider what happens if the number of bears decreases too quickly. Since there are now fewer bears, fish populations can increase. But, more fish will place a strain on the plants that they feed on. These plants also provide oxygen for other water-dwelling creatures.

Changing the population of one life-form can have drastic effects on others. In this chapter, we explore ways that computers can help us understand this potential impact.

11.3   What Is a Simulation?

Earlier, we used a "dartboard" simulation to calculate an approximation for the value of pi. That simulation used a random number generator to place darts on a dartboard as if the darts were being thrown by a player. Although the locations of the darts changed each time we ran the simulation, we were able to consistently use the relative dart locations in calculating a value for pi.

A **computer simulation** is a computer program that is designed to model some specific aspects of a real situation or system. Computer simulations will often utilize random numbers as a way of introducing some realistic variability into the underlying model. The results can then be used to gain information about the way a real system behaves. The complexity of the computer simulation is dependent on the complexity of the underlying reality as well as the specific characteristics we are interested in representing.

One of the most common types of simulation is one in which a "real world" relationship is modeled, typically between two or more life-forms that must coexist and depend on one another in some fashion. These relationships, often referred to as **predator–prey relationships**, suggest that one life-form (the predator) preys on another (the prey) in order to survive. As the number of predators increases or decreases, it may in turn cause the number of prey to increase or decrease. Examples such as foxes and rabbits, big fish and little fish, ladybugs and aphids, and whales and plankton are common. In each of these cases one life-form consumes another and the existence of one depends on the other.

In this chapter, we will construct a computer simulation that will graphically show a world that is inhabited by both predator and prey. In particular, we will model bears and fish. There will be rules that each must live by and as time progresses, individuals will live, breed, die, and move about. We will be able to observe the impact of initial conditions as well as the interaction of one life-form with another as the simulation plays out.

11.4   Rules of the Game

Our computer simulation models a world that contains two types of individual life-forms: bears and fish. We can think of the world as a two-dimensional "grid" with a fixed size for each dimension. Life-forms will only be able to live at specific locations within the grid.

Each life-form will be described by a set of rules that governs how it lives. To start, a group of life-forms will be placed in the world at random locations. The simulation will progress by allowing one of the life-forms to live for one time unit. During this unit of time, all other life-forms are in "suspended animation." This means that at any given time the life-form will be in one of two states: (1) alive or (2) suspended. The particular life-form will be chosen at random from the collection of all possible life-forms. Each time a life-form is in the alive state it must reevaluate its surroundings because it is likely that the rest of the world will have changed during the previous time units. It is in this way that the simulation takes on a sense of reality.

Fish will be allowed to breed, move, and die. Once a fish has been in the alive state twelve times, it may attempt to breed. To do so, it will randomly pick an adjacent location. If that location is empty, a new fish will appear. If the location is occupied, the fish will have to wait until next time and try again.

Regardless of whether a fish breeds, it will next try to move. When a fish moves, it will randomly pick an adjacent location. If that location is empty, the fish will move to this new location. If the location is occupied, the fish will remain in its current location.

One additional environmental characteristic that will affect fish is overcrowding. If a fish discovers that there are two or more other fish living adjacent, then the fish will die. This means that even in the complete absence of bears, fish will self-regulate to some extent. In addition, note that in this version of the simulation fish never need to eat.

Bears will breed, move, eat, and die. Breeding will take place in much the same fashion as described above for fish. The only difference will be that bears need to be in the alive state eight times before they can start the breeding process. Bears will move in exactly the same manner as fish.

Bears will not be impacted by overcrowding but they will need to eat. In order to eat, a bear will need to determine whether there are fish living in an adjacent location. If there are, then the bear will randomly pick one of the fish and "eat" it. In order to consume the fish, the bear will move to the location currently occupied by the chosen fish. If there are no adjacent fish, the bear will begin to starve. Any bear that has been in the alive state and starving ten times in a row will die.

11.5 Design

We will begin by coming up with a basic design for our simulation based on the previous description. The first step is to identify those parts of the problem that correspond to **objects**. One of the easiest ways to start the process of object identification is to consider the prominent **nouns** that appear in the description of the problem. In this case, words like *bear*, *fish*, and *world* seem like good choices. The nouns that you identify now will likely become Python **classes** when we implement the design.

Next, we need to analyze each noun and come up with a list of things that it should know and a list of actions that it can perform. The list of things that an object should know will become **instance variables**. The list of things that an object can do will become **methods**. This process will be very helpful in deciding how objects will interact with one another. You may not identify all the instance variables and methods immediately, but you can always go back and add more later as you discover additional information about the problem.

The following lists provide a first attempt to identify the characteristic properties for the nouns previously identified:

- A world should know
  - The maximum X and Y dimensions.
  - A collection of all life-forms present.
  - A grid with the locations of each specific life-form.

- A world should be able to
  - Return the dimensions of the world.
  - Add a new life-form at a specific location.
  - Delete a life-form wherever it is.
  - Move a life-form from one world location to another.
  - Check a world location to see if it is empty.
  - Return the life-form at a specific location.
  - Allow a life-form to live for one time unit.
  - Draw itself.

- A bear should know
  - The world it belongs to.
  - Its specific world location given as (x, y).
  - How long it has gone without food.
  - How long it has gone without breeding.

- A bear should be able to
  - Return its location, both the x and y value.
  - Set its location, both the x and y value.
  - Set the world that it belongs to.
  - Appear if it is newly born.
  - Hide if it dies.
  - Move from one location to another.
  - Live for one time unit (includes breeding, eating, moving, and dying).

- A fish should know
  - The world it belongs to.

- Its specific location given as (x, y).
- How long it has gone without breeding.
- A fish should be able to
  - Return its location, both the x and y value.
  - Set its location, both the x and y value.
  - Set the world that it belongs to.
  - Appear if it is newly born.
  - Hide if it dies.
  - Move from one location to another.
  - Live for one time unit (includes breeding, moving, and dying).

Figure 11.1 shows a summary of these results in a tabular form. Each table consists of the name of the class, a list of instance variables, and a list of methods. Names have been chosen that are consistent with the previous descriptions. Note that we have included

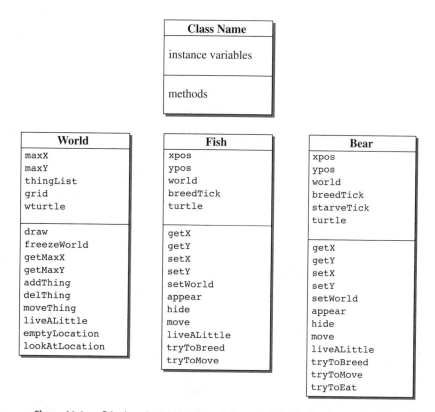

Figure 11.1 Listing instance variables and methods for each class

an extra instance variable, a turtle, in each class. Since we want this to be a graphical simulation, it will be necessary to include instances of the **Turtle** in any class that will have some type of drawing capability.

11.6   Implementation

We will create our simulation in Python by first implementing the instance variables and methods of the classes as described previously. Once we have the classes in place, we can complete the simulation by simply creating a world, adding life-forms to it, and then allowing the life-forms to live. The longer we let the simulation run, the more interesting the results may become.

11.6.1   The World Class

We will begin by implementing the **World** class. Recall that the **World** class will maintain dimensions as well as a list of the life-forms that are present. It will also have a grid to track the life-form positions. A **Turtle** will be used to set the initial coordinates for the world and to draw the grid.

Implementation of the grid will require some additional thought. The grid will maintain the exact two-dimensional position of each life-form. Each entry in the grid may contain a reference to a life-form. For those grid positions that do not contain a life-form, we will use the **None** value.

Figure 11.2 shows an example 12 by 6 grid with three life-forms present. Each position of the grid will be addressed by a unique (x, y) pair. There are bears living at positions $(2, 4)$ and $(11, 5)$, and a fish is currently at position $(5, 0)$.

One of the easiest ways to implement a collection in Python is to use a list. However, since lists are one-dimensional, we need to be creative in order to represent the grid's two-dimensional structure. The solution will be to implement the rows and columns of the grid using a "list of lists" structure. In order to do this, we need to make a decision whether the grid is actually a collection of rows or a collection of columns. Once we make this decision, the code that we write will simply need to be consistent with that decision.

Our choice will be to think of the grid as a collection of rows (list of rows). In computer science this is known as **row major storage**. Each row will in turn be a list of items, one for each column. The entries will either be a reference to a life-form or **None**. Figure 11.3 shows a Python variable called g that is assigned to a list of six lists. This list of lists is designed to represent the information from Figure 11.2.

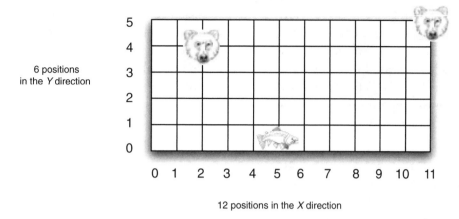

Figure 11.2   A grid with three items

g = [[None,None,None,None,None,FISH,None,None,None,None,None,None] ,

[None,None,None,None,None,None,None,None,None,None,None,None] ,

[None,None,None,None,None,None,None,None,None,None,None,None] ,

[None,None,None,None,None,None,None,None,None,None,None,None] ,

[None,None,BEAR,None,None,None,None,None,None,None,None,None] ,

[None,None,None,None,None,None,None,None,None,None,None,BEAR]   ]

Figure 11.3   A list of lists representation for the example grid

Each item in the list **g** corresponds to a row in the grid. Row 0 can be accessed by g[0], row 1 by g[1], and so on. Within each row there are 12 items. To access a specific item simply requires another list index. For example, the fish is shown in position $(5, 0)$. To access this position, we would use g[0] to access row 0 and then use [5] to access the sixth item in the list. Putting this all together would give g[0][5] as the complete access to that item.

Generalizing this pattern, if we want to access the item at any (x, y) location, the list of lists grid location will be given by g[y][x]. It is important to note that since we decided that our rows would be "stored together," the first index will be the row or y value and the second index will be the column or x value. The two bears can therefore be accessed by g[4][2] and g[5][11].

Listing 11.1 shows the constructor for the World class. It creates six instance variables: (1) maxX, (2) maxY, (3) thingList, (4) wturtle, (5) wscreen, and (6) grid. Initially grid is an empty list. Lines 7–11 show a nested iteration used to create the list of lists implementation. Each row is first created by repeatedly appending None to an empty list. That entire list is then appended to the list of lists (self.grid). Recall from a discussion in Chapter 4 that simply using the repetition operator will result in references to the same list, obviously not what we want or need here.

```
1  def __init__(self, mx, my):
2      self.maxX = mx
3      self.maxY = my
4      self.thingList = []
5      self.grid = []
6
7      for arow in range(self.maxY):
8          row = []
9          for acol in range(self.maxX):
10             row.append(None)
11         self.grid.append(row)
12
13     self.wturtle = turtle.Turtle()
14     self.wscreen = turtle.Screen()
15     self.wscreen.setworldcoordinates(0,0,self.maxX-1,self.maxY-1)
16     self.wscreen.addshape("Bear.gif")
17     self.wscreen.addshape("Fish.gif")
18     self.wturtle.hideturtle()
```

Listing 11.1   The World class constructor

The remainder of the constructor (lines 13–18) modifies the coordinate system and adds two new shapes that will be used later as icons for fish and bears. The wturtle is hidden so that the default triangle shape is no longer present.

The draw method (Listing 11.2) will use wturtle to draw the grid system assuming the maximum x and y dimensions. It first draws the outer boundaries of the grid and then goes back and fills in the horizontal and vertical lines.

The other World methods are shown in Listing 11.3. These will allow us to access or change some aspect of the simulation world. The simple accessor methods getMaxX and getMaxY will return the maximum dimensions, emptyLocation will return True or False depending on whether there is a life-form at that particular location in the grid, and lookAtLocation will return the value at a particular grid location.

```
1   def draw(self):
2       self.wscreen.tracer(0)
3       self.wturtle.forward(self.maxX-1)
4       self.wturtle.left(90)
5       self.wturtle.forward(self.maxY-1)
6       self.wturtle.left(90)
7       self.wturtle.forward(self.maxX-1)
8       self.wturtle.left(90)
9       self.wturtle.forward(self.maxY-1)
10      self.wturtle.left(90)
11      for i in range(self.maxY-1):
12          self.wturtle.forward(self.maxX-1)
13          self.wturtle.backward(self.maxX-1)
14          self.wturtle.left(90)
15          self.wturtle.forward(1)
16          self.wturtle.right(90)
17      self.wturtle.forward(1)
18      self.wturtle.right(90)
19      for i in range(self.maxX-2):
20          self.wturtle.forward(self.maxY-1)
21          self.wturtle.backward(self.maxY-1)
22          self.wturtle.left(90)
23          self.wturtle.forward(1)
24          self.wturtle.right(90)
25      self.wscreen.tracer(1)
```

Listing 11.2   The `draw` method

The `freezeWorld` method is used at the end of the simulation. It calls the `exitonclick` method of `wscreen` to allow the graphics window to remain drawn after the simulation has ended. Clicking on the window will then exit the simulation.

A new life-form is added to the world by `addThing`, lines 4–10. It needs the life-form and the (x, y) position where the life-form should be placed. Some of the methods that are called belong to the life-form itself and have not yet been described. We will come back to these at a later time. For now, line 7 adds the life-form to the grid and line 9 appends the life-form to the list of life-forms maintained by the world.

Removing a life-form from the simulation world requires that it be taken off the grid and also removed from the life-form list. This is done in the `delThing` method. Line 14 sets the appropriate grid reference to `None`. Line 15 uses the list method `remove` to delete the fish or bear from the list of life-forms maintained by the world.

```
1   def freezeWorld(self):
2       self.wscreen.exitonclick()
3
4   def addThing(self, athing, x, y):
5       athing.setX(x)
6       athing.setY(y)
7       self.grid[y][x] = athing
8       athing.setWorld(self)
9       self.thingList.append(athing)
10      athing.appear()
11
12  def delThing(self,athing):
13      athing.hide()
14      self.grid[athing.getY()][athing.getX()] = None
15      self.thingList.remove(athing)
16
17  def moveThing(self,oldx,oldy,newx,newy):
18      self.grid[newy][newx] = self.grid[oldy][oldx]
19      self.grid[oldy][oldx] = None
20
21  def getMaxX(self):
22      return self.maxX
23
24  def getMaxY(self):
25      return self.maxY
26
27  def liveALittle(self):
28      if self.thingList != [ ]:
29          athing = random.randrange(len(self.thingList))
30          randomthing = self.thingList[athing]
31          randomthing.liveALittle()
32
33  def emptyLocation(self,x,y):
34      if self.grid[y][x] == None:
35          return True
36      else:
37          return False
38
39  def lookAtLocation(self,x,y):
40      return self.grid[y][x]
```

Listing 11.3   The rest of the World class

The `liveALittle` method, lines 27–31, does the majority of the simulation work. As long as there are still life-forms remaining, the world will pick a random life-form from the list that it maintains (lines 29–30). Once a random life-form has been chosen, it is allowed to live as was described earlier. The details are dependent on the type of life-form that was chosen. Note that the world lets only one life-form live during every call to `liveALittle`.

Exercises

11.1 Implement the `World` using column major storage for the grid of locations. In other words, store the columns together in lists instead of the rows.

11.2 Add two additional instance variables, `bearCount` and `fishCount`, to the `World` class. Also add methods `getNumBears`, `getNumFish`, `incBears`, `decBears`, `incFish`, and `decFish` to increment and decrement the appropriate counters by one.

11.3 Add a method `showCounts` to show the count of bears and fish you added in Exercise 11.2. You may want to use the `write` method of `wturtle` for this task.

11.6.2 The `Fish` Class

In this simulation, fish are the prey. They will try to breed, move around, and inevitably may end up in the vicinity of a bear who will likely eat them for dinner. Fish need to know where they are and how long it has been since they have given birth. In addition, since this is a graphical simulation, each fish will have an instance of `Turtle` so that it can be displayed.

In Listing 11.4, which shows the constructor for the `Fish` class, `self.xpos` and `self.ypos` are initialized to $(0, 0)$ but will be set later when the fish is placed in the world. Likewise, each fish will have a reference back to the world that they live in. Line 10 sets this reference to `None`. This will also be set when the fish are added to the world.

The next group of methods for the `Fish` class will be the simple accessor and mutator methods used by other objects as they interact with `Fish` objects (see Listing 11.5). They allow "getting" and "setting" of values as well as some basic `Turtle` function. The `appear` and `move` methods need a bit of explanation. When a `Fish` is first created, it will be added to the world at a specific location and then told to appear. The `appear` method will take care of moving the underlying `Turtle` object and then showing the icon in the simulation display.

```
1  class Fish:
2      def __init__(self):
3          self.turtle = turtle.Turtle()
4          self.turtle.up()
5          self.turtle.hideturtle()
6          self.turtle.shape("Fish.gif")
7
8          self.xpos = 0
9          self.ypos = 0
10         self.world = None
11
12         self.breedTick = 0
```

Listing 11.4   The constructor for the Fish class

```
1  def setX(self,newx):
2      self.xpos = newx
3
4  def setY(self,newy):
5      self.ypos = newy
6
7  def getX(self):
8      return self.xpos
9
10 def getY(self):
11     return self.ypos
12
13 def setWorld(self,aworld):
14     self.world = aworld
15
16 def appear(self):
17     self.turtle.goto(self.xpos, self.ypos)
18     self.turtle.showturtle()
19
20 def hide(self):
21     self.turtle.hideturtle()
22
23 def move(self,newx,newy):
24     self.world.moveThing(self.xpos,self.ypos,newx,newy)
25     self.xpos = newx
26     self.ypos = newy
27     self.turtle.goto(self.xpos, self.ypos)
```

Listing 11.5   The simple accessor and mutator methods of the Fish class

Once the `Fish` object is in the simulation, it can be moved to a new location using the `move` method. This method not only moves the underlying `Turtle` but also changes the x and y positions of the `Fish` object. From the `Fish` object's perspective, these are the two things that must happen for it to move. It is important to note that the world must also move the object in its underlying representation.

The most important method in the `Fish` class is `liveALittle`. This method is responsible for what happens to a `Fish` each time it is allowed to live for a time unit. Recall from our description that fish can die if they are crowded by too many other fish. If that is not the case, then they will try to breed and then finally try to move. Of course, if a fish dies due to overcrowding, it will not attempt to breed or move.

The first thing this method needs to do is count the number of `Fish` that are at adjacent locations in order to decide if overcrowding is occurring. This will require that we design a process that allows us to find all of the locations that are adjacent to a given location. For this task, we will use a list of offsets. Each offset is a tuple containing an amount to adjust the x coordinate and an amount to adjust the y coordinate. Figure 11.4 shows the (x, y) values for any location and the eight locations that occur around it. Note that from the original (x, y) it is possible to compute the coordinates of all adjacent locations.

Figure 11.5 shows how we can take the coordinates, reduce them to an offset tuple, and then simply create a list of these offset tuples. Now it is just a matter of iterating through the `offsetList` and adjusting the original (x, y) position by the appropriate tuple component.

Listing 11.6 shows the `liveALittle` method. Line 2 creates the list of offset tuples and line 5 initializes a variable to count the number of neighboring fish. Lines 7–13 are performed for

$(x-1, y+1)$	$(x+0, y+1)$	$(x+1, y+1)$
$(x-1, y+0)$	(x, y)	$(x+1, y+0)$
$(x-1, y-1)$	$(x+0, y-1)$	$(x+1, y-1)$

Figure 11.4 Coordinates of the eight adjacent locations around a specific (x, y)

(−1, +1)	(0, +1)	(+1, +1)
(−1, 0)	(x, y)	(+1, +0)
(−1, −1)	(0, −1)	(+1, −1)

Figure 11.5   Coordinates of the eight adjacent locations around a specific (x, y)

```
1  def liveALittle(self):
2      offsetList = [(-1,1) ,(0,1) ,(1,1),
3                    (-1,0)         ,(1,0),
4                    (-1,-1),(0,-1),(1,-1)]
5      adjfish = 0
6      for offset in offsetList:
7          newx = self.xpos + offset[0]
8          newy = self.ypos + offset[1]
9          if 0 <= newx < self.world.getMaxX()   and
10             0 <= newy < self.world.getMaxY():
11             if (not self.world.emptyLocation(newx,newy)) and
12                 isinstance(self.world.lookAtLocation(newx,newy),Fish):
13                 adjfish = adjfish + 1
14
15      if adjfish >= 2:
16          self.world.delThing(self)
17      else:
18          self.breedTick = self.breedTick + 1
19          if self.breedTick >= 12:
20              self.tryToBreed()
21
22          self.tryToMove()
```

Listing 11.6   The liveALittle method

each offset in `offsetList`. First, new x and y values are computed from the current (x, y) location and the current offset tuple. Line 10 checks to see if this new location is actually a legal location. It is possible that we can generate an illegal location if the original (x, y) was on a boundary.

If the location is legal, then it can be checked for a life-form. Finally, we use the built-in `isinstance` function to ask if an object is an instance of a particular class. In this case, we want to count only those objects that are instances of the `Fish` class. Line 13 increments the `adjfish` counter if this is the case.

Once we have counted the adjacent `Fish`, line 15 checks to see if there is overcrowding according to the rules described earlier. If so, `world` is told to delete the fish (`self`). Since `self` is a reference to the actual fish, `world` can use the reference to locate and remove the object from `thingList`. This may look odd to you since we have always used `self` as a formal parameter rather than as an actual parameter. However, if you trace the call to `delThing` in Listing 11.3, you will see that `self` is assigned to the formal parameter `athing`.

If no overcrowding is taking place, the next activity is to check whether the fish has been active for enough time units to try to breed. According to the rules, it must wait 12 time units before trying to breed. Regardless of whether the fish is successful in breeding, it then tries to move to a new location.

If it is determined that the `Fish` can try to breed, the `tryToBreed` method is called (Listing 11.7). According to the rules, this method must first pick a random adjacent location. To do this, we can use the same offset list technique that we used earlier. In this case, instead of iterating through all of the offsets, we will simply pick one. In order to choose a random element of the list, we will first choose a random integer in the range of index values using the length of the `offsetList` as the upper bound. Once we compute this new (x, y) position, we must be sure that it is in the actual range of legal coordinates. If it is not, we must try again. The *while* loop (line 9) continues to choose random offset pairs until a legal result is obtained.

Once a new random location has been determined, the rules state that it must be empty in order for breeding to take place. Line 16 checks the location to see if any life-forms are present. If they are not, a new `Fish` is created and added to the world at that location. Recall that the `addThing` method sets the (x, y) and world values and makes the fish appear in its initial position in the graphical display.

The `tryToMove` method (Listing 11.8) has much of the same functionality as `tryToBreed`. It must first pick a random adjacent location and check if it is empty. If it is, the fish is allowed to move using the `move` method.

```python
def tryToBreed(self):
    offsetList = [(-1,1) ,(0,1) ,(1,1),
                  (-1,0)          ,(1,0),
                  (-1,-1),(0,-1),(1,-1)]
    randomOffsetIndex = random.randrange(len(offsetList))
    randomOffset = offsetList[randomOffsetIndex]
    nextx = self.xpos + randomOffset[0]
    nexty = self.ypos + randomOffset[1]
    while not (0 <= nextx < self.world.getMaxX() and
               0 <= nexty < self.world.getMaxY() ):
        randomOffsetIndex = random.randrange(len(offsetList))
        randomOffset = offsetList[randomOffsetIndex]
        nextx = self.xpos + randomOffset[0]
        nexty = self.ypos + randomOffset[1]

    if self.world.emptyLocation(nextx,nexty):
        childThing = Fish()
        self.world.addThing(childThing,nextx,nexty)
        self.breedTick = 0
```

Listing 11.7   The `tryToBreed` method

```python
def tryToMove(self):
    offsetList = [(-1,1) ,(0,1) ,(1,1),
                  (-1,0)          ,(1,0),
                  (-1,-1),(0,-1),(1,-1)]
    randomOffsetIndex = random.randrange(len(offsetList))
    randomOffset = offsetList[randomOffsetIndex]
    nextx = self.xpos + randomOffset[0]
    nexty = self.ypos + randomOffset[1]
    while not(0 <= nextx < self.world.getMaxX() and
              0 <= nexty < self.world.getMaxY() ):
        randomOffsetIndex = random.randrange(len(offsetList))
        randomOffset = offsetList[randomOffsetIndex]
        nextx = self.xpos + randomOffset[0]
        nexty = self.ypos + randomOffset[1]

    if self.world.emptyLocation(nextx,nexty):
        self.move(nextx,nexty)
```

Listing 11.8   The `tryToMove` method

Exercises

11.4 Make the `offsetList` an instance variable of the `Fish` class.

11.5 Modify the `liveALittle` method to use instance variables for the number of fish that constitute overcrowding, and the number of time units that must pass before breeding is allowed. Also modify the `Fish` constructor to have parameters to initialize the new instance variables.

11.6 Add getter and setter methods for the instance variables you created in the previous exercise.

11.7 Modify the `tryToMove` method to allow the fish to try up to four random locations for its move.

11.6.3 The `Bear` Class

The `Bear` class is implemented in much the same way as the `Fish` class. In fact, many of the methods are identical. We will focus on those methods that are either different or are new. The obvious place to start is with the `liveALittle` method and the constructor. As described earlier, bears will not be impacted by overcrowding. The first thing they will do is try to breed. The other important difference is that bears will eat fish if fish are available. However, any bear that does not get enough food will starve and die. This means that the constructor for the `Bear` class will need to include one more instance variable that will keep track of the number of time units since the bear's last meal.

Listings 11.9 and 11.10 show these modifications. The obvious difference between this constructor and the `Fish` constructor is the graphics icon used as a turtle shape and the inclusion of the `starveTick` instance variable. The first three lines of the `liveALittle` method suggest that bears must wait for eight time units before attempting to breed (recall that fish waited for 12). Implementation of the `tryToBreed` method is identical to the `Fish` class.

The next step in the `liveALittle` method allows a bear to try to eat a fish (line 6). The `tryToEat` method shown in Listing 11.11 is new. Recall that bears will check in the adjacent locations to see if there are any fish present. If so, the bear will pick one of the fish at random and eat it. This means that the bear moves to the location currently occupied by the fish and the fish dies. If there are no fish present, the bear starves a bit more.

```
1  class Bear:
2      def __init__(self):
3          self.turtle = turtle.Turtle()
4          self.turtle.up()
5          self.turtle.hideturtle()
6          self.turtle.shape("Bear.gif")
7
8          self.xpos = 0
9          self.ypos = 0
10         self.world = None
11
12         self.starveTick = 0
13         self.breedTick = 0
```

Listing 11.9   The constructor method in the Bear class

```
1  def liveALittle(self):
2      self.breedTick = self.breedTick + 1
3      if self.breedTick >= 8:
4          self.tryToBreed()
5
6      self.tryToEat()
7
8      if self.starveTick == 10:
9          self.world.delThing(self)
10     else:
11         self.tryToMove()
```

Listing 11.10   The liveALittle method in the Bear class

As before, we will use the offset list technique to check the adjacent locations for Fish. However, instead of just counting the number of Fish that are present, we will create a list of adjacent fish. Line 5 creates an initially empty list and line 13 adds the neighboring Fish to the list. The details for computing the adjacent (x, y) locations and checking the instance type are the same as we used to look for neighboring fish in the test for overcrowding.

Line 15 checks to see if there are any Fish adjacent to the bear. If not, then starveTick is incremented (line 24). If there are fish present, one is chosen at random by once again picking a random index value (line 16). Since the bear must move to the location of the chosen fish (in order to eat it), we must get the current (x, y) location of the randomly chosen fish by using getX and getY. Lines 20–21 tell the world to delete the fish and tell the bear to move to the location formerly occupied by the fish. Since the bear has now eaten, it is no longer starving and starveTick can be reset to zero (line 22).

```
1  def tryToEat(self):
2      offsetList = [(-1,1) ,(0,1) ,(1,1),
3                    (-1,0)         ,(1,0),
4                    (-1,-1),(0,-1),(1,-1)]
5      adjprey = []
6      for offset in offsetList:
7          newx = self.xpos + offset[0]
8          newy = self.ypos + offset[1]
9          if 0 <= newx < self.world.getMaxX() and
10             0 <= newy < self.world.getMaxY():
11             if (not self.world.emptyLocation(newx,newy)) and
12                    isinstance(self.world.lookAtLocation(newx,newy),Fish):
13                 adjprey.append(self.world.lookAtLocation(newx,newy))
14
15      if len(adjprey)>0:
16          randomprey = adjprey[random.randrange(len(adjprey))]
17          preyx = randomprey.getX()
18          preyy = randomprey.getY()
19
20          self.world.delThing(randomprey)
21          self.move(preyx,preyy)
22          self.starveTick = 0
23      else:
24          self.starveTick = self.starveTick + 1
```

Listing 11.11 The `tryToEat` method

Bears move in exactly the same way as fish. The `tryToMove` method is identical in both classes. Remember that they check adjacent locations and can move only if one is available. It is also important to note that in the `liveALittle` method for `Bear`, the `tryToMove` method is done regardless of whether the bear eats. This means that it is possible to have the bear move twice during a time unit, once to eat and then again when it moves normally.

Exercises

11.8 Make the `offsetList` an instance variable of the `Bear` class.

11.9 Modify the `liveALittle` method to use instance variables for the number of time units that must pass before a bear starves, and the number of time units that must pass before breeding is allowed. Also modify the `Bear` constructor to have parameters to initialize the new instance variables.

11.10 Add getter and setter methods for the instance variables you created in the previous exercise.

11.11 Modify the `tryToMove` method to allow the bear to be more intelligent about the direction it moves. Perhaps the bear can look farther out to see if there are any fish in some direction.

11.6.4   Main Simulation

We can now turn our attention to implementing a function that will be responsible for setting up the entire simulation and starting it. Recall that once it is in execution, the simulation itself dictates how it progresses due to the random numbers that are generated. This main function will need to do four things:

1. Set initial constants pertaining to the number of bears and fish, the size of the world, and the length of the simulation.

2. Create an instance of the `World`.

3. Create the specified number of bears and fish and place them at random locations in the world.

4. Let the world live for the specified number of time units.

Listing 11.12 shows the complete `mainSimulation` function. In this case we initialize the world with ten bears and ten fish. Line 8 creates a `World`, called `myworld` with dimensions as defined. The grid for `myworld` is then drawn (line 9).

Lines 11–18 will create and place the `Fish` objects in the world. Note that once a fish has been created, a random (x, y) location must be generated. Since we do not want more than one life-form living at a specific location, we must check to see if the location is empty before using it. If it is not empty, we continue to randomly generate random (x, y) locations (line 24). For our purposes here, we assume that there will always be enough space to find an empty location.

Bears are created and placed in the same way (lines 20–27). Figure 11.6 shows the one possible way that the life-forms can be placed in the world. Of course, due to the random nature of the initial location selection, subsequent runs of the simulation will likely look different at the start.

```
1   def mainSimulation ():
2       numberOfBears = 10
3       numberOfFish = 10
4       worldLifeTime = 2500
5       worldWidth = 50
6       worldHeight = 25
7
8       myworld = World(worldWidth , worldHeight )
9       myworld.draw ()
10
11      for i in range(numberOfFish ):
12          newfish = Fish ()
13          x = random.randrange(myworld.getMaxX ())
14          y = random.randrange(myworld.getMaxY ())
15          while not myworld.emptyLocation (x,y):
16              x = random.randrange(myworld.getMaxX ())
17              y = random.randrange(myworld.getMaxY ())
18          myworld.addThing(newfish ,x,y)
19
20      for i in range(numberOfBears ):
21          newbear = Bear ()
22          x = random.randrange(myworld.getMaxX ())
23          y = random.randrange(myworld.getMaxY ())
24          while not myworld.emptyLocation (x,y):
25              x = random.randrange(myworld.getMaxX ())
26              y = random.randrange(myworld.getMaxY ())
27          myworld.addThing(newbear ,x,y)
28
29      for i in range(worldLifeTime ):
30          myworld.liveALittle ()
31
32      myworld.freezeWorld ()
```

Listing 11.12   The `mainSimulation` function

Most of the work is then accomplished by lines 29–30. For each time unit, myWorld's `liveALittle` method is called. Recall that this means that a random life-form will be chosen to live for that time unit. The final line of the function simply puts the world into a wait mode so that we can observe the final state of the simulation. When you click in the simulation window, it will close and the function will exit.

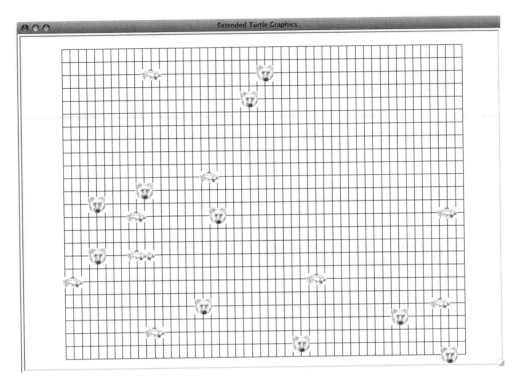

Figure 11.6 The initial simulation

Exercises

11.12 Modify `addThing` and `delThing` to automatically update the fish and bear counters you added in an earlier exercise.

11.13 Run the simulation with different numbers of bears and fish. What do you observe about the number of bears and fish over time?

11.14 Modify `mainSimulation` to create bears and fish using different constants for the time to breed and time to starve. This will allow each fish to behave slightly differently.

11.15 Modify the simulation so that it will automatically stop if the number of bears or fish go above or below some thresholds that you define.

11.16 Modify the `liveALittle` method of the `World` so that all bears and fish get a chance to live each time unit. To make it fair, you should randomly shuffle `thingList` each time unit.

11.17 Modify the `mainSimulation` function to create two lists. One list will keep track of the number of fish that are alive in each time unit, the other will keep track of the number of bears. When the simulation is done, this data should be written to a file. The file should have three columns: one column for the time, one for the number of fish, and one for the number of bears.

11.18 Write a function to read the file produced by the previous exercise. This function should produce a graph that shows how the number of bears and fish change over time.

11.7 Growing Plants

In our initial description of the bears and fish model, we mentioned that fish could also be predators in that they could eat plants that exist in the water. If there are not enough plants available, the fish would starve and die. It is relatively easy to include another class to represent the plants by taking code that already exists and simply "repackaging" it as required for a plant.

We can begin by realizing that plants will not be able to move. In addition, we will not have them eat anything. So, the only action that they really carry out when they live is breeding. Listing 11.13 shows the `liveALittle` method for the `Plant` class. Note that we are assuming that plants can attempt to breed after five time units.

```
def liveALittle(self):
        self.breedTick = self.breedTick + 1
        if self.breedTick >= 5:
            self.tryToBreed()
```

Listing 11.13   The `liveALittle` method in the `Plant` class

The only other change that we need to make is the inclusion of a `tryToEat` method as part of the `Fish` class. This method would be identical to the `tryToEat` method of the `Bear` class except for the one modification that fish eat plants. Listing 11.14 shows the modified line of code that would be used.

```
    if isinstance(self.world.lookAtLocation(ix,iy),Plant):
```

Listing 11.14   The modified `liveALittle` method in the `Fish` class

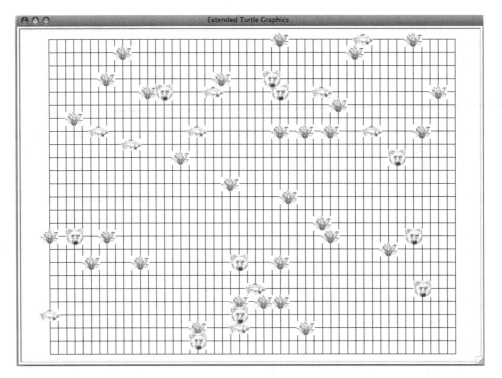

Figure 11.7   The initial simulation including plants

Finally, we need to modify the main function so that plants are also added to the simulation at random locations. Figure 11.7 shows a possible initial scenario that includes plants as well as the bears and fish from before.

Exercises

11.19 Create a **Plant** class that is similar to the **Fish** class using the modifications suggested in Section 11.7.

11.20 Modify the **liveALittle** method of the **Fish** class so that fish can try to eat plants. You will need to add a **starveTick** counter for the fish.

11.21 Modify the main simulation to create some initial number of plants and place them in the World.

11.22 Modify the **Plant** class to implement some kind of overcrowding mechanism.

11.8 A Note on Inheritance

As you consider the implementation for the Fish, Bear, and Plant classes, you have probably noticed that there are a number of duplications. Each class includes methods that are identical. For example, getX, getY, setX, setY, appear, and hide are all implemented the same way regardless of the class.

This observation leads us to think about the similarities among all life-forms in our simulation. It would make sense if we could somehow take all of this duplication, put it in one place, and have all of the life-forms share it. This new implementation would allow us to efficiently add and modify functionality.

The solution that we are proposing is called **inheritance**—an object-oriented programming technique that is supported by many programming languages including Python. We introduce this new technique in the next chapter and will ask you to reconsider the simulation as a programming exercise.

11.9 Summary

In this chapter we designed and implemented a large, multiclass graphical simulation. To start, we considered a description of the problem. We picked out the important subjects (nouns) and began to implement classes, one for each. In order to design a class, we described those things that instances of a class would need to know about themselves (the instance variables) and those things that instances of a class would need to be able to do (the methods). After creating each class, we implemented a function that established many objects and let each one perform methods as defined by the initial rules of the simulation. By using random numbers, we were able to provide a degree of uncertainty so that no two runs of our simulation would look the same.

Key Terms

class	instance variables	predator–prey relationships
column major storage	methods	random number generator
computer simulation	nouns	row major storage
inheritance	object	

Python Keywords

class	if	random	self
def	isinstance	randrange	while
for	None	range	

Bibliography

[Fla02] Gary William Flake. *The Computational Beauty of Nature.* MIT Press, 2002.

[KE85] Richard Knight and L. L. Eberhardt. Population dynamics of yellowstone grizzly bears. *Ecology*, 1985.

Programming Exercises

11.1 Modify the simulation so that `world` consists of two kinds of locations, water and land. Fish and plants can live only in the water and bears can go in the water but only to eat fish.

11.2 Modify the simulation to give bears and fish an energy instance variable. Each time a bear or fish eats, it increases its energy level. If the energy level drops to zero, the bear or fish dies. If the energy level is sufficiently high, then the bear or fish can breed. Bears and fish should lose energy as they move and breed.

11.3 Add a `Berry` class so that the bears have another food source. This class should behave much like the `Plant` class.

11.4 Choose another real-world predator–prey ecosystem and implement a simulation.

CHAPTER 12

Your Father Was a Rectangle

12.1 Objectives

- To introduce the concept of inheritance
- To create a working object-oriented graphics package
- To provide another example of object-oriented design

12.2 Introduction

So far in this book we have relied on our trusty turtle for any graphics we want to add to our programs. However, most computer graphics programs do not use a turtle. Common drawing programs that you may be familiar with, including Visio or OmniGraffle, allow users to select the shapes they want to include in their drawing from a palette of available shapes. For simple drawing programs, this palette may include lines, circles, squares, triangles, and other simple shapes. For more advanced drawing programs, such as architecture programs or computer-aided design (CAD) programs, the palette may include sophisticated shapes like cabinets, bathroom fixtures, or even specific parts needed for a car. These kinds of drawing programs are typically called object-oriented drawing programs.

Object-oriented drawing programs are easy to use. If your drawing calls for a square, you simply drag a square from the palette of shapes and drop it into your drawing in the appropriate place. If your drawing calls for a circle, or any other shape, you drag the circle into position. Once a shape is placed in the drawing, the user can change attributes of the shape, such as its size, color, outline, or position.

Our goal for this chapter is to design an object-oriented graphics module for Python that will allow you to write graphics programs by creating simple graphical shapes and placing them on a drawing canvas. The shapes will be exactly the same as the shapes you would use if you were making a drawing program such as the ones described previously, except that we will not go so far as to write the code that would let a user drag the objects from a palette.

To be clear about where we are going in this chapter, consider the simple Python function, drawHouse, shown in Listing 12.1. The code draws a blue filled rectangle as the main part of a house, along with a brown door and a peaked roof. In addition, it draws a yellow sun that slowly moves across the sky. The picture drawn by the code in Listing 12.1 is shown in Figure 12.1.

```python
def drawHouse():
    myCanvas = Canvas(800,600)
    house = Rectangle(Point(-100,-100),Point(100,100))
    house.setFill('blue')
    door = Rectangle(Point(-50,-100),Point(0,75))
    door.setFill('brown')
    roof1 = Line(Point(-100,100),Point(0,200))
    roof2 = Line(Point(0,200),Point(100,100))
    roof1.setWidth(3)
    roof2.setWidth(3)
    myCanvas.draw(house)
    myCanvas.draw(door)
    myCanvas.draw(roof1)
    myCanvas.draw(roof2)
    sun = Circle(Point(-150,250),20)
    sun.setFill('yellow')
    myCanvas.draw(sun)
    for i in range(-150,150):     # move the sun across the sky
        sun.move(1,0)
```

Listing 12.1   Using geometric objects to draw a house

In the rest of this chapter we will design and implement a set of classes that enable us to write the function in Listing 12.1. Along the way we will learn about a powerful programming concept called **inheritance**.

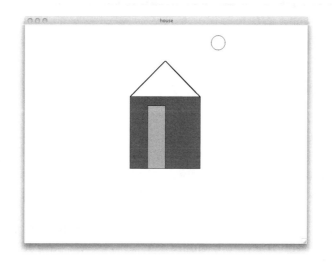

Figure 12.1 Using object-oriented graphics to draw a simple scene

12.3 First Design

When designing a project like our graphics module, it is a good idea to begin by making a list of the different kinds of objects involved and the relationships between those objects. As we make the list of objects, we will try to identify two important kinds of relationships between the objects. The relationships we are looking for are IS-A and HAS-A.

The **IS-A relationship** describes two objects where one object is a more specific instance of the other. For example, a square *is a* more specific instance of a rectangle, and a circle *is a* more specific instance of an ellipse. As we identify these IS-A relationships, we also look for functionality that each of the instances have in common.

A **HAS-A relationship** describes two objects where one object uses another object. For example, if you think about a circle, each circle *has a* center point. A rectangle *has a* lower-left-corner point and an upper-right-corner point.

With these definitions in mind let us now create a list of objects for our graphics module. An initial set of objects might look like the following:

- Square
- Circle
- Oval
- Rectangle

- Triangle
- Polygon
- Line
- Point
- Canvas

As you begin to think about the words in the list, you will recognize that there are IS-A relationships between several of them. A Rectangle *is a* Polygon. A Square *is a* Rectangle. A Triangle *is a* Polygon. A Circle *is a*n Oval. You may also recognize that all of the words we have just mentioned are shapes. The word *shapes* is not on our list of objects, but it may be a good idea to add it because it is an abstraction of many of the words we have listed. As you begin to design an application, this will often be the case. As you start the design process, and as you begin to organize the objects you have identified, you will very often uncover new, more abstract objects.

The next step is to arrange our words into a diagram that makes the IS-A relationships explicit. Figure 12.2 illustrates the relationships between the objects we have discussed so far. This diagram is often referred to as a hierarchical diagram because of the vertical relationships between the objects. The most abstract or general object is at the top of the hierarchy and the most specific objects are at the bottom.

When you look at the diagram in Figure 12.2 and think about the words on our list, you may have some questions: What about Point, Line, and Canvas? Where do these objects belong? Should Lines and Points be included in the shapes hierarchy? Is there another abstraction that we could use to relate Lines and Points to the others?

We might determine that although Lines and Points are not shapes, they are geometric objects. In addition, shapes are also geometric objects and so we might create another abstraction called GeometricObject.

And another question might be asked: What about the Canvas? The Canvas is not a GeometricObject, or a Shape. However the Canvas is the place where we will draw our lines, points, and other shapes. The relationship between Canvas and GeometricObject is a HAS-A relationship. A Canvas may contain many geometric objects. This new hierarchy can be seen in Figure 12.3.

With this hierarchy of objects complete, we can begin to think about implementing the objects as Python classes. The difference between this implementation and the implementations we have seen in previous chapters is that in this case we will use the hierarchical relationships to avoid the duplication of code that we saw in "Bears, Fish, and Plants, Oh My!" (Chapter 11).

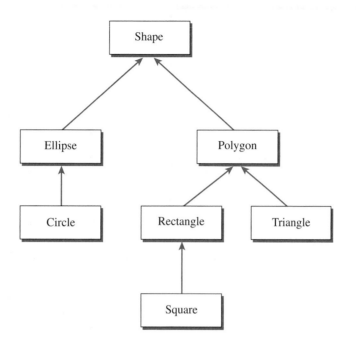

Figure 12.2   A simple object hierarchy

In object-oriented programming, the IS-A links in Figure 12.3 define an **inheritance hierarchy**. Inheritance is the idea that a more general class is a **parent class** of a more specific class (a **child class**). The parent class may have methods that can be shared with any child. This idea of shared methods is how we avoid duplicating code.

In our example, the `Rectangle` class is a child of the `Shape` class. In object-oriented programming terms, this means that any methods that we write for the `Shape` class are inherited by the `Rectangle` class and the rest of the classes that are below `Shape` in the inheritance hierarchy. When two classes are connected by an IS-A link, we call a class that is directly above another class in the inheritance hierarchy a **superclass**. The class where the IS-A link originates is called the **subclass**.

In the next stage of our design we need to ask the following questions:

- What things should each object know?
- What things should each object be able to do?

The things we want each object to know will lead us to the set of **instance variables**. The things that each object can do will give us the set of **methods** we need to write.

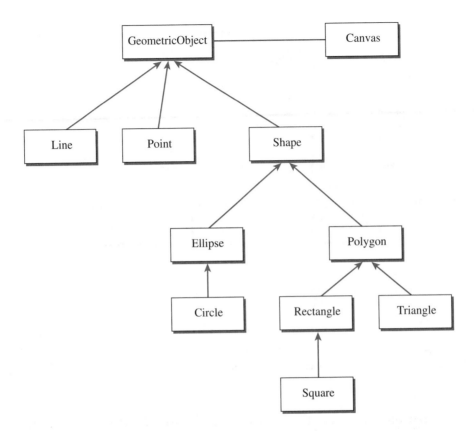

Figure 12.3   An expanded object hierarchy

There are several things we want our objects to remember about themselves:

- Fill color
- Outline color
- Position on the canvas
- Line width

If you look back at the `drawHouse` function in Listing 12.1, you will quickly come up with a list of things that our shapes should be able to do:

- Set or change the outline color: `setOutline(color)`.
- Set or change the fill color: `setFill(color)`.
- Move to a new position on the canvas: `move(dx,dy)`.
- Set or change the width of a line or outline: `setWidth(w)`.
- Set or change the color of a line or point: `setColor(color)`.

We are now at the point where we can talk about the advantages of using inheritance. Since all shapes have the same set of attributes, we can create the instance variables, and write the methods to modify those instance variables in the Shape class. We can do this because whenever a method is defined in a superclass the method can also be called by an instance of the subclass, or even any of the subclasses of the subclass. This can save us an enormous amount of work and is one of the reasons that spending time up front doing a good design is so important.

It is good programming practice to learn how to develop a large program like this one step at a time. To help us with this task, we will write a simple test program that uses just a small part of the overall functionality we want to create. Once we get this simple program working, we can move on to something more complicated. Writing programs this way is much easier and more fun than trying to write all the code for a large program first and then trying to figure out where things went wrong.

One of the easiest programs to write that moves us a long way toward our end goal is to simply draw a line on the screen. This program is shown in Listing 12.2. Although the program looks simple, it actually forces us to do some more design on the classes Point, Line, GeometricObject, and Canvas.

```
1   myCanvas = Canvas(800,600)
2   myLine = Line(Point(-100,-100),Point(100,100))
3   myCanvas.draw(myLine)
```

Listing 12.2   Drawing a line

The Canvas class is responsible in some way for drawing a GeometricObject. How *will* Canvas do this? The answer is by using a turtle. That is the only tool we have right now for drawing anything. In addition, the turtle comes with a built-in window for drawing. With all of the turtle's functionality, implementing the Canvas class should be pretty easy. But it does mean that one of the instance variables of the Canvas will be a Turtle. We will also have to write a draw method for the Canvas that can take any shape we give it and draw it using the turtle.

The GeometricObject class has instance variables for lineColor and lineWidth. We also know that the GeometricObject class will need methods for getting and setting the lineColor and lineWidth instance variables. Although we will not change the color or width in our simple test program, we will still implement the methods now.

The Point class is an abstraction for a geometric point in our two-dimensional coordinate system. The two instance variables that are unique to a point are the x coordinate and the y coordinate. In addition, the Point class inherits the lineColor and lineWidth instance variables from GeometricObject. This means that a Point has the following instance variables: x, y, lineColor, and lineWidth. The Point class provides three simple methods: getX returns the x coordinate, getY returns the y coordinate, and getCoord returns the x and y coordinates as a tuple.

The Line class has two instance variables: a beginning point and an ending point. Like Point, Line inherits the instance variables lineColor and lineWidth from GeometricObject, so we do not have to explicitly implement them as part of the Line class.

Figure 12.4 shows our inheritance hierarchy with the details of instance variables and methods for each class added to the diagram.

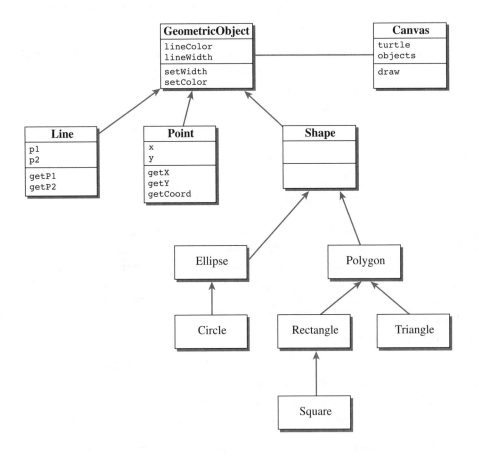

Figure 12.4   Instance variables and methods

12.4   Basic Implementation

Let's begin with a top-down implementation of the portion of the class hierarchy needed to implement the program in Listing 12.2. We will start with the `Canvas` class (shown in Listing 12.3), which serves the same purpose for our graphics module as it does for the turtle. It is a place for us to draw `GeometricObjects`. In fact since we are using the turtle to do all of our behind-the-scenes drawing, we will simply make use of the same window and canvas as the turtle. This decision saves us a lot of work but also has some important ramifications for our program. For example, it means that we will use the same coordinate system as the turtle does.

12.4.1   Canvas

The most difficult task in writing our `Canvas` class is writing the constructor. As you have previously learned, the constructor method is always named `__init__`. The job of the constructor for `Canvas` is to create an instance of a `Turtle` and store a reference to it in an instance variable called `turtle`. We will also create an instance variable called `screen` that will allow us to configure the canvas.

Once we have initialized the instance variables for the class, we set the width and height of the `Canvas` using the `screen` method `setup`. Finally, because the people who will be using our graphics classes may not know anything about turtle graphics, we will hide the turtle using the `hideturtle` method. We do not want them to know that a `turtle` is actually doing the work.

```
1  class Canvas:
2      def __init__(self,w,h):
3          self.turtle = turtle.Turtle()
4          self.screen = turtle.Screen()
5          self.width = w
6          self.height = h
7
8          self.screen.setup(width=self.width,height=self.height)
9          self.turtle.hideturtle()
10
11     def draw(self,gObject):
12         self.turtle.up()
13         self.screen.tracer(0)
14         gObject._draw(self.turtle)
15         self.screen.tracer(1)
```

Listing 12.3   The canvas class

The final method of our `Canvas` class is the `draw` method, which is simple to implement but exposes one of the most powerful and important parts of object-oriented programming. Notice that `draw` accepts a geometric object `gObject` as a parameter. After putting the turtle into a state with its tail up, and tracing off, the only thing the draw method does is call the `_draw` method on the `gObject`, passing our turtle as a parameter! It is important to realize that the `draw` method belongs to the `Canvas`, while the `_draw` method belongs to the `GeometricObject`. Although `_draw` may look strange to you, it is a perfectly legal name for a function. We use `_draw` in this case to differentiate it from the `draw` method, and to prevent programmers from inadvertently calling the `draw` method directly on a `GeometricObject`.

If you think about it for a while, you may realize that the formal parameter of the `draw` method can be any `GeometricObject`. This means that the `Canvas` does not know whether it has to draw a `Point`, a `Line`, or any other `Shape`. We can solve this problem by using the following code:

```
if isinstance(gObject,Point):
    # code to draw a point
elif isinstance(gObject,Line):
    # code to draw a line
elif isinstance(gObject,Circle):
    # code to draw a circle
...
else:
    print ('unknown geometric object')
```

While using `isinstance` to check the type of `gObject` would certainly work, object-oriented programming provides us with **polymorphism**—a much more powerful way to handle exactly this kind of problem that allows us to write a `_draw` method for each of our specific geometric objects. Python is smart enough to call the right method, depending on the type of object that is referenced by the `gObject` variable. As you will soon see, we will implement a `_draw` method for the classes `Point`, `Line`, and `GeometricObject`. After we have implemented these methods, we discuss the underlying mechanism that Python uses to implement polymorphism.

12.4.2   GeometricObject

Let's continue our implementation by writing the `GeometricObject` class. `GeometricObject` and `Canvas` are peers at the top level of our inheritance hierarchy. The most important thing to point out in the implementation of GeometricObject, as shown in Listing 12.4, is the _draw method. All the _draw method does is print an error message. The reason for this is because we should never actually create an instance of the GeometricObject class.

The GeometricObject class is called an **abstract class**. We created this class because it is an abstraction of its child classes: Point, Line, Rectangle, and others. An abstract class provides us with one place to define instance variables and methods that are used by all of the child classes. The GeometricObject class contains two instance variables: lineColor and lineWidth. Because the instance variables are initialized by the GeometricObject constructor, they do not need to be initialized by any of the child classes.

```
1   class GeometricObject:
2       def __init__(self):
3           self.lineColor = 'black'
4           self.lineWidth = 1
5
6       def getColor(self):
7           return self.lineColor
8
9       def getWidth(self):
10          return self.lineWidth
11
12      def setColor(self,color):
13          self.lineColor = color
14
15      def setWidth(self,width):
16          self.lineWidth = width
17
18      def _draw(self,someturtle):
19          print("Error: You must define _draw in subclass")
```

Listing 12.4   The geometricObject class

12.4.3   Point

The Point class is important because it is *used* by all other GeometricObjects for positioning. For example, the Line class uses two Point objects to anchor the ends of the Line. The Rectangle class uses two Point objects to position the opposing corners of the Rectangle, and so on.

The code for the `Point` class is given in Listing 12.5. The `Point` class is a child of `GeometricObject`, so the class statement designates `GeometricObject` as the parent. The syntax we use to designate one class as the parent of another is to place the parent in parentheses after the child. You can see this on line 1 of Listing 12.5.

Another way that we can speak about the parent–child relationship between classes is to say that `Point` *extends* `GeometricObject`. This can be a helpful way to think about the relationship because `Point` begins with the instance variables and methods provided by `GeometricObject` and adds new instance variables and methods of its own.

There are two key ideas to understand in the `Point` class. First, the line

```
super().__init__()
```

makes sure that the `__init__` method in the parent class is called and that the instance variables inherited from `GeometricObject` have their proper initial values. The **super** function returns a special super-object that knows how to properly call the `__init__` method for the parent class.

The `_draw` method implements the drawing of a `Point`, using the turtle that is passed as a parameter. The important thing to see here is that the turtle is moved to the right place on the canvas with its tail up using the `goto` method. The parameters passed to `goto` are the instance variables `self.x` and `self.y`. Once the turtle is in position, a dot is drawn using the instance variables `self.lineWidth` and `self.lineColor`.

12.4.4   Line

The `Line` class is very similar to the `Point` class with the exception that `Line` has two instance variables that are `Points`. The other difference is that `_draw` draws a line rather than a simple point. Notice that we need to make two calls to the turtle to set the line color and the line width. This is an important step because we cannot make any assumptions about what color or line width the turtle is set to use. The code for the `Line` class is given in Listing 12.6.

12.4.5   Testing Our Implementation

With our first four classes written, let's try our first test program and see what we can learn about our implementation. Assume that all of the classes we have defined so far are stored in `draw.py`. Session 12.1 creates a `Canvas` and a `Line`, and it draws the line. If everything works, you should see a window with a diagonal line in it.

```
1  class Point(GeometricObject):
2      def __init__(self, x,y):
3          super().__init__()
4          self.x = x
5          self.y = y
6
7      def getCoord(self):
8          return (self.x,self.y)
9
10     def getX(self):
11         return self.x
12
13     def getY(self):
14         return self.y
15
16     def _draw(self,turtle):
17         turtle.goto(self.x,self.y)
18         turtle.dot(self.lineWidth,self.lineColor)
```

Listing 12.5   The Point class

```
1  class Line(GeometricObject):
2      def __init__(self, p1,p2):
3          super().__init__()
4          self.p1 = p1
5          self.p2 = p2
6
7      def getP1(self):
8          return self.p1
9
10     def getP2(self):
11         return self.p2
12
13     def _draw(self,turtle):
14         turtle.color(self.getColor())
15         turtle.width(self.getWidth())
16         turtle.goto(self.p1.getCoord())
17         turtle.down()
18         turtle.goto(self.p2.getCoord())
```

Listing 12.6   The Line class

```
>>> from draw import *
>>> myCanvas = Canvas(800,600)
>>> myLine = Line(Point(-100,-100),Point(100,100))
>>> myCanvas.draw(myLine)
```

Session 12.1   First test of graphics classes

Let's continue to explore this example and see what we can learn about the objects we have created. Session 12.2 illustrates the use of some of the methods we have just defined. First, let's verify that `myLine` has the default color and width. Next, let's get one of the Points used to create the line and check its x and y coordinates, along with its width and color.

```
>>> myLine
<draw.Line object at 0x106f6b0>
>>> myCanvas
<draw.Canvas instance at 0x1070328>
>>> isinstance(myLine,Line)
True
>>> myLine.getColor()
'black'
>>> myLine.getWidth()
1
>>> p = myLine.getP1()
>>> p
<draw.Point object at 0x6c950>
>>> p.getX()
-100
>>> p.getY()
-100
>>> p.getWidth()
1
>>> p.getColor()
'black'
```

Session 12.2   Investigating objects

Exercises

12.1 Modify the test program to change the line color and width.

12.2 Rewrite the `Point` class, but rather than storing the coordinate information as separate numbers, store the coordinates as a tuple. When you are done, use your `Point` class in place of the `Point` class we have written and make sure the test program still works.

12.3 Modify the `Line` class so that a line can be either solid or dashed.

12.4 Write a program that plots a sine wave using instances of the `Point` class.

12.5 Create an instance of a `GraphicsObject` and then try to draw it. Do you get an error message?

12.5   Understanding Inheritance

To better understand how inheritance works, we can look behind the scenes at how Python keeps track of instance variables and methods. Each class and instance of a class has some special instance variables we can use to see how Python finds the right method to call or the right instance variable. The first of these is the `__bases__` instance variable. This variable tells us the names of the parent of any class. For example, in Session 12.3 you can see that the parent class of `Line` is `GeometricObject`. The parent of `GeometricObject` is `object`, and `object` has no parent. This succession of child to parent links is very important for Python when a method is called that was defined in a parent class. By default, Python uses the special class `object` at the top of the inheritance hierarchy.

The name `__bases__` comes from the term base class, which is an alternative way of thinking about the parent–child relationship. Some programmers say that the parent class is the base class, and the child class extends the base class. In our hierarchy, `GeometricObject` is the base class of `Line`. The idea is that `Line` has all the functionality of `GeometricObject` plus new functionality that extends the base.

```
>>> Line.__bases__
(<class 'draw.GeometricObject'>,)
>>> GeometricObject.__bases__
(<class 'object'>,)
>>> object.__bases__
()
>>> Line.__dict__.keys()
['getP1', '__module__', 'getP2', '_draw', '__doc__', '__init__']
>>> GeometricObject.__dict__.keys()
['__module__', 'setColor', 'getColor', '_draw', 'getWidth', '__weakref__',
 '__dict__', 'setWidth', '__doc__', '__init__']
>>> Line.__dict__['getP1']
<function getP1 at 0x14b8430>
>>> myLine.__class__
<class 'draw.Line'>
>>> myLine.__dict__.keys()
['p2', 'lineWidth', 'p1', 'lineColor']
```

Session 12.3   Investigating the inheritance hierarchy

Another instance variable that each class maintains is the __dict__ variable. This instance variable is a dictionary that keeps track of the methods defined for the class. For example, in Session 12.3 you can see that the dictionary of methods for the Line class has keys that correspond to the name of every method we defined.

Instances of Python objects also have some special instance variables. Every object has an instance variable __class__, which contains a reference to the class that the object is an instance of. In Session 12.3, you can see that myLine.__class__ refers to the class Line. In addition, the __dict__ variable for instances of classes contains a dictionary of user-defined instance variables. For example, Session 12.3 shows that an *instance* of the Line class also has a __dict__ instance variable that contains keys for p2, lineWidth, p1, and lineColor.

Putting all of these special variables together, we can see in more detail how inheritance works in Python. Figure 12.5 shows a reference diagram to illustrate the chain of events in the Python interpreter for the expression myLine.getWidth().

When Python evaluates the expression myLine.getWidth(), the first step is to dereference

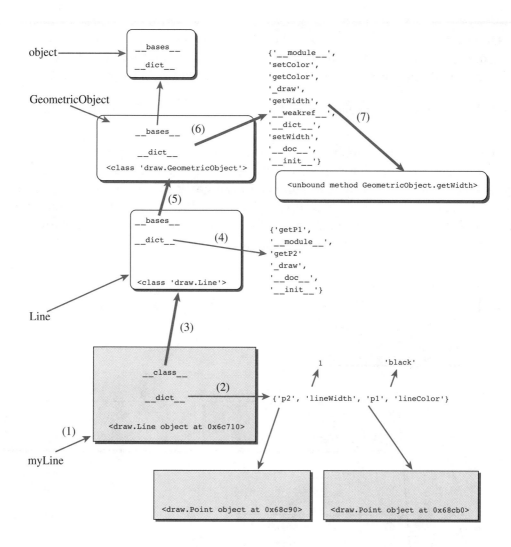

Figure 12.5 A reference diagram for following an inheritance chain. The numbered arrows indicate the order of the search operation

the name `myLine`. Python next tries to dereference the name `getWidth` using the following chain of lookups:

1. If `__dict__` in `myLine` contains `getWidth` as a key, stop searching and use it.

2. Otherwise, follow the `__class__` link; if `__dict__` in the class object contains `getWidth` as a key, stop searching and use it.

3. Otherwise, follow the __bases__ link to the parent class (GeometricObject). If __dict__ contains getWidth as a key, stop searching and use it. This last step can be repeated indefinitely until all of the classes listed in __bases__ have been tried.

4. If all base classes are exhausted and getWidth is not found, then generate an error.

Once the name getWidth is dereferenced, the next step is to apply the function call operators ( ). Since we are applying the call operators to a method of a class, we take the value of myLine and pass it as the first parameter to the getWidth function. In the getWidth function, myLine is called self. Figure 12.6 illustrates the binding of myLine as an actual parameter to the formal parameter self. The main thing to notice is that myLine and self both reference the same instance of a Line.

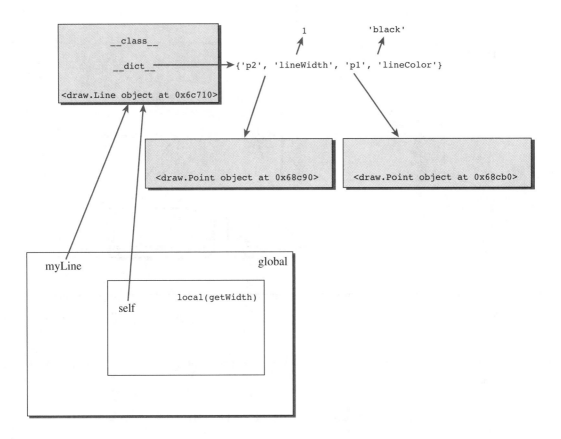

Figure 12.6   The self parameter with an inherited method

Exercises

12.6 Using the reference diagram in Figure 12.5, trace the series of reference links that Python uses to evaluate the expression `self.lineWidth(5)`.

12.7 Using the reference diagram in Figure 12.5, trace the series of reference links that Python uses to evaluate the expression `myLine._draw()`.

12.8 Draw a reference diagram illustrating the sequence of lookups required for the statement `myLine.getP1().getX()`.

12.9 In the Python shell, follow the sequence of lookups to find the location in memory of `myLine.p1`.

12.6   Limitations

Now that you have a better understanding of how inheritance works, let's try a slightly more difficult test program. Listing 12.7 contains a simple function called `test2` to draw two thick lines that cross. Once the lines are drawn, the color of the first line is changed to red. What do you think the final picture should look like?

```
1   def test2():
2       myCanvas = Canvas(500,500)
3       myLine = Line(Point(-100,-100),Point(100,100))
4       myOtherLine = Line(Point(-100,100),Point(100,-100))
5       myLine.setWidth(4)
6       myOtherLine.setWidth(4)
7       myCanvas.draw(myLine)
8       myCanvas.draw(myOtherLine)
9       myLine.setColor('red')
```

Listing 12.7   Drawing two lines that cross

If you think that the result should be two crossing black lines, you are correct. Why didn't the call to `setColor` actually change the color of the line? Calling `setColor` only modifies the `lineColor` instance variable; it does not change the way the line appears on the screen. In order to change the appearance of the line on the screen, we need to redraw it. Although the obvious fix for this small program is to move the `setColor` call in front of the call to `draw`, that is not an acceptable general solution.

Another solution is that every time we change the color or thickness of the line we have to tell the canvas to draw the line again. This solution can produce unintended consequences. For example, we can simply add one more line to the program in Listing 12.7 to call `myCanvas.draw(myLine)`. Now the line is red, but it is in front of the other line. If we want the black line to be in front of the red line, we need to redraw the black line as well. If this is a complicated drawing, this can turn into a very complicated set of dependencies.

The behavior that we really want can be specified as follows:

1. If the object is not drawn yet, simply change the value of the instance variable.

2. If the object is already visible, change the attribute and redraw all the objects on the screen in the same order as they were originally drawn.

One solution to this problem would be to add a call to `_draw` in the `setColor` and `setWidth` methods. However, that gives us the same problem with the order of drawing we just mentioned. There is another problem with this approach as well. In order to draw the line, we need a turtle. As you may remember, the turtle is passed as a parameter to the `_draw` method. However, when we call the `setWidth` method, we do not (and should not!) have a reference to a turtle object. A final problem is that requirement 1 stipulates that if the line has not yet been drawn the only thing that `setColor` should do is change the value of the color instance variable.

12.7   An Improved Implementation

The solution to the problem outlined previously is valuable to understand because it will help you recognize the principles behind many professional graphics systems, including the TKinter graphics system used by Python. It also helps you understand what is happening in the graphics system used in the Java programming language. Another benefit of the solution is that once you have the mechanism in place to solve the current problem, you will be able to implement a `move` method for all graphics objects very easily.

The solution to the problem begins with three additional instance variables. One variable will allow us to keep track of whether the object has been drawn. We might call this instance variable `visible`. The second instance variable will be used to keep track of the `Canvas` on which the object is drawn. The third instance variable, `visibleObjects`, will allow the `Canvas` to remember a list of the objects it has drawn.

To better understand the importance of these three instance variables, let's look at a new way of thinking about what will happen when we make a call like the following: `theCanvas.draw(myLine)`.

1. Set the value of the `visible` instance variable of the line to `True`.

2. Set the value of the `myCanvas` instance variable of the line to point to `theCanvas`. At the moment this may seem circular to you, but hopefully it will become clear when we talk about what happens when you call `setColor`.

3. Call the line's `_draw` method.

4. Add the line object to the `visibleObjects` instance variable of the canvas.

At the end of this sequence, the line will be drawn on the canvas. But more importantly, the line will now "remember" which canvas it was drawn on, and the canvas will know all the objects that have been drawn on it.

Next let's consider the sequence of events when we make a call to change the color or width of the line such as: `myLine.setColor('red')`.

1. Modify the `lineColor` instance variable of the line to have the new value of `'red'`.

2. If the `visible` instance variable is `True`, then use the `myCanvas` instance variable to call the method `drawAll` on the canvas.

The `drawAll` method clears the canvas and redraws all objects on the canvas in the same order as they were drawn originally. It is true that we may not need to redraw all the objects on the canvas, but it would be more work to figure out which objects need to be redrawn than it would be to simply redraw everything. The new design for our classes is shown in Figure 12.7. This figure includes all the new instance variables and methods we have discussed.

Even though we have made some major improvements to the functionality of the `Point` and `Line` classes, we will see that we changed only the `Canvas` and `GeometricObject` classes. Listing 12.8 presents the new version of the `Canvas` class. Compared with our earlier implementation in Listing 12.3, we have added two new methods: `drawAll` and `addShape`. In addition, we have made small modifications to `draw` and `__init__`.

The modifications to `__init__` and `draw` involve initializing and updating the `visibleObjects` instance variable. When a canvas is first created, the list of objects drawn on the canvas is initialized to an empty list. Whenever `draw` is called, the `GraphicsObject` passed as a parameter is appended to the end of the list. In this way all objects that are visible on the canvas are stored in the `visibleObjects` list, and the order that they were drawn is preserved.

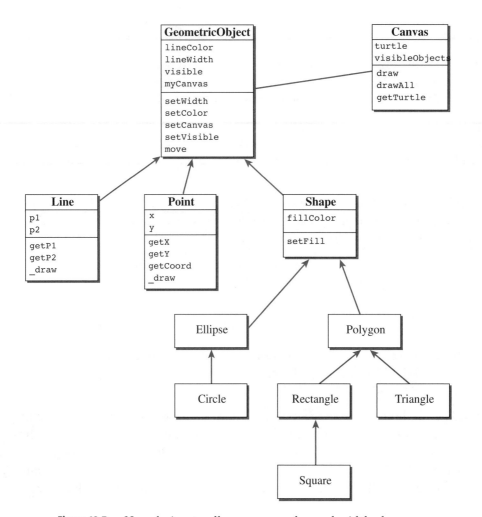

Figure 12.7   New design to allow proper color and width changes

The `addShape` method is simply a convenient way to add an object to the `visibleObjects` list. The reason we do not simply call `visibleObjects.append` directly is that by consistently using the `addShape` method we limit any dependencies on how we represent the objects drawn on the canvas to one method. Imagine that some time in the future you decide to use a dictionary, rather than a list, to keep track of the objects on the canvas. If you had used `visibleObjects.append` in several places, each one of those places would need to be changed to accommodate the new representation. However, since we have been clever and used the `addShape` method, we would need to change only the way we add an object to the canvas in one place.

```
1  class Canvas:
2      def __init__(self,w,h):
3          self.width = w
4          self.height = h
5          self.visibleObjects = []
6          self.turtle = turtle.Turtle()
7          self.turtle.setup(width=self.width,height=self.height)
8          self.turtle.hideturtle()
9
10     def drawAll(self):
11         self.turtle.reset()
12         self.turtle.tracer(0)
13         for shape in self.visibleObjects:
14             shape._draw(self.turtle)
15         self.turtle.tracer(1)
16         self.turtle.hideturtle()
17
18     def addShape(self,shape):
19         self.visibleObjects.append(shape)
20
21     def draw(self,gObject):
22         gObject.setCanvas(self)
23         gObject.setVisible(True)
24         self.turtle.up()
25         self.turtle.tracer(0)
26         gObject._draw(self.turtle)
27         self.turtle.tracer(1)
28         self.addShape(gObject)
```

Listing 12.8   A new improved `Canvas` class

The biggest addition to the `Canvas` class is the `drawAll` method. The main purpose of this method is to iterate over all the `GeometricObject` objects on the `visibleObjects` list and have each perform its `_draw` method. By doing this, we can completely recreate whatever picture we have on the canvas by calling a single method. This loop demonstrates polymorphism in object-oriented programming in a very powerful way. Notice that we do not need to keep a separate list of lines, points, and other shapes. We need only one list of objects, and since each object provides a `_draw` method, Python finds the correct `_draw` method for each object.

You may also notice that the first line of the method calls `self.screen.reset()`. The reset method of the screen erases anything the turtle has previously drawn to give us a blank canvas, and puts the turtle in the center of the canvas again.

The new `GeometricObject` class is shown in Listing 12.9. The changes to `GeometricObject` are fairly small. We have added two new setter methods: `setVisible` and `setCanvas`. The setColor and setWidth methods have been modified to call the drawAll method whenever the object being changed is visible.

```
 1    class GeometricObject:
 2
 3        def __init__(self):
 4            self.lineColor = 'black'
 5            self.lineWidth = 1
 6            self.visible = False
 7            self.myCanvas = None
 8
 9        def setColor(self,color):
10            self.lineColor = color
11            if self.visible:
12                self.myCanvas.drawAll()
13
14        def setWidth(self,width):
15            self.lineWidth = width
16            if self.visible:
17                self.myCanvas.drawAll()
18
19        def getColor(self):
20            return self.lineColor
21
22        def getWidth(self):
23            return self.lineWidth
24
25        def _draw(self):
26            print ("Error: You must define _draw in subclass")
27
28        def setVisible(self,vFlag):
29            self.visible = vFlag
30
31        def setCanvas(self,theCanvas):
32            self.myCanvas = theCanvas
```

Listing 12.9   A new improved GeometricObject class

Exercises

12.10 Write an "undraw" method to remove a GeometricObject from the canvas.

12.11 Add the ability to move objects.

12.12 Since each object has a reference to the canvas it is drawn on, it would no longer be necessary to pass a reference to a turtle as a parameter to **_draw**. Modify the classes to remove this parameter.

12.8   Implementing Polygons

We have neglected a large part of our initial inheritance hierarchy in order to focus on a few key implementation details. Now that we have made it possible to properly modify the color, line width, and visibility of Points and Lines we can turn our attention to adding new graphical objects. You will see that inheritance is going to make it fairly easy to add new objects that are quite powerful without writing a lot of code.

Let's begin by working down the inheritance hierarchy, starting with **Shape**. **Shape** is going to be an abstract class that will hold an instance variable that will let us know whether an instance of **Shape** should appear as an outline or whether the shape should be filled in with a color.

The next class to consider is **Polygon**, which can be either abstract or concrete. That is, we can probably imagine creating an instance of a **Polygon** to represent some irregular multisided closed shape. In fact, we can just stop with **Polygon** and implement squares, triangles, octagons, etc., as polygons. This is one of those design decisions that has no right or wrong answer. If we choose to make **Polygon** abstract, then we need to add explicit child classes for every possible polygon we might want to use in an application. If we choose to allow **Polygon** to be concrete, then we can implement some child classes to make it easy to construct the most common polygons. We will choose the latter approach and make **Polygon** a concrete class.

For each of our shapes, the most important method for us to write is **_draw**. If we think carefully, we can implement a single draw method to draw any polygon. The big question is, how can we represent the shape of a polygon? The answer is that we can represent any polygon using a list of points. A triangle has three points corresponding to its three corners. A square has four points corresponding to its four corners and so on. In addition to knowing the position of the corners of our polygon, it is also important to specify them in some order, so that we can go from corner to corner and get an outline of the shape. If the corners are randomly ordered, we may just get a bunch of random lines.

There are two logical choices for the order in which to specify the corners: clockwise and counterclockwise. Most graphics systems use a counterclockwise ordering for the corners of a polygon for reasons that do not matter to us right now.

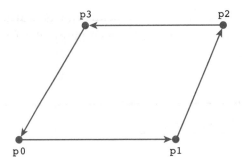

Figure 12.8   A correctly drawn polygon with corners specified in counterclockwise order

A counterclockwise ordering means that we can draw any polygon by drawing lines between points that are adjacent to each other in our ordered list of points. Figure 12.8 shows an example parallelogram with four points. These four points could be stored in a list such as [p0, p1, p2, p3]. We can draw lines from p0 to p1, from p1 to p2, and p2 to p3 since they are next to one another in the list. However, this will give us only three of the four sides, so we must also draw a line from p3 to p0 to complete the shape.

If we had specified the corners of our polygon in the order [p0, p1, p3, p2], we would get a completely different shape that is not a polygon at all. The incorrect shape is shown in Figure 12.9.

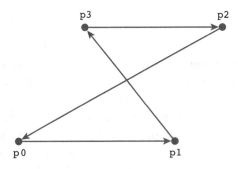

Figure 12.9   An incorrectly drawn polygon due to random corner positions

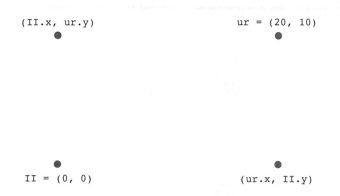

Figure 12.10   Using the information from lower-left and upper-right to determine other corners

To implement the _draw method for any polygon, you can simply iterate over the list of corners and have the turtle go from point to point. When you run out of points in the list, you must have the turtle draw one final line back to the first point on the list. If a polygon has a fillColor other than None, then you will need to call the begin_fill and end_fill methods of the turtle before and after you start drawing lines.

Now that you know how to represent and draw any polygon, what about Rectangle, Triangle, and Square? The key for these three classes is how we write our constructor. For an arbitrary polygon, the constructor must take a list of points. For a specific polygon, we can make it a bit more user friendly. For example, the constructor for Triangle can take three points, and the constructors for the Square and Rectangle can each take just two points.

The points needed to specify a rectangle are simply the lower-left corner and the upper-right corner. If you know the lower-left and upper-right, you can figure out the position of the other two corners quite easily, as shown in Figure 12.10. You can see examples of the constructors for a rectangle in Listing 12.1. The constructor for the Square is identical to the constructor for Rectangle except that it should check that the lengths of all sides are the same.

A new version of our class hierarchy is shown in Figure 12.11. We are not going to show you the Python implementation for Polygon. Implementing the rest of the hierarchy is left as an exercise for you.

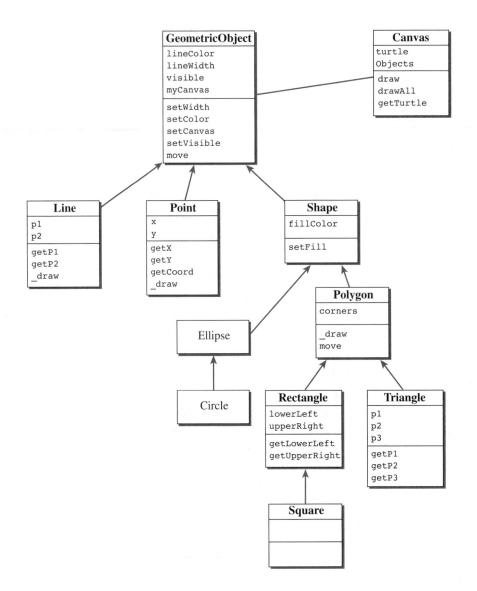

Figure 12.11   Inheritance hierarchy including details for polygons

Exercises

12.13 Implement the design for `Polygon` and its children.

12.14 Implement additional `Polygon` convenience classes such as `Square`, `Triangle`, `Rectangle`, and `Octagon`.

12.9   Summary

In this chapter we learned about inheritance, the ability to design and implement classes so that they take advantage of natural relationships that may exist between them. These relationships provide a way for us to organize our classes. Parent classes contain general details (instance variables and methods) that pertain to an object. Child classes contain details that allow objects to be more specific. This child–parent relationship, called an IS-A relationship, allows child objects to have all the functionality of parent objects while adding specific additional details.

Key Terms

abstract class	inheritance hierarchy	polymorphism
base class	instance variables	subclass
child class	IS-A relationship	superclass
HAS-A relationship	methods	
inheritance	parent class	

Python Keywords

`class`	`None`	`self`
`isinstance`	`object`	`super`

Programming Exercises

12.1 Design and implement the Ellipse part of the shape hierarchy.

12.2 Design and implement a `Text` class for the `GeometricObject` hierarchy.

12.3 Test your entire set of classes using Listing 12.1.

12.4 Using our graphics module, implement your own scene.

12.5 Using our graphics module, draw a rectangle and a circle inside the rectangle. Now have the circle move inside the rectangle. If the circle touches the wall of the rectangle, it should bounce off the wall in the appropriate direction.

12.6 Reimplement the bear and fish simulation from Chapter 11 using inheritance. *Hint:* You will want to create an abstract class called `LifeForm` that captures the commonalities of bears and fish.

CHAPTER 13

Video Games

13.1 Objectives

- To write an event-driven program
- To understand and write callback functions
- To practice with lists of objects
- To see another pattern for using inheritance
- To learn about static variables

13.2 Introduction

So far the programs we have written have a beginning, a middle, and an end. We know the order in which things will happen because we have implemented the steps in a linear fashion. But that is not the way that most programs work. Think of the programs you use on a daily basis—from your web browser and word processor, to video games. These programs do not have a beginning, a middle, and an end. Rather they sit there and wait for you to click your mouse or press a key. When you take some action, the program responds with its own action. The order of the actions is determined by you, not the program.

13.2.1 Event-Driven Programming

Programs that wait for an event to occur and then respond to the event by taking an action are called **event-driven programs**. In this chapter you are going to learn how to write event-driven programs using the `turtle` module. When writing event-driven programs, one of the most important concepts is that of a **callback function**, which is just like any other function except that it is designed to be called in response to an event.

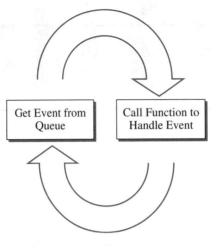

Figure 13.1   The event loop

Let's look at this idea of events in a bit more detail. The main structure of an event-driven program is an **event loop**, which does the following:

- Checks the event queue for the next event.
- Calls the callback function to handle the event.

Figure 13.1 illustrates the idea behind the event loop graphically. You will notice that there is some similarity between this event loop diagram and the read–eval–print loop that Python uses. One of the differences is that in event-driven programming we use a **queue**—a data structure that works something like a to-do list to keep track of events that need to be handled. A queue allows you to remove the first thing on your to-do list and to add things at the end. In this way a queue enforces a first-come first-served strategy for handling events. You will learn much more about queues and their usefulness in a data structures class.

13.2.2   Simulating an Event Loop

The event loop in Figure 13.1 looks pretty simple, but there is one important piece of the puzzle not shown in the diagram—that is, how do we as programmers control which function is called for a particular event? Of course, if we were writing the event loop, we could do it easily with some **if** statements. But since we are not writing the event loop, and do not even have access to the source code for the event loop, there must be some other way.

The way that this control problem is solved is to have the event-processing system provide us with a way to register a function that we want to be called when a specific event occurs. For example, we might tell the event-processing system to call function A when the mouse is clicked and function B when a key is pressed on the keyboard.

To illustrate how this all works, let's write a simple simulation of an event-processing system. Our event processor will have the following functions:

- Add an 'event' to the queue.
- Register a function to be called in response to an event.
- Run the simulation.

```
1    class EventHandler:
2        def __init__(self):
3            self.queue = []
4            self.eventKeeper = {}
5
6        def addEvent(self, eventName):
7            self.queue.append(eventName)
8
9        def registerCallback(self, event, func):
10            self.eventKeeper[event] = func
11
12        def run(self):
13            while(True):
14                if len(self.queue) > 0:
15                    nextEvent = self.queue.pop(0)
16                    self.eventKeeper[nextEvent]()
17                else:
18                    print('queue is empty')
```

Listing 13.1   A simple event-processing simulation

Listing 13.1 implements a simple class to illustrate an event-processing loop. Although the code is short and simple, there are some powerful things happening. In the `__init__` method we set up two important instance variables: `self.queue`, which will hold the list of events that need to be processed, and `self.eventKeeper`, which is a dictionary that maps events to their callback functions. Suppose that we have two events: `'mouse'` and `'key'`. We can store a reference to the callback function for the mouse event in `self.eventKeeper` using the string `'mouse'` as the key. We can then simply call the function using the rather odd-looking expression `self.eventKeeper['mouse']()`.

If we break that expression apart, it is not so mysterious. Python first evaluates `self`, then it finds the `eventKeeper` dictionary. The square brackets tell Python to look up the key `'mouse'` in the dictionary. The dictionary lookup returns a reference to the function stored there. Finally, the left and right parentheses let Python know that it should call the referenced object as a function.

Let's give our simulation a try. You can follow along in Session 13.1. First, we will define two simple callback functions. We will call the functions myMouse and myKey to handle mouse and key events respectively. Although these two functions are simple, keep in mind that they could do anything you want them to do. Second, we will register our callback functions with the event handler. As you can see in Listing 13.1, all this does is store a reference to the function in the eventKeeper dictionary. Third, we will add some events using the addEvent method.

```
>>> def myMouse():
        print('Oh no the mouse was clicked.')

>>> def myKey():
        print('A key has been pressed')

>>> eh = EventHandler()
>>> eh.registerCallback('key',myKey)
>>> eh.registerCallback('mouse',myMouse)
>>> eh.addEvent('mouse')
>>> eh.addEvent('key')
>>> eh.addEvent('mouse')
>>> eh.run()
Oh no the mouse was clicked.
A key has been pressed
Oh no the mouse was clicked.
queue is empty
queue is empty
queue is empty
...
>>>
```

Session 13.1   Testing the event processing simulation

With the callback functions registered and some events added to the queue, we tell the event handler to run. Note that the **run** method does something that we have never tried to do on purpose before. The **run** method enters an infinite loop. In each pass through the loop, we check the length of the event queue to see if there are entries. If there are entries on the queue, then the first one is removed and the appropriate callback function is called. If there are no events on the queue, then the message **queue is empty** is printed.

Remember that `queue is empty` will be printed forever or until you stop the program from running.

13.2.3   A Multithreaded Event Loop

The problem with the code in Listing 13.1 is that once you call the run method the program goes into an infinite loop. The only events that will ever be processed are events that you placed on the event queue before you called the run method. In practice, this is not the case. The event loop runs simultaneously with other code that is capable of putting events on the event queue. The term **multithreaded** program implies that one program can have multiple things happening at the same time. All modern desktop applications are multithreaded applications, including the `turtle` module.

Figure 13.2 illustrates the difference between single-threaded and multithreaded execution. In the top sequence, there is a single **thread** of execution, which means that once the run method is started nothing else can happen. The start call in the multithreaded diagram starts a new thread and calls the run method inside the new thread. The new thread runs in parallel with the old thread. With two threads of execution, events can be added in one thread while the run method is executing in the other.

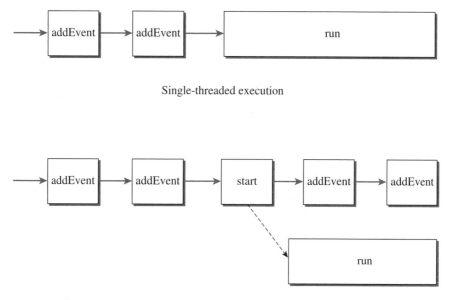

Figure 13.2   Comparing single and multithreaded execution

Inheritance makes it possible to convert a single-threaded EventHandler class to a multi-threaded class very easily. Even though we do not know anything about how threads work behind the scenes, we can make our class multithreaded by having it inherit from the class Thread. This is an extremely powerful pattern that we will revisit when we implement our video game. For now we can just use the code shown in Listing 13.2. Notice that there are only a couple of small changes between Listing 13.1 and 13.2. The first change is that we now import the Thread class from the threading module. The second change is that we import time, and the third is in the class declaration. Instead of inheriting from object we now inherit from Thread.

By inheriting from Thread, we gain access to some additional methods. For our purposes, the start method is the only one we need to worry about. Start creates a new thread and calls the run method of the class inside that new thread. Once the run command starts, it enters an infinite loop just as before, except for this time, if there are no events on the event queue, the function time.sleep is called. The time.sleep function causes the thread to pause for the number of seconds passed as a parameter.

```python
from threading import Thread
import time

class EventHandler(Thread):
    def __init__(self):
        super().__init__()
        self.queue = []
        self.eventKeeper = {}

    def addEvent(self, eventName):
        self.queue.append(eventName)

    def registerCallback(self, event, func):
        self.eventKeeper[event] = func

    def run(self):
        while(True):
            if len(self.queue) > 0:
                nextEvent = self.queue.pop(0)
                callBack = self.eventKeeper[nextEvent]
                callBack()
            else:
                time.sleep(1)
```

Listing 13.2   A multithreaded event handler

We can test the multithreaded version of our event loop as shown in Session 13.2. As you can see, once the **start** method is called the three original events are handled as before. However, with the **run** method executing in its own thread we can now type additional Python statements that will be executed by the original thread.

```
>>> eh = EventHandler()
>>> eh.addEvent('mouse')
>>> eh.addEvent('key')
>>> eh.addEvent('mouse')
>>> eh.registerCallback('key',myKey)
>>> eh.registerCallback('mouse',myMouse)
>>> eh.start()
Oh no the mouse was clicked.
A key has been pressed
Oh no the mouse was clicked.
>>> eh.addEvent('mouse')
Oh no the mouse was clicked.
>>> eh.addEvent('key')
A key has been pressed
>>> eh.addEvent('mouse')
Oh no the mouse was clicked.
```

Session 13.2   A multithreaded event loop example

Exercises

13.1 Write your own callback functions for `'mouse'` and `'key'` events. Register these events with the **EventHandler** and rerun the simulation.

13.2 Add a third event type called `'timer'`. Supply a simple callback function for the timer.

13.3 Draw a reference diagram to illustrate how a dictionary of callback functions works.

13.4 Devise a way to modify the simulation so that you can have a key event and pass the name of the key as a parameter to the callback function.

13.5 Devise a way to modify the simulation so that you can have a mouse event and pass simulated window coordinates of the mouse to the callback function.

13.6 Modify the simulation to support the timer event. When you add a timer event, you should supply the number of seconds until the timer expires. When the timer goes off, it should call the timer callback function.

13.3   Event-Driven Programming with `turtle`

The `turtle` module provides three methods to register callbacks for key, mouse, and timer events. The callback functions are

- `onkey`
- `onclick`
- `ontimer`

We will need to master the use of all three of these kinds of callbacks to successfully write our video game. In this section we will investigate the use of these callbacks in more detail.

13.3.1   A Simple Etch-a-Sketch

Let's begin our investigation of event-driven turtle programming by creating a simple drawing program. Previously we have used the turtle to draw by writing a fixed set of commands that the turtle followed. Now we would like to create a program where the user can draw just by using the arrow keys. Each arrow key will have the following effect:

- UP: The turtle goes forward 5 pixels.
- LEFT: The turtle turns counterclockwise by 10 degrees.
- RIGHT: The turtle turns clockwise by 10 degrees.
- DOWN: The turtle backs up 5 pixels.

In addition, pressing the "q" key will cause the program to quit. Note that the arrow keys go by the special names `Up`, `Down`, `Left`, and `Right`.

The `turtle` module allows us to add a callback function for any key by using the `onkey` method of a `Screen` object. This method takes two parameters: the first is a reference to a function and the second is the name of a key. For example, `myScreen.onkey(myKey,'a')` sets up a callback so that when the 'a' key is pressed the function `myKey` is called. This approach allows us to set up a different callback function for each key on the keyboard.

One important question remains: What about parameters? The first solution that might occur to you is to have the callback function for the left arrow call the turtle method `left`. But the `left` method requires a parameter. Now you might think that the solution is to set up the callback by using `myScreen.onkey(myTurtle.left(5),'Left')`. But this would result in an error. Why? If you think about how Python evaluates the statement, you will realize that call-by-assignment parameter passing evaluates the parameters to a function call. Python will actually try to evaluate `myTurtle.left(5)`, which will return the value `None`. The `onkey` method wants to have a reference to a function.

Different callback functions will have different conventions for how many parameters they take. In the `turtle` module, the callback functions for key callbacks cannot accept any parameters. So we will have to implement our callbacks with zero parameters and have them call the turtle methods with the appropriate parameters. With this in mind we will need to write five different callback functions for our program, one for each of the arrow keys and one for the "q" key. In the case of the arrow keys, the callback functions will be very short. All we need to do is call the appropriate turtle function. The callback functions are shown on lines 19–32 of Listing 13.3.

The most interesting part for us is the `__init__` method. In `__init__` we create a turtle, initialize its colors, create a screen, and set up the callback functions. The final line of `__init__` calls the screen method `listen`, which specifically tells the screen to start listening for keyboard events.

The final method is `main`. All this method does is call the `turtle.mainloop` function. By now you can probably guess what kind of a loop `mainloop` is. It is the event loop for the turtle.

To run this little drawing program, all you need to do is load the `Etch` class as defined in Listing 13.3 and then execute the following two commands:

```
>>> draw = Etch()
>>> draw.main()
```

Once the program is running, you can make a drawing by pressing the arrow keys to move the turtle around the window.

The program in Listing 13.3 uses **composition**—a style of object-oriented programming in which the `Etch` class uses a turtle to do the bulk of the work and therefore has a reference to a turtle as an instance variable. This is a common and useful way to think about programming. However, there is another way to think about this problem using

```
1  import turtle
2
3  class Etch:
4      def __init__(self):
5          self.myT = turtle.Turtle()
6          self.myScreen = turtle.Screen()
7          self.myT.color('blue')
8          self.myT.pensize(2)
9          self.myT.speed(0)
10         self.distance = 5
11         self.turn = 10
12         self.myScreen.onkey(self.fwd,"Up")
13         self.myScreen.onkey(self.bkwd,"Down")
14         self.myScreen.onkey(self.left,"Left")
15         self.myScreen.onkey(self.right,"Right")
16         self.myScreen.onkey(self.quit,"q")
17         self.myScreen.listen()
18
19     def fwd(self):
20         self.myT.forward(self.distance)
21
22     def bkwd(self):
23         self.myT.backward(self.distance)
24
25     def left(self):
26         self.myT.left(self.turn)
27
28     def right(self):
29         self.myT.right(self.turn)
30
31     def quit(self):
32         self.myScreen.bye()
33
34     def main(self):
35         turtle.mainloop()
```

Listing 13.3   A simple drawing program

inheritance. The inheritance view of this problem would say that an Etch is a special kind of Turtle, and therefore our Etch class would inherit from Turtle.

Listing 13.4 shows how to implement our drawing program using inheritance. The main difference between this program and the previous one is that we do not explicitly create a

```
1    from turtle import Turtle, mainloop
2
3    class Etch(Turtle):
4        def __init__(self):
5            super().__init__()
6            self.screen = self.getscreen()
7            self.color('blue')
8            self.pensize(2)
9            self.speed(0)
10           self.distance = 5
11           self.turn = 10
12           self.screen.onkey(self.fwd,"Up")
13           self.screen.onkey(self.bkwd,"Down")
14           self.screen.onkey(self.left5,"Left")
15           self.screen.onkey(self.right5,"Right")
16           self.screen.onkey(self.quit,"q")
17           self.screen.listen()
18           self.main()
19
20       def fwd(self):
21           self.forward(self.distance)
22
23       def bkwd(self):
24           self.backward(self.distance)
25
26       def left5(self):
27           self.left(self.turn)
28
29       def right5(self):
30           self.right(self.turn)
31
32       def quit(self):
33           self.screen.bye()
34
35       def main(self):
36           mainloop()
37
38   if __name__ == '__main__':
39       etch = Etch()
```

Listing 13.4 The drawing program implemented with inheritance

reference to a turtle inside the Etch class. The reason is that an Etch IS-A Turtle. So, the real work of creating the window and the Turtle part of our Etch object happens on lines 5 and 6. Notice that this also simplifies the rest of the code because we can now simply call self.forward rather than self.myT.forward.

It is important to mention that neither implementation of Etch is "right" or "wrong." The programs in Listings 13.3 and 13.4 are two alternative ways of accomplishing the same goal. Each has advantages and disadvantages.

Exercises

13.7 Add a new key event to the Etch program to allow the turtle to pick up or put down its tail.

13.8 Add a key event and reset function to the Etch program that clears the screen and returns the turtle to the home position.

13.9 The Etch program in Listing 13.4 could be made even cleaner by using polymorphism and a default parameter. Rather than implementing a fwd method that calls self.forward, you can replace the definition of forward using a default parameter for the distance. The implementation of the forward method would use the super function to call the turtle's implementation of forward passing the default parameter. Rewrite the Etch implementation using forward, backward, left, and right with default parameters.

13.3.2   Placing Turtles

We will continue our investigation of event-driven programming by looking at how our programs can respond to mouse click events. To set up a callback for a mouse click, we call the onclick method and simply pass it the function to call whenever the mouse is clicked. The main difference between the keyboard callbacks and the mouse callbacks is that the function we write to accept mouse callbacks must accept two parameters. The two parameters will specify the x and y coordinates of where the cursor was when the mouse was clicked.

As a first example, let's write an application to place turtles in the window. Wherever the user clicks the mouse, a new turtle will appear. The number of turtles the user is allowed to create is passed as a parameter during startup time. Once the maximum number of turtles have been placed, no more turtles should be created.

To solve this problem we create a class called TurtlePlace, which will have three methods (see Listing 13.5). The __init__ method will create the initial window, and unfortunately an initial turtle. We will simply hide the initial turtle. The __init__ method will also call onclick to arrange for the second method placeTurtle to be called whenever the mouse is clicked. In addition, __init__ sets up a turtle counter so we can keep track of how

```
1  from turtle import Turtle, mainloop
2  import random
3
4  class TurtlePlace:
5      def __init__(self, maxTurtles, hWall=200, vWall=200):
6          self.bigT = Turtle()
7          self.bigTscreen = self.bigT.getscreen()
8          self.bigT.shape('turtle')
9          self.turtleList = []
10         self.bigTscreen.onclick(self.placeTurtle)
11         self.bigT.hideturtle()
12         self.numTurtles = 0
13         self.maxTurtles = maxTurtles
14         self.hWall = hWall
15         self.vWall = vWall
16         self.drawField(hWall, vWall)
17         mainloop()
18
19     def placeTurtle(self, x, y):
20         newT = Turtle()
21         newTscreen = newT.getscreen()
22         newTscreen.tracer(0)
23         newT.up()
24         newT.goto(x, y)
25         newT.shape('turtle')
26         newT.setheading(random.randint(1, 359))
27         newTscreen.tracer(1)
28         self.numTurtles = self.numTurtles + 1
29         self.turtleList.append(newT)
30         if self.numTurtles >= self.maxTurtles:
31             self.bigTscreen.onclick(None)
32
33     def drawField(self, hWall, vWall):
34         self.bigTscreen.tracer(0)
35         self.bigT.up()
36         self.bigT.goto(-hWall, -vWall)
37         self.bigT.down()
38         for i in range(4):
39             self.bigT.forward(2*hWall)
40             self.bigT.left(90)
41         self.bigTscreen.tracer(1)
```

Listing 13.5 A turtle placement program

many turtles we have created so far. Finally, the third method called `drawField` draws a rectangle for the turtles to live in. Once the setup is done, `__init__` calls `mainloop` to begin processing events.

The `placeTurtle` method will create a new turtle at position `(x,y)` in the window. It updates the number of turtles created, gives the turtle a random heading, and gives the turtle a fancy shape. The last thing that `placeTurtle` does is check to see if `maxTurtles` have been created. If the limit on turtles is reached, then `placeTurtle` calls `onClick` and passes `None` as the function to call. Passing `None` to the `onClick` function effectively cancels the callback mechanism so that `placeTurtle` will no longer be called when the mouse is clicked.

To test the `TurtlePlace` implementation, you simply create an instance of `TurtlePlace`. Because `mainloop` is called on the last line of the `__init__` method, `__init__` will never return and the event loop is started.

Exercises

13.10 Modify the `placeTurtle` method so that turtles cannot be placed outside the boundary box.

13.11 Modify the `TurtlePlace` class so that after all the turtles have been created subsequent mouse clicks cause all the turtles to turn and move 10 units toward the point that the mouse was clicked on.

13.12 Add an `onclick` event to `Etch` that causes the turtle to move to wherever the mouse was clicked.

13.13 Modify the drawing package from Chapter 12 to allow a user to place geometric objects on a canvas.

13.14 Create a program to draw a regression line through a set of points. The user should be able to click in the window to create a set of points. When the user clicks in a certain part of the window, you should calculate and draw a best-fit line through the points. You will find the equations needed for calculating the regression line in Chapter 4.

13.3.3   Bouncing Turtles

The final event we examine is `ontimer`, in which we will use a timer to animate the turtles we have placed in the window using the `TurtlePlace` program. The `ontimer` method takes two parameters. The first parameter is the callback function, and the second parameter is the number of milliseconds to wait before calling the function. Timer callback functions have no parameters.

For this part of our program we would like to have the turtles that we placed in the last section move. We can animate a turtle by calling the forward method every few milliseconds. Furthermore, we want the turtles to bounce off the walls of an imaginary box and off each other as they move around.

There are a couple of ways we can approach this problem. The first way, which we leave for you to implement later, is to take advantage of the self.turtleList instance variable, which keeps track of all the turtles that have been created. Every so many milliseconds, a timer callback function iterates over all the turtles on the list and call the forward method on each turtle. We classify this approach to the solution as the composition approach.

Let's look at an alternative solution using inheritance. Suppose that rather than making a plain old Turtle we make a special kind of turtle called an AnimatedTurtle. Once an AnimatedTurtle is created, it automatically begins to wander around the box, bouncing off the walls and the other turtles.

Because the animated turtle class is not meant to be controlled like a regular turtle, we are not going to add any methods that we expect the user to call. The important point to note in the AnimatedTurtle class is on line 9 of Listing 13.6. The ontimer method is called to set up a callback for __moveOneStep in 100 milliseconds.

The __moveOneStep method checks to see if the turtle has run into one of the boundary walls, moves forward by 5 units, and then calls ontimer again. It is important to remember that a timer callback is good for only one interval; it does not repeat. Therefore, the last thing we would want to do is reset the timer callback to call again after another 100 milliseconds.

We use the two underscores in the name __moveOneStep to ensure that the method cannot be called from outside the AnimatedTurtle class. Names that begin with two underscores undergo **mangling** by Python. The effect of mangling a name is to hide it from any functions outside the class.

In order to integrate the TurtlePlace class with the AnimatedTurtle class, we need to modify the placeTurtle method so that it creates an AnimatedTurtle rather than a plain Turtle. The AnimatedTurtle also requires that we pass its boundaries as parameters. The new placeTurtle method is shown in Listing 13.7.

At this point we must load both the modified TurtlePlace and AnimatedTurtle turtle classes. Once the classes are loaded, it is easy to start the whole program by simply

```
1  class AnimatedTurtle(Turtle):
2      def __init__(self,hWall,vWall):
3          super().__init__()
4          self.scr = self.getscreen()
5          self.xmin = -vWall
6          self.xmax = vWall
7          self.ymin = -hWall
8          self.ymax = hWall
9          self.scr.ontimer(self.__moveOneStep,100)
10
11     def __moveOneStep(self):
12         self.__computeNewHeading()
13         self.forward(5)
14         self.scr.ontimer(self.__moveOneStep,100)
15
16     def __computeNewHeading(self):
17         xpos,ypos = self.position()
18         oldHead = self.heading()
19         newHead = oldHead
20
21         if xpos > self.xmax or xpos < self.xmin:
22             newHead = 180-oldHead
23         if  ypos > self.ymax or ypos < self.ymin:
24             newHead = 360-oldHead
25         if newHead != oldHead:
26             self.setheading(newHead)
```

Listing 13.6   A class to implement an animated turtle

```
1      def placeTurtle(self,x,y):
2          newT = AnimatedTurtle(self.hWall,self.vWall)
3          newTscreen = newT.getscreen()
4          newTscreen.tracer(0)
5          newT.up()
6          newT.goto(x,y)
7          newT.shape('turtle')
8          newT.setheading(random.randint(1,359))
9          newTscreen.tracer(1)
10         self.numTurtles = self.numTurtles + 1
11         self.turtleList.append(newT)
12         if self.numTurtles >= self.maxTurtles:
13             self.bigTscreen.onclick(None)
```

Listing 13.7   A modified `placeTurtle` method

typing `TurtlePlace(5,200,200)`. This statement simply creates a new instance of the `TurtlePlace` class that allows us to create five new turtles in a box that is 400 by 400 units.

The turtles bounce off the walls, but at this point they go right through each other if their paths cross. Clearly this is not a realistic simulation of turtle behavior. The next step to make our program more realistic is to add the ability for turtles to bounce off each other.

There is no magic to this part of the solution. To find out if a turtle has "hit" another turtle, we are going to have to check the distance between the turtle that is currently moving, and all the other turtles. You might be tempted to think that there must be a very elegant solution to this problem. In fact, for this application a simple brute force check of all other turtles will be just fine.

The question is how to keep track of all the turtles. Of course, we will want to use a list, but where will that list be kept? Who is responsible for adding turtles to the list, and how can we ensure that each `AnimatedTurtle` has access to the list of all other turtles? We could use the `turtleList` instance variable in the `TurtlePlace` class, but then every animated turtle would need to have a reference to an instance of `TurtlePlace`.

The answer is to use a **static variable**—a variable that is shared by all instances of a class and is available to all the methods in the class. Listing 13.8 creates a static variable on line 3. As you can see, static variables are defined inside the class but outside any method definition.

With the static variable `allTurtles` defined, the `__init__` method can add new turtles to this list as they are created using the statement `AnimatedTurtle.allTurtles.append(self)`. Similarly the `__checkCollisions` method can now access the list of all turtles by referencing the variable `AnimatedTurtle.allTurtles`. Notice that when we reference a static variable, we use the class name rather than `self`. The beauty of the static variable approach is that it keeps the accounting of all the animated turtles inside the `AnimatedTurtle` class.

To calculate the approximate distance between two turtles, we will use the `distance` method provided by the `turtle` module. The `distance` method calculates the distance between the center points of the two turtles, but in order to have our simulation look more realistic we really need to think of the distance between the edges of the circles that circumscribe the two turtles. In other words, if the edges of the circles touch, we should consider that the two turtles have collided.

With this in mind, take a look at the `__checkCollisions` method in Listing 13.8. You will see that the method uses two loops. One loop iterates over all the turtles on the

```
 1  class AnimatedTurtle(Turtle):
 2
 3      allTurtles = []
 4
 5      def __init__(self,hWall,vWall):
 6          super().__init__()
 7          self.scr = self.getscreen()
 8          self.xmin = -vWall+10
 9          self.xmax = vWall-10
10          self.ymin = -hWall+10
11          self.ymax = hWall-10
12          self.scr.ontimer(self.__moveOneStep,100)
13          AnimatedTurtle.allTurtles.append(self)
14
15      def __moveOneStep(self):
16          self.__computeNewHeading()
17          self.forward(5)
18          self.__checkCollisions()
19          self.scr.ontimer(self.__moveOneStep,100)
20
21      def __computeNewHeading(self):
22          xpos,ypos = self.position()
23          oldHead = self.heading()
24          newHead = oldHead
25
26          if xpos > self.xmax or xpos < self.xmin:
27              newHead = 180-oldHead
28          if  ypos > self.ymax or ypos < self.ymin:
29              newHead = 360-oldHead
30          if newHead != oldHead:
31              self.setheading(newHead)
32
33      def __checkCollisions(self):
34          for otherT in AnimatedTurtle.allTurtles:
35              if self != otherT:
36                  if self.distance(otherT) < 20:
37                      tempHeading = self.heading()
38                      self.setheading(otherT.heading())
39                      otherT.setheading(tempHeading)
40                      while self.distance(otherT) < 20:
41                          self.forward(1)
42                          otherT.forward(1)
```

Listing 13.8   An `AnimatedTurtle` class with turtle–turtle collision detection

`AnimatedTurtle.allTurtles` list. The statement `if self != otherT` ensures that we do not compute the distance between the same turtle using two different references. If the turtles are too close, then we bounce them off each other by exchanging their headings. This assumes that turtles collide in a perfectly elastic collision, which may not be the case in nature but is easy to program. Finally, we have a *while* loop that moves the turtles forward along their new headings to make sure they are not inside the collision distance anymore. If we leave the *while* loop out, we can get some funny-looking simulations where the turtles may appear to be stuck together for a short time.

Exercises

13.15 Modify the `__init__` method to give each new turtle a random color.

13.16 Add start and stop methods to the `AnimatedTurtle` class.

13.17 Add a speed method that allows you to alter the speed of a turtle by changing the number of milliseconds passed to the `ontimer` method.

13.18 Add a "q" key event to the bouncing turtles program. Pressing "q" should cause the program to exit.

13.19 Add a mouse event to the bouncing turtles program so that if you click on a turtle that is moving it stops, and if you click on a turtle that is stopped it starts.

13.20 Rewrite the bouncing turtles program using composition rather than inheritance. After you are done, compare the two solutions. What are the strengths and weaknesses of each approach?

13.4 Creating Your Own Video Game

By now you should have a pretty good understanding of event-driven programming using the `turtle` module. We will finish this chapter by pulling everything together to create a simple video game—our own version of the old space invaders game, where aliens fall from the sky and you must shoot them with a laser cannon. Every time you shoot an alien, you get some points; every time an alien falls to the ground, you lose points. Figure 13.3 shows a screenshot of the game in action.

You can see in the figure the three main objects we are going to implement to make our video game work. At the bottom center of the window is the laser cannon. The little aliens are the enemies, and the small circles are the bombs that have been shot from the laser

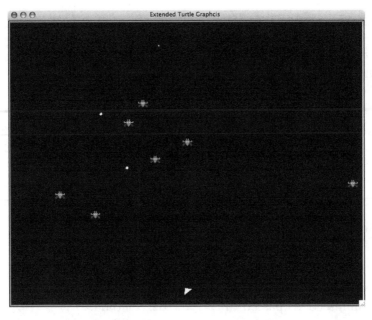

Figure 13.3   Space invaders

cannon. These three things will become our three main classes: `LaserCannon`, `Alien`, and `Bomb`. Each of these classes inherits from the `Turtle` class, so we can control each element of our game as a `Turtle`. The different appearance of each object comes from using the turtle `shape` method that allows us to use image files and even shapes you draw yourself to represent a turtle.

The next step is to identify the capabilities of each of our new classes. The `LaserCannon` must be able to do two things:

- Aim at `Alien`s.
- Fire `Bomb`s.

A `Bomb` must be able to do three things:

- Move in the direction it was fired.
- Detect when it hits an Alien.
- Detect when it disappears out of the window.

An `Alien` must be able to do two things:

- Move from the top of the screen to the bottom.
- Detect when it reaches the bottom of the screen.

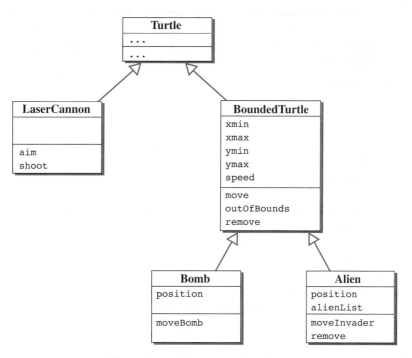

Figure 13.4   Space invaders design

This high-level design is captured in Figure 13.4.

13.4.1   The LaserCannon Class

Let's look at the implementation of the LaserCannon class in more detail (see Listing 13.9). This should look somewhat familiar to you after studying the bouncing turtles example from the previous section. The LaserCannon will serve as our initial turtle so it will create the window for all the other turtles that come later. In the __init__ method, we create a turtle, change its color, set the background color for the entire window, and set our world coordinate system so that $y = 0$ is at the bottom of the window.

In addition, there are three callback functions to install: aim, shoot, and exit. The aim method takes care of adjusting the aim of the laser cannon. A mouse click causes the laser cannon to aim toward the position of the cursor where the mouse was clicked. The shoot method is called when the "s" key is pressed. The shoot method is very short in that it only creates a new Bomb. As you will see later in Listing 13.12, the constructor for Bomb takes care of all the rest.

If you want to test incrementally, you can load the `LaserCannon` class now and create an instance of `LaserCannon`. You should get a window with a triangular laser cannon at the bottom center. If you call the `mainloop` function, you can try aiming and shooting. You can aim the cannon with the mouse, but if you try to fire you will get an error because we have not written the Bomb class yet.

```python
class LaserCannon(Turtle):
    def __init__(self,xmin,xmax,ymin,ymax):
        super().__init__()
        self.screen = self.getscreen()
        self.screen.bgcolor('light green')
        self.screen.setworldcoordinates(xmin,ymin,xmax,ymax)
        self.screen.onclick(self.aim,1)
        self.screen.onkey(self.shoot,"s")
        self.screen.onkey(self.quit,'q')

    def aim(self,x,y):
        heading = self.towards(x,y)
        self.setheading(heading)

    def shoot(self):
        Bomb(self.heading(),5)

    def quit(self):
        self.screen.bye()
```

Listing 13.9   The `LaserCannon` class

13.4.2   The `BoundedTurtle` Class

The `BoundedTurtle` class is an abstract class that is the parent of `Alien` and `Bomb`. The difference between a regular turtle and a `BoundedTurtle` is that the `BoundedTurtle` knows when it is outside the window. When the turtle is outside the window, it disappears.

Listing 13.10 shows the code for the `BoundedTurtle` class. In the `outOfBounds` method, the statement `xpos,ypos = self.position()` is equivalent to two statements that get the x and y coordinates of the turtle separately. `position` returns a tuple but the assignment statement unpacks the tuple and assigns the corresponding elements to the variables on the left-hand side. The `outOfBounds` returns `True` or `False` depending on whether the turtle has gone outside its boundaries.

The `move` method checks to see if the turtle is out of bounds. If the turtle stays in bounds, the timer is reset so that the turtle will move again in 200 milliseconds. If the turtle is out of bounds, it is hidden and the timer is not reset, which means that the turtle will no longer move.

```
class BoundedTurtle(Turtle):
    def __init__(self, speed, xmin=-200,xmax=200,ymin=0,ymax=400):
        super().__init__()
        self.xmin = xmin
        self.xmax = xmax
        self.ymin = ymin
        self.ymax = ymax
        self.speed = speed

    def outOfBounds(self):
        xpos,ypos = self.position()
        out = False
        if xpos < self.xmin or xpos > self.xmax:
            out = True
        if ypos < self.ymin or ypos > self.ymax:
            out = True
        return out

    def move(self):
        self.forward(self.speed)
        if self.outOfBounds():
            self.remove()
        else:
            self.getscreen().ontimer(self.move,200)

    def remove(self):
        self.hideturtle()
```

Listing 13.10   Bounded turtles can check whether they are out of bounds

13.4.3 The Alien Class

The next class we will implement is the Alien class. Our aliens need to be able to move down the screen, and they need to be able to remove themselves from the game when they are hit by a Bomb.

As in the bouncing turtle simulation, we are going to need to keep track of all aliens so that when a bomb moves we can test whether it has hit any of the aliens. We will use the static variable alienList to keep track of all the aliens.

To keep things simple, we want only one method to add or remove aliens from the `alienList`. We will do this in the `Alien` constructor. When a new alien is created, we append the new alien to the list. When an alien is hit by a bomb, we set the `alive` instance variable for that alien to `False`.

Since the `Bomb` class needs to know which aliens it can blow up, it will need to get a list of all the live aliens. To do this, the `Alien` class will provide a **static method** called `getAliens` to return this list. Just like a static variable provides a single variable for the class, a static method is shared by the whole class.

Listing 13.11 shows the code for the `Alien` class. Notice that there is no `self` parameter in the formal parameter list of the static method `getAliens`. You will also notice that to create a static method we use a special bit of Python syntax called a **decorator**. In this case, the decorator is `@staticmethod`. The `@staticmethod` decorator tells the Python interpreter

```python
class Alien(BoundedTurtle):
    alienList = []

    @staticmethod
    def getAliens():
        return [x for x in Alien.alienList if x.alive]

    def __init__(self,speed,xmin,xmax,ymin,ymax):
        super().__init__(speed,xmin,xmax,ymin,ymax)
        self.getscreen().tracer(0)
        self.up()
        if 'PurpleAlien.gif' not in self.getscreen().getshapes():
            self.getscreen().addshape('PurpleAlien.gif')
        self.shape('PurpleAlien.gif')
        self.goto(random.randint(xmin-1,xmax-1),ymax-20)
        self.setheading(random.randint(250,290))
        self.getscreen().tracer(1)
        Alien.alienList = [x for x in Alien.alienList if x.alive]
        Alien.alienList.append(self)
        self.alive = True
        self.getscreen().ontimer(self.move,200)

    def remove(self):
        self.alive = False
        self.hideturtle()
```

Listing 13.11   The `Alien` class

that there is no need for an instance variable to be passed as an implicit parameter to the function getAliens. So we can call the method using Alien.getAliens() without needing an instance of the Aliens class. Aliens.getAliens returns all the live aliens by constructing a brand new list created from the instances of Alien where alive is True. Like static attributes, static methods are useful when you have a method that belongs inside a class but does not apply to any particular instance of the class.

The other Python construct that is part of the getAliens method is the list comprehension, which provides a concise way to create a list without using a for loop with an append inside it. Session 13.3 illustrates some uses of list comprehensions. It is also legal to apply Python operators to the variable you are using to create the list. For example, to create a list of the first five numbers squared, you could write [x**2 for x in range(5)].

```
>>> movies = [ 'aliens', 'starwars', 'bourne' ]
>>>
>>> [x.capitalize() for x in movies]
>>> ['Aliens', 'Starwars', 'Bourne']
>>>
>>> [x[-1] for x in movies if len(x) > 6]
>>> ['s']
>>>
>>> [x[-1] for x in movies if len(x) <= 6]
>>> ['s', 'e']
```

Session 13.3   Using list comprehensions

The getAliens method on line 6 of Listing 13.11 uses a list comprehension and is equivalent to the getAliens method shown here.

```
def getAliens():
    myList = []
    for x in Alien.alienList:
        if x.alive:
            myList.append(x)
    return myList
```

The __init__ method contains a couple of important things to notice. First, it is the only method that we will allow to modify the alienList. This ensures that we avoid the situation where one callback method could be adding to the list while another is trying to remove from the list. This could happen if a bomb hit an alien at the same time as another alien was being created.

Second, we use a list comprehension to filter out all the dead aliens every time a new alien is created. This is a performance improvement to keep the list nice and short. The other statement to look at is the conditional on lines 12 and 13. This statement simply checks to see if the `'PurpleAlien.gif'` file has been loaded. If it has been loaded once, it is not necessary to load it again since the **addshape** method is really loading a list of shapes that works for all the turtles in the same window.

The `move` method for an **Alien** is inherited from the **BoundedTurtle** class. Although the `move` method is inherited from **BoundedTurtle**, polymorphism ensures that the `remove` method of the **Alien** class is called when an alien moves out of bounds.

The `remove` method marks the alien as dead and hides it so it is no longer seen. By setting `alive = False`, the alien stays on the list but will not be included in any calculations with bombs that are shot from the laser cannon.

13.4.4   The Bomb Class

Our final class is the Bomb. This class is no more complicated than the bouncing turtle. A bomb is created with an initial heading corresponding to the direction the cannon was pointing. Once the bomb is created, it continues moving in the direction it was pointed. If it runs into an alien, the bomb explodes, the alien is marked as dead, and the bomb hides itself and ceases to move. The entire Bomb class is shown in Listing 13.12.

13.4.5   Putting All the Pieces Together

To pull all the pieces of the game together and start things running, we will create one final class, **AlienInvaders**, which will act as the main application. The complete code for the **AlienInvaders** class is found in Listing 13.13. The main task of this class is to create a **LaserCannon**, and to set up a timer to add aliens to the playing field at regular intervals. These tasks are implemented in the **play** method.

To play the game, we need only execute the two commands shown in Session 13.4. Of course, these should be added to the bottom of the file with all of the class definitions so we can run everything with a single command.

```
 1  class Bomb(BoundedTurtle):
 2      def __init__(self, initHeading, speed):
 3          super().__init__(speed)
 4          self.initHeading = initHeading
 5          self.resizemode('user')
 6          self.color('red','red')
 7          self.shape('circle')
 8          self.setheading(initHeading)
 9          self.up()
10          self.turtlesize(.25)
11          self.getscreen().ontimer(self.move,100)
12
13      def move(self):
14          exploded = False
15          self.forward(self.speed)
16          for i in Alien.getAliens():
17              if self.distance(i) < 5:
18                  i.remove()
19                  exploded = True
20          if self.outOfBounds() or exploded:
21              self.remove()
22          else:
23              self.getscreen().ontimer(self.move,100)
24
25      def distance(self,other):
26          p1 = self.position()
27          p2 = other.position()
28          a = p1[0]-p2[0]
29          b = p1[1]-p2[1]
30          dist = math.sqrt(a**2 + b**2)
31          return dist
```

Listing 13.12   The Bomb

```
1  class AlienInvaders:
2      def __init__(self,xmin,xmax,ymin,ymax):
3          super().__init__()
4          self.xmin = xmin
5          self.xmax = xmax
6          self.ymin = ymin
7          self.ymax = ymax
8
9      def play(self):
10         self.mainWin = LaserCannon(self.xmin,self.xmax,
11                                   self.ymin,self.ymax).getscreen()
12         self.mainWin.ontimer(self.addAlien,1000)
13         self.mainWin.listen()
14         mainloop()
15
16     def addAlien(self):
17         if len(Alien.getAliens()) < 7:
18             Alien(1,self.xmin,self.xmax,self.ymin,self.ymax)
19         self.mainWin.ontimer(self.addAlien,1000)
```

Listing 13.13   Putting it all together

```
>>> game = AlienInvaders(-200,200,0,400)
>>> game.play()
```

Session 13.4   Running the aliens game

Exercises

13.21 Modify the space invaders game to keep score. The user should earn 10 points for each invader hit and should lose 10 points for each invader that falls to the ground.

13.22 Modify the invaders game to increase the difficulty level as the score gets higher. That is, there should be more invaders on the screen, and they should move faster.

13.23 Modify the invaders game to use the arrow keys instead of a mouse click to aim the laser cannon.

13.24 Modify the invaders game so that if an alien lands on the laser cannon the game is over.

13.25 Modify the invaders game so that the laser cannon always shoots straight up but can be slid back and forth across the bottom of the window.

13.26 Modify the invaders game to have a button that resets the score and all invaders.

13.5   Summary

In this chapter we extended our discussion of object-oriented programming by introducing event-driven programming that would implement a simple video game. We designed our video game by creating classes to represent the components of the game. Functions were tied to mouse clicks and keys so that action would occur when those input events took place.

As part of the implementation, we used a static variable that could be shared by each instance of the class. We also created a static method that did not belong to any one instance of the class but could access data defined in the class. Finally, we used timers to place the video game in motion.

Key Terms

callback function	inheritance	static method
composition	list comprehension	static variable
decorator	multithreaded	thread
event-driven program	name mangling	
event loop	queue	

Bibliography

[pyg]   Pygame—Python Game Development. Retrieved from: www.pygame.org.

[Ril03]   Sean Riley. *Game Programming with Python*. Charles River Media, 2003.

Python Keywords

@staticmethod	def	sys
class	if	

Programming Exercises

13.1 Write your own video game. Here are some simple games to think about:

- One player pong
- One player brickout
- Frogger
- Race track
- Asteroids
- Two player pong
- Tank battle

Your game should keep score and utilize each of the callbacks discussed in this chapter.

APPENDIX A

Installing the Required Software

All of the Python software used in this book is free and open source. The following sections will give you pointers about where to find the software as well as some links to instructions for installing this software. Since software is always a moving target and the versions of Python and some of the modules we use in this book are bound to change, we will not try to give you specific instructions for installing Python on every operating system and platform.

A.1 Installing Python

The latest version of Python is always available from `www.python.org`. However, you should note that we have written this book using Python 3.x. Python 3.x represents a big change in Python. Although many of the programs in this book may work with previous versions of Python, you are strongly encouraged to use Python 3.x.

Mac OS X

If you have a Mac and are using OS X 10.5 or a later version, Python 2.x is already installed on your machine and you do not need to do anything to install it. If you have an earlier version of OS X, you will have Python 2.3. In any case you should download and install version 3.x from the python.org website. You will find very helpful instructions and links to videos that explain the process at: `http://wiki.python.org/moin/BeginnersGuide/Download`. You will also find a link to download the OS X installer at `http://python.org/download/releases`.

Windows

If you are running Windows XP or Windows Vista, you will need to download and install Python. You will find very helpful instructions and links to videos that explain the process at `http://wiki.python.org/moin/BeginnersGuide/Download`. You can also find a quick link to the Windows installer at `http://python.org`.

Linux

If you are running Linux, the chances are very good that you already have Python installed. You can see what version you have installed by typing the command `python` or `python3` from the command line. You should see something like the following:

```
Python 3.x.0 (#1, May  2 2007, 08:13:46)
[GCC 4.1.0 (SUSE Linux)] on linux2
Type "help", "copyright", "credits" or "license" for more information.
>>>
```

If Python 3.x is not installed on your Linux box, you will need to download and install it. You can find helpful instructions at: `http://wiki.python.org/moin/BeginnersGuide/Download`. A source tarball can be found at `http://python.org/download/releases`.

A.2   Installing the Python Image Library and `cImage`

The image library used in Chapter 6 relies on two Python modules. The first module you will need for image processing is `cImage.py`. This module is available from `http://knuth.luther.edu/~bmiller/python.html`. Click the link to download `cImage.py`. Move the `cImage.py` file to your `site-packages` directory, which is part of your Python installation. On Windows, you will find it inside the `C:\Python30\lib` folder. On OS X you will find it in the `/Library/Frameworks/Python.framework/versions/3.0/lib/python3.0/` folder. On Linux, it will likely be in `/usr/lib/python3.0`. If you have trouble locating the site-packages folder, an alternative is to put a copy of `cImage.py` in the folder of the project you are working on. Python will be able to find `cImage.py` in either location. The `cImage` module will work with `gif` and `ppm` files with no additional modules required.

The second module, called the Python Image Library (PIL), can be installed to allow image processing of `jpeg` files. You can download PIL from `http://www.pythonware.com/products/pil/`. Make sure you download the version of PIL that is designated for your version of Python. If you are running Windows, download the binary installer and simply click on the downloaded file to run the installer. Follow the instructions on the screen. To install PIL for either OS X or Linux, download the source kit.

To install PIL from the source kit, you will need to unpack the source archive. Currently the source is archived in a file called `Imaging-1.1.6.tar.gz`. You can unpack it with the command `tar zxf Imaging-1.1.6.tar.gz`. This will create a folder called `Imaging-1.1.6`. Inside the folder you will find a file called `setup.py`. Run the command `python setup.py install`. This will compile and install PIL for you.

APPENDIX B

Python Quick Reference

This quick reference provides an overview of the primary Python constructs used in this book. It is not a detailed reference but rather a compendium of tables and syntax. These are described in much more detail within the book. Further, more detailed documentation can be found at `http://python.org/release/3.2/library`.

B.1 Python Reserved Words

The words shown in Table B.1 are reserved by Python. You should not use any of these words as identifiers in your program. If you do, you will get a `SyntaxError`.

and	continue	else	for	import	not	return
assert	def	except	from	in	or	try
break	del	exec	global	is	pass	while
class	elif	finally	if	lambda	raise	

Table B.1 Python's reserved words

B.2   Numeric Data Types

Python has three numeric data types:

- Integers
- Floating points
- Complex numbers

Table B.2 shows the most common operators for numeric data types.

Operation Name	Operator	Explanation
Addition	+	Calculate the sum of two values.
Subtraction	-	Calculate the difference of two values.
Multiplication	*	Calculate the product of two values.
Division	/	Calculate the quotient of two values.
Integer division	//	Calculate the integer quotient of two integers.
Remainder	%	Find the remainder after performing a division on two integers.
Exponentiation	**	(x ** y) Calculate x raised to the y power.

Table B.2   Arithmetic operators in python

B.3   Sequences

Python has three sequential data types: Strings, Lists, and Tuples. Table B.3 summarizes the operators that apply to all sequences.

Operation Name	Operator	Explanation
Indexing	[ ]	Access an element of a sequence.
Concatenation	+	Combine sequences together.
Repetition	*	Concatenate a repeated number of times.
Membership	in	Ask whether an item is in a sequence.
Membership	not in	Ask whether an item is not in a sequence.
Length	len	Ask the number of items in the sequence.
Slicing	[:]	Extract a part of a sequence.

Table B.3   Operations on any sequence in Python

B.3.1 String

Strings are immutable sequences of characters that are indexed by integers, starting at zero. To create string literals, you can enclose them in single, double, or triple quotes as follows:

```
a = "Don't say Hello"
b = 'She said "Hello World!"'
c = """He Said "You Don't say!" didn't he?"""
```

Table B.4 summarizes the more useful string methods.

Method	Use	Explanation
center	astring.center(w)	Returns the string astring but surrounded by spaces to make the length of astring w.
count	astring.count(item)	Returns the number of occurrences of item in astring.
ljust	astring.ljust(w)	Returns astring left-justified in a field of width w.
rjust	astring.rjust(w)	Returns astring right-justified in a field of width w.
upper	astring.upper()	Returns astring in all uppercase.
lower	astring.lower()	Returns astring in all lowercase.
index	astring.index(item)	Returns the index of the first occurrence of item in astring, or an error if not found.
find	astring.find(item)	Returns the index of the first occurrence of item in astring, or −1 if not found.
replace	astring.replace(old,new)	Replaces all occurrences of old substring with new substring in astring.
split	astring.split(schar)	Returns a list of substrings, split at schar.

Table B.4   Summary of string methods

B.3.2 List

Lists are mutable sequences of references to any object. They are indexed by integers starting with zero. You can create a list as follows.

```
>>> emptyList = []
>>> myList = [1, 2, 3.0, 'hello', 5, 6]
```

```
>>> newList = list("hello")
>>> newList
['h', 'e', 'l', 'l', 'o']
```

Table B.5 summarizes the most useful list methods. You can convert the sequences to lists using the `list` function. You can also create sequences using the following `range` function.

Method Name	Use	Explanation
append	alist.append(item)	Adds a new item to the end of a list
insert	alist.insert(i,item)	Inserts an item at the ith position in a list
pop	alist.pop()	Removes and returns the last item in a list
pop	alist.pop(i)	Removes and returns the ith item in a list
sort	alist.sort(key=keyfun,cmp=cmpfun)	Modifies a list to be sorted
reverse	alist.reverse()	Modifies a list to be in reverse order
index	alist.index(item)	Returns the index of the first occurrence of item
count	alist.count(item)	Returns the number of occurrences of item
remove	alist.remove(item)	Removes the first occurrence of item

Table B.5   Methods provided by lists in Python

range(stop) Creates a sequence of numbers starting at 0 and going up to stop–1.

range(start,stop) Creates a sequence of numbers starting at start and going up to stop–1.

range(start,stop,step) Creates a sequence of numbers starting at start and going up to stop–1 counting by step.

```
>>> list(range(10))
[0, 1, 2, 3, 4, 5, 6, 7, 8, 9]
>>> list(range(1,11))
[1, 2, 3, 4, 5, 6, 7, 8, 9, 10]
>>> list(range(10,0,-1))
[10, 9, 8, 7, 6, 5, 4, 3, 2, 1]
```

B.3.3   Tuple

Tuples are immutable sequences of references to any object. You can create a tuple as follows:

```
>>> t = (1,2,3)
>>> u = ('a','b')
>>> y = tuple([1,2,3])
>>> y
(1, 2, 3)
>>> z = tuple('abc')
>>> z
('a', 'b', 'c')
```

Tuples support the same operators as lists, such as indexing and slicing. The main difference is that you cannot use an operator in a way that would modify the tuple. You may not use any of the list methods with a tuple.

The `zip` function can be used to create a list of tuples from two or more sequences. For example:

```
>>> list(zip('hello',range(len('hello'))))
[('h', 0), ('e', 1), ('l', 2), ('l', 3), ('o', 4)]
>>> list(zip([1,2,3],[4,5,6]))
[(1, 4), (2, 5), (3, 6)]
>>> list(zip('abc','def','ghi'))
[('a', 'd', 'g'), ('b', 'e', 'h'), ('c', 'f', 'i')]
>>>
```

B.4   Dictionaries

A dictionary is an unordered collection of objects that are referenced by their keys. You can create a Python dictionary as follows:

```
>>> emptyDict = {}
>>> myD = { 'a':123, 'b':789, 'c':'246 }
>>> myD['d'] = 359
>>> myD
{'a': 123, 'c': '246', 'b': 789, 'd': 359}
```

The Python dictionary methods are summarized in Table B.6.

Method Name	Use	Explanation
keys	adict.keys()	Returns a `dict_keys` object of keys in the dictionary.
values	adict.values()	Returns a `dict_values` object of values in the dictionary.
items	adict.items()	Returns a `dict_items` object of key-value tuples.
get	adict.get(k)	Returns the value associated with k, `None` otherwise.
get	adict.get(k,alt)	Returns the value associated with k, `alt` otherwise.
in	key in adict	Returns `True` if key is in the dictionary, `False` otherwise.
not in	key not in adict	Returns `True` if key is not in the dictionary, `False` otherwise.
index	adict[key]	Returns the value associated with `key`.
del	del adict[key]	Removes the entry from the dictionary.

Table B.6   Methods provided by dictionaries in Python

B.5   Files

Files are sequences of characters that are stored on the disk. It is also useful to think of files as sequences of lines. Table B.7 summarizes `File` methods.

Method Name	Use	Explanation
open	open(filename,'r')	Open a file called `filename` and use it for reading. This will return a reference to a file object.
open	open(filename,'w')	Open a file called `filename` and use it for writing. This will also return a reference to a file object.
close	filevariable.close()	File use is complete.
write	filevar.write(astring)	Add `astring` to the end of the file. `filevar` must refer to a file that has been opened for writing.
read(n)	filevar.read(n)	Reads and returns a string of n characters, or the entire file as a single string if n is not provided.
readline(n)	filevar.readline(n)	Returns the next line of the file with all text up to and including the newline character. If n is provided as a parameter, then only n characters will be returned if the line is longer than n.
readlines(n)	filevar.readlines(n)	Returns a list of n strings, each representing a single line of the file. If n is not provided, then all lines of the file are returned.

Table B.7   Methods provided by a file object

The following program opens a file and reads it line by line, printing each line of the file.

```
f = open('myfile.dat')
line = f.readline()
while line:
    print(line)
    line = f.readline()

f.close()
```

It is also possible to read and print a file using a simple `for` loop:

```
f = open('myfile.dat')
for line in f:
    print(line)
```

B.6 Formatting Output

Python allows you to format strings using the format operator %. For example:

```
>>> print('%d + %d = %d' % (2,3,5))
2 + 3 = 5
```

Tables B.8 and B.9 show the various format characters that can be used. It is also possible to control the width of the field used by any of the format strings.

Character	Output Format
d,i	Integer or long integer.
u	Unsigned integer.
f	Floating point as m.ddddd.
e	Floating point as m.dddde+/−xx.
E	Floating point as m.ddddE+/−xx.
g	Use %e for exponents less than −4 or greater than precision; otherwise use %f.
c	Single character.
s	String, or any Python data object that can be converted to a string by using the `str` function.
%	Insert a literal % character.

Table B.8   String formatting conversion characters

Modifier	Example	Description
number	%20d	Put the value in a field width of 20.
-	%-20d	Put the value in a field 20 characters wide, left-justified.
+	%+20d	Put the value in a field 20 characters wide, right-justified.
0	%020d	Put the value in a field 20 characters wide, fill in with leading zeros.
.	%10.2f	Put the value in a field 20 characters wide with 2 characters to the right of the decimal point.
(name)	%(name)d	Get the value from the supplied dictionary using name as the key.

Table B.9   Additional formatting options

B.7 Iteration

B.7.1 Simple Iteration over Collections of Data

The *for* statement allows you to easily iterate over any collection of data using the form:

```
for item in sequence:
    statement1
    statement2
    ...
```

The next three examples show you how to iterate over strings, lists, and tuples. In this example, the variable i will be bound to a new integer created by the range function each time through the loop.

```
for i in range(n):
    statement1
    statement2
    ...
```

In this example, the loop variable i will be bound to the next element in the list each time through the loop.

```
for i in ['a', 1, 'b', 2, 'c', 3]:
    statement1
    statement2
    ...
```

In this example, the loop variable i is bound to each character of the string.

```
for ch in "hello world":
    statement1
    statement2
    ...
```

It is also possible to iterate over a dictionary. The following examples show you two common patterns:

```
for i in myDictionary:
    print(myDictionary[i])
```

In this case, the loop variable i is bound to each of the keys contained in the dictionary myDictionary. It is also possible to iterate over keys and values simultaneously using the following:

```
for key,value in myDictionary.items():
    print(key, value)
```

In this example, the key value pairs are pulled out of the dictionary ahead of time using the items method.

B.7.2   Iteration with *while*

The *while* loop is an indefinite loop. It will continue to perform the statements in the body of the loop until the condition becomes False. If the condition is never False, then the loop is an infinite loop and will continue forever.

```
while <condition>:
    statement 1
    statement 2
        ...
```

B.7.3 List Comprehensions

List comprehensions allow you to create lists by embedding a *for* loop in a list creation expression. It is more convenient than writing out a *for* loop and using the append method. Here is the general format for a list comprehension:

```
[<expression> for <item1> in <sequence1>
              for <item2> in <sequence2>
              ...
              if <condition> ]
```

Here are some examples of simple list comprehensions:

```
>>> x = [1,2,3]
>>> y = ['a','b','c']
>>> [a*a for a in x]
[1, 4, 9]
>>> [a for a in x if a%2 != 0]
[1, 3]
>>> [(a,b) for a in x for b in y]
[(1, 'a'), (1, 'b'), (1, 'c'),
 (2, 'a'), (2, 'b'), (2, 'c'),
 (3, 'a'), (3, 'b'), (3, 'c')]
```

B.8 Boolean Expressions

B.8.1 Relational Operators

A simple Boolean expression can be constructed using any of the relational operators shown in Table B.10.

Relational Operator	Meaning
$<$	Less than
$<=$	Less than or equal to
$>$	Greater than
$>=$	Greater than or equal to
$==$	Equal
$!=$	Not equal

Table B.10   Relational operators and their meaning

B.8.2   Compound Boolean Expressions

Multiple Boolean expressions can be joined using the logical operators **and**, **or**, and **not** as shown in Table B.11.

x and y	If x is **False** return x; otherwise return y.
x or y	If x is **False** return y; otherwise return x.
not x	If x is **False** return **True**; otherwise return **False**.

Table B.11   Logical operator behavior

B.9   Selection

B.9.1   Binary Selection

```
if <condition>:
   <statements>
else:
   <statements>
```

B.9.2   Unary Selection

```
if <condition>:
   <statements>
```

B.9.3   Nested Selection with `elif`

```
if <condition>:
    <statements>
elif <condition>:
    <statements>
elif <condition>:
    <statements>
elif <condition>:
    <statements>
else:
    <statements>
```

B.10   Python Modules

B.10.1   Math

Table B.12 summarizes the main math functions used in this book.

Method name	Use	Explanation
cos	math.cos(x)	Returns the cosine of x where x is in radians.
sin	math.sin(x)	Returns the sine of x where x is in radians.
tan	math.tan(x)	Returns the tangent of x where x is in radians.
degrees	math.degrees(r)	Converts r radians to degrees.
radians	math.radians(d)	Converts d degrees to radians.
sqrt	math.sqrt(x)	Returns the square root of x.

Table B.12   Simple math functions

B.10.2   Random Numbers

Table B.13 summarizes the main functions from the random module used in this book.

Method name	Use	Explanation
random	random.random()	Returns a random number between 0.0 and 1.0.
randint	random.randint(1,3)	Returns a random number in the range 1,3 including the endpoints.
randrange	random.randrange(4)	Returns a random number in the range 0,3. Uses the same syntax as the range function for specifying ranges of numbers.
gauss	random.gauss(mu,sigma)	Returns a random number from a Gaussian distribution that has mean of mu (μ) and standard deviation of sigma (σ).
shuffle	random.shuffle(myList)	Returns a copy of myList with the elements of the list shuffled into random order.

Table B.13   Random number generation

B.10.3   Regular Expression Patterns

The following is a list of some simple regular expression patterns:

.   Match any character.

[abc]   Match a, b, or c.

[^abc]   Match any characters other than a, b, or c.

[abc]+   Match one or more occurrences of the characters abc. For example, b or aba or ccba.

[abc]+[de]*   Match zero or more occurrences of the characters abc. For example, b or aba or bd or abae.

(*regex*)   Create a capture group.

Table B.14 summarizes the main regular expression methods.

Method name	Use	Explanation
match	re.match('[abc]XY.')	Matches any string that starts with a, b, or c followed by XY followed by any character. Returns a match object on success or None.
sub	re.sub('[tv]','X', 'vxyzbgtt')	Returns 'XxyzbgXX'. Similar to replace, except that regular expression matching is used.
findall	{re.findall('[bc]+', 'abcdefedcba')	Returns ['bc','cb']. Returns a list of all substrings matching the regular expression.
groups	matchObj.groups()	Returns a list of all capture groups matched. matchObj is created by a call to match.
group	matchObj.group(2)	Returns a single capture group. matchObj is created by a call to match.

Table B.14   Regular expression module functions

B.11 Defining Functions

```
def functionName(param1,param2,...):
    statement1
    statement2
    ...
```

B.12 Defining Classes

```
class classname:

    def method1()
        ...

    def method2()
        ...
    ...
```

B.13 Common Error Messages

Learning how to read and understand error messages can save a lot of time and trouble once you know what to look for.

One of the most common errors is the syntax error, which indicates that you have written a line of code that does not follow the rules of Python's grammar. It is the equivalent of not ending a sentence with a period or forgetting to capitalize the first word of a sentence. Here is an example of a syntax error that is due to a missing : at the end of the line def foo(x,y). It is also very common to get a syntax error like this when you are using an if statement.

```
>>> def foo(x,y)
  File "<stdin>", line 1
    def foo(x,y)
               ^
SyntaxError: invalid syntax
```

Another common error is to use a variable that you have not yet assigned a value to. The following example shows the use of the variable **spam** when spam has no value. Note that this error message starts with the word `Traceback`, which can help you pinpoint exactly the line and the function where an error occurs. The traceback is followed by the error message itself. This message tells you that `'spam'` is undefined. Since the only way to define a variable in Python is to assign a value to it, this should help you realize that you have not done so.

```
>>> 4 + spam*3
Traceback (most recent call last):
  File "<stdin>", line 1, in ?
NameError: name 'spam' is not defined
```

Let's look at another example of a traceback using a simple Python program we have saved in the file `test.py` (Listing B.1). When we run this program we get the following output:

```
hello
Traceback (most recent call last):
  File "test.py", line 11, in <module>
    main()
  File "test.py", line 8, in main
    x = foo()
  File "test.py", line 3, in foo
    b = a + spam
NameError: global name 'spam' is not defined
```

```
1    def foo():
2        a = 1 + 2
3        b = a + spam
4        return b
5
6    def main():
7        print('hello')
8        x = foo()
9        print(x)
10
11   main()
```

Listing B.1   A simple Python traceback

The first line of the traceback points to line 11 of the file `test.py`. This is where `main()` is called. The next line of the file points to line 8 where `foo()` is called and the last line points to line 3 where we find the expression b = a + spam. Once again Python tells us that spam is not defined and it gives us exactly the line that contains the error.

When working with a mixture of strings and numeric data types it is possible to try to "add" two things together that you should not. The next example shows an expression that tries to add a string and an integer together. Python does not know whether it should convert '2' to an integer and add two integers together, or to convert 2 to a string and concatenate two strings together. It will thus give you this error message:

```
>>> '2' + 2
Traceback (most recent call last):
  File "<stdin>", line 1, in ?
TypeError: cannot concatenate 'str' and 'int' objects
```

Here is another situation where Python cannot figure out what to add:

```
>>> def bar():
...     return 2 * 5
...
>>> a = 3 + bar
Traceback (most recent call last):
  File "<stdin>", line 1, in <module>
TypeError: unsupported operand type(s) for +: 'int' and 'function'
```

In this case, the statement a = 3 + bar is missing the parentheses after the function named bar. Even though bar does not require any parameters, Python does not know that it should call the function without the "call operators" ().

Here is an example of using the call operators on an object that is not a function:

```
>>> b = 1
>>> c = 2 + b()
Traceback (most recent call last):
  File "<stdin>", line 1, in <module>
TypeError: 'int' object is not callable
```

The next error is pretty easy to recognize, but it happens quite commonly.

```
>>> 10 * (1/0)
Traceback (most recent call last):
  File "<stdin>", line 1, in ?
ZeroDivisionError: int division or modulo by zero
```

Finally, here is an example of the error message you get when you attempt to iterate over something that is not a sequence. In this case d is an integer rather than a string, list, tuple, dictionary, or file.

```
>>> for i in d:
...     print(i)
...
Traceback (most recent call last):
  File "<stdin>", line 1, in <module>
TypeError: 'int' object is not iterable
```

APPENDIX C

turtle **Reference**

The definitive guide to the turtle module can be found at `http://docs.python.org/release/3.2/library/turtle.html`.

C.1 Basic Move and Draw

forward(distance) Move forward along current heading by `distance` units.

back(distance) Move backward along current heading by `distance` units.

right(angle) Turn the turtle right by `angle` degrees.

left(angle) Turn the turtle left by `angle` degrees.

goto(pos,y=None) Move the turtle to an absolute position. If the tail is down then a line will be drawn. The turtle's orientation does not change. The position may be specified by a pair of numbers, or a tuple representing the `x,y` coordinates.

setx(x) Move the turtle to absolute position `x,y` where `x` is specified as a parameter and `y` does not change.

sety(y) Move the turtle to absolute position `x,y` where `y` is specified as a parameter and `x` does not change.

setheading(to_angle) Set the turtle facing the given heading. Some common directions in degrees include `0` = right, `90` = up, `180` = left, `270` = down.

circle(radius,extent) Draw a circle or part of a circle.

dot(size=None,*color) Make a dot at the current position.

```
dot(30)
dot(40,'blue')
```

write(text, move=False, align='left', font=('Arial', 8, 'normal')) Write some text to the screen. If move is False, the text will start at the turtle's current position and the turtle will not move. Align can be 'left', 'right', or 'center'. The font specification allows you to choose a font and size for the message.

C.2   Turtle State

position() Return the turtle's current location as an (x,y) tuple.

towards(pos, y=None) Return the angle between the turtle's current heading and the location passed as a parameter.

```
towards(number,number)
towards((number,number))
towards(otherTurtle)
```

xcor() Return the current x coordinate of the turtle.

ycor() Return the current y coordinate of the turtle.

heading() Return the current heading of the turtle.

distance(pos, y=None) Return the distance from the turtle's current location and the location passed as a parameter.

```
distance(number,number)
distance((number,number))
distance(otherTurtle)
```

C.3   Drawing State

down() Put the turtle's tail down.

up() Raise the turtle's tail up.

width(width=None) Change the width of the line to draw. If no parameter is passed the method will return the width of the line.

C.4   Filling

begin_fill() Call `begin_fill` before drawing the shape you want filled in.

end_fill() Call `end_fill` after you draw the shape you want filled in. For example, you can use the following code to create a filled square:

```
turtle.begin_fill()
for i in range(4):
    turtle.forward(100)
    turtle.right(90)
turtle.end_fill()
```

C.5   More Drawing Control

reset() Delete all drawing from the window. Re-center the turtle and set all turtle variables back to their default values.

clear() Delete all the turtle's drawing but leave the turtle at current position.

C.6   Controlling the Shape and Appearance

The turtle is not limited to the triangular shape you see by default. The turtle can appear as a turtle, or any other shape that you can draw with the turtle. In addition, any `gif` file can be used to provide the turtle with a shape. Once you have added a shape to your program, any turtle can use that shape by name.

addshape(name, shape=None) Adds a new shape to the dictionary of turtle shape names and shapes. The arguments are interpreted as follows:

- Name is the name of a `gif` file and shape is `None`. Then the image is installed using the `gif` file name as the dictionary key.
- If name is a string and shape is a tuple of pairs of coordinates, then the tuple of pairs is used to create a polygon to use as the turtle shape. It is stored in the dictionary with **name** used as the key.
- Name is a string and shape is a shape object. Then name is the key and the shape object is the shape.

resizemode(rmode=None) Set resize mode to one of the following values: `auto`, `user`, or `noresize`. Each resize mode has the following effect: `auto` adapts the appearance of the turtle according to the value of pensize. `user` adapts the appearance of the turtle according to the values of `stretchfactor` and outline width. Both of these can be set by `turtlesize`. `noresize` forces the turtle to stay the same size. If no parameter is passed, then the method returns the current mode.

turtlesize(stretchfactor=None, outline=None) If the `resizemode` is `user`, then the turtle will be displayed `stretchfactor` times as big as the original turtle using a pen width of `outline`.

getshapes() Return a list of all keys currently in the shape dictionary.

polystart() Start recording the vertices of a polygon.

polyend() Stop recording the vertices of a polygon.

getpoly() Return the last recorded polygon. This polygon is an object that can be passed to `addshape`.

shape(name=None) Return or set the turtle shape. There are three default shapes for the turtle `'arrow'`, `'turtle'`, and `'circle'`. You can make your own shapes as shown in the following example.

```
turtle.polystart()
for i in range(4):
    turtle.forward(10)
    turtle.right(90)
turtle.polyend()
squareShape = turtle.getpoly()
turtle.addshape('squarepants',squareShape)
turtle.shape('squarepants')
```

hideturtle() Make the turtle invisible.

showturtle() Make the turtle visible.

C.7 Measurement Settings

degrees(fullcircle=360.0) Change the angle measurement units to degrees. For some applications it may be convenient for a full circle to have a different number of degrees. For example, you might want to make a circle have 100 degrees to make it easy to map percentages to portions of a circle. You can modify this using the `fullcircle` parameter.

radians() Change all angle measurement units to radians.

C.8 Drawing Speed

speed(speed=None) If no parameter is given, return the current speed of the turtle. Otherwise set the speed to an integer value between 1 and 10, where 1 is slow and 10 is fast. The fastest speed can be obtained by calling speed with a parameter of 0.

tracer(flag=None, delay=None) `tracer` can be called in two ways. In the first, tracer can be called with either `True` or `False`. If `False` is passed as a parameter, then no animation is done. `True` turns on animation using the speed specified. In the second, `tracer` can be passed a single integer. If a single integer n is passed, then only every nth update is really performed when animating the turtle. To conclude, the second parameter specifies a delay value. (See below.)

delay(delay=None) Set or return the drawing delay in milliseconds.

update() Update the screen with all drawing. This is very useful when `tracer` is set to 0.

C.9 Color

bgcolor(*args) Set or return the background color of the window. The color can be set in several ways:

bgcolor("colorname") Most reasonable color names are recognized.

bgcolor(r,g,b)   r, g, and b are floating point numbers between 0.0 and 1.0.

bgcolor((r,g,b))   r, g, and b are floating point numbers between 0.0 and 1.0.

bgpic(picname=None) Set the background of the window to use the image in the filename.

pencolor(*args) Set the color of the pen, using the same options as `bgcolor`.

```
pencolor(color1,color2)
pencolor((r1,g1,b1),(r2,g2,b2))
pencolor(r1,g1,b1,r2,g2,b2)
```

See `color` for more explanation.

fillcolor(*args) Set the current fillcolor using the same options as `bgcolor`.

color(*args) When called without parameters, returns the current pen and fill colors. Otherwise you can use this method to set the pencolor and fillcolor in one call. Legal ways to call this method include `color(r1,g1,b1,r2,g2,b2)` or `color((r1,g1,b1),` `(r2,g2,b2))`, or `color(string1,string2)`. The first group of numbers sets the pen color and the second set of numbers sets the fill color.

colormode(cmode=None) Change the specification of red-green-blue colors to floating point values between 0 and 1 or to integer values between 0 and 255. Calling `colormode(255)` changes to integer mode.

```
colormode(255)
color(200,149,58)
colormode(1.0)
color(.75, .69, .02)
```

C.10   Events

onclick(fun, btn=1) Bind a function to a mouse click, so that `fun` is called whenever the button is pressed. Note that `fun` must accept two parameters that will give the position of the mouse when the button was clicked.

onkey(fun, key=None) Bind a function to a key press. `fun` must be defined with no parameters.

listen(xdummy=None, ydummy=None) Give the current turtle's canvas focus so it can listen for key events. Key events will not be recognized until this function is called. This `listen` method is defined to take two dummy parameters, so `listen` can be bound to a mouse click event.

ontimer(fun, t=0) Bind a function to a timer event. fun must be defined with no parameters. The time value is specified in milliseconds.

C.11 Miscellaneous

turtles() Return a list of all the turtles in the window.

clearscreen(), resetscreen() Reset all turtles in the window to their initial positions.

screensize(canvwidth=None,canvheight=None) Resize the canvas that the turtles are drawing on to height and width.

screen_height(self) Return the height of the turtle canvas.

screen_width(self) Return the width of the turtle canvas.

window_height(self) Return the height of the window containing the canvas.

window_width(self) Return the width of the window containing the canvas.

bye() Close the turtle graphics window.

exitonclick() Wait for a mouse click inside the window, then close and exit.

winsize(w, h, lr=-20, tb=-40) Reset the geometry of the turtle graphics window. Width and height are the width and height of the window. lr and tb can be used to place the top-right or bottom-left corner of the window on the monitor screen. Positive values are used for left and top while negative values indicate bottom and right.

setworldcoordinates(llx,lly,urx,ury) Modify the world coordinates of the canvas that the turtle draws on. This will automatically scale the canvas between llx and urx in the x direction and lly and ury in the y direction.

INDEX